D1671398

ARIS AND PHILLIPS CLASSICAL TEXTS

JUVENAL

Satires Book III

Edited with a Translation and Commentary by

John Godwin

LIVERPOOL UNIVERSITY PRESS

First published 2022 by
Liverpool University Press
4 Cambridge Street
Liverpool
L69 7ZU

www.liverpooluniversitypress.co.uk

Copyright © 2022 John Godwin

The right of J. Godwin to be identified as the author of this book has been asserted by him in accordance with the Copyright, Designs and Patents Act 1988.

All rights reserved. No part of this book may be reproduced, stored in a retrieval system, or transmitted, in any form or by any means, electronic, mechanical, photocopying, recording, or otherwise, without the prior written permission of the publisher.

British Library Cataloguing-in-Publication data
A British Library CIP record is available

ISBN 978-1-80085-486-4 hardback
eISBN 978-1-80085-487-1

Typeset by Tara Montane

Printed and bound by CPI (UK) Ltd, Croydon CR0 4YY

Cover image: Dancer, detail of mosaic from the Domus of Stone Carpets, Ravenna, iStock.com/seraficus.

CONTENTS

To Heather

uxori dilectissimae

PREFACE

Juvenal is the last and in many ways the greatest of the four major Roman verse satirists, and if this book has one overarching aim it is to offer more evidence of Juvenal's status as one of the finest satirists the world has seen and one of the best wielders of Latin to have survived from the ancient world. His narrator snarls and sneers at the topsy-turvy world around him with the eloquence of a fine orator, the word-play of an adept poet and the imagination of a literary firebrand. His words recreate the world about him in hyperbolic terms and his deft management of the genre keeps the reader constantly uncertain of just how seriously we can take what he is saying with such studied and elegant venom. His Latin sometimes reads as if it were spat onto the page with little preparation, and yet there is nothing random in the way he uses the Latin language and the hexameter metre in which he composed. We know little about his life, but that matters little when we have a text as glowing with fire, energy and elegance as this to work on.

Book III is the middle volume of the five books of Satires and shows something of a transition between the earlier stance of the raging, sneering underdog and the more ironic and distanced voice of the later books. The poet continues to cast a critical eye on society at large, with especial focus on the workings of patronage, the demise of the aristocracy and the plight of the intellectual. The tone here is often more questioning and judicious, and yet this poet has if anything increased his ability to amuse and to shock.

The purpose of this book is to help readers to enjoy this poetry, to understand the ideas being discussed and also to appreciate the literary qualities of the Latin. Little previous knowledge of the languages, history and culture of the ancient world is assumed, and (as in all the books in this series) the commentary is keyed to the English translation. The notes also attempt, however, to cater for readers who are studying the poems in Latin, and where the text is more than usually opaque I have sought to elucidate the syntax. My understanding of the text has relied heavily and all too obviously on the centuries of massive scholarship which have been dedicated to it right up to the present day: and I am only sorry that Franco Bellandi's major edition of *Satire* 9 arrived too late to be taken account of. The translation is as close to the Latin as I could produce while keeping the sense and the flow of the sentences but makes no literary claims for itself. My text, apparatus and sigla are based on those of Clausen and Willis, and readings which differ from the OCT are discussed in the commentary notes.

I have been very fortunate to receive help from many people in working on this text: Jim Adams, Eleanor Dickey, Giuseppe Dimatteo, William Dominik, Peter Tennant, Alex Hardie and Martin Winkler all generously shared their ideas and their research with me. Giuseppe Dimatteo read through all the sections on *Satire* 8 and Roland Mayer and the series editor Alan Sommerstein both heroically read through the entire book: all three saved me from error on many occasions and are in no way to blame for any faults which remain. I have once again enjoyed the unstinting editorial help of Clare Litt and her team at Liverpool University Press who have refused to allow a global pandemic to interrupt their meticulous and efficient handling of inquiries and who have once again been a pleasure to work for. The book is dedicated to my wife Heather who has endured the presence of Juvenal in our household for many years and who has been a beacon of sanity and support throughout the lengthy writing process.

John Godwin
Shrewsbury 2021

INTRODUCTION

I. Who was Juvenal?

We know almost nothing about the life of Decimus Iunius Iuvenalis and his very 'anonymity' has been the subject of two major recent studies of his work.[1] Umbricius (at 3.319) invites Juvenal to visit him in Cumae whenever he is on his way from Rome to Aquinum, suggesting that the poet had property there, as well as a pied-à-terre in Rome, all of which suggests a measure of prosperity: and there is an inscription from Aquinum (*CIL* 10.5382) which lists a 'Juvenal' as being a tribune of a cohort of Dalmatian troops and a priest of the cult of the deified emperor Vespasian, but serious doubt has been cast[2] on whether this refers to 'our' poet. Three poems by his contemporary Martial are addressed to him as a friend (7.24.1) and as 'eloquent' (*facundus* 7.91.1) or living the life of a city *cliens* (12.18) – but epigram is not the most reliable of historical sources and these are slim pickings. Juvenal does not dedicate his work to a patron (unlike (e.g.) Virgil and Horace) and so we can surmise that he was rich enough not to need financial support; and his early rhetorical education – the mark of a wealthy upbringing – is both asserted (1.15–17) and proved in the language of his text. Where he appears to be speaking for himself he may well be putting on a performance (see below on 'the poet and the *persona*') and we need to exercise caution in taking his words at face value.

Scholars have dated his work from *termini post quem:*[3] in his first book he alludes to the assassination of Domitian in AD 96 (4.153), the exile of Marius Priscus in AD 100 (1.49–50) and to the publication of Tacitus' *Histories* in AD 105–110 (2.102–3), all of which suggests that he published that book after AD 110. In *Satire* 6 he alludes to events of AD 113–117 which places that book after AD 117, and the 'Caesar' whose accession is applauded in the opening line of Book 3 is generally assumed to be Hadrian who came to power in AD 117. This being so, it

---

1   Uden (2015), Geue (2017)

2   Syme (1979) 1–5

3   For more on the dating of the different books see Uden (2015) 219–26

is plausible that the poet was born somewhere between 55 and 68 AD, and I am tempted by Syme's suggestion of 67 as his year of birth[4]. There is nothing in Book 4 which helps us to date it, but it is not unreasonable to suppose that it was composed in the period around AD 120. There are chronological markers which place Book 5 in or after the year 127.[5]

II.   What did Juvenal write?

Juvenal left us five books of verse *Saturae*. This literary form was said by the Romans to be a Roman invention ('Satire is entirely our own' Quintilian (10.1.93)) and had a long history in a series of very different hands. Early satire such as that of Lucilius (180–102 BC) has only survived in fragments but what we have shows a sharp line in wit and a caustic ability to attack his contemporaries. He attacked people by name and recounted his own sexual exploits; he denounced gluttony and political chicanery, and borrowed philosophical ideas while also mocking philosophical jargon. *ars est celare artem*: Lucilius often reads as if he is improvising his lines but there is a good deal of conscious artistry at work in the ribald and raucous polemic, although Horace (*Satires* 1.4.11) was later to call his work 'a muddy river from which much should have been removed'. He also presents himself in a more or less ironic manner as the (anti-)hero of his own narrative, and thus introduces a very personal voice into the poetic language.

The tradition of verse satire was continued by Horace (65–8 BC), although he called his satirical poems *sermones* ('conversations', the first book of which was published in about 35 BC) rather than *saturae*. His is a gentler sort of satire after the savagery of Lucilius, and he more often appears as an ironic self-satirist than as the scourge of other people. He famously (*Satires* 1.5) tells us how he made an assignation with a servant-girl, only to be stood up by her and end up 'staining his nightshirt'; and his account of how he tried to free himself from a boring social-climber in 1.9 is a study in how good manners can cause us grief. He links his mode of writing with the ribald comedy of 5th century Athens (1.4) and he certainly speaks frankly and crudely about sex (1.2) and food (2.2) in language worthy of an Aristophanes, but he

---

4   For discussion see Syme (1958) 774–75
5   13.16–18, 14.196, 15.27

avoids overt political satire and so (for instance) his account of the journey to Brundisium – where the fate of the world was to be decided with a treaty between Mark Antony and Octavian – avoids making much of the politics and concentrates instead on incidental details in an arch and ironic manner. His targets are ones which Juvenal also shares – such as hypocrisy and ambition – and the set-piece descriptions of events such as the dinner-party (2.8) give us a vivid glimpse into the social world in which Horace, the freedman's son, always (no doubt) felt himself to be something of an outsider. He made good use of a variety of styles in his poems: parody of epic, philosophical discourse in the manner of a didactic poet, vivid raconteurish descriptions of Roman life, and even animal fables such as the famous tale of the town mouse and country mouse (2.6). He clearly found the composition of this sort of accessible verse philosophy congenial and went on to compose a second book of *Sermones* (published in 30 BC), his first book of hexameter *Epistles* in 20 BC and the final three *Epistles* (Book 2 and the *Ars Poetica*) sometime after that.

The Octavian who was going to meet Antony at Brundisium in Horace's *Satire* 1.5 was to be Rome's first emperor, of course, and the republic into which Horace was born was to be transformed into the Roman Empire. Writing under the emperor Nero (who ruled from AD 54–68), the satirist Persius (AD 34–62) composed only six satires – a meagre 650 lines in all – but took the genre in a new direction with his use of Stoic philosophy as the inspiration for his work. His poetry is involved and obscure but deals with the stock themes – food, poetry, sex, power, gods – and offers a more astringent and assertive model of satirical argument after the relaxed voice of Horace.

A tributary of this tradition was the so-called 'Menippean' satires of Varro (116–27 BC) which were a blend of prose and verse, described by Cicero (*Acad.* 1.8) as 'a bit of philosophy with a dash of humour and dialogue': this combination of prose and verse in satire was to be imitated much later by Seneca and Petronius in the age of Persius. Petronius[6] wrote a prosimetric picaresque novel *Satyricon* which combines narrative and direct speech, ideas and the life of the streets. Its title is not in fact to do with 'satire' but rather with the fabled half-men half-goats known as 'Satyrs' who were servants of the god Bacchus – often drunk and always

---

6 See *OCD* s.v. 'Petronius Arbiter'

disorderly – and the plot centres around the lives of young men finding their way in a debauched and decadent social world. The philosopher, dramatist and essayist Lucius Annaeus Seneca was tutor to the young emperor Nero until he was forced to commit suicide in AD 65 on suspicion of being involved in the Pisonian conspiracy against the emperor. His spoof on the deification of the previous emperor Claudius – the *Apocolocyntosis* or 'Pumpkinification' of Claudius – is (like the *Satyricon*) a Menippean mixture of prose and verse and is one of the most effective pieces of comic literature to have survived from the ancient world.

Juvenal left us sixteen poems (the last of which is incomplete) divided up into five books. Book 1 (*Satires* 1–5) establishes the poet as a man of 'savage indignation' railing against the evils of the city around him and the appalling behaviour of his contemporaries. In his first Satire he denounces bad poetry and expresses the need to write satire to expose the vicious and unfair world he lives in: 'it is difficult <u>not</u> to write satire'. The other four *Satires* attack hypocrites who pretend to be austere Stoic philosophers but who love perverted sex in private (*Satire* 2), the living conditions endured by poorer Romans (*Satire* 3), the absurdities of the imperial court (*Satire* 4) and the humiliation of the poor *cliens* who attends a dinner party given by his rich patron (*Satire* 5). Book II (*Satire* 6) is a single poem arguing against marriage and inveighing against the wickedness and crassness of women. Book III (*Satires* 7–9) sees the poet lament the failure of the Romans to reward adequately the literary professions, such as poets, speech-writers and teachers (*Satire* 7), the failure of the Roman aristocracy to live up to the social elevation which they claim (*Satire* 8) and the failure of the patronage system to prevent the mutual sexual exploitation of clients and their patrons (*Satire* 9). Book IV (*Satires* 10–12) deals with ethical concerns rather than simply scandalised exposure of folly and vice: the folly of praying for what appear to be advantages – such as wealth, power, long life and beauty which will only deliver misery (*Satire* 10), the need to live within one's means (*Satire* 11) and to cultivate true friendship (*Satire* 12). Book V (*Satires* 13–16) deals with the two false gods of money and power, promoting people over property and urging us to educate ourselves, our children and each other in habits of friendship and love rather than selfish greed while also exploring the ugly side of human nature to a degree not seen since the early poems.

Book III is thus central in Juvenal's *oeuvre* and has been seen by many as marking a turning away from savage indignation towards a more philosophical and ironic viewpoint.[7] The book has a great deal of internal variety, but also a good deal of common ground in that all three poems bemoan the attitudes of the so-called upper classes: in *Satire* 7 they are rebuked for not supporting the arts, in 8 they are rebuked for not living up to their delusions of moral and political grandeur and in 9 they are rebuked for abusing their role as patrons. *Satire* 7 presents us with a view of artistic inspiration and even (7.53–71) literary genius which needs and deserves support from the rich, *Satire* 8 sees the behaviour of the rich and 'noble' as being below that of the worst in society, while Naevolus and his patron in *Satire* 9 make up the two halves of the pantomime horse which is the mutually exploitative patronage system in one particular case. Naevolus and his patron deserve each other and it is difficult to feel sympathy for either, but the provincials in *Satire* 8 (87–141) are depicted as helpless in the face of senatorial rapacity in a system where the governors are on the make and their wives are harpies (8.129–30). The 'intellectuals' in *Satire* 7 also provoke ambivalent reactions in the reader: the teacher's lot (7.150–243) is not a happy one for sure, but serving up 'rehashed cabbage' (7.154) to students whom the teacher clearly despises (7.159–61) is not going to make us respect their professional commitment. The speaker of *Satire* 7 is motivated throughout by an envious money-conscious attitude towards those better-off than himself and seems to think (like Naevolus in 9) that the world owes him a living while being unwilling or unable to earn it by talent or by hard work. *Satire* 8 varies this pattern by showing us how the rich and famous manage to stay rich and famous even though they do so simply by ruthless despoiling of the provinces, by trading on the greatness of ancestors long dead and (in the case of the emperor) by flagrant disregard for what was decent and fitting in a governor. None of this is a million miles away from the 'underdog' stance of the first book of *Satires*, in which the speaker was jostled aside by slaves and foreigners and forced to watch as upstarts lord it over native citizens, was fed dreadful food by a patron who was dining on turbot and who saw the moral standards of Roman greatness being washed away by a flood of foreigners. The difference between Book III and the earlier satires is (as Braund says

---

7   See on this most obviously Braund (1988)

(2004) 296) one of tone rather than one of content as the satirist speaks more in sorrow than in anger at the abuses under scrutiny.

III.   Style – how did Juvenal write?

Juvenal's lines sometimes read as if they came tumbling out of the poet's head in a flood of extempore bile, but their artistry is no less acute for being concealed. His methods of composition and expression are deeply indebted both to the rhetorical tradition[8] and to the long history of Greek and Latin literature[9] to which he was clearly indebted and with which he was obviously familiar. They include:

(a) **Irony**. Socratic irony was often the dissembling of knowledge, the pretence that Socrates knew only his own ignorance and needed to be educated by his interlocutor: this allowed him to ask men such as Laches, Gorgias and Protagoras for advice and so expose their ignorance as (even) greater than his own, leaving the audience in a state of *aporia* and his interlocutors sometimes in a state of sullen rage. Juvenal uses this form of Socratic irony to great effect in *Satire* 9 where the speaker coaxes self-condemnatory words out of the mouth of Naevolus. The speaker also uses heavy sarcasm on occasions (e.g. 7.78). Less specific forms of irony[10] include the poet's dramatisation of his own character within his own text, often espousing views which are ridiculous or absurdly exaggerated in order to present the speaker himself as a target for his own satire – effectively debunking his own words by their very style. The poems in this book all present us with a 'Juvenal' who is giving advice to the reader/addressee, but there is ample scope for seeing the 'Juvenal' speaking as a fictive *persona* (see below) who may even be part of the joke rather than simply its mouthpiece: the poems can of course be read as tracts delivered by a poet speaking for himself, but can also be conversations in which the character of the speaker may be being sent up as much as his quarry.[11] This is particularly so with sexual matters: *Satire* 6, for instance, shows an excess of misogyny and a prurient fascination

---

8   See Kenney (1963) and (2012) 124–36
9   See Highet (1951)
10   See Muecke (1970)
11   For this tension with regard to *Satire* 7 see e.g. Tennant (1996) responding to Braund (1988) 24–68

with sex which belies its own prudish disapproval, rather like the poet's rejection of the hideous cannibalism in Satire 15 which he nonetheless describes with lip-smacking prurience, or the tantalising stance of *Satire 7* in which a writer complains eloquently and successfully about the status of the writer and teachers are quoted as complaining of their pupils in terms which can make the reader side with the kids. Irony usually depends on the reader being alert to the fun being had either by the speaker's withering sarcasm (as at 7.78, 7.180) or else at the speaker's expense – such as the sardonic *Realpolitik* about provincial government at 8.98–126 or the pompous ass bragging of his lineage at 8.44–6. This ironic way of reading the text is hugely important as it relies on the judgement of the individual reader to be aware of the satirical nuances and to be less ready to swallow the lines uncritically, but (by the same token) it is a way of reading a passage which will provoke disagreement as to the sense and the meaning which the ironic text both conveys and conceals. For the larger questions surrounding the *persona* theory, see below (IV 'The Poet and the Persona').

(b) **Parody and allusion to epic**. This is the humorous imitation of literary form in which the salient characteristics of the target are exaggerated and so rendered comic – such as the riff on Horace's description of the wise man at 7.190–4 or the caustic use of lightly rewritten lines from epic at 9.37 (Homer) and 9.69, 9.102 (Virgil). In the first of these a familiar line from Homer's *Odyssey* is adapted to the situation of the speaker: at 9.102 the speaker uses a line from Virgil to gently poke fun at the pretensions of the interlocutor. Naevolus is much given to epic in his self-dramatisation (see 9.37n.) but he also mourns the passing of time in language taken straight from love elegy and the poetry of the symposium (9.127–9).

Parody of style is frequent in Juvenal. Classical epic was written in the same metre as these satires, and so it is easy for the satirist to slip into a higher register and so send up the genre by allowing the satirical *persona* to speak like a Lucan or a Statius. Juvenal is master of this: he makes use of epic allusions (9.37n., 8.269–71) and the occasional epic periphrasis (7.25, where 'fire' is called 'the husband of Venus' referring to Vulcan (god of fire)), but also loves to build up an epic atmosphere only to deflate it with bathos (e.g. 7.6–7). At 8.56 he addresses the pretentiously

well-born man as 'offspring of the Trojans' (*Teucrorum proles*), in a nod
to Virgil (*Aeneid* 6.648) while Naevolus regularly shows off his learning
with his allusions to epic (9.37, 9.64–5, 9.149–50)

(c) The **'grand style'** (*genus grande*).[12] The poet of the satires had clearly
enjoyed a rhetorical education as he himself tells us (1.15–17) and his
use of the 'grand style' of oratory is shown in such literary devices as:

(i)   his use of rhetorical questions (e.g. 7.81, 103–104, 146, 8.24–5,
        192–93) which add a touch of high drama and forensic indignation.
        In lamenting the lack of old-style patrons for poets, Juvenal lists
        (7.94–5) a string of the great men of the past, asking 'who will
        these days be to you a Maecenas, a Proculeius…?'. Shortly after
        (7.98–9) he uses apostrophe (see below) to address historians as
        a class and then (7.103-4) gives us a neat tricolon crescendo of
        rhetorical questions to hammer home the point. Satire 8 opens with
        the punchy three-word rhetorical question *stemmata quid faciunt*?
        ('what use are family trees?') which is as arresting as the opening
        question of *Hamlet*.
(ii)   apostrophe, where the poet addresses absent character(s) directly:
        at 7.205 the poet addresses the city of Athens while at 8.185 he
        rounds on a bankrupt called Damasippus to accuse him of hiring
        out his voice in the theatre. Naevolus uses this device a good deal
        while he constructs an imaginary conversation with his patron
        (9.85–90).
(iii)   sententious generalisations summing up an argument in a memorable
        and pithy phrase, often pompous and bombastic as in the proud
        claim (9.79–80) that 'in many homes where a marriage is rickety
        – on the point of falling apart and all but dissolved – an adulterer
        has saved it' or the authoritative blanket judgement (8.73–4) that
        'empathy is a rare commodity in that income-bracket' or similarly
        'Eloquence is not often found in threadbare clothing' (7.145).
(iv)   the balanced word-order known as the 'golden line', where a central
        verb is framed by a pair of nouns and a pair of adjectives: see for
        instance 8.18 (*frangenda miseram funestat imagine gentem*) and
        cf. the similar pattern at 7.92 (*praefectos Pelopea facit Philomela
        tribunos*).

---

12   See De Decker (1913), Braun (1989), Santorelli (2016)

(v)   pointed antitheses, where stark contrasts are drawn for enhanced effect, such as Naevolus' harsh comparison (9.45–6) of himself with an agricultural slave ('The slave who ploughs a field will be less of a wretch than the one who ploughs his master') or the wonderfully neat couplet on the power of *Fortuna* (7.197–8): 'If Fortune wants, you will become a consul from being a teacher of rhetoric: / in the same way, if she wants, the consul will become a teacher'. Especially pithy and pointed is the damning comparison (8.55) of the 'herm' and Rubellius Blandus ('the herm has a marble head, while you are a living statue').

(vi)   diminutive forms of nouns and adjectives, lending a homely, almost intimate tone to the language such as 9.61 where the poor child has his little toy houses (*casulis*) and his little puppy (*catello*) to play with.

(vii)   anaphora or rhetorical repetition of important words to raise the oratorical temperature. This is used to great effect at 7.81 ('what will any amount of glory do for Serranus and famished Saleius, if glory is all they get?') where the key word *gloria* is used in metrically strong positions in the same line: see also the peremptory repetition of the singular imperative *pone* at 8.88–9 and the sententious repetition of forms of *fatum* ('fate') at 9.32. Sometimes (as at 7.213–4, 8.159–60) the repetition is to draw attention to an individual .

(viii) hyperbole[13] or comic exaggeration is common, such as 9.12–17 where Naevolus' dishevelled appearance is drawn in grotesquely exaggerated terms or 8.85-6 where the lavish lifestyle is taken to extremes of greed and luxury. This can take the form of caricature as at 9.103-4 where the list of potential informers includes animals and even marble: and the pithy language can amount to a cartoon image as at 9.136 ('my stomach is fed by my cock').

(ix)   characterisation by putting words into the mouths of others: from the impatient parent at 7.242 to the pompous ass at 8.44–6, the straw-man of 8.163–4, the calculating patron at 9.39 and 63: and above all that superb creation Naevolus, whose speeches are masterpieces of doublethink and petulant pleading.

---

13 See Fredericks (1979)

(x)   Juvenal generally avoids primary obscenities[14] but has a wonderful
      ability to be rude without being crude. He can describe sexual acts
      without using sexual terms (such as the autoerotic fumblings of
      pupils at 7.241) and in his 'one excursion into scatology' (Jenkyns
      (1982) 200) where he fixes our attention on sodomy at 9.43–4 he
      does so using perfectly respectable Latin. He can also use innuendo
      where the precise meaning is coloured with a sexual overtone as
      at 7.212, 8.162, 9.5.
(xi) Juvenal likes to combine words in an arresting way, often coining
      two-word oxymora which baffle and bemuse the reader: see for
      example the *mulio consul* ('muleteer consul') at 8.148, the *uernam
      equitem* ('home-bred knight') at 9.10, the *citharoedo principe*
      ('lyre-playing emperor') at 8.198.

To illustrate some of the above in action, look at 8.231–9:

> *quid, Catilina, tuis natalibus atque Cethegi*
> *inueniet quisquam sublimius? arma tamen uos*
> *nocturna et flammas domibus templisque paratis,*
> *ut bracatorum pueri Senonumque minores,*
> *ausi quod liceat tunica punire molesta*   235
> *sed uigilat consul uexillaque uestra coercet.*
> *hic nouus Arpinas, ignobilis et modo Romae*
> *municipalis eques, galeatum ponit ubique*
> *praesidium attonitis et in omni monte laborat.*

('What, Catiline, can anyone find more elevated than your lineage
or that of Cethegus? Yet still you plan night-time assaults, arson
against homes and temples like the sons of the trousered Gauls and
offspring of the Senones, and you had the nerve to do something
deserving punishment in the shirt of pain. But the consul is awake
and puts a stop to your standards. This new man from Arpinum, not
a noble and only recently arrived in Rome as a municipal knight – he
positions a helmeted guard everywhere to protect the thunderstruck
people and he toils on every hill.')

---

14   Courtney (2013) 34–35, Jenkyns (1982) 197–202

The paragraph is built around contrasts. The noble birth of a Catiline versus the ignoble birth of a Cicero: the villainy of 'noble' Catiline compared with the arson of foreign tribes: the cunning insidious plot of the villain and the Herculean labours of the consul. The speaker opens with a direct apostrophe (231–3) to the long dead Catiline contained in a rhetorical question. The lengthy ponderous phrasing of the opening (*quid ... sublimius*) then gives way to the short words and syncopated rhythm of *arma tamen uos* as the speaker suggests the stealthy setting of the night-time attack. Line 233 is worthy of Cicero himself with the emotional charge of 'homes and temples' having arson prepared against them leading in to the sneering comparison of the noble Catilinarians and the 'trousered Gauls and offspring of the Senones' who deserved a most ignominious (and painful) death. The speaker does not spell out the form of execution beyond the allusion to the *tunica molesta* ('shirt of pain'), assuming that the audience would be familiar with the term, just as the Gallic wearing of trousers was well-known and here declaimed with pompous relish in the string of long syllables (*brācātōrum* where the final syllable is also lengthened before the following word). Line 236 quotes Cicero more directly with a string of alliterative words and the great man simply rendered by his title of *consul*. That individual is then unpacked in the following lines with a string of descriptive terms of cumulative force. Cicero was a *nouus* (*homo*) – the first man in his family to hold the office of consul – from Arpinum, who had not been long in Rome (*modo Romae*) and was therefore *municipalis*. This last term is joined with *eques* in a form of description common in Juvenal (cf. (xi) above): both terms 'carry a sting' (Courtney) but juxtaposing the two together makes the sting all the sharper. The catalogue of ignobility is all there to point up the surprise that this nobody from out of town managed to do the impossible: hyperbole shows the consul putting troops 'everywhere' and managing to toil on 'every' hill to protect the 'thunderstruck' citizens – *attonitis* summing up the whole citizen body in a single epithet of terror. Key words are placed for effect: *galeatum* ('helmeted') is no idle filler but shows that these troops were now in sight of their foe and thus in real and present danger, *praesidium* was one of Cicero's favourite words to describe the 'protection' he offered them and *laborat* ('toils') even raises our hero to the rank of a Hercules.

IV. The poet and the persona: why did Juvenal write?

Satire in the modern world usually attacks named individuals and institutions. It is a topical genre which dates fast and which depends on the reader knowing a good deal about the background if they are to see the point. Roman verse satire on the contrary is a literary and rhetorical genre which takes its material and much of its inspiration from the past rather than the present. The poet himself claims (1.170–171) only to attack the dead and most of the people he describes in this collection (such as Nero, Marius, and Cicero) were long dead before the poet was even born: an excellent example of the way in which history quickly becomes literature. Furthermore the poetic form makes use of literary intertexts which were (and remain) part of the cultural milieu. This means that the demands on the reader are high, as is the case with most satire: readers are expected to understand the historical themes and also pick up the allusions to earlier writers, to admire the way in which Juvenal picks up names, themes, literary allusions from the past and reworks them into what sounds like a tract for the times. The poet alludes to his rhetorical education and much of the material addressed in *Satire* 8 in particular was staple material from the world of the rhetorical exercises of the schools, but readers are also expected to spot direct quotations from epic and to understand allusions to epic and tragedy as well as pastoral and oratory.

These poems are, then, artifacts and their formal and stylistic effects render them less rather than more effective as in any sense capable of changing the world. They exaggerate wildly and create a caricature of reality, they ventriloquise straw men, they play with forms of argumentation which are clever rather than practical, and they deliver all this in a verse form which is routinely 'higher' than Juvenal's three great predecessors in the genre and whose style dazzles with a literary brilliance which reduces any protreptic purpose almost to nothing. In Juvenal's hands, satire is raised to epic heights: this creates a jarring conflict between form and content which is both humorous and also bewildering. Above all it casts an ironic sheen over the words which makes readers wonder exactly how seriously we can take this writer who shows off his literary talent while also wagging his finger in apparent disapproval.

It may be that this is to miss the point. Juvenal might be pulling out all the rhetorical stops simply because he cares to keep our attention and persuade us, and many readers have over the centuries read him in this way. There is no *a priori* reason why the text should not express real feelings in the powerful form of verse satire. The fact that different views are expressed in different poems is not a serious challenge to this as (a) we can all change our minds and (b) some of those views are delivered by named individuals (such as Laronia in 2) whom the poet casts as having different views. The fact that the theses are sometimes familiar from the rhetorical schools is also immaterial: the poet could be seeking to inject new fire into the smouldering ashes of old arguments for personal reasons, and anyway those theses were chosen by the schools because they raised issues of deep importance to society.

The other way to read these poems is to see the 'indignation' which 'drives' him to verse (1.79) and which makes it difficult *not* to write satire (1.30) as perhaps a pose to lure the reader in; the enraged old-testament prophet is in fact a character invented by the writer and the audience may choose to laugh either *with* or *at* the speaker so long as they enjoy the poem. In the last century Anderson in a ground-breaking work[15] urged that the poet is a performer and that he is creating a character who is the narrator and the speaker of the words being uttered: this 'character' is referred to by Anderson as a *persona* (which literally means 'mask' and alludes to the theatrical nature of the text) and is the creation of the poet and is not therefore to be taken as identical with the man writing the words on the page. Just as we do not demand total sincerity on the part of a songwriter who may express feelings in a song which he does not personally share, so also this poet may be conjuring up what are more or less set-piece declamations which are delivered 'in character' behind the mask of savage indignation or shocked *humanitas* which is the satirist's stock in trade.[16]

Clearly this sort of judgement has to be made in reading many works of literature. When a Horace or a Catullus expresses love, we can choose to read the poem as an expression of the poet's real feeling for real persons, or else we can read it as a love-poem in the tradition of love poetry and with no need for a referent in the 'real' world. If the writer has done a good job then readers often are led to think that the writer is bursting to

---

15 Anderson, W. S. (1982) esp. 293–339
16 On the *persona* theory see also Keane (1989), Braund (1996), Schmitz (2019) 11–30

express genuine emotions ('feelings in search of a form') when it may in fact be the other way round ('form in search of a feeling') as the artist, working with a form (such as a sonnet or an elegy), or a particular metre, will find that feelings emerge from his emotional depths and colour his work with emotion which is itself freely invented. Writers have (after all) to write about something, and there is always the strong possibility that writers produce what the public will enjoy rather than what they are burning personally to impart.

This argument is more acute perhaps in discussing other poets such as Horace. After all, there is no doubt that Juvenal exaggerates wildly and risks his credibility by his hyperbole. His sensible words about youthful indiscretions (8.163–6, complete with an unnamed interlocutor feeding him the lines and an elegant one-line image of 'some misbehaviour should be trimmed with the first beard') give way to a prurient and tabloid account of 'fatty' Lateranus (whose name means 'bricky') keeping sordid company with 'sailors, thieves and runaways… executioners and coffin-makers and the idle drums of the eunuch-priest flat on his back' (8.174–6). Our speaker who is arguing against aristocratic snobbery is the biggest snob of them all and has no time at all for the values of 'equal freedom for all' which Lateranus is enjoying in a bibulous sense at the bar of the Syrian Jew. The moralising about Lateranus is thus seen as part of a role being played, an emotion being spun by this master-rhetorician who can both summon up our own feelings and then calm them down, and who can thus dazzle us with his own self-characterising display as a sententious and wrong-headed ranter. In *Satire* 9 Juvenal puts words into the mouth of Naevolus, a swaggering sexual buccaneer who is clearly past his prime, and the speaker both leads Naevolus on with a show of sympathy and then cuts him down for his naiveté. This perfectly illustrates the capacity of satire to be 'staged' and read as the script of a performance rather than as a *cri de coeur* from an anguished moralist.

The same line of reasoning could also be used to get the poet off the hook in the eyes of many modern readers who will find many of the ideas repellent. *Satire* 6 is a sustained exercise in misogyny, purporting to give advice to a certain Postumus to avoid getting married as all the different classes of women are hideous. This sort of misogyny is not without parallel in the ancient world,[17] but it is still pretty strong stuff

---

17   E.g. Semonides Fr. 7W

and it is a difficult poem to read without feeling readerly revulsion. If, however, one were to see it as ironic mockery of misogyny rather than the real thing – assuming that the poet, in other words, adopts a 'mask' (*persona*) of 'woman-hater' and then writes a poem which such a man would deliver – then the purpose of the poem becomes the very opposite of what it appears to be. Far from espousing these revolting ideas, Juvenal is exposing the attitudes he expresses to ridicule as they are so obviously wrong. It makes no sense to accuse Euripides of hating women because his character Hippolytus does[18] even though the contemporary comic poet Aristophanes invents characters who think exactly that.[19] There is much to be said for this. Juvenal is writing in a tradition of epideictic oratory (where the point was to demonstrate oratorical subtlety rather than to prove a specific case) and with the memory of his own rhetorical training as a composer of *suasoriae* or 'set-piece speeches' such as he mocks in 1.17–18. James Uden[20] has explored the oratorical and intellectual world of the Second Sophistic in which Juvenal lived, and it would be a dull reader who did not realise this. Furthermore, in a fascinating pair of recent books,[21] the stylised form of speech has recently been examined as a study in anonymising the author – a process whereby he hides behind his own text and does not allow us to glimpse his reality behind the tissue of the words.

This is not, however, the last word by any means. The *persona* which the poet adopts may not be co-extensive with the poet himself, but it is the poet who chooses which *persona* to adopt and there is still scope for reading the text as in some ways revelatory of the mind of the writer and his readers in the time at which the work was composed. Some of the points being made are over-stated but still resonate with us today and continue to haunt our thinking – what is worth dying or killing for? is there any value in money? – while others let us glimpse a world in which social values of 'nobility' and masculinity are questioned and discussed in language which is unparalleled for its frankness and power to make us think.

---

18 Euripides *Hippolytus* 616–668
19 *Thesmophoriazuai* 85
20 Uden (2015) esp. 129–35
21 Uden (2015), Geue (2017a): see Godwin (2017) and Schmitz (2019b) for some qualifications of this theory.

Readers must ultimately read the poems and decide the extent to which they are tongue-in-cheek or hand-on-heart, whether they are ironic rhetoric or examples of genuine emotion captured in expressive language. There is, after all, no single way to read a poem. Roman literature was created with generic and metrical propriety, such that epic was always in hexameters and generally avoided vulgarities, while love-poetry tended to be in elegiac couplets and certain stock figures recur: but there is also a marked resistance to this restraint on the part of many writers who at all times need to avoid the tedium of predictability and who seek to foil the expectations of their audience. Juvenal obviously wrote within the tradition of verse satire, but beyond that he resists categorisation. The one area where he is totally devoted to a single purpose is as a writer, and he uses the many skills of his trade to keep the readers on their toes and to surprise us with his skill. When he makes points which are facetious or plain wrong, then we end up admiring the style precisely because the content is faulty ('how does he manage to argue *that*?!'). It is then that the mask slips to reveal the grinning manipulator behind it. The fact that the poet hides behind the poetry is no surprise: but then it would be an odd poet who did not also wish to be noticed as the author of great literature. Weak writing is one-sided and monothematic and the elusive quality of Juvenal's thought is a mark of his greatness as a writer: we might also feel that if (as the satirist seems to be suggesting) we live in a topsy-turvy world where all around is bad, mad, and sad, then at least we have the consolations of the poetry itself in which the views are so vividly and eloquently expressed.

V. The metre

Spoken Latin had a stress accent, whereby one syllable in a word was given greater weight, as in English 'Juvenal'. The first syllable was stressed if the word had two syllables (*prodest*): if the word had more than two syllables the stress is placed on the penultimate syllable if that syllable is heavy – i.e. one containing a long vowel or diphthong or else 'closed' by a consonant – but if the penultimate syllable is light then the stress goes on the antepenultimate syllable. So for instance the opening lines of satire 8 are stressed thus:

stemmata quid faciunt? quid prodest, Pontice, longo
sanguine censeri, pictos ostendere uultus.

Heavy syllables were reckoned to take longer to say than light ones, and so all Latin (prose and verse) was spoken with this alternating pattern of light and heavy syllables.

Roman poets used this system of 'light' and 'heavy' syllables to adopt something close to the quantitative syllables of Greek poetry, where the rhythm of the verse is dictated by the 'quantity' of the syllables. Thus in Roman poetry a syllable is reckoned to be a vowel sound, followed either by nothing (an 'open' syllable) or by a consonant (a 'closed' syllable): usually a single consonant following a vowel is reckoned to be the first consonant of the following syllable (e.g. *ca-li-gi-ne*) and does not affect the length of the preceding syllable; but where two or more consonants follow a vowel, whether in the same word or in different words, the first one is included in the first syllable (*men-sa*) which is thus 'closed' and becomes lengthened – the exceptions being combinations of mute and liquid consonants within the same word (*b, c, g, p, t* followed by *r*, and *c, p, t,* followed by *l*) where both letters may optionally be considered as belonging to the following syllable (*ma-tris*) and need not lengthen the preceding one. Diphthongs (*ae, eu, au,* etc.) are always long by nature: single vowels may be long or short in length and may vary with inflection (e.g. the final *-a* of *mensa* is long by nature in the ablative case, short in the nominative).

–   means a heavy syllable
∪   means a light syllable
x   means a syllable which may be either heavy or light
// means the caesura (word-end in the middle of a foot
    of a hexameter).

The **hexameter** is the 'epic' metre used by Homer and all later epic and didactic poets: it also became (after Lucilius) the metre of all verse satire. The line is divided into six 'feet', each of which is either a dactyl (a heavy syllable followed by two light syllables (–∪∪ in conventional notation)) or a spondee (two heavy syllables (– –)). The last foot is always dissyllabic, and the last syllable of all may be either heavy or light. The metrical analysis of a line is called 'scansion' and a typical hexameter line (8.1) may be scanned thus:

–∪∪/ – ∪∪ /–// – / – – / – ∪∪/ – – /
stēmmătă/ quīd făcĭ/ŭnt? quīd /prōdēst/Pōntĭcĕ /lōngō

where the // sign shows the 'caesura' – the word-break in the middle of a
foot – which occurs in the third foot or (less often) the fourth (e.g. 7.80,
7.91, 7.106, 7.126, 8.155, 8.169, 9.116, 9.132). It may also occur between
the two short syllables of a dactyl in the third foot and then be followed
by a further caesura in the fourth, as at (e.g.) 7.19, 7.32, 7.61, 8.12, 9.10,
9.39, 9.123, 9.137. In cases where a word ending with a vowel (or a vowel
+ *m* such as *rotam*) is followed by a word beginning with a vowel or *h*,
the two syllables usually merge ('elide') into a single syllable, as at 8.148
where *rotam adstringit* is scanned as *rot(am) adstringit* (four syllables),
or 9.147 where *quando ego* is read *quand(o) ego* (three syllables).

Ictus and Accent

As discussed above, Latin words had a stress accent, and Latin verse
divides a line into 'feet' in which the first syllable has a metrical weight
or 'ictus'. These two forms of accent could either coincide or they could
clash in the same word: line 130 of Satire 9, for instance is spoken thus:

   ne͜ trepida nu͜mquam pa͟thicus ti͟bi de͟rit ami͟cus

but scanned metrically as:

   nē *trepid/ā num/quām pathi/cūs tibi /dērit a/mīcus*

In this line the speech accent and the metrical ictus or 'downbeat' clash
a good deal until we get to the last two feet where they coincide. This
final congruence of ictus and accent is common, but is broken on many
occasions when the poet ends the line with shorter words which carry their
own accent and which thus produces a syncopated rhythm as at 8.231:

   *inue͜ni/et qui͟s/quam sub/li͟mius/ **a͟rma** ta͟m/en uo͟s*

Here there is congruence of ictus and accent in the fourth foot and the
first syllable of the fifth foot but then a jarring clash at the end of the line.

One strength of the hexameter is its versatility in the variation of quick
and slow rhythms and also its readiness to vary the ending of the phrases
and resist the urge to end the phrase with the ending of the line – a device
known as enjambement (see e.g. 8.31–2, where the enjambed *insignis*
comes at the end of the question but in identical stressed position as
indignus in the line above, or 8.122 where the laudable instruction 'do
not cause harm' is rendered ironic by the enjambed qualifier *fortibus et*

miseris – 'to people who are strong and desperate'). Rhythmic effects can be obvious: the spondees at 7.230 enact the weight of linguistic rules laid on the hapless teacher, just as spondees give grandeur to the massive row of ancestors at 8.3 or the pompous sententiousness of 8.84, while dactyls assume an air of urgency as at 7.27 or humour at 9.6. The fifth foot of a hexameter is almost always a dactyl but Juvenal (along with other poets) uses the fifth foot spondee for special effects as at 9.111 where the slaves exact slow vengeance on their masters or at 8.218 where it creates an archaic tone in keeping with the archaic material under discussion.[22]

VI.   The transmission of the text[23]

It is possible to view Juvenal as something of a literary loner in his own time. Unlike writers such as Virgil who quickly became widely read and widely admired, Juvenal went largely unnoticed amongst his contemporaries and only the roughly contemporary poet Martial mentions him by name as a man (but not as a poet). This obscurity changed in the latter half of the fourth century, when an edition of his poetry was produced, and he is mentioned and quoted by Servius (the great commentator on Virgil) and the Christian apologist Lactantius (240–320) who cites 10.365–6 approvingly. It is not surprising that the more sententious and censorious lines of Juvenal were music to the ears of anti-pagan Christians. More impressive still, he began to be admired and imitated by poets such as Ausonius (AD 310–94) and later on Paulinus and Prudentius who all saw the poetic worth as well as the proto-Christian potential of the poems and who borrowed and adapted some of Juvenal's best phrases. Christian apologists such as Jerome and Augustine used his satirical venom as ammunition against pagan immorality, while the historian Ammianus tells us (28.4.14) that he was the poet read by people who do not read poetry – a sentiment which rings true when one reads the opening of *Satire* 1 with its condemnation of (other) poets' pretentious poetry. The earliest commentary on a text of the poet was produced sometime between AD 350 and 420, and after that time the survival of Juvenal was never in doubt.

---

22   For more on this topic see Courtney (2013) 38, Kenney in Braund and Osgood (2012) 135
23   For fuller information on the manuscript tradition see Tarrant in Reynolds and Wilson (1984), Parker in Braund and Osgood (2012) 137–61, Griffith (1968)

The transmission of ancient literature was done by laborious and highly fallible copying out by scribes. Errors and variant readings crept into the system and by the time of our earliest manuscript (P) from the ninth century many lines had been corrupted, emended, interpolated or omitted. Interestingly, all the manuscripts of Juvenal break off suddenly at 16.60 and this suggests either that the poet died with his last poem incomplete or else all the surviving manuscripts rely on one single version of the text which lacked its final pages. There are over 500 extant manuscripts of the poet – a number which shows how much he was read – and they are usually grouped into these categories:

Pithoeanus (P) named after the 16th-century scholar Pithou (who wrote his name on it) and housed in the Medical School at Montpellier. This is regarded as the most reliable (that is, least prone to error) of the manuscripts. A large number of manuscripts of lesser reliability derive from a different source and are usually referred to as Φ.

The central dilemma for any editor of this text is to decide whether to follow P over Φ (as at 8.167, 8.195, 9.68) or Φ over P (as at 7.23, 9.132): or sometimes whether they are both wrong and one should adopt a newer reading (e.g. 7.42, 9.106). I have preferred in this edition to produce a readable text wherever possible and indicated in the *apparatus criticus* where the text printed is the fruit of modern judgement rather than more ancient sources. Interpolations are also common in ancient poetry: sometimes marginal notes in a text were inserted into the text by the scribe copying it and then found themselves part of the text as may have happened at 7.15. Some modern scholars[24] would excise more than others and I have marked up the relevant passages with square brackets but left them in place for readers to make their own judgement.

For this edition I have relied heavily on the textual work of others. The text is largely that of Clausen, with such emendations as I have thought preferable to his readings. I have made use of the sigla which appear in the OCT throughout this book. In the Latin text I have used dictionary forms of words wherever possible and assimilated prefixes accordingly: so I have printed *uulgi* rather than *uolgi* and *affixit* rather than *adfixit*.

---

24   See Tarrant (2016) 85–104, (1987) 297, Courtney (1975)

BIBLIOGRAPHY

Editions of the text

Braund S. M. (1996) *Juvenal Satires Book 1* (Cambridge, Cambridge University Press).

Braund S. M. (2004) *Juvenal and Persius* (Cambridge, MA, Harvard University Press (Loeb Classical Library)).

Clausen W. V. (1992) *A. Persi Flacci et D. Iuni Iuvenalis Saturae* (Oxford Classical Text).

Courtney E. (1980, reprinted 2013) *A Commentary on the Satires of Juvenal* (California).

Dimatteo G. (2014) *Giovenale 'Satira' 8 Introduzione, testo, traduzione e commento* (Berlin/Boston, De Gruyter).

Duff J. D. (rep. 1975) *Juvenal Satires* (Cambridge, Cambridge University Press).

Ferguson J. (1979) *Juvenal the Satires* (London, Macmillan).

Friedländer L. (1895) *D. Iunii Iuvenalis Saturarum Libri V* (Leipzig: repr. Nabu Press 2014).

Godwin J. (2016) *Juvenal Satires Book IV* (Liverpool, Liverpool University Press).

Godwin J. (2020) *Juvenal Satires Book V* (Liverpool, Liverpool University Press).

Hardy E. G. (1963) *The Satires of Juvenal* (London).

Housman A. E. (1931) *D. Iunii Iuvenalis Saturae* (Cambridge, Cambridge University Press).

Mayor J. E. B. (1886–89) *Thirteen Satires of Juvenal* (London).

Ramsay G. G. (1918) *Juvenal and Persius* (Cambridge, Mass., Harvard University Press).

Stramaglia A. (2008) *Giovenale, Satire 1, 7, 12, 16. Storia di un poeta* (Bologna: Pàtron Editore).

Watson L. and Watson P. (2014) *Juvenal Satire 6* (Cambridge, Cambridge University Press).

Willis J. (1997) *Iuuenalis Saturae* (Stuttgart: Teubner).

Abbreviations

AG   Allen J. H. and Greenough J. B., *New Latin Grammar*
        (New York, 2006).
CAH   *The Cambridge Ancient History* (2nd edn, Cambridge, 2000).
CGL   *Corpus Grammaticorum Latinorum* (1831–: Leipzig, Teubner).
CIL   *Corpus Inscriptionum Latinorum* (1853–).
FLP   Courtney E *The Fragmentary Latin Poets*
        (Oxford, Oxford University Press, 2003).
K-S   Kühner R. and Stegmann C., *Ausführliche Grammatik*
        der Lateinischen Sprache (Hannover, 1971).
KRS   Kirk G. S., Raven J. E. and Schofield M. (2nd edn)
        The Presocratic Philosophers (Cambridge, 1983)
LS   Long A. A. and Sedley D. N. *The Hellenistic Philosophers*
        (2 vols, Cambridge,1987)
LSJ   Liddell, H. G. and Scott R. *A Greek-English Lexicon*
        (9th edn, Oxford 1968)
NLS   Woodcock E. C. (1959) *A New Latin Syntax* (London, Methuen)
OCD   *The Oxford Classical Dictionary* (3rd edn).
OLD   *The Oxford Latin Dictionary.*

Bibliography Of Works Cited

Adams J. N. (1982) *The Latin Sexual Vocabulary* (London, Duckworth).
Alexander W. H. (1947) 'Juvenal 7.126–8'. *Classical Philology* 42: 123–24.
Allen W. (1972) 'Ovid's *Cantare* and Cicero's *Cantores Euphorionis*'.
    Transactions and Proceedings of the American Philological Association
    103: 1–14.
Anderson W. S. (1955) 'Juvenal: Evidence on the Years AD 117–28'. *Classical*
    Philology 50: 255–57.
Anderson W. S. (1982) *Essays on Roman Satire* (Princeton, Princeton
    University Press).
Andrews A. C. (1948) 'Oysters as a Food in Greece and Rome'. *Classical*
    Journal 43: 299–303.
Ash R. (2007) *Tacitus Histories Book 2* (Cambridge, Cambridge University
    Press).
Austin R. (1971) *P. Vergil Maronis Aeneidos Liber Primus* (Oxford, Oxford
    University Press).

Austin R. (1977) *P. Vergil Maronis Aeneidos Liber Sextus* (Oxford, Oxford University Press).

Balsdon J. P. V. D. (1969) *Life and Leisure in Ancient Rome* (London, Bodley Head).

Barton T. (1994) *Ancient Astrology* (London/New York, Routledge).

Beard M. (1994) 'The Roman and the Foreign: the Cult of the "Great Mother" in Imperial Rome'. In Thomas N. and Humphrey C. (1994) *Shamanism, History and the State* (Michigan, University of Michigan Press).

Beard M., North J. and Price S. (1998) *Religions of Rome* (Cambridge, Cambridge University Press).

Beard M. (2007) *The Roman Triumph* (Cambridge Mass., Harvard University Press).

Beard M. (2008) *Pompeii: the Life of a Roman Town* (London, Profile Books).

Bellandi F. (2009) 'Naevolus cliens'. In Plaza M. (ed.) *Persius and Juvenal: Oxford Readings in Classical Studies* (Oxford: Oxford University Press).

Bernstein N. (2017) *Seneca: Hercules Furens* (London, Bloomsbury).

Bond S. (2014) 'Altering Infamy: Status, Violence, and Civic Exclusion in Late Antiquity'. *Classical Antiquity* 33: 1–30.

Bonner S. (1949) *Roman Declamation in the Late Republic and Early Empire* (Liverpool, University Press of Liverpool).

Bonner S. (1977) *Education in Ancient Rome* (London, Methuen).

Bowersock G. W. (1969) *Greek Sophists in the Roman Empire* (Oxford, Oxford University Press).

Boyle A. J. (2017) *Seneca Thyestes* (Oxford, Oxford University Press).

Braun L. (1989) 'Juvenal und die Überredungskunst', *Aufstieg und Niedergang der römichen Welt* II. 33.1: 770–810.

Braund S. H. (1981) 'Juvenal 8.58–59'. *Classical Quarterly* 31: 221–23.

Braund S. H. (1988) *Beyond Anger: a Study of Juvenal's Third Book of Satires* (Cambridge: Cambridge University Press).

Braund S. H. (1989) 'City and Country in Roman Satire'. In Braund S. H. (ed.) *Satire and Society in Ancient Rome* (Exeter, University of Exeter Press).

Braund S. H. (1992) *Roman Verse Satire* (*Greece and Rome* New Surveys in the Classics 23: Oxford, Oxford University Press).

Braund S. M. (1996) *The Roman Satirists and their Masks* (London, Bristol Classical Press).

Braund S. (2009) *Seneca de Clementia* (Oxford, Oxford University Press).

Braund S. and Osgood J. (2012) *A Companion to Persius and Juvenal* (Malden/Oxford, Wiley-Blackwell).

Brink C. O. (1971) *Horace on Poetry: the Ars Poetica* (Cambridge, Cambridge University Press).

Brown P. G. McC. (1972) 'Two Passages in Juvenal's Eighth Satire'. *Classical Quarterly* 22: 374–75.

Brunt P. A. (1961) 'Charges of Provincial Maladministration under the Early Principate'. *Historia*: 10: 189–227.

Brunt P. A. (1975) 'Did Imperial Rome Disarm Her Subjects?'. *Phoenix* 29: 260–70.

Burton G. P. (1975) 'Proconsuls, Assizes and the Administration of Justice under the Empire'. *The Journal of Roman Studies* 65: 92–106.

Butrica J. L. (2006) '*Criso* and *Ceueo*'. *Glotta* 82: 25–35.

Cameron A. (1976) *Circus Factions: Blues and Greens at Rome and Byzantium* (Oxford, Oxford University Press).

Carcopino J. (1956) *Daily Life in Ancient Rome* (Harmondsworth, Penguin).

Cary M. and Nock A. D. (1927) 'Magic Spears'. *Classical Quarterly* 21: 122–27.

Clarke M. L. (1953) *Rhetoric at Rome* (London, Cohen and West).

Clarke M. L. (1973) 'Juvenal 7. 242–3'. *The Classical Review* 23: 12.

Coleman K. M. (1990) 'Fatal Charades: Roman Executions Staged as Mythological Enactments'. *The Journal of Roman Studies* 80: 44–73.

Copley F. O. (1956) *Exclusus Amator: a Study in Latin Love Poetry* (Michigan, Scholars Press).

Corbier M. (2007) 'Painting and familial and genealogical memory (Pliny, *Natural History* 35, 1–14)'. *Bulletin of the Institute of Classical Studies*, Suppl. 100, vita vigilia est: Essays in Honour of Barbara Levick pp. 69–83.

Courtney E. (1966) 'Juvenaliana'. *Bulletin of the Institute of Classical Studies* 13: 38–43.

Courtney E. (1975) 'The Interpolations in Juvenal'. *Bulletin of the Institute of Classical Studies* 22: 147–62.

Cramer F. H. (1951) 'Expulsion of astrologers from ancient Rome'. *Classica et Mediaevalia* 12: 9–50.

Cramer F. H. (1954) *Astrology in Roman Law and Politics* (Philadelphia, American Philosophical Society).

Crook J. A. (1967) *Law and Life of Rome* (London, Thames and Hudson).

Crook J. A. (1995) *Legal Advocacy in the Roman World* (Ithaca, Cornell University Press).

Dalzell A. (1955) 'C. Asinius Pollio and the early history of public recitation in Rome'. *Hermathena* 86: 20–28.

Davey F. (1971) 'Juvenal 7.242f.'. *Classical Review* 21: 11.

Demougeot E. (1978) 'L'invasion des Cimbres-Teutons-Ambrons et les Romains'. *Latomus* 37: 910–938.

De Decker J. (1913) *Juvenalis Declamans: étude sur la rhétorique déclamatoire dans les Satires de Juvénal* (Ghent, Gand).

De Ste Croix G. E. M. (1981) *The Class Struggle in the Ancient Greek World* (London, Duckworth).

Dewar M. (2014) *Leisured Resistance: Villas, Literature and Politics in the Roman World* (London, Bloomsbury).

Dickey E. (2012) *The Colloquia of the Hermeneumata Pseudodositheana* (Cambridge, Cambridge University Press).

Dimatteo G. (2009) 'Onomastica, mito, satira: Iuv. 8, 30–38'. In Bonadeo A., Canobbio A. and Gasti F. (eds) *Filellenismo e Identità Romana In Età Flavia* (*Atti della VIII Giornata ghisleriana di Filologia classica*: Pavia) 135–54.

Dimatteo G. (2015) 'Una preghiera al nobile perduto: nota a Iuv. 8.26–30' *Philologus* 159: 188–95.

Dodds E. R. (2nd edn, 1960) *Euripides Bacchae* (Oxford, Oxford University Press).

Dodds E. R. (1973) *The Greeks and the Irrational* (California, University of California Press).

Dover K. J. (1974) *Greek Popular Morality in the Time of Plato and Aristotle* (Oxford, Oxford University Press).

Dunbabin R. L. (1925) 'Notes on Latin Authors'. *Classical Review* 39: 111–13.

Dyck A. R. (2008) *Cicero Catilinarians* (Cambridge, Cambridge University Press).

Dyck A. R. (2013) *Cicero Pro Marco Caelio* (Cambridge, Cambridge University Press).

Eden P. T. (1984) *Seneca Apocolocyntosis* (Cambridge: Cambridge University Press).

Eden P. T. (1985) 'Juvenalia'. *Mnemosyne* 38: 334–52.

Edwards C. (1993) *The Politics of Immorality in Ancient Rome* (Cambridge, Cambridge University Press).

Edwards C. (1997) 'Unspeakable Professions: Public Performance and Prostitution in Ancient Rome'. In Hallett J. P. and Skinner M. B. *Roman Sexualities* (Princeton, Princeton University Press) 66–95.

Edwards C. (2007) *Death in Ancient Rome* (Yale, Yale University Press).

Fantham R. E. (1989) 'Mime: The Missing Link in Roman Literary History'. *The Classical World* 82: 153–63.

Feldherr A. (2000) 'Non inter nota sepulcra: Catullus 101 and Roman Funerary Ritual'. *Classical Antiquity* 19: 209–31.

Finglass P. J. (2007) *Sophocles Electra* (Cambridge, Cambridge University Press).

Finglass P. J. (2018) *Sophocles Oedipus the King* (Cambridge, Cambridge University Press).

Flores Militello V. (2019) *tali dignus amico: Die Darstellung des patronus-cliens Verhältnisses bei Horaz, Martial und Juvenal* (Tübingen, Narr).

Flower H. (1996) *Ancestor Masks and Aristocratic Power in Roman Culture* (Oxford, Oxford University Press).

Fordyce C. (1961) *Catullus: a Commentary* (Oxford, Oxford University Press).

Fowler D. P. (2002) *Lucretius on Atomic Motion: a Commentary on* De rerum natura *2.1–332* (Oxford, Oxford University Press).

Franklin J. L. (1987) 'Pantomimists at Pompeii: Actius Anicetus and His Troupe'. *American Journal of Philology* 108: 95–107.

Fredericks S. C. (1971) 'Rhetoric and Morality in Juvenal's 8th Satire'. *Transactions and Proceedings of the American Philological Association* 102: 111–32.

Fredericks S. C. (1979) 'The Irony of Overstatement in the Satires of Juvenal'. *Illinois Classical Studies* 4: 178–91.

Freeman H. A. (1984) 'Critical Notes on some Passages in Juvenal'. *Rheinisches Museum* 127: 344–50.

Friedländer L. trans. Magnus L. A. (repr. 1968) *Roman Life and Manners under the Early Empire* (London, Barnes and Noble).

Galinsky G. K. (1972) *The Herakles Theme* (Oxford, Oxford University Press).

Gallivan P. A. (1973) 'Nero's Liberation of Greece'. *Hermes* 101: 230–34.

Garzetti A. (1974) *From Tiberius to the Antonines* (London, Methuen).

Geddes A. G. (1984) 'Who's Who in 'Homeric' Society?'. *The Classical Quarterly* 34: 17–36.

Gelzer M. trans. R. Seager (1969) *The Roman Nobility* (Oxford, Basil Blackwell).

Geue T. (2017) *Juvenal and the Poetics of Anonymity* (Cambridge, Cambridge University Press)

Gibson R. K. (2020) *Man of High Empire: the Life of Pliny the Younger* (New York, Oxford University Press).

Godwin J. (1995) *Catullus Poems 61–68* (Warminster, Aris and Phillips).

Godwin J. (2017) Review of Uden (2015). *Latomus* 76: 1159–62.

Golden M. (2004) *Sport in the Ancient World from A to Z* (London, Routledge).

Gow A. S. F. (1950) *Theocritus edited with a Translation and Commentary* (2 vols, Cambridge, Cambridge University Press).

Gowers E. (1993) *The Loaded Table: Representations of Food in Roman Literature* (Oxford, Oxford University Press).

Gowers E. (2012) *Horace Satires Book I* (Cambridge, Cambridge University Press).

Green W. M. (1931) 'The Rustic Festival of Osiris'. *Classical Weekly* 24: 83–84.

Griffin, J. (1985) *Latin Poets and Roman Life* (London, Duckworth).

Griffin M. T. (1984) *Nero: the End of a Dynasty* (London, Batsford).

Griffith J. G. (1962) 'Juvenal and Stage-Struck Patricians'. *Mnemosyne* 15: 256–61.

Griffith J. G. (1968) 'A Taxonomic Study of the Manuscript Tradition of Juvenal', *Museum Helveticum* 25: 101–138.

Griffith J. G. (1969) 'Frustula Iuvenaliana'. *Classical Quarterly* 19: 379–87.

Griffith M. (2006) 'Horsepower and Donkeywork: Equids and the Ancient Greek Imagination'. *Classical Philology* 101: 185–246.

Griffith M. (1983) *Aeschylus Prometheus Bound* (Cambridge, Cambridge University Press).

Gschlößl R. (2007) 'Göttinnen zwischen Orient und Okzident: Der Austausch der Kulturen ließ in der Spätantike Religionen verschmelzen'. *Antike Welt* 38: 91–97.

Guthrie W. K. C. (1971) *The Sophists* (Cambridge, Cambridge University Press).

Hardie A. (1990) 'Juvenal and the Condition of Letters: the Seventh Satire'. *Papers of the Leeds International Latin Seminar* 6: 145–209.

Harris W. V. (1980) 'Towards a Study of the Roman Slave Trade'. *Memoirs of the American Academy in Rome* 36: 117–40.

Harrison E. L. (1964) 'Was Gorgias a Sophist?'. *Phoenix* 18: 183–92.

Harrison S. J. (1991) *Vergil Aeneid 10* (Oxford, Oxford University Press).

Harrison S. J. (2015) 'Notes on the Text of Juvenal'. *Melita Classica* 2: 9–15.

Harrison S. J. (2017) *Horace Odes Book II* (Cambridge, Cambridge University Press).

Hassall M. W. C. (1970) 'Batavians and the Roman Conquest of Britain'. *Britannia* 1: 131–36.

Helmbold W. C. (1952) 'Atakta'. *Mnemosyne* 5: 224–27.

Helmbold W. C. and O'Neil E. N. (1959) 'The Form and Purpose of Juvenal's Seventh Satire'. *Classical Philology* 54: 100–108.

Henderson J. (1991) *The Maculate Muse* (Oxford/New York, Oxford University Press).

Henderson J. (1997) *Figuring out Roman Nobility: Juvenal's Eighth Satire* (Exeter, University of Exeter Press).

Hendry M. (1999) 'Epidaurus, Epirus, … Epidamnus? Vergil *Georgics* 3.44'. *Harvard Studies in Classical Philology* 99: 295–300.

Highet G. (1951) 'Juvenal's Bookcase'. *American Journal of Philology* 72: 369–94.

Highet G. (1952) 'Notes on Juvenal'. *The Classical Review* 2: 70–71.

Highet G. (1954) *Juvenal the Satirist* (Oxford, Oxford University Press).

Hill H. (1969) 'Nobilitas in the Imperial Period'. *Historia* 18: 230–50.

Hillner J. (2003) 'Domus, Family, and Inheritance: The Senatorial Family House in Late Antique Rome'. *The Journal of Roman Studies* 93: 129–45.

Hinard F. (1976) 'Remarques sur les "praecones" et le "praeconium" dans la Rome de la fin de la République'. *Latomus* 35: 730–46.

Hopkins K. (1978) *Conquerors and Slaves* (Cambridge, Cambridge University Press).

Hopkins K. (1983) *Death and Renewal* (Cambridge, Cambridge University Press).

Hopman M. (2003) 'Satire in Green: Marked Clothing and the Technique of Indignatio at Juvenal 5.141–45'. *The American Journal of Philology* 124: 557–74.

Jenkyns R. (1982) *Three Classical Poets* (London, Duckworth).

Jenkyns R. (1998) *Virgil's Experience* (Oxford, Oxford University Press).

Jones F. (1982) 'A note on Juvenal 7.86'. *Classical Quarterly* 32: 478–79.

Jones F. (1989) 'Juvenal 7'. In Deroux C. (ed.) *Studies in Latin Literature and Roman History* V (Collection Latomus) 444–63.

Jones C. P. (1972) 'Juvenal 8.220'. *The Classical Review* 22: 313.

Keane C. (2010) 'Persona and Satiric Career in Juvenal'. In Hardie P. and Moore H. *Classical Literary Careers and their Reception* (Cambridge, Cambridge University Press) 105–117.

Keane C. (2003) 'Theatre, Spectacle, and the Satirist in Juvenal'. *Phoenix* 57: 257–75.

Keane C. (2006) *Figuring Genre in Roman Satire* (Oxford/New York, Oxford University Press).

Kenney E. J. (1963) 'Juvenal: Satirist or Rhetorician?'. *Latomus* 22: 704–20.

Kenney E. J. (2012) 'Satiric Textures: Style, Meter and Rhetoric'. In Braund and Osgood (2012) 113–36.

Kerferd G. B. (1981) *The Sophistic Movement* (Cambridge, Cambridge University Press).

Killeen J. F. (1969) 'Juvenal 7.1126ff.'. *Glotta* 67: 265–66.

Kilpatrick R. S. (1973) 'Juvenal's 'Patchwork' Satires: 4 and 7'. *Yale Classical Studies* 23: 229–41.

Kißel W. (1990) *Aulus Persius Flaccus Satiren* (Heidelberg, Winter).

Lane Fox R. (2020) *The Invention of Medicine: from Homer to Hippocrates* (London, Allen Lane).

Latham J. (2012) 'Fabulous clap-trap: Roman Masculinity, the Cult of Magna Mater, and Literary Constructions of the galli at Rome from the Late Republic to Late Antiquity'. *The Journal of Religion* 92: 84–122.

Lattimore R. (1962) *Themes in Greek and Latin Epitaphs* (Urbana, University of Illinois Press).

Levick B. (1985) 'L. Verginius Rufus and the Four Emperors'. *Rheinisches Museum für Philologie* 128: 318–46.

Lloyd G. E. R. (2003) *In the Grip of Disease* (Oxford, Oxford University Press).

Lyne R. O. A. M. (1980) *The Latin Love Poets from Catullus to Horace* (Oxford, Oxford University Press).

McGill S. (2020) *Virgil Aeneid Book XI* (Cambridge, Cambridge University Press).

Marrou H. I. (1956) *A History of Education in Antiquity* (Wisconsin, University of Wisconsin Press).

Marshall A. J. (1975) 'Tacitus and the Governor's Lady: A Note on Annals iii. 33–4'. *Greece & Rome* 22: 11–18.

Martyn J. R. C. (1964) 'Juvenal on Latin Oratory'. *Hermes* 92: 121–23.

Mayer R. (1982) 'What Caused Poppaea's Death?'. *Historia* 31: 248–49.

Mayer R. (2001) *Tacitus: Dialogus* (Cambridge, Cambridge University Press).

Mayer R. (2012) *Horace Odes Book 1* (Cambridge, Cambridge University Press).

Millar F. (1984) 'Condemnation to Hard Labour in the Roman Empire, from the Julio-Claudians to Constantine'. *Papers of the British School at Rome* 52: 124–47.

Morford M. (2002) *The Roman Philosophers* (London, Routledge).

Muecke D. C. (1970) *Irony* (London, Methuen).

Mussehl J. (1919) 'Bedeutung und Geschichte des Verbums cēvēre'. *Hermes* 54: 387–408.

Mynors R. A. B. (1990) *Virgil Georgics* (Oxford, Oxford University Press).

Nappa C. (2013) 'Money, Marius Priscus, and *infamia* in Juvenal's First Satire'. *Rheinisches Museum für Philologie* 156: 406–409.

Nisbet R. G. M. (1995) *Collected Papers on Latin Literature* (Oxford, Oxford University Press).

Nisbet R. G. M. and Hubbard M. (1970) *A Commentary on Horace Odes Book I* (Oxford, Oxford University Press).

Nisbet R. G. M. and Hubbard M. (1978) *A Commentary on Horace Odes Book II* (Oxford, Oxford University Press).

Nisbet R. G. M. and Rudd N. (2004) *A Commentary on Horace Odes Book III* (Oxford, Oxford University Press).

Norden E. (1957) *P. Vergilius Maro Aeneis Buch VI* (Stuttgart, Teubner).

Ogilvie R. M. (1965) *A Commentary on Livy Books 1–5* (Oxford, Oxford University Press).

Ogilvie R. M. (1981) *The Romans and their Gods* (London, Chatto and Windus).

Otto A. (1890) *Sprichwörter und sprichwörtlichen Redensarten der Römer* (Leipzig).

Owen S. G. (1905) 'On the Tunica Retiarii. (Juvenal II. 143 ff.; VIII. 199 ff.; VI. Bodleian Fragment 9 ff.)'. *The Classical Review* 19: 354–57.

Paoli U. E. (1990) *Rome: Its People, Life and Customs* (Bristol, Bristol Classical Press).

Pelling C. B. R. (2016) 'Herodotus, Polycrates – and maybe Stesimbrotus too?'. *The Journal of Hellenic Studies* 136: 113–20.

Pelling C. B. R. (2019) *Herodotus and the Question Why* (Texas, University of Texas Press).

Plaza M. (2006) *The Function of Humour in Roman Verse Satire* (Oxford, Oxford University Press).

Powell J. G. F. (1988) *Cicero Cato Maior de Senectute* (Cambridge, Cambridge University Press).

Power T. (2010) 'Pliny, Letters 5.10 and the Literary Career of Suetonius'. *Journal of Roman Studies* 100: 140–62.

Prag J. R. W. (2007) 'Auxilia and Gymnasia: A Sicilian Model of Roman Imperialism'. *The Journal of Roman Studies* 97: 68–100.

Purcell N. (1995) 'Literate Games: Roman urban society and the game of alea'. *Past and Present* 147: 3–37.

Quincey J. H. (1959) 'Juvenal "Satire" VIII 192–6'. *Mnemosyne* 12: 139–40.

Radermacher L. (1904) 'zur siebentem Satire Juvenals'. *Rheinisches Museum für Philologie* 59: 525–31.

Radin M. (1920) 'The *lex Pompeia* and the *poena cullei*'. *Journal of Roman Studies* 10: 119–30.

Reeve M. R. (1971) 'Eleven Notes'. *Classical Review* 21: 324–29.

Reeve M. R. (1983) 'Commentaries on Juvenal'. *Classical Review* 33: 27–34.

Reynolds L. D. and Wilson N. G. (1967) *Scribes and Scholars: a Guide to the Transmission of Greek and Latin Literature* (Oxford, Oxford University Press).

Ronnick M. V. (1996) 'Lucan's marble gardens: Juvenal Satire 7.79f.'. *Scholia* 5: 89–90.

Rosen R. M. (2007) *Making Mockery: the Poetics of Ancient Satire* (Oxford, Oxford University Press).

Rudd N. (1976) *Lines of Enquiry: Studies in Latin Poetry* (Cambridge, Cambridge University Press).

Russell D. A. and Winterbottom M. (1972) *Ancient Literary Criticism: the Principal Texts in New Translations* (Oxford, Oxford University Press).

Saller R. P. (1983a) 'Martial on Patronage and Literature'. *The Classical Quarterly* 33: 246–57.

Saller R. P. (1983b) 'The Meaning of *faenus* in Juvenal's Ninth Satire'. *Proceedings of the Cambridge Philological Society* N.S. 29: 72–76.

Sandbach F. H. (1975) *The Stoics* (London, Chatto and Windus).

Santorelli B. (2016) 'Juvenal and declamatory *inuentio*' In Stramaglia A., Grazzini S. and Dimatteo G. (eds) *Giovenale tra storia, poesia e ideologia* (Berlin/Boston: de Gruyter).

Schmeling G. (2011) *A Commentary on the Satyrika of Petronius* (Oxford, Oxford University Press).

Schmidt K. H. (1967) 'Keltisches Wortgut im Lateinischen'. *Glotta* 44: 151–74.

Schmitz C. (2019a) *Juvenal* (Hildesheim, Georg Olms Verlag).

Schmitz C. (2019b) Review of Geue (2017). *Journal of Roman Studies* 109: 415–16.

Scullard H. H. (1963) *From the Gracchi to Nero* (London, Methuen).

Scullard H. H. (1981) *Festivals and Ceremonies of the Roman Republic* (London, Thames and Hudson).

Seaford R. A. S. (1984) 'The Last Bath of Agamemnon'. *Classical Quarterly* 34: 247–54.

Shackleton Bailey D. R. (1965) *Cicero's Letters to Atticus* vol. 1 (Cambridge, Cambridge University Press).

Shaw B. D. (2001) 'Raising and Killing Children: Two Roman Myths'. *Mnemosyne* 54: 31–77.

Spaeth B. S. (1996) *The Roman Goddess Ceres* (Austin, University of Texas Press).

Steel C. (2004) 'Being Economical with the Truth: what really happened at Lampsacus?' In Powell J. and Paterson J. (eds) *Cicero the Advocate* (Oxford, Oxford University Press).

Sullivan J. (2001) 'A Note on the Death of Socrates' *Classical Quarterly* 51: 608–10.

Syme R. (1939) *The Roman Revolution* (Oxford, Oxford University Press).

Syme R. (1958) *Tacitus* (Oxford, Oxford University Press).

Syme R. (1958b) 'Sabinus the Muleteer'. *Latomus* 17:73–80.

Syme R. (1970) 'Domitius Corbulo'. *The Journal of Roman Studies* 60: 27–39.

Syme R. (1979) 'The *Patria* of Juvenal'. *Classical Philology* 74: 1–15.

Syme R. (1982) 'The Marriage of Rubellius Blandus'. *American Journal of Philology* 103: 62–85.

Syme R. (1986) *The Augustan Aristocracy* (Oxford, Oxford University Press).

Syme R. (1991) *Roman Papers* vol. 6. Ed. A. R. Birley (Oxford, Oxford University Press).

Tarrant R. (1987) 'Towards a typology of interpolation in Latin poetry'. *Transactions of the American Philological Association* 117: 281–98.

Tarrant R. (2012) *Virgil Aeneid Book XII* (Cambridge, Cambridge University Press).

Tarrant R. (2016) *Texts, Editors and Readers: Methods and Problems in Latin Textual Criticism* (Cambridge, Cambridge University Press).

Tempest K. (2011) *Cicero: Politics and Persuasion in Ancient Rome* (London/New York, Continuum).

Tennant P. (1996) 'Tongue in cheek for 243 Lines? The Question of Juvenal's Sincerity in his Seventh Satire'. *Scholia* 5: 72–88.

Tennant P. (2003) 'Queering the Patron's Pitch: the Real Satirical Target of Juvenal's Ninth Satire' in: Basson A. F. and Dominik W. J. (eds) *Literature, Art, History: Studies on Classical Antiquity and its Tradition in Honour of W. J. Henderson* (Frankfurt am Main/New York, Peter Lang).

Thompson D. W. (1936) *A Glossary of Greek Birds* (Oxford, Oxford University Press).

Thompson H. J. (1920) 'Communis Sensus'. *The Classical Review* 34: 18–21.

Thurmond D. L. (2017) *From Vines to Wines in Classical Rome: a Handbook of Viticulture and Oenology in Rome and the Roman West* (Leiden, Brill).

Torelli M. (1968) 'The Cursus Honorum of M. Hirrius Fronto Neratius Pansa'. *Journal of Roman Studies* 58: 170–75.

Townend G. B. (1973) 'The Literary Substrata to Juvenal's Satires'. *The Journal of Roman Studies* 63: 148–60.

Toynbee J. M. C. (1948) 'Beasts and their Names in the Roman Empire'. *Papers of the British School at Rome* 16: 24–37.

Toynbee J. M. C. (1973 repr. 2013) *Animals in Roman Life and Art* (London, Pen and Sword).

Treggiari S. (1991) *Roman Marriage*: iusti coniuges *from the time of Cicero to the time of Ulpian* (Oxford, Oxford University Press).

Uden J. (2015) *The Invisible Satirist: Juvenal and Second-Century Rome* (New York, Oxford University Press).

Vessey D. W. T. C. (1973) 'The Stoics and Nobility: a Philosophical Theme'. *Latomus* 32: 332–44.

Virlouvet C. (1995) *Tessera Frumentaria: les Procédures de Distribution du Blé public à Rome à la Fin de la République et au Début de l'Empire* (Rome, École Francaise de Rome).

Vout C. (1996) 'The Myth of the Toga: Understanding the History of Roman Dress'. *Greece and Rome* 43: 204–220.

Wallace-Hadrill A. (1981) 'Family and Inheritance in the Augustan Marriage Laws'. *Proceedings of the Cambridge Philological Society* N.S. 27: 58–80.

Walsh P. G. (1961) *Livy: his Historical Aims and Methods* (Cambridge, Cambridge University Press).

Watson G. R. (1969) *The Roman Soldier* (London, Thames and Hudson).

Watson L. C. (2003) *A Commentary on Horace's Epodes* (Oxford, Oxford University Press).

Watson P. (1983) 'Puella and Virgo'. *Glotta* 61: 119–43.

Watt W. S. (2002) 'Notes on Juvenal'. *Hermes* 130: 299–305.

West M. L. (1966) *Hesiod: Theogony* (Oxford, Oxford University Press).

West M. L. (1978) *Hesiod: Works and Days* (Oxford, Oxford University Press).

White P. (1978) 'Amicitia and the Profession of Poetry in Early Imperial Rome'. *The Journal of Roman Studies* 68: 74–92.

Wiesen D. S. (1971) 'Classis Numerosa: Juvenal, Satire 7. 151'. *Classical Quarterly* 21: 506–508.

Wiesen D. S. (1973) 'Juvenal and the Intellectuals'. *Hermes* 101: 464–83.

Williams G. W. (1959) 'Dogs and Leather'. *Classical Review* 9: 97–100.

Williams C. A. (1999) *Roman Homosexuality: Ideologies of Masculinity in Classical Antiquity* (New York, Oxford University Press).

Winkler M. M. (1983) *The Persona in Three Satires of Juvenal* (Hildesheim, Olms).

Winsbury R. (2009) *The Roman Book* (London, Bloomsbury).

Winterbottom M. (2004) 'Perorations'. In Powell J. and Patterson J. (eds) *Cicero the Advocate* (Oxford, Oxford University Press).

Wirszubski Ch. (1968) *Libertas as a Political Idea at Rome during the Late Republic and Early Principate* (Cambridge, Cambridge University Press).

Wiseman T. P. (1985) *Catullus and his World* (Cambridge, Cambridge University Press).

Witt R. E. (1971) *Isis in the Graeco-Roman World* (London, Thames and Hudson).

Yavetz Z. (1984) 'The *Res Gestae* and Augustus' Public Image'. In Millar F. and Segal E. *Caesar Augustus: Seven Aspects* (Oxford, Oxford University Press).

JUVENAL

SATIRES

BOOK III

SATIRE VII

et spes et ratio studiorum in Caesare tantum;
solus enim tristes hac tempestate Camenas
respexit, cum iam celebres notique poetae
balneolum Gabiis, Romae conducere furnos
temptarent, nec foedum alii nec turpe putarent   5
praecones fieri, cum desertis Aganippes
uallibus esuriens migraret in atria Clio.
nam si Pieria quadrans tibi nullus in umbra
ostendatur, ames nomen uictumque Machaerae
et uendas potius commissa quod auctio uendit   10
stantibus, oenophorum, tripedes, armaria, cistas,
Alcithoen Pacci, Thebas et Terea Fausti.
hoc satius quam si dicas sub iudice 'uidi'
quod non uidisti; faciant equites Asiani,
[quamquam et Cappadoces faciant equitesque Bithyni]   15
altera quos nudo traducit gallica talo.
nemo tamen studiis indignum ferre laborem
cogetur posthac, nectit quicumque canoris
eloquium uocale modis laurumque momordit.
hoc agite, o iuuenes! circumspicit et stimulat uos   20
materiamque sibi ducis indulgentia quaerit.
si qua aliunde putas rerum expectanda tuarum

3   celebres notique *PAG*: noti celebresque *Φ*: multi celebresque *LZ*
8   umbra *PGU*: arca *Φ*
11   tripedes *PFG*: tripodes *Φ*
12   Alcithoen *GO*: alcitheon *PS*: alcinoen *Φ*: Halcyonem *C. Valesius*   Pacci *PS*:
     bacchi *Φ*
15   *del. Guyet*
16   gallica *PSGU*: gallia *ΦΣ*
20–21   *damnauit Guyet*
20   uos *PFG*: nos *Φ*
22   expectanda *Φ*: spectanda *P*: speranda *Housman*: experanda *Lond.mus.Brit.
     Burn.* 192

SATIRE VII

The hope and the justification for the life of the mind rests
    solely on Caesar:
he alone has shown concern for the wretched Muses in these times,
when by now famous and well-known poets
would seek to rent a bath-house in Gabii, or bake-houses in Rome
and others did not think it disgusting or degrading   5
to become auctioneers, since the vales of Aganippe have been
abandoned and famished Clio was moving into the salerooms.
For if not a penny is shown to you in the Pierian shade
then you have to embrace the name and the lifestyle of Machaera
and settle for selling whatever the tooth-and-nail auction sells   10
to its bystanders – winejar, three-legged pieces, cupboards, trunks,
Paccius' *Alcithoe*, the *Thebans* and *Tereus* of Faustus.
This is preferable to saying under the eye of the judge 'I saw it'
about something you did not see; let the Asian knights do that
[although both Cappadocians and Bithynian knights do it]   15
who are betrayed by one of their shoes leaving an ankle bare.
Nobody however will be forced to put up with work which is
    unworthy
of his intellect in years to come – nobody who weaves a verbal
    utterance
in melodious metres and who has chewed the laurel.
To work then, young men! The kindness of our leader is looking
    around and urging   20
you on, in the hunt for material for his favour.
If you think you should expect your fortunes can be shored up
    from another source

praesidia atque ideo croceae membrana tabellae
impletur, lignorum aliquid posce ocius et quae
componis dona Veneris, Telesine, marito,   25
aut claude et positos tinea pertunde libellos.
frange miser calamum uigilataque proelia dele,
qui facis in parua sublimia carmina cella,
ut dignus uenias hederis et imagine macra.
spes nulla ulterior; didicit iam diues auarus   30
tantum admirari, tantum laudare disertos,
ut pueri Iunonis auem. sed defluit aetas
et pelagi patiens et cassidis atque ligonis.
taedia tunc subeunt animos, tunc seque suamque
Terpsichoren odit facunda et nuda senectus.   35
accipe nunc artes ne quid tibi conferat iste,
quem colis et Musarum et Apollinis aede relicta.
ipse facit uersus atque uni cedit Homero
propter mille annos. tu si dulcedine famae
succensus recites, maculosas commodat aedes.   40
haec longe ferrata domus seruire iubetur
in qua sollicitas imitatur ianua porcas.
scit dare libertos extrema in parte sedentes
ordinis et magnas comitum disponere uoces;
nemo dabit regum quanti subsellia constant   45
et quae conducto pendent anabathra tigillo
quaeque reportandis posita est orchestra cathedris.
nos tamen hoc agimus tenuique in puluere sulcos
ducimus et litus sterili uersamus aratro.

23   croceae … tabellae *Φ*: crocea … tabellae *P*: crocea … tabella *F*
24   impletur *Φ*: implentur *PSΣ*
25   componis *PAGU*: conscribis *Φ*
27   calamum *P Vat.Reg. 2029*: calamos *Φ*
39   tu *Hermann*: et *P*: aut *Φ*
40   maculosas *Heinrich*: maculosos *F:* maculonus *Φ*: maculonis *PG*
41   haec *P*: ac *Φ*
42   porcas *Jessen*: portas *codd.*

and that's why the parchment of your yellow page is being filled up,
then ask right now for some firewood and donate your
compositions to the husband of Venus, Telesinus;   25
or else store and lock the books up and get them punched through
    by a bookworm.
You wretch, snap your pen and destroy those midnight-oil battles;
you who create lofty poems in a tiny garret
in the hope of coming out worthy of the ivy and a skinny bust.
There is no further hope: the rich miser has learned by now   30
just to admire, just to praise intellectuals,
as kids admire Juno's bird. Meanwhile your time of life,
which would be able to stand the sea, the helmet and the mattock,
    is flowing away.
It's then that boredom invades the heart, then that your old age,
eloquent but stripped bare, detests itself and its Muse.   35
Listen now to the tricks he uses to avoid giving you anything – that
man whom you cultivate, leaving the temple of the Muses
    and Apollo.
He produces verses himself and only defers to Homer
for the sake of the thousand years between them. If you are ablaze
    for the sweetness
of public renown and give a recitation, he lets you have a shoddy
    house for it.   40
This house, out in the sticks and all chained up, is ordered to be
    at your service
and its door makes the noise of panicking pigs.
He knows how to give you freedmen to sit on the ends
of the rows and he knows how to put the loud voices of the
    claque at your disposal;
but none of these princes will give you the price of the benches   45
and the hanging gallery with its hired scaffolding
and the front rows set out with thrones which must be returned
    after the event.
And yet we carry on doing this, ploughing furrows in the thin dust
and turning over the seashore with an unprofitable plough.

nam si discedas, laqueo tenet ambitioso 50
[consuetudo mali tenet insanabile multos]
scribendi cacoethes et aegro in corde senescit.
sed uatem egregium, cui non sit publica uena,
qui nihil expositum soleat deducere, nec qui
communi feriat carmen triuiale moneta, 55
hunc, qualem nequeo monstrare et sentio tantum,
anxietate carens animus facit, omnis acerbi
impatiens, cupidus siluarum aptusque bibendis
fontibus Aonidum. neque enim cantare sub antro
Pierio thyrsumque potest contingere maesta 60
paupertas atque aeris inops, quo nocte dieque
corpus eget: satur est cum dicit Horatius 'euhoe.'
quis locus ingenio, nisi cum se carmine solo
uexant et dominis Cirrhae Nysaeque feruntur
pectora uestra duas non admittentia curas? 65
magnae mentis opus nec de lodice paranda
attonitae currus et equos faciesque deorum
aspicere et qualis Rutulum confundat Erinys.
nam si Vergilio puer et tolerabile desset
hospitium, caderent omnes a crinibus hydri, 70
surda nihil gemeret graue bucina. poscimus ut sit
non minor antiquo Rubrenus Lappa coturno,
cuius et alueolos et laenam pignerat Atreus?

50   ambitioso *Braund*: ambitiosi *codd.*: ambitiosum *Jahn*
50–51   laqueo … mali *deleuit Housman*
51   *omisit L, deleuit Jahn*
54   nihil *SΦ*: nil *P*
60   maesta *PAL*; sana *GHKTUΣ*: saeua *FOZ*
63   quis *Φ*: qui *P*
73   alueolos *PFΣ*: albiolos *Φ*

For if you escaped, then a cancer of writing holds you in a
    binding noose   50
[the habit of misfortune holds many men incurably]
and grows old in the sick heart.
But the poet of genius who does not quarry the common
    vein of inspiration,
who is not in the habit of turning out a commonplace and does not
knock out a banal poem from the public mint –   55
I cannot point out anyone like this but can only feel his
    existence – he
is made by a mind which has no anxiety and is completely
    free of all
bitterness, a mind which desires the woods and which is fit
    to drink from
the springs of the Muses. For unhappy poverty cannot sing under
    the shade of
the Pierian cave nor touch the thyrsus, since it lacks the money
    which the body   60
needs night and day. Horace is stuffed full of food when he
    says 'euhoe'.
What scope is there for original genius if your hearts are not
    troubled
by poetry alone, moving to the beat of the masters
    of Cirrha and Nysa
and not giving any room to more than one concern?   65
It is the task of a great mind – one which is not distressed
    about the buying
of a blanket – to gaze upon chariots, horses, features of gods
and the sort of Fury which confounded the Rutulian.
For if Virgil had no slave-boy and no acceptable
accommodation, then all the snakes would fall from
    the Fury's hair,   70
and the trumpet would wail its deep tones unheard.
    Do we demand
that Rubrenus Lappa be no less than the tragedians of old
when his *Atreus* has been pawned against his plates
    and his cloak?

non habet infelix Numitor quod mittat amico,
Quintillae quod donet habet, nec defuit illi   75
unde emeret multa pascendum carne leonem
iam domitum; constat leuiori belua sumptu
nimirum et capiunt plus intestina poetae.
contentus fama iaceat Lucanus in hortis
marmoreis, at Serrano tenuique Saleio   80
gloria quantalibet quid erit, si gloria tantum est?
curritur ad uocem iucundam et carmen amicae
Thebaidos, laetam cum fecit Statius Urbem
promisitque diem: tanta dulcedine captos
afficit ille animos tantaque libidine uulgi   85
auditur. sed cum fregit subsellia uersu
esurit, intactam Paridi nisi uendit Agauen.
ille et militiae multis largitus honorem
semenstri uatum digitos circumligat auro.
quod non dant proceres, dabit histrio. tu Camerinos   90
et Baream, tu nobilium magna atria curas?
praefectos Pelopea facit, Philomela tribunos.
haud tamen inuideas uati quem pulpita pascunt.
quis tibi Maecenas, quis nunc erit aut Proculeius
aut Fabius, quis Cotta iterum, quis Lentulus alter?   95
tum par ingenio pretium, tunc utile multis
pallere et uinum toto nescire Decembri.
uester porro labor fecundior, historiarum
scriptores? perit hic plus temporis atque olei plus.
nullo quippe modo millensima pagina surgit   100

---

80   at *PSΣ*: et *Φ*   saleio *SFGHOZ*: saleno *P*: salino *AKLTUΣ*
87   uendit *PΦ*: uendat *AKOT*
88   largitus *GVat.3286*: largitur *PΦ*:
91   Baream *PSF*: bareas *Φ*
93   *deleuit Markland*
96   tum *P*: tunc *Φ*
99   perit *PFG*: petit *Φ*
100   nullo quippe modo *PGLOUZ*: namque oblita modo *A*: namque oblita modi
     FHKT

Unfortunate Numitor has nothing to send to his client
but he has gifts for Quintilla and did not lack the funds 75
to buy a lion – previously tamed – which needed feeding with
lots of meat; a beast supposedly costs less in outlay
and the guts of a poet hold more food.
Lucan may be lying in his marbled gardens, content with his
    reputation,
but what will any amount of glory do for Serranus and 80
famished Saleius, if glory is all they get?
People run to hear the lovely voice and the poetry of his darling
Thebaid, when Statius has made the city happy
and fixed a date; he grips their hearts, taken captive by
so much sweetness, and is listened to with so much ardent desire 85
from the crowd. But when he has brought the house down
    with his reading
he goes hungry if he does not sell his virginal *Agaue* to Paris – the
man who lavishes military honours on many a man,
who puts (for six months' service) the gold ring on poets' fingers.
An actor will give what great men do not. Do you
    cultivate the Camerini 90
and Barea, do you seek out the grand entrance-halls of
    noble men?
Pelopea is what makes men prefects, *Philomela* makes
    them tribunes.
But do not be jealous of a bard who is fed by the stage.
Who will be a Maecenas to you, who will now be a Proculeius
or a Fabius, who will be a second Cotta or Lentulus reborn? 95
In those times the pay matched the talent, in those days many
    found it
useful to go pale and disown wine for the whole of December.
Is your hard work then more productive, you writers of
histories? More time and midnight oil goes to waste in this
    enterprise.
With no limit applied, the thousandth page rises up 100

omnibus et crescit multa damnosa papyro;
sic ingens rerum numerus iubet atque operum lex.
quae tamen inde seges? terrae quis fructus apertae?
quis dabit historico quantum daret acta legenti?
'sed genus ignauum, quod lecto gaudet et umbra.'   105
dic igitur quid causidicis ciuilia praestent
officia et magno comites in fasce libelli.
ipsi magna sonant, sed tum cum creditor audit
praecipue, uel si tetigit latus acrior illo
qui uenit ad dubium grandi cum codice nomen.   110
tunc immensa caui spirant mendacia folles
conspuiturque sinus; ueram deprendere messem
si libet, hinc centum patrimonia causidicorum,
parte alia solum russati pone Lacertae.
consedere duces, surgis tu pallidus Aiax   115
dicturus dubia pro libertate bubulco
iudice. rumpe miser tensum iecur, ut tibi lasso
figantur uirides, scalarum gloria, palmae.
quod uocis pretium? siccus petasunculus et uas
pelamydum aut ueteres, Maurorum epimenia, bulbi   120
aut uinum Tiberi deuectum, quinque lagonae
si quater egisti. si contigit aureus unus,
inde cadunt partes ex foedere pragmaticorum.
'Aemilio dabitur quantum licet, et melius nos
egimus.' huius enim stat currus aeneus, alti   125
quadriiuges in uestibulis, atque ipse feroci
bellatore sedens curuatum hastile minatur
eminus et statua meditatur proelia lusca.

105   lecto *PFGH*: tecto *Φ*
106   praestent *PAGU*: praestant *ΦΣ*
108   tum *PAOU*: tunc *Φ*
109   *deleuit Jahn*
114   Lacertae *Φ*: lacernae *PS Arou et fortasse G*
120   aut *PΦ*: et *AKLT*
121   lagonae *PFGH*: lagoenae *Φ*
123   ex *PAGLU*: in *Φ*
124   licet *PT Arou.*: libet *GLU*: petet *Φ*   et *mss.*: at *Ruperti, Cramer*

in every case and grows ruinous with heaps of papyrus.
The massive number of facts and the rule of the genre
  dictate this.
But what is the harvest of all this? what is the fruit of this
  ploughed field?
Who will give a historian as much as he would give to a man
  reading out the gazette?
'But they are a lazy breed, enjoying their days on the couch
  in the shade.'   105
Tell me then what reward barristers get for their civic
duties, with their briefs going with them in a big bundle.
They make a big sound, but especially so when a creditor of theirs
is listening, or if someone who is here with a huge account-book
  to chase up a contested
debt taps them on the flank with still greater urgency.   110
Then his hollow bellows breathe out measureless falsehoods
and his bosom is spattered; if you wish to uncover the real earnings,
then put the estates of one hundred barristers on one side
and on the other the property just of the Lizard dressed in red.
The chiefs have sat down, you get up, a pale-faced Ajax,   115
to plead for contested liberty before a peasant
judiciary. You poor man, burst your tense liver open just to ensure
  that when you are
exhausted green palms might be pinned up as the glory of your
  staircase.
What is the price of your voice? A dry little pork shoulder
  and a jar
of tunny-fish, or else ancient onions – monthly rations for Moors
  – or   120
wine brought down the Tiber, five flagons if you have spoken
  four times. If you do get a single gold coin
the solicitors take their share of it according to the deal.
'Aemilius will get as much as is permitted, and yet we pleaded
better.' Why? this man has a bronze chariot standing there, a lofty 125
four-horse team in his entrance-halls, and himself sitting on
his fierce warhorse, aiming his drooping spear
from afar and planning his battles as a one-eyed statue.

sic Pedo conturbat, Matho deficit, exitus hic est
Tongilii, magno cum rhinocerote lauari 130
qui solet et uexat lutulenta balnea turba
perque forum iuuenes longo premit assere Maedos
empturus pueros, argentum, murrina, uillas;
spondet enim Tyrio stlattaria purpura filo.
[et tamen est illis hoc utile. purpura uendit] 135
causidicum uendunt amethystina; conuenit illi
et strepitu et facie maioris uiuere census,
sed finem impensae non seruat prodiga Roma.
fidimus eloquio? Ciceroni nemo ducentos
nunc dederit nummos, nisi fulserit anulus ingens. 140
respicit haec primum qui litigat, an tibi serui
octo, decem comites, an post te sella, togati
ante pedes. ideo conducta Paulus agebat
sardonyche, atque ideo pluris quam Gallus agebat,
quam Basilus. rara in tenui facundia panno. 145
quando licet Basilo flentem producere matrem?
quis bene dicentem Basilum ferat? accipiat te
Gallia uel potius nutricula causidicorum
Africa, si placuit mercedem ponere linguae.
declamare doces? o ferrea pectora Vetti, 150
cum perimit saeuos classis numerosa tyrannos.
nam quaecumque sedens modo legerat, haec eadem stans
perferet atque eadem cantabit uersibus isdem.
occidit miseros crambe repetita magistros.

134 *transposuit post 137 Courtney*
135 *om. U, del. Knoche*
136 illi *P Arou. Mico Sang.*: illis *Φ*
138 *del. Guyet*
139 fidimus eloquio *PGArou.*: ut redeant ueteres *Φ*
142 post te *PGL*: poste *Arou. Sang.*: posite *FH*: posita *Φ*
144 Gallus *PFGHU Arou*: Cossus *Φ*
146 producere *PAGTU*: deducere *Φ*
149 ponere *P Arou.*: inponere *Φ Ant.*: poscere *Buecheler*
151 cum *mss*: cui *Jahn*
153 isdem *ΦP*: idem *AGU*

This is how Pedo goes bankrupt, how Matho fails, this is the
    end for
Tongilius who likes to be washed with a huge rhinoceros-horn,   130
who disturbs the baths with his muddy mob and who
weighs down his Maedian youths with the long litter-pole
    through the forum,
on his way to buy slave-boys, silver, myrrhine vessels, villas:
for the pirate purple with its Tyrian thread stands as his guarantor.
[Yet this is also useful for them. Purple sells]   135
a barrister, and crimson garb does too. It pays him
to live with the racket and the appearance of inflated wealth,
but spendthrift Rome sets no limit to his expenditure.
Do we trust oratory? Nobody would give even two hundred
to Cicero these days – unless he had a massive gleaming ring.   140
This is what anyone going to court looks at first – whether you
    have eight
slaves, ten companions, whether you have a litter-chair
    following you, with
toga-clad men walking in front. That is why Paulus used
    to plead with a rented
sardonyx, and that is why he earned more for his pleading
    than Gallus did,
and more than Basilus. Eloquence is not often found
    in threadbare clothing.   145
When may Basilus bring out a weeping mother into court?
Who would make do with Basilus for all his fine speaking?
    Get yourself
to Gaul or even better that wet-nurse of barristers
Africa, if you have decided to monetise your tongue.

Do you teach rhetoric? Oh for the iron-clad heart of Vettius   150
when his chanting class slays savage tyrants.
For whatever the student had just read sitting down, this same
    stuff he will
perform standing up and sing the same stuff in the same lines.
The rehashed cabbage murders the wretched teachers.

quis color et quod sit causae genus atque ubi summa   155
quaestio, quae ueniant diuersa parte sagittae,
nosse uolunt omnes, mercedem soluere nemo.
'mercedem appellas? quid enim scio?' 'culpa docentis
scilicet arguitur, quod laeuae parte mamillae
nil salit Arcadico iuueni, cuius mihi sexta   160
quaque die miserum dirus caput Hannibal implet,
quidquid id est de quo deliberat, an petat Urbem
a Cannis, an post nimbos et fulmina cautus
circumagat madidas a tempestate cohortes.
quantum uis stipulare et protinus accipe: quid do   165
ut totiens illum pater audiat?' haec alii sex
uel plures uno conclamant ore sophistae
et ueras agitant lites raptore relicto;
fusa uenena silent, malus ingratusque maritus
et quae iam ueteres sanant mortaria caecos.   170
ergo sibi dabit ipse rudem, si nostra mouebunt
consilia, et uitae diuersum iter ingredietur
ad pugnam qui rhetorica descendit ab umbra,
summula ne pereat qua uilis tessera uenit
frumenti; quippe haec merces lautissima. tempta   175
Chrysogonus quanti doceat uel Pollio quanti
lautorum pueros, artem scindes Theodori.
balnea sescentis et pluris porticus in qua
gestetur dominus quotiens pluit. anne serenum
expectet spargatque luto iumenta recenti?   180

154   crambe *G:* grambe *FH*: cambre *Φ Ant.*: crambre *P Arou.*
156   diuersa *AGLOU*: diuersa e *uel* diuersae *PFHKTZ Arou*
       parte *Φ*: forte *P Arou*: fronte *Vat.3286 Ant.*
157   uolunt *Φ Ant.:* uelunt *P Arou*: uelint *Pithoeus*
159   laeuae *mss*: leue *P Arou*: laeua *AFGHU*: laeua in *KLOTZ*
166   haec *PGU Ant. Arou*: ast haec *FH*: ast *Φ*
167   uel *PS Arou*: ut *H*: et *Φ*
177   scindes *Jahn*: scindens *PSΦΣ*
180   spargatque *mss.*: spargatue *Heinrich*

What gloss to put on the speech, what the genre of the case is,
    where is the key 155
point, what arrows might come from the other side – they
all want to know this, but none of them wants to pay up.
'You're asking to be paid? What have I learned?' 'I suppose it's
    alleged to be
the fault of the teacher that in the area of his left breast
the bumpkin youth has no pulse; his 'Hannibal the Dread' 160
fills my poor head every sixth day
no matter what he is pondering – whether to go to the city
after Cannae, whether after the storm-clouds and thunderbolts
    he should be cautious
and wheel round his troops who are soaked from the storm.
Name your fee – as much as you like – and have it at once.
    What would I give 165
for his father to hear him as often as I have?' This is what
    another six
or more professors shout out with one voice
and mount real court-cases, abandoning 'the rapist';
'poured poisons' are silent, as is the 'bad thankless husband'
and 'preparations which heal cases of chronic blindness'. 170

He will accordingly take retirement, if our advice convinces
him, and will enter upon a different way of life, this man
who comes down from the shades of rhetoric to fight it out
to ensure that he does not lose the pittance with which the
    cheap token
for corn is bought, since this is the most lavish fee he can
    expect. Find out 175
how much Chrysogonus and Pollio get for teaching the sons
    of the
posh folk and you will then rip up the *Handbook* of Theodorus.
Bathrooms cost six hundred thousand – more for the colonnade
    in which
the master may ride whenever it rains. Is he to wait for calm
weather or else spatter his animals with fresh mud? 180

hic potius, namque hic mundae nitet ungula mulae.
parte alia longis Numidarum fulta columnis
surgat et algentem rapiat cenatio solem.
quanticumque domus, ueniet qui fercula docte
componit, ueniet qui pulmentaria condit.   185
hos inter sumptus sestertia Quintiliano,
ut multum, duo sufficient: res nulla minoris
constabit patri quam filius. 'unde igitur tot
Quintilianus habet saltus?' exempla nouorum
fatorum transi. felix et pulcher et acer,   190
felix et [sapiens et nobilis et generosus
appositam] nigrae lunam subtexit alutae;
felix orator quoque maximus et iaculator
etsi perfrixit cantat bene. distat enim quae
sidera te excipiant modo primos incipientem   195
edere uagitus et adhuc a matre rubentem.
si Fortuna uolet, fies de rhetore consul;
si uolet haec eadem, fiet de consule rhetor.
Ventidius quid enim? quid Tullius? anne aliud quam
sidus et occulti miranda potentia fati?   200
seruis regna dabunt, captiuis fata triumphum.
felix ille tamen coruo quoque rarior albo.
paenituit multos uanae sterilisque cathedrae,
sicut Tharsimachi probat exitus atque Secundi
Carrinatis; et hunc inopem uidistis, Athenae,   205
nil praeter gelidas ausae conferre cicutas.
di maiorum umbris tenuem et sine pondere terram
spirantesque crocos et in urna perpetuum uer,

---

181   *omisit Laur. 34, 39, del. Heinrich*
185   conponit *GT Ant.:* conponat *PΦ*   condit *PΦ Ant.:* condat *LOU:* condet *H Vat.Urb.342*
191–2   sapiens ... appositam *del. Reeve*
192   *del. Jahn, Scholte*
194   etsi *Eden:* et si *mss.:* et nisi *Courtney:* et ni *Weidner*
197   fies *Φ Ant. Sang.:* fiet *P*
204   tharsimachi *P:* thresimachi *Φ:* lisimachi *FH.* uersum omisit *T.*

Preferably ride here, since here the hoof of his clean mule shines.
In another part of the house let him have a dining room, shored
    up on long columns from
Numidia, rise up and catch the sun in cold weather.
No matter how much the house costs, there will be someone
    to set out the dishes
skilfully, someone will come who flavours the food.   185
Amongst this expense two thousand sesterces (a considerable sum)
    will suffice
for Quintilian. Nothing will cost the father less than his
son. 'In that case where does
Quintilian get so many estates?' Pass over cases of unprecedented
fortune. The fortunate man is handsome and energetic,   190
the fortunate man is [also wise and noble and well-born] and
weaves the moon [attached] to his black shoe;
the fortunate man is also the greatest orator and javelin-thrower
who sings well even if he has caught a cold. What makes the
    difference is
which stars greet you when you are just starting to utter your   195
first wailing and are still glowing red from your mother.
    If Fortune wants, you will become a consul from being
    a teacher of rhetoric:
in the same way, if she wants, the consul will become a teacher.
What about Ventidius? What of Tullius? Does this show
    anything other than the
work of the star and the amazing power of hidden destiny?   200
Destiny will give kingship to slaves, triumph to captives.
The fortunate man is still rarer than a white crow, however.
Many have regretted their unprofitable and barren professor's chair,
as proved by the demise of Thrasymachus and Carrinas
Secundus; Athens, you saw this man too in poverty   205
and had the nerve to offer him nothing but chilly hemlock.
May the gods lay thin and weightless earth on the souls of our
    ancestors,
blooming crocuses and everlasting spring in the burial-urn,

qui praeceptorem sancti uoluere parentis
esse loco. metuens uirgae iam grandis Achilles   210
cantabat patriis in montibus et cui non tunc
eliceret risum citharoedi cauda magistri;
sed Rufum atque alios caedit sua quemque iuuentus,
Rufum, quem totiens Ciceronem Allobroga dixit.
quis gremio Celadi doctique Palaemonis affert   215
quantum grammaticus meruit labor? et tamen ex hoc,
quodcumque est (minus est autem quam rhetoris aera),
discipuli custos praemordet acoenonoetus
et qui dispensat frangit sibi. cede, Palaemon,
et patere inde aliquid decrescere, non aliter quam   220
institor hibernae tegetis niueique cadurci,
dummodo non pereat mediae quod noctis ab hora
sedisti, qua nemo faber, qua nemo sederet
qui docet obliquo lanam deducere ferro,
dummodo non pereat totidem olfecisse lucernas   225
quot stabant pueri, cum totus decolor esset
Flaccus et haereret nigro fuligo Maroni.
rara tamen merces quae cognitione tribuni
non egeat. sed uos saeuas imponite leges,
ut praeceptori uerborum regula constet,   230
ut legat historias, auctores nouerit omnes
tamquam ungues digitosque suos, ut forte rogatus,
dum petit aut thermas aut Phoebi balnea, dicat
nutricem Anchisae, nomen patriamque nouercae
Anchemoli, dicat quot Acestes uixerit annis,   235

---

214   quem *PGU Sang. Σ*: qui *Φ*
215   celadi *PGU*: enceladi *Φ Sang.*
218   acoenonoetus *P Vat. Reg. 2029*: acoenonoetos *G*: acoenonetos *U*
219   frangit *FGHUZΣ*: frangat *PA*: franget *KLOT*
223   sederet *P*: sedebit *FGHU*: sedebat *Φ*
224   docet *mss.*: solet *Scholte*
235   anchemoli *Vat. Reg. 2029*: anchemori *GKU*: archemoli *Paris. 7906*:
      archemori *PSΦ*
      annis *PA*: annus *FH*: annos *Φ*

since those men wanted the teacher to be in the position
  of a respected
parent. Achilles was by now a grown man but still feared
  the cane   210
as he sang in his father's mountains, and would not even then
  find that
the tail of his lyre-playing master would give him the giggles:
but Rufus and other man are each flogged by their own young
  charges,
Rufus, whom they so often called the 'Cicero of the Allobroges.'
Who puts into the pocket of Celadus and the learned Palaemon   215
as much as their pedagogical labour deserves? Yet out of this,
whatever it is (and it is less than the cash of a teacher of rhetoric)
the pupil's ungracious bodyguard has a nibble first
and the cashier also breaks a bit off for himself. Give in,
  Palaemon,
and just let some deductions be made from it, like the   220
street-seller of a winter mat or a snowy mattress,
so long as you don't lose payment for sitting from the midnight
hour, an hour when no smith would sit, nor anyone
who teaches people to card wool with a slanting metal frame:
so long as you don't lose the fee for smelling as many lamps   225
as there were boys standing there, when your Flaccus was all
discoloured and the soot was sticking to your blackened Virgil.
It's not often however that pay is given without
  needing the investigation
of a tribune. Yet you (parents) impose harsh conditions on him:
the teacher's command of grammar is to be unfailing,   230
he should read the stories and know all the authors
as he knows his own nails and toes, in case he is asked,
while he is making for the hot baths or the bath-house of
  Phoebus, to name
the nurse of Anchises, the name and native-land of the stepmother
of Anchemolus, to state how many years Acestes lived   235

quot Siculi Phrygibus uini donauerit urnas.
exigite ut mores teneros ceu pollice ducat,
ut si quis cera uultum facit; exigite ut sit
et pater ipsius coetus, ne turpia ludant,
ne faciant uicibus. non est leue tot puerorum 240
obseruare manus oculosque in fine trementes.
'haec' inquit 'cura; sed cum se uerterit annus,
accipe, uictori populus quod postulat, aurum.'

236   siculi *PGL*: siculis *U*: siculus *Φ*
242   cura sed *G*: cura *F*: curas et *PΦ*. *uersum omisit Z*

and how many jars of Sicilian wine he gave to the Phrygians.
Demand of him that he shape, as if with his thumb, their tender
   characters
like someone making a face out of wax: demand that he be
the father of the actual gang, to stop them playing dirty games
and doing it taking turns. It is no easy matter with so many boys   240
to keep an eye on their hands and their eyes quivering as they
   climax.
'That's your job' says the parent 'but when the year turns around
take home the gold which the people demand for a victorious
   fighter.'

SATIRE VIII

stemmata quid faciunt? quid prodest, Pontice, longo
sanguine censeri, pictos ostendere uultus
maiorum et stantes in curribus Aemilianos
et Curios iam dimidios umerosque minorem
Coruinum et Galbam auriculis nasoque carentem,   5
quis fructus generis tabula iactare capaci
censorem posse ac multa contingere uirga
fumosos equitum cum dictatore magistros,
si coram Lepidis male uiuitur? effigies quo
tot bellatorum, si luditur alea pernox   10
ante Numantinos, si dormire incipis ortu
luciferi, quo signa duces et castra mouebant?
cur Allobrogicis et magna gaudeat ara
natus in Herculeo Fabius lare, si cupidus, si
uanus et Euganea quantumuis mollior agna,   15
si tenerum attritus Catinensi pumice lumbum
squalentes traducit auos emptorque ueneni
frangenda miseram funestat imagine gentem?
tota licet ueteres exornent undique cerae
atria, nobilitas sola est atque unica uirtus.   20
Paulus uel Cossus uel Drusus moribus esto,
hos ante effigies maiorum pone tuorum,
praecedant ipsas illi te consule uirgas.

---

4 umerosque *P*: humeroque *Dresd.155*: nasumque *Φ*
5–6 *om. G, del Hermann*
5 coruinum *P Dresd.155*: coruini *Φ*
6–8 *del. Guyet*
7 *habent PG, om. Φ* censorem *Harrison*: coruinum *P*: coruini *G*: pontifices
  Housman
 posse ac *Withof, Housman*: posthac *P*: post haec *GK*:
8 fumosos *PFG*: famosos *Φ*
11 ortu *PGΣ*: ortus *Φ*
17 traducit *PSAGUΣ*: producit *FHLOZ* producat *KT*

SATIRE VIII

What use are family trees? What's to be gained, Ponticus by being
assessed with a long blood-line, with showing off painted faces
of your ancestors – Aemiliani standing in their chariots,
Curii now chopped in half, a Corvinus smaller in the shoulders
and a Galba lacking his ears and his nose –   5
what profit is there from being able to brag about a censor in your
extensive family tree, joining, with many a branch, smoky
    Cavalry Officers
with a dictator, if your life in the presence of the Lepidi is
    a bad one? What use are
images of so many war-heroes if the dice are played all night long   10
in front of Numantini, if you only start to sleep at the rising
of Lucifer – a time when generals used to stir their standards
    and their camp?
Why should a Fabius, born in the house of Hercules, crow about
the Allobroges and the Great Altar if he is greedy,
if he is a fool and softer than any Euganean lamb,   15
if he has his groin rubbed smooth with Catanian pumice
and so betrays his hairy ancestors? If as a poison-dealer
he pollutes his pathetic clan and his image ought to be smashed?
Even though ancient wax masks decorate your whole entrance
    hall,
the one and only nobility is virtue.   20
Be a Paulus or a Cossus or a Drusus in your behaviour;
put these men before the images of your ancestors
and let them walk in front of the rods when you are consul.

prima mihi debes animi bona. sanctus haberi
iustitiaeque tenax factis dictisque mereris?   25
agnosco procerem; salue Gaetulice, seu tu
Silanus: quocumque alio de sanguine rarus
ciuis et egregius patriae contingis ouanti,
exclamare libet populus quod clamat Osiri
inuento. quis enim generosum dixerit hunc qui   30
indignus genere et praeclaro nomine tantum
insignis? nanum cuiusdam Atlanta uocamus,
Aethiopem Cycnum, prauam extortamque puellam
Europen; canibus pigris scabieque uetusta
leuibus et siccae lambentibus ora lucernae   35
nomen erit pardus, tigris, leo, si quid adhuc est
quod fremat in terris uiolentius. ergo cauebis
et metues ne tu sic Creticus aut Camerinus.
his ego quem monui? tecum est mihi sermo, Rubelli
Blande. tumes alto Drusorum stemmate, tamquam   40
feceris ipse aliquid propter quod nobilis esses,
ut te conciperet quae sanguine fulget Iuli,
non quae uentoso conducta sub aggere texit.
'uos humiles' inquis 'uulgi pars ultima nostri,
quorum nemo queat patriam monstrare parentis,   45
ast ego Cecropides.' uiuas et originis huius
gaudia longa feras. tamen ima plebe Quiritem
facundum inuenies, solet hic defendere causas

27   alio *PΦ* alto *Richards*
33   prauam *PΦ*: paruam *ALO*
37   fremat *PΦ*: fremit *ALT*
38   sic *Lond. mus. Brit. Add. 11997*: si *P*: sis *Φ*
40   stemmate *PAFGHU*: sanguine *KLOTZ*
44   inquis *AKLO*: inquit *PΦ*

The first thing you must show (I think) is goodness of heart.
   Do you deserve to be
considered unimpeachable, never letting go of justice in your
   deeds and words? 25
I salute you as a leader of men: hail, Gaetulicus, or you
Silanus – or from whatever other blood-line – you turn out
   to be a rare
and outstanding citizen to your exultant fatherland and
I want to shout out what the crowd shouts when Osiris has been
found. For who would call this man 'noble' if he is 30
a disgrace to his family and only distinguished by virtue
   of his glorious
title? We do call somebody's dwarf 'Atlas',
the Ethiopian 'Swan', the twisted and deformed girl
'Europa': dogs which are idle, smooth-skinned with chronic
mange, which lick the rim of the dry lamp – they 35
will be given the name 'leopard', 'tiger', 'lion' or anything else
which roars more violently on the earth. For that reason you
   will beware
and be anxious not to be a 'Creticus' or a 'Camarinus' only
   in that way.
Who have I been warning with these words? My conversation
   is with you,
Rubellius Blandus. You are puffed up with the lofty pedigree
   of the Drusi, as if 40
you have personally done something to make you noble,
so that a woman glowing with Julian blood conceived you
rather than one who did weaving for hire under the windy
   embankment.
'You are inferiors' you say 'the lowest section of our people,
and none of you could point out the fatherland of your parent, 45
whilst I am a Cecropid'. Long life to you and may you enjoy
   long-lasting
joy from this pedigree of yours. You will however find in the
   lowest class
an articulate citizen, and this man has the habit of defending
   the case

nobilis indocti; ueniet de plebe togata
qui iuris nodos et legum aenigmata soluat;   50
hinc petit Euphraten iuuenis domitique Bataui
custodes aquilas armis industrius; at tu
nil nisi Cecropides truncoque simillimus Hermae.
nullo quippe alio uincis discrimine quam quod
illi marmoreum caput est, tua uiuit imago.   55
dic mihi, Teucrorum proles, animalia muta
quis generosa putet nisi fortia. nempe uolucrem
sic laudamus equum, facili cui plurima palma
feruet et exultat rauco uictoria circo;
nobilis hic, quocumque uenit de gramine, cuius   60
clara fuga ante alios et primus in aequore puluis.
sed uenale pecus Coryphaei posteritas et
Hirpini, si rara iugo uictoria sedit.
nil ibi maiorum respectus, gratia nulla
umbrarum; dominos pretiis mutare iubentur   65
exiguis, trito et ducunt epiraedia collo
segnipedes dignique molam uersare nepotes.
ergo ut miremur te, non tua, priuum aliquid da
quod possim titulis incidere praeter honores
quos illis damus ac dedimus, quibus omnia debes.   70
haec satis ad iuuenem quem nobis fama superbum
tradit et inflatum plenumque Nerone propinquo;
rarus enim ferme sensus communis in illa
fortuna. sed te censeri laude tuorum,

49   plebe *PSAGLU*: gente *Φ*: pube *Housman*   togata *codd.*: togatus *Scriverius*
51   hinc *GU, Weidner*: hic *PΦS*
57   putet *PAFL*: putat *Φ*
62   coryphaei *GU²Σ*: cor•c• *P*: corythae *Φ*
66   trito et *Goth. 2.52, Laur. 34.34.*: et trito *P Sang*: trito *AGU*: tritoque *Φ*
67   nepotes *PFGHU*: nepotis *Φ*
68   priuum *Salmasius*: primum *codd.*

of the uneducated nobleman. There will arise from the
    toga-wearing plebs
a man to untie statutory knots and legal puzzles;   50
a youth from this class, tireless in fighting, makes for the
    Euphrates and for the eagles
 which watch over the conquered Batavian: but you are
nothing but a Cecropid, looking just like a stunted Herm.
You are superior by no criterion at all except that
the herm has a marble head, while you are a living statue.   55
Tell me, o offspring of the Trojans, who could think that dumb
    animals
are well-bred unless they are strong? That is why we praise
    the swift
horse – the one who wins easily and who has many a triumph
    seething
and celebrating in the hoarse Circus;
whatever grass it comes from, this one is 'pedigree' whose   60
running is clear of the rest and its dust is first on the track.
The descendants of Coryphaeus and Hirpinus are just beasts up
    for sale
if Victory sits but rarely on their yoke.
No regard for ancestors there, no favour conferred by their
shades; these slow-footed scions are told to change their masters   65
for tiny fees and drag carriages with worn necks,
fit only to turn the millstone.
And so, to make us admire you and not just what you have,
    give me something
individual which I could chisel onto your tablet besides those titles
which we give (and have given) to those men to whom
    you owe everything.   70
That is enough to say to the young man who – as his reputation
    reports – was
proud and puffed up and full of his connections to Nero;
for empathy is a rare commodity in that
income-bracket. I would not be happy to see you assessed on
    the glory of your

Pontice, noluerim sic ut nihil ipse futurae   75
laudis agas. miserum est aliorum incumbere famae,
ne collapsa ruant subductis tecta columnis.
stratus humi palmes uiduas desiderat ulmos.
esto bonus miles, tutor bonus, arbiter idem
integer; ambiguae si quando citabere testis   80
incertaeque rei, Phalaris licet imperet ut sis
falsus et admoto dictet periuria tauro,
summum crede nefas animam praeferre pudori
et propter uitam uiuendi perdere causas.
dignus morte perit, cenet licet ostrea centum   85
Gaurana et Cosmi toto mergatur aeno.
expectata diu tandem prouincia cum te
rectorem accipiet, pone irae frena modumque,
pone et auaritiae, miserere inopum sociorum:
ossa uides rerum uacuis exsucta medullis.   90
respice quid moneant leges, quid curia mandet,
praemia quanta bonos maneant, quam fulmine iusto
et Capito et Tutor ruerint damnante senatu,
piratae Cilicum. sed quid damnatio confert?
praeconem, Chaerippe, tuis circumspice pannis,   95
cum Pansa eripiat quidquid tibi Natta reliquit,
iamque tace; furor est post omnia perdere naulum.
non idem gemitus olim neque uulnus erat par
damnorum sociis florentibus et modo uictis.

78   desiderat *PΦ Sang.*: desideret *FGHU, Beer*
88   accipiet *Φ*: accipiat *PAF Sang.*
90   rerum *PFGHU*: regum *Φ*
93   tutor *ΦΣ*: numitor *PS Mico*
98   neque *PAF*: nec *SΦ*

people, Ponticus, with you doing nothing to secure glory
   in the future.   75
It is pathetic to depend on the renown of others
in case the columns are pulled down and the roof crashes in ruins.
The vine-shoot strewn on the ground longs for the bereaved
   elm-trees.
Be a good soldier, a good guardian and also an honest
judge; if ever you are summoned as a witness in a dubious   80
and unclear case – even though Phalaris orders you to lie
and dictates perjuries with his bull moved into position –
think it the height of wickedness to prefer existence to honour
and to ruin the reasons for living for the sake of your life.
The man who deserves death is not alive, even though he dines
   on one hundred   85
Gauran oysters and bathes in a bronze tub full of Cosmus' perfume.
When finally the province that you have been waiting for
   so long
welcomes you as its governor, then rein in and moderate
   your anger,
set a limit to your greed, take pity on the penniless allies;
you see the bones of their property sucked out, their marrows
   empty.   90
Keep an eye on what the laws advocate, what the senate-house
   stipulates,
how great are the benefits which await good men and with how
   righteous a lightning-bolt
both Capito and Tutor were ruined when the senate condemned
   them,
those pirates of the Cilicians. But what good came
   of the condemnation?
Chaerippus, look out an auctioneer for your rags   95
since Pansa is snatching whatever Natta left you,
and now stop speaking up: it is madness after losing all else to
   lose your fare.
The groaning was not the same, nor was the injury of their losses
   as great
when the allies were thriving and had only just been conquered.

plena domus tunc omnis, et ingens stabat aceruus   100
nummorum, Spartana chlamys, conchylia Coa,
et cum Parrhasii tabulis signisque Myronis
Phidiacum uiuebat ebur, nec non Polycliti
multus ubique labor, rarae sine Mentore mensae.
inde Dolabella atque audax Antonius, inde   105
sacrilegus Verres referebant nauibus altis
occulta spolia et plures de pace triumphos.
nunc sociis iuga pauca boum, grex paruus equarum,
et pater armenti capto eripietur agello,
ipsi deinde Lares, si quod spectabile signum .   110
[si quis in aedicula deus unicus; haec etenim sunt
pro summis, nam sunt haec maxima. despicias tu]
forsitan imbelles Rhodios unctamque Corinthon
despicias merito: quid resinata iuuentus
cruraque totius facient tibi leuia gentis?   115
horrida uitanda est Hispania, Gallicus axis
Illyricumque latus; parce et messoribus illis
qui saturant Urbem Circo scaenaeque uacantem;
quanta autem inde feres tam dirae praemia culpae,
cum tenues nuper Marius discinxerit Afros?   120
curandum in primis ne magna iniuria fiat
fortibus et miseris. tollas licet omne quod usquam est
auri atque argenti, scutum gladiumque relinques.
et iaculum et galeam; spoliatis arma supersunt.
quod modo proposui, non est sententia, uerum est;   125
credite me uobis folium recitare Sibyllae.

105   Dolabella *Φ*: Dolabellae *Ruperti*: dolo bellans *Eden*.   audax *Knoche*: atque
      hinc *mss*: rapax   *Nisbet*: astuque *Eden*: praedoque *Braund*: hinc atque hinc
      Weidner
111–112   *deleuit Manso.*
111   etenim sunt *mss*: retinentes *Courtney* rapientur *Dimatteo*
119–21   *deleuit Jachmann*
123–4   scutum – galeam *deleuit Hermann*
123   relinques *Φ*: relinquas *PST*
124   *deleuit Lachmann.* iaculum *P. Vat. 3286* iacula *Φ*

Every house in those days was full of stuff, there stood a huge
    heap   100
of cash, a cloak from Sparta and purple from Cos,
and along with paintings by Parrhasius and Myron's statues
the ivory of Phidias lived, and everywhere were many
works of Polyclitus, and hardly any tables without a Mentor.
From there Dolabella and ruthless Antonius, from there   105
the impious Verres would bring back in their tall ships
hidden spoils and more triumphs over the peaceful.
These days the allies will have a few head of cattle, a small herd
    of mares
and the sire of the herd snatched from them when the little estate
    is taken,
and even the Household Gods, if there is a statue worth looking at 110
[if any single god is in the little shrine: for these things are
as good as it gets, for these are now the biggest. You might despise]
perhaps the unwarlike Rhodians and oiled Corinth
you might rightly despise: what will the resin-smeared youth
and the hairless legs of a whole people do to you?   115
You should avoid hairy Spain, the Gallic region
and the flank of Illyricum: and spare those harvesters
who glut the city when it is on holiday to enjoy the races
    and the stage;Besides, what amount of pay-off will you get
    for such appalling behaviour
now that Marius has not long ago stripped the Africans
    to the bone?   120
The first priority is to ensure that no wrong is done to people
    who are
strong and desperate. Even if you lift all the gold and silver
    which is
anywhere to be found, you will still leave them their shield
    and sword
[and spear and helmet: even plundered people keep their weapons.]
What I have just set down is not opinion, it is true: 125
believe that I am reading aloud to you a page of the Sibyl.

si tibi sancta cohors comitum, si nemo tribunal
uendit acersecomes, si nullum in coniuge crimen
nec per conuentus et cuncta per oppida curuis
unguibus ire parat nummos raptura Celaeno,   130
tum licet a Pico numeres genus, altaque si te
nomina delectant omnem Titanida pugnam
inter maiores ipsumque Promethea ponas.
[de quocumque uoles proauom tibi sumito libro.]
quod si praecipitem rapit ambitio atque libido,   135
si frangis uirgas sociorum in sanguine, si te
delectant hebetes lasso lictore secures,
incipit ipsorum contra te stare parentum
nobilitas claramque facem praeferre pudendis.
omne animi uitium tanto conspectius in se   140
crimen habet, quanto maior qui peccat habetur.
quo mihi te, solitum falsas signare tabellas,
in templis quae fecit auus statuamque parentis
ante triumphalem? quo, si nocturnus adulter
tempora Santonico uelas adoperta cucullo?   145
praeter maiorum cineres atque ossa uolucri
carpento rapitur pinguis Lateranus, et ipse,
ipse rotam adstringit sufflamine mulio consul,
nocte quidem, sed Luna uidet, sed sidera testes
intendunt oculos. finitum tempus honoris   150
cum fuerit, clara Lateranus luce flagellum
sumet et occursum numquam trepidabit amici

131   tum *KLOTZ*: tu *PSAFGHU*: tunc *Vat.Pal. 1701*
133   ponas *PAL Sang.*: pingas *Φ*
134   *deleuit Ribbeck*
135   ambitio *PG Sang.*: ambitus *Φ*
147   Lateranus *PSGU*: Damasippus *ΦΣ*
148   sufflamine mulio *GUSang.*: sufflamine multo *Laur. 34.40*: multo sufflamine
      PΦ
151   Lateranus *PGU*: Damasippus *ΦΣ*
152   numquam *PAGU*: nusquam *Φ*

If you have a team of staff who are not corrupt, if no
    long-haired youth
sells your verdict, if there is no blame in your wife
and she does not set out to go through the district courts and all
    the towns
with curved talons, out for cash like a Harpy,   130
then you may count your ancestry from Picus and (if lofty
    names are
what pleases you) you can name the whole Titan phalanx
and Prometheus himself amongst your ancestors.
[take your great-grandfather from whichever book you like.]
But if it's a thirst for power and sex which drives you headlong,   135
if you shatter rods in the blood of our allies, and if
you are pleased by axes blunted in the hands of an exhausted
    lictor,
then the pedigree of your actual parents begins to oppose you
and to hold a bright torch to your shameful deeds.
Every moral failing faces more public charges against itself   140
the greater the reputation of the sinner himself.
What use are you, tell me, if you are in the habit of sealing
    fake wills
in temples which your grandfather built and in front of a statue
of your parent celebrating a triumph? If you are an adulterer
    by night
shrouding your brow with a Gallic cap?   145
Fat Lateranus races
    in his flying mule-cart past the ashes and bones
of his ancestors and the man himself
personally slows the wheel with the brake – a muleteer consul –
by night for sure, but the moon sees him, but the stars
sharpen their eyes to witness. When his period of office   150
has finished, Lateranus will take up his lash in bright daylight
and will never be nervous of meeting a friend

iam senis ac uirga prior adnuet atque maniplos
soluet et infundet iumentis hordea lassis.
interea, dum lanatas robumque iuuencum 155
more Numae caedit, Iouis ante altaria iurat
solam Eponam et facies olida ad praesepia pictas.
sed cum peruigiles placet instaurare popinas,
obuius assiduo Syrophoenix udus amomo
currit – Idymaeae Syrophoenix incola portae 160
hospitis adfectu dominum regemque salutans –
et cum uenali Cyane succincta lagona.
defensor culpae dicet mihi 'fecimus et nos
haec iuuenes.' esto, desisti nempe nec ultra
fouisti errorem. breue sit quod turpiter audes, 165
quaedam cum prima resecentur crimina barba.
indulge ueniam pueris: Lateranus ad illos
thermarum calices inscriptaque lintea uadit
maturus bello Armeniae Syriaeque tuendis
amnibus et Rheno atque Histro. praestare Neronem 170
securum ualet haec aetas. mitte Ostia, Caesar,
mitte, sed in magna legatum quaere popina:
inuenies aliquo cum percussore iacentem,
permixtum nautis et furibus ac fugitiuis,
inter carnifices et fabros sandapilarum 175
et resupinati cessantia tympana galli.
aequa ibi libertas, communia pocula, lectus
non alius cuiquam, nec mensa remotior ulli.
quid facias talem sortitus, Pontice, seruum?
nempe in Lucanos aut Tusca ergastula mittas. 180
at uos, Troiugenae, uobis ignoscitis et quae

155   robumque *PS Sang, Σ*: toruumque *Φ* rubumque *GU*
159   adsiduo *codd.*: Assyrio *Dorleans*. udus *Φ*: unctus *A*
159–60   Syrophoenix…Idymaeae *om. F del. Hermann*
161   salutans *Leo* salutat *ΦP*
163   dicet *GT*: dicit *Φ*
166   resecentur PAGLOU: resecantur *FHKTZ*
170   amnibus *codd.*: finibus *Markland.*
170–174   et … et *PAGU Sang.*: aut … aut *Φ*

who is now old, and he will take the initiative in greeting him
   with his stick
and untie the hay-bundles and pour out the barley for the weary
   beasts.
Meanwhile, while he slaughters woolly animals and a ruby bull   155
in the manner of Numa, when he is in front of Jupiter's altars
   he swears oaths
only by Epona and the images painted on the stinking stables.
When he chooses to revisit his all-night diners
the Phoenician, awash with constant perfume,
runs to meet him – the Phoenician who lives at the Jewish gate   160
with his host's welcome greeting him as master and lord – along
with Cyane, her skirt hitched up with her bottle for sale.
Someone will excuse this misbehaviour and say 'we too did
this when we were young'. Yes – but you stopped and did not
indulge the waywardness any further. Let shameless
   adventuring be short-lived   165
and some misbehaviour should be trimmed with the first beard.
Make allowances for the sins of youth: but Lateranus marches
   off to those
bath-house boozers and slogan-clad awnings
when he is ready for war, for defending the rivers of Armenia
   and Syria
and the Rhine and the Danube. This time of life has the
   power to secure   170
Nero's safety. Send your governor to Ostia, Caesar,
send him – but look for him in some massive tavern:you will
   find him lying with some assassin
mingled with sailors, thieves and runaways
amongst executioners and coffin-makers   175
and the idle drums of the eunuch-priest flat on his back.
it's equal freedom for all there, shared cups, not separate
couches for some nor a table set aside for anyone.
What would you do if fate gave you a slave of that sort, Ponticus?
You would send him to the folk in Lucania or the Etrurian
   dungeons, surely.   180
But you, scions of the Trojans, you pardon yourselves and so what
   would be

turpia cerdoni Volesos Brutumque decebunt.
quid si numquam adeo foedis adeoque pudendis
utimur exemplis, ut non peiora supersint?
consumptis opibus uocem, Damasippe, locasti   185
sipario, clamosum ageres ut Phasma Catulli.
Laureolum uelox etiam bene Lentulus egit,
iudice me dignus uera cruce. nec tamen ipsi
ignoscas populo; populi frons durior huius,
qui sedet et spectat triscurria patriciorum,   190
planipedes audit Fabios, ridere potest qui
Mamercorum alapas. quanti sua funera uendant
quid refert? uendunt nullo cogente Nerone,
nec dubitant celsi praetoris uendere ludis.
finge tamen gladios inde atque hinc pulpita poni,   195
quid satius? mortem sic quisquam exhorruit, ut sit
zelotypus Thymeles, stupidi collega Corinthi?
res haut mira tamen citharoedo principe mimus
nobilis. haec ultra quid erit nisi ludus? et illic
dedecus Urbis habes, nec murmillonis in armis   200
nec clipeo Gracchum pugnantem aut falce supina;
damnat enim tales habitus [sed damnat et odit,
nec galea faciem abscondit]: mouet ecce tridentem.
postquam uibrata pendentia retia dextra
nequiquam effudit, nudum ad spectacula uoltum   205

182   Uolesos *Φ*: uolusos *O Vat.Reg.2029*: uolsos *P*.   Brutumque *Φ*: rutulumque
       GU
192   funera *PAU*: uerbera *Courtney*
194   *del. Ruperti*
195   poni *P*: pone *Φ*: ponunt *FH*
196   sic *O Vat. Pal.1701 Σ*: si *PΦ*   praestare…aetas *del. Nisbet*
198   mimus *GU*: natus *Φ*
201   pugnantem aut *PSAGU*: aut pugnantem *Φ*
202   *del. Guyet*
202   sed *PAGU*: et *Φ*
202–3   sed damnat … abscondit: *deleuit Hermann*
203   faciem *PAGU*: frontem *Φ*
204   uibrata *codd.*: librata *Courtney*

disgraceful for a labourer is sure to be honourable for the Volesi
    or a Brutus.
What if we never find cases which are so disgusting, so shameless
that there are not even worse ones around?
When you had spent up all your money, Damasippus, you hired
    out your voice   185
to the mime-show, to play the noisy ghost of Catullus.
Speedy Lentulus played Laureolus quite well in fact,
and in my opinion deserved a real crucifixion. Do not however
    pardon
the crowd themselves: these people have a brazen front
and can sit watching the triple-buffooneries of patricians,   190
listen to barefoot Fabii and can laugh at the slapstick at the
    expense of the
Mamerci. What does it matter how much they sell their
    'deaths' for?
They sell them without being forced to do so by Nero
and have no qualms about selling them at the games of the lofty
    praetor.
Imagine that either execution or the stage are set up as
    alternatives –   195
which is preferable? Has anyone trembled at death so much
    that he would be
Thymele's jealous husband, the colleague of the clown Corinthus?
An aristocrat acting in a mime is nothing to be surprised at
    when the emperor is
a lyre-player. Beyond this what will there be except the
    gladiatorial school? There too
you have the disgrace of the city – Gracchus fighting neither
    in the weapons of   200
murmillo nor with shield or curved blade;
he scorns gear like that [but scorns and hates it
and does not hide his face in a helmet]: look – he is brandishing
    a trident.
After he has steadied his right hand and cast his dangling net
to no avail, he lifts up his bare face to the crowd   205

erigit et tota fugit agnoscendus harena.
credamus tunicae, de faucibus aurea cum se
porrigat et longo iactetur spira galero.
ergo ignominiam grauiorem pertulit omni
uolnere cum Graccho iussus pugnare secutor.   210
libera si dentur populo suffragia, quis tam
perditus ut dubitet Senecam praeferre Neroni?
cuius supplicio non debuit una parari
simia nec serpens unus nec culleus unus.
par Agamemnonidae crimen, sed causa facit rem   215
dissimilem. quippe ille deis auctoribus ultor
patris erat caesi media inter pocula, sed nec
Electrae iugulo se polluit aut Spartani
sanguine coniugii, nullis aconita propinquis
miscuit, in scena numquam cantauit Oresten,   220
Troica non scripsit. quid enim Verginius armis
debuit ulcisci magis aut cum Vindice Galba,
quod Nero tam saeua crudaque tyrannide fecit?
haec opera atque hae sunt generosi principis artes,
gaudentis foedo peregrina ad pulpita cantu   225
prostitui Graiaeque apium meruisse coronae.
maiorum effigies habeant insignia uocis,
ante pedes Domiti longum tu pone Thyestae
syrma uel Antigones seu personam Melanippes,
et de marmoreo citharam suspende colosso.   230
    quid, Catilina, tuis natalibus atque Cethegi
inueniet quisquam sublimius? arma tamen uos
nocturna et flammas domibus templisque paratis,
ut bracatorum pueri Senonumque minores,
ausi quod liceat tunica punire molesta.   235

220   Oresten *Weidner*: Orestes *codd.*
223   *del. Knoche.* quod *Vat.Urb.342* quid *PΦ*
224   hae sunt *PAE*: haec sunt *U Vat. 3192*: illae sunt *FH*: illae *KLOTZ*
225   cantu *PGU et test. Prisc GL 2.419*: saltu *Φ*
229   Antigones *Φ*: Antigonae *P Mico.* seu *Vat. 3192, Vat. 3286*: tu *Φ*: aut
      Hermann
233   paratis *P Lond. Mus. Brit. Reg 15 B XII*: parastis *Φ*

and runs all over the arena for all to recognise him.
Let's believe the tunic, as it stretches golden from his throat
and the ribbon bouncing from his high hat.
In this way the *secutor* who was told to fight with Gracchus
endured shame worse than any injury could inflict.   210
If the people were given free votes, who would be so
beyond help as to hesitate about choosing Seneca over Nero?
Not just one monkey needed to be acquired to punish that
man, nor one snake or one sack.
His crime was the equal of Agamemnon's son, but the motive
      makes the case   215
very different. Orestes, you see, was told by gods to avenge
his father who had been butchered at a banquet; but he did not
pollute himself with Electra's blood nor with that of his
Spartan wife, he prepared poison for no relatives
and he never sang the part of Orestes on stage   220
nor wrote *Troica*. For what should Verginius with his forces,
or Galba with Vindex, have avenged more, of all that
Nero did in so brutal and savage a tyranny? These are the deeds,
      these the accomplishments of the noble emperor
who got pleasure from prostituting himself on foreign stages
      with his foul   225
singing and winning the parsley that makes up a Greek crown.
Let the statues of your ancestors wear the trophies of your voice,
place in front of Domitius' feet the long robe of Thyestes
or of Antigone or the mask of Melanippe,
and dangle your lyre from the marble colossus.   230
What, Catiline, can anyone find more elevated than
your lineage or that of Cethegus? Yet still you plan night-time
assaults, arson against homes and temples
like the sons of the trousered Gauls and offspring of the Senones,
      and you
had the nerve to do something deserving punishment in the
      shirt of pain.   235

sed uigilat consul uexillaque uestra coercet.
hic nouus Arpinas, ignobilis et modo Romae
municipalis eques, galeatum ponit ubique
praesidium attonitis et in omni monte laborat.
tantum igitur muros intra toga contulit illi   240
nominis ac tituli, quantum sibi Leucade, quantum
Thessaliae campis Octauius abstulit udo
caedibus adsiduis gladio; sed Roma parentem,
Roma patrem patriae Ciceronem libera dixit.
Arpinas alius Volscorum in monte solebat   245
poscere mercedes alieno lassus aratro;
nodosam post haec frangebat uertice uitem,
si lentus pigra muniret castra dolabra.
hic tamen et Cimbros et summa pericula rerum
excipit et solus trepidantem protegit Urbem,   250
atque ideo, postquam ad Cimbros stragemque uolabant
qui numquam attigerant maiora cadauera corui,
nobilis ornatur lauro collega secunda.
plebeiae Deciorum animae, plebeia fuerunt
nomina; pro totis legionibus hi tamen et pro   255
omnibus auxiliis atque omni pube Latina
sufficiunt dis infernis Terraeque parenti.
[pluris enim Decii quam quae seruantur ab illis.]
ancilla natus trabeam et diadema Quirini
et fasces meruit, regum ultimus ille bonorum.   260
prodita laxabant portarum claustra tyrannis
exulibus iuuenes ipsius consulis et quos
magnum aliquid dubia pro libertate deceret,
quod miraretur cum Coclite Mucius et quae
imperii fines Tiberinum uirgo natauit.   265
occulta ad patres produxit crimina seruus

---

241   sibi *Jahn*: in *PSGU*: non *Φ*: unda *Weidner*: uix *Hermann, Ribbeck*: ima *Eden*
251   Cimbros *codd*: cumulos *Nisbet*
256   pube *PSAGU*: plebe *Φ*
258   *del. Markland et Dobree*
266   produxit *P Lond. Mus. Brit. Reg 15 B XII*: eduxit *Φ*: conduxit *A Vat. 2810*

But the consul is awake and puts a stop to your standards.
This new man from Arpinum, not a noble and only recently
    arrived in Rome
as a municipal knight – he positions a helmeted guard
    everywhere to protect
the thunderstruck people and he toils on every hill.
In this way within the walls the toga gained him as much   240
name and title as Octavius got for himself at Leucas
and the plains of Thessaly with his sword dripping
with constant bloodshed; but Rome called Cicero 'parent',
a free Rome called him 'father of the fatherland'.
Another man from Arpinum used to work for wages   245
on the Volscian hills, exhausted with working another man's
    plough;
after this he would have a knotty vine-staff broken on his head
if he was slow in fortifying the camp with a sluggish pick-axe.
    Yet this man takes on the Cimbri and the utmost state emergency
and he alone protects the quivering city   250
and so, when the crows flew down to the Cimbri and the
    slaughter – crows
which had never tasted bigger corpses than these –
his aristocratic colleague is adorned with second laurels.
The souls of the Decii were plebeian, their names were
plebeian: and yet these men satisfy the gods of the underworld   255
and mother Earth on behalf of all the legions, all the
allies and the entire youth of Latium.
[for the Decii are worth more than all that is saved by them.]
A man born of a slave-girl deserved the robe and the crown of
    Quirinus
and his rods of office, he being the last of the good kings.   260
The men who betrayed and tried to undo the locks on the gates
    to the tyrants
in exile were the sons of the consul himself – men who should have
been doing something great for their still shaky freedom,
something to impress Mucius and Cocles and that girl
who swam the Tiber (the border of the empire in those days).   265
It was a slave who revealed the hidden crimes to the senators,

matronis lugendus; at illos uerbera iustis
afficiunt poenis et legum prima securis.
    malo pater tibi sit Thersites, dummodo tu sis
Aeacidae similis Volcaniaque arma capessas,   270
quam te Thersitae similem producat Achilles.
et tamen, ut longe repetas longeque reuoluas
nomen, ab infami gentem deducis asylo;
maiorum primus, quisquis fuit ille, tuorum
aut pastor fuit aut illud quod dicere nolo.   275

a slave who deserved to be mourned by ladies; while those
   men are rightly
punished with flogging and the first legal axe.
I prefer you to have Thersites for a father (so long as you are
like the grandson of Aeacus and seize the armour of Vulcan)   270
than for Achilles to produce you as a man like Thersites.
Yet all the same, if you go back a long way and unwind your name
a long way, you still trace your descent from the notorious asylum:
the first of your ancestors, whoever he was, was
either a shepherd or else something I am not inclined to name.   275

SATIRE IX

scire uelim quare totiens mihi, Naeuole, tristis
occurras fronte obducta ceu Marsya uictus.
quid tibi cum uultu, qualem deprensus habebat
Rauola dum Rhodopes uda terit inguina barba?
nos colaphum incutimus lambenti crustula seruo.   5
non erit hac facie miserabilior Crepereius
Pollio, qui triplicem usuram praestare paratus
circumit et fatuos non inuenit. unde repente
tot rugae? certe modico contentus agebas
uernam equitem, conuiua ioco mordente facetus   10
et salibus uehemens intra pomeria natis.
omnia nunc contra: uultus grauis, horrida siccae
silua comae, nullus tota nitor in cute, qualem
Bruttia praestabat calidi tibi fascia uisci,
sed fruticante pilo neglecta et squalida crura.   15
quid macies aegri ueteris, quem tempore longo
torret quarta dies olimque domestica febris?
deprendas animi tormenta latentis in aegro
corpore, deprendas et gaudia; sumit utrumque
inde habitum facies. igitur flexisse uideris   20
propositum et uitae contrarius ire priori.
nuper enim, ut repeto, fanum Isidis et Ganymedem

---

2 uictus *mss*: uinctus *Jortinus*
5 *del. Guyet*
6 erit *PAGU*: erat *SΦ*
14 *uersum et post 13 et post 11 scriptum exhibent GU.* Bruttia *codd.*: brustia
    prestabat calidi
circum *P*: praestabat calidi circumlita *ΦGU*
17 torret *PΦ*: torquet *recentiores*

SATIRE IX

Speaker: I would like to know, Naevolus, why you are so often miserable when
you run into me, your brow clouded over like defeated Marsyas.
Why does your face look like the one that Ravola had when
    he was caught
rubbing Rhodope's groin with his wet beard?
We give a slap to any slave who licks the pastries.   5
Crepereius Pollio will not turn out to have a face more pathetic
than this one – and he goes round, ready to stump up three times
    the rate of interest
but finds no idiots to take it on. Where did such a lot of wrinkles
suddenly come from? You certainly used to be content with
    a modest lifestyle
playing the role of home-bred knight, a smooth dinner-guest with
    biting wit,   10
forceful with your jokes all produced within these city-limits.
Everything is now the opposite of that: your face is grave,
    you have a bristling
forest of dry hair, nowhere on your skin is there any of that
    gloss which
the Bruttian strip of hot pitch would offer you –
in fact your legs are neglected and filthy with sprouting hair.   15
Why do you have the emaciation of a chronic invalid who for
    a long time
has been roasted every three days with a well-established
    fever which shares his home?
You could uncover the pains of the mind as it lies hidden in the sick
body, and you could uncover the joys too: the face puts on
both appearances to suit. You seem therefore to have changed
    your   20
lifestyle and to be moving in the opposite direction to your
    former life.
Not long ago, as I recall, you used to be a regular at the shrine
    of Isis,

Pacis et aduectae secreta Palatia matris
et Cererem (nam quo non prostat femina templo?)
notior Aufidio moechus celebrare solebas,   25
quodque taces, ipsos etiam inclinare maritos.
'utile et hoc multis uitae genus, at mihi nullum
inde operae pretium. pingues aliquando lacernas,
[munimenta togae, duri crassique coloris]
et male percussas textoris pectine Galli   30
accipimus, tenue argentum uenaeque secundae.
fata regunt homines, fatum est et partibus illis
quas sinus abscondit. nam si tibi sidera cessant,
nil faciet longi mensura incognita nerui,
quamuis te nudum spumanti Virro labello   35
uiderit et blandae assidue densaeque tabellae
sollicitent, αὐτὸς γὰρ ἐφέλκεται ἄνδρα κίναιδος.
quod tamen ulterius monstrum quam mollis auarus?
"haec tribui, deinde illa dedi, mox plura tulisti."
computat et ceuet. ponatur calculus, adsint   40
cum tabula pueri; numera sestertia quinque
omnibus in rebus, numerentur deinde labores.
an facile et pronum est agere intra uiscera penem
legitimum atque illic hesternae occurrere cenae?
seruus erit minus ille miser qui foderit agrum   45
quam dominum. sed tu sane tenerum et puerum te
et pulchrum et dignum cyatho caeloque putabas.
uos humili asseculae, uos indulgebitis umquam
cultori, iam nec morbo donare parati?
en cui tu uiridem umbellam, cui sucina mittas   50

23   secreta *mss*: sacrata *Lubinus*.   matris *mss*: matri *Nisbet*
25   celebrare *Φ*: scelerare *P*
26   quodque taces *PSFGHO*: quodque taceo *U*: quod taceo utque *AKLTZ*
29   *deleuit Ribbeck*
33   cessant *PGHUZΣ*: cessent *Φ*
40   et ceuet *GU*: atque ceuet *Vat. Pal. 1703*: atque cauet *Φ*
43–4   *om. Vat. Pal. 1703*
46   quam *PGTU*: non *ΦΣ*.   tenerum *PSAGT*: tener *Φ*
49   parati *codd.*: paratis *Braund*

at Ganymede in Peace's temple, at the secret Palace of the
    foreign Mother
and at Ceres' (is there any temple in which a woman does not
    go up for sale?)
better-known than Aufidius as an adulterer, and   25
(something you kept quiet about) you used to bend their
    husbands over too.
Naevolus: 'Many find this way of life rewarding, but to me it is not
worth the effort. Now and then we get greasy cloaks
[toga-protectors, made of hard and rough material]
which have been badly beaten out by the comb of a Gallic weaver,   30
or slivers of silver from an inferior seam.
The fates govern human lives, fate is in charge even of those parts
which the clothing conceals. For if the stars let you down
then the unprecedented length of your massive penis
    will get you nowhere,
even though Virro with drooling lips has seen you naked   35
and his frequent coaxing love-letters constantly
harass you 'for the man is drawn by the actual faggot'.
But what monster is lower than a stingy effeminate?
'I gave you this, then I gave you that, then you got even more.'
He does his sums and wiggles his arse. Let the reckoning be
    done, let the   40
slaves attend with the accounts: count the five thousand sesterces
paid in all, and then let the exertions be reckoned up.
Or is it easy and no effort at all to drive a decent penis inside
the guts and there run into yesterday's dinner?
The slave who ploughs a field will be less of a wretch than the one 45
who ploughs his master. But you surely used to think of yourself
    as a delicate boy,
a fine figure and deserving of the heavens and the cup.
Will you men ever gratify a supporter of slender means, or
a follower of yours, since these days you are not even prepared
    to pay for your infirmity?
Look, that's the man to send a green parasol to – or large amber 50

grandia, natalis quotiens redit aut madidum uer
incipit et strata positus longaque cathedra
munera femineis tractat secreta kalendis.
dic, passer, cui tot montes, tot praedia seruas
Apula, tot miluos intra tua pascua lassas?   55
te Trifolinus ager fecundis uitibus implet
suspectumque iugum Cumis et Gaurus inanis –
nam quis plura linit uicturo dolia musto?
quantum erat exhausti lumbos donare clientis
iugeribus paucis? melius nunc rusticus infans   60
cum matre et casulis et collusore catello
cymbala pulsantis legatum fiet amici?
"improbus es cum poscis" ait. sed pensio clamat
"posce," sed appellat puer unicus ut Polyphemi
lata acies per quam sollers euasit Vlixes.   65
alter emendus erit, namque hic non sufficit, ambo
pascendi. quid agam bruma spirante? quid, oro,
quid dicam scapulis puerorum aquilone Decembri
et pedibus? "durate atque expectate cicadas"?
uerum, ut dissimules, ut mittas cetera, quanto   70
metiris pretio quod, ni tibi deditus essem
deuotusque cliens, uxor tua uirgo maneret?
scis certe quibus ista modis, quam saepe rogaris
et quae pollicitus. fugientem nempe puellam

53   tractat *PG Servius*: tractas Φ
54   tot praedia *PAGLU*: cui praedia Φ
55   lassas *GU*: lassos *PS$\Phi\Sigma$*
60   melius nunc *Housman*: meliusne hic *PΦ*: melius, dic *Castiglione*
62   legatum *PGHTΣ*: legatus Φ
63   es Φ est *PAL*: poscis *PGOU* poscit Φ. ait *PAGLOZ*: ais *HKTU*
68   puerorum *PA*: seruorum Φ. aquilone *PAGU*: mense Φ
74   nempe *Housman*: saepe *mss.*

balls whenever his birthday comes round again or rainy spring
starts and he positions himself on his long cushioned chair
handling his secret gifts on the ladies' day.
Tell me, little bird, for whom you are saving so many mountains,
    so many Apulian
estates, for whom are you tiring out so many kites within
    your pasturelands?   55
Your lands at Trifolium keep you full with their fertile vines
and the ridge overlooking Cumae and hollow Gaurus -
for who seals more jars for the survival of the wine-juice?
How much would it have cost to reward the groin of your
    drained client
with a few plots of land? Is it better in that case that the rural
    child   60
with his mother, his little cottages and his playfellow the puppy
will go as a legacy to your friend who beats the cymbals?
'You're a pain when you ask for things' he said. But my rent
    yells out
'ask him!' and my slave stakes his demands – my slave
    as single as the
wide eye of Polyphemus which let crafty Ulysses make
    his escape.   65
I need to buy another one, for this one is not enough,
    but then both
will need feeding. What am I to do when winter blows?
    What, I ask you,
what am I to say to the shoulders and feet of the slaves
    in the icy blast
of December? 'stay firm and await the cicadas'?
But even though you pretend otherwise, though you ignore
    all the rest,   70
what price do you put on the fact that if I were not your obedient
and loyal client, your wife would still be a virgin?
You cannot have forgotten in what ways and how often you
    asked me for that,
and what you promised. The girl was actually running away
    from you

amplexu rapui; tabulas quoque ruperat et iam   75
migrabat; tota uix hoc ego nocte redemi
te plorante foris. testis mihi lectulus et tu,
ad quem peruenit lecti sonus et dominae uox.
instabile ac dirimi coeptum et iam paene solutum
coniugium in multis domibus seruauit adulter.   80
quo te circumagas? quae prima aut ultima ponas?
nullum ergo meritum est, ingrate ac perfide, nullum
quod tibi filiolus uel filia nascitur ex me?
tollis enim et libris actorum spargere gaudes
argumenta uiri. foribus suspende coronas: 85
iam pater es, dedimus quod famae opponere possis.
iura parentis habes, propter me scriberis heres,
legatum omne capis nec non et dulce caducum.
commoda praeterea iungentur multa caducis,
si numerum, si tres impleuero.' iusta doloris,   90
Naeuole, causa tui; contra tamen ille quid affert?
'neglegit atque alium bipedem sibi quaerit asellum.
haec soli commissa tibi celare memento
et tacitus nostras intra te fige querellas;
nam res mortifera est inimicus pumice leuis.   95
qui modo secretum commiserat, ardet et odit,
tamquam prodiderim quidquid scio. sumere ferrum,
fuste aperire caput, candelam apponere ualuis

---

76   migrabat *Highet*: signabat *mss*: signabant *Eden*
84   libris *mss*: titulis *Servius*. actorum *PSAHLΣ*: auctorum *Φ*: fastorum *G*:
      astorum *U*
89   iungentur *PGU*: iunguntur *Φ*

when I took her in an embrace. She had smashed the contract too
   and was just 75
about to move out. I bought her back for you with great difficulty
   all night long
while you were weeping outside the door. The couch is my witness –
   and you are – as the noise
of the bed and the voice of the mistress got through to you.
In many homes where a marriage is rickety – on the point
   of falling apart
and all but dissolved – an adulterer has saved it. 80
Where can you turn to? Which would you place first, which last?
Do I get no thanks then, ungrateful bastard, no thanks
for letting your little son or daughter be born by me?
You bring them up, you love spreading the proof of your
manhood in the newspapers. Hang up garlands over the doors: 85
you are now a father, I have given you something to counter
   the gossip.You have the parental privileges, because of me
   you are written into a will as heir,
you get the whole legacy and what's more you get the sweet
   extras too.
More pleasant things will be added to the extras besides
if I make up the number to three.' 90
<u>Speaker</u>:
You have fair reason to feel pain, Naevolus. What does he bring
   up in answer?
<u>Naevolus</u>:
'He ignores me and looks out for another two-legged donkey
   for himself.
Don't forget to keep this under wraps, entrusted to you alone
and lock my complaints inside yourself in total silence;
for an enemy made smooth with the pumice-stone is lethal. 95
The man who has just entrusted me with his secret burns
   with hatred,
thinking that I have betrayed whatever I know. He has no
   qualms about
taking up the sword, opening my head up with a club, setting
   a torch

non dubitat. nec contemnas aut despicias quod
his opibus numquam cara est annona ueneni. 100
ergo occulta teges ut curia Martis Athenis.'
    o Corydon, Corydon, secretum diuitis ullum
esse putas? serui ut taceant, iumenta loquentur
et canis et postes et marmora. claude fenestras,
uela tegant rimas, iunge ostia, tolle lucernam 105
e medio fac eant omnes, prope nemo recumbat;
quod tamen ad cantum galli facit ille secundi
proximus ante diem caupo sciet, audiet et quae
finxerunt pariter libarius, archimagiri,
carptores. quod enim dubitant componere crimen 110
in dominos, quotiens rumoribus ulciscuntur
baltea? nec derit qui te per compita quaerat
nolentem et miseram uinosus inebriet aurem.
illos ergo roges quidquid paulo ante petebas
a nobis, taceant illi. sed prodere malunt 115
arcanum quam subrepti potare Falerni
pro populo faciens quantum Saufeia bibebat.
uiuendum recte, cum propter plurima, tum est his
[idcirco ut possis linguam contemnere serui.]
praecipue causis, ut linguas mancipiorum 120
contemnas; nam lingua mali pars pessima serui.
deterior tamen hic qui liber non erit illis
quorum animas et farre suo custodit et aere.
'utile consilium modo, sed commune, dedisti.
nunc mihi quid suades post damnum temporis et spes 125
deceptas? festinat enim decurrere uelox

99–100   nec ... opibus *deleuit Ribbeck*
100   cara est *PGΣ*: careas *Φ*: caras *U*
105   tolle lucernam *Nisbet*: tollite lumen *PAKOTZ*: tollito lumen *GHU*
106   fac eant *Haupt*: taceant *P*: clament *Φ*: abeant *Hermann*
109   libarius ignotus apud *Plathnerum*: librarius *PΦ*
118   recte *Φ*: recte est *PA*.   tum est his *Housman* tunc est *PA* tunc his *Φ*
119   *uersum hic ponunt PA, post 123 Φ, om. Vat. Pal. 1700, damnauit Pithoeus*
122–3   *deleuit Pinzger*

to the doorway. Don't think it of no importance or ignore the
    fact that
for wealth like his the cost of poison is never high.   100
So guard the secrets like the Senate of Mars in Athens would.'
Speaker:
O Corydon, Corydon, do you think a rich man ever has
a secret? Even if the slaves kept quiet, the beasts will talk
and the dog and the door-posts and the slabs of marble. Close
    the shutters,
have curtains cover up the gaps, seal the doors, put out the lamp,   105
make everyone leave the place, let nobody recline nearby;
what the man does at the second crowing of the cockerel
his neighbour the inn-keeper will know of it before dawn:
    and he will hear also
what has been made up by the pastry-cook, the head chefs
the carvers. For what crime do they hesitate to invent   110
against their masters, since gossip is their revenge
for being flogged? Some boozed-up bloke is also sure to look
    for you at the crossroads
(even if you don't want to hear him) and souse your unhappy ear.
So try asking them what you just now asked me –
to keep silent. They prefer spreading secrets   115
to swigging the stolen Falernian in the amounts
that Saufeia used to drink when doing a public ritual.
You should live an upright life for lots of reasons, but also
[so that you can despise the tongue of your slave]
especially so that you despise the tongues of slaves;   120
for the tongue is the worst part of a bad slave.
Worse off is the man who will never be free of the people
whose lives he preserves with his food and his money.'
Naevolus: 'The advice you have just given me is useful but trite.
What do you recommend now after the wastage of time and
    the duping   125
of my hopes? For the swift little flower which is the shortest part

flosculus angustae miseraeque breuissima uitae
portio; dum bibimus, dum serta, unguenta, puellas
poscimus, obrepit non intellecta senectus.'
ne trepida, numquam pathicus tibi derit amicus   130
stantibus et saluis his collibus; undique ad illos
conueniunt et carpentis et nauibus omnes
qui digito scalpunt uno caput. altera maior
spes superest, tu tantum erucis imprime dentem.
[gratus eris, tu tantum erucis imprime dentem.]   134a
    'haec exempla para felicibus; at mea Clotho
et Lachesis gaudent, si pascitur inguine uenter.
o parui nostrique Lares, quos ture minuto
aut farre et tenui soleo exorare corona,
quando ego figam aliquid quo sit mihi tuta senectus
a tegete et baculo? uiginti milia faenus   140
pigneribus positis, argenti uascula puri,
sed quae Fabricius censor notet, et duo fortes
de grege Moesorum, qui me ceruice locata
securum iubeant clamoso insistere circo;
sit mihi praeterea curuus caelator, et alter   145
qui multas facies pingit cito; sufficiunt haec.
quando ego pauper ero? uotum miserabile, nec spes
his saltem; nam cum pro me Fortuna uocatur,
affixit ceras illa de naue petitas
quae Siculos cantus effugit remige surdo.'   150

132   conueniunt Φ: conuenient PAΣ
134   tu tantum erucis inprime dentem PΦ: turbae, properat quae crescere, molli
       Housman
134A   *habent PA, om.* Φ
143   locata Φ: locatum *Heinrich*
146   pingit PG: pingat Φ
148   uocatur PA rogatur Φ
149   affixit PA: affigit Φ

of our cramped and miserable life, is hurrying to its end.
While we are drinking, while we are demanding garlands,
   scents, girls
old age creeps up on us unawares.'
<u>Speaker</u>: 'Have no fear: you will never go short of a faggot
   friend   130
while these hills are safe and standing. They are coming
   to them from all over
in their carriages and their ships – all the men
who scratch their head with one finger. Another and greater
hope is available – you just bite on the rocket-wort.
[You will be popular, you just bite on the rocket-wort.]
<u>Naevolus</u>: 'Give those role-models to the fortunate men.
   My Clotho   135
and Lachesis are happy if my stomach is fed by my cock.
Oh tiny household gods of mine, whom I tend to pray to
with small bits of incense or grain and a skinny garland,
when will I get something to keep my old age safe
from the mat and stick? Twenty thousand at interest   140
with pledges secure, goblets of pure silver
(the sort which the censor Fabricius would mark down) and
   two strong men
from the tribe of the Moesi, to put their necks in position
and bid me take my place in the bellowing Circus;
Let me also have a stooping engraver, and another man   145
who can paint many pictures in a trice: this will be enough.
When will I be poor? A pathetic prayer: no hope
even for those things. For when Fortune is summoned on my account
she has stuffed her ears with wax which she got from that ship
which dodged the Sicilian singing by means of deaf rowers.'   150

COMMENTARIES

SATIRE VII

This is a programmatic poem to open the new book. Seen in one way it shows the underdog of Satire 1 now wearing the toga of a man of letters but still complaining of being poor: he laments the death of financial support given to writers with typically nostalgic evocation of the 'golden age' when Augustan poets enjoyed Augustus' patronage (as contrasted with modern patrons who give fine words but little cash), and spends much of the rest of the poem describing how the so-called 'professional' men of letters (barristers and teachers) all find themselves struggling to be paid for their onerous work. The people who should be paying them – the parents of the students for instance – care more about their interior design than about their offspring (178–188) and the poem ends with the image of the humble teacher working for a year to receive what a gladiator can get for one fight (242–3). Some of the themes of social criticism are here for sure – the old aristocracy is represented by Aemilius (124–7) who is reduced to being a one-eyed old statue with a drooping spear, with the real power going to the actors (87–92), the musicians (176–7) and chancers like Tongilius with their rhino-horn oil flasks and exotic purple clothing (130–138), and the poet Lucan, who enjoyed independent means, is sneered at in his 'marble gardens' (79–80).

The criticism is however not one-sided. The opening line sets up a red herring – seeming to plead for patronage from the emperor but in fact being a simple expression of hope that 'Caesar' might help since nobody else will. There are some wonderful ironic vignettes which undermine any sentimental view of the undeserving poor – such as the professors of oratory all leaving their fictitious cases to take up 'real' oratory to secure their fees (166–70), the people's poet Statius (82–7) pimping out his work to the actor Paris, Horace with his full belly shouting out in Bacchic delight (62) and historians turning out industrial quantities of papyrus-leaves (98–105). The teachers who claim to deserve better than they get are in fact appallingly dull men who puff themselves up as *sophistae* (167), complain of their pupils' endless declamations as so much 'rehashed cabbage' (154) but do nothing to enliven the fare themselves and simply mock their stupid students (158–60) in grossly abusive language. They complain about pushy parents making demands but seem reluctant to master their subject and see their moral tutoring in grotesquely sexual terms (240–1). They demand the respect which they naively claim was given to their (mythological) predecessors (207–12) but they give no respect either to their students or to their employers. Do they deserve any better than they are getting?

It could be argued that the poem is a study in sterility: what is the point of putting words together in the liberal arts any more? Images of agricultural (in)fertility are found (48–9, 103, 112), the gardens of Lucan are made of stone (79–80) and papyrus plants are wasted on writing histories (100–101): teachers of rhetoric are told to retire and retrain in the 'real' world (171–3) and men of letters are seen (105) as an idle breed 'enjoying their days on the couch in the shade' who should give it all up and burn their work (22–29). Everybody here is (it seems) venal and the world is only divided up into the abusers and the abused. Seeking preferment is a labour of Sisyphus. Is this an exercise in nihilism?

One answer to that is the poem itself, and this is what makes Satire 7 programmatic. If the poet had truly felt that writing poetry was a waste of time then he would hardly have written a poem to say so (although he enjoys the irony of hinting as much). If there are no material rewards in terms of money and/or status for the liberal arts, then the poet is well advised to steer clear of them and devote himself to – satire. The poem thus embodies the answer to its own question, giving us the gloriously entertaining and imaginative vision of a literary milieu at war with the world and with itself. In this topsy-turvy merry-go-round world of Fortune, poets and actors vie for preference (87), teachers blame students and students blame teachers (158–60), teachers have to apply their own lessons to be paid for their own teaching, money has to be flaunted in order to be earned (135–6, 139–149), consuls become teachers and teachers become consuls (197–201), pupils flog the masters (213) and poets end up running a bath-house (4) or auction-rooms (7) where they even sell the works of other writers (12) and where ex-slaves now parade as knights (16). The tone of this poem (see Rudd (1976) 84–118) is deliberately elusive and the care behind its composition shows a poet at the top of his craft, manipulating language and imagery in a way which is both playful *and* serious and eliciting both pleasure and puzzlement in his readers. The dominant mode in this poem is that of irony: a literary form which draws attention to itself *qua* literary form and which pleases and teases the reader in equal measure with its studied ambivalence

(Braund (1988) 68). The only area in which there is no ambivalence is in the quality of the literary achievement which transcends and almost justifies the ramshackle dystopia it so eloquently describes.

Further discussion includes: Radermacher L. (1904), Highet (1954) 106–12, Helmbold W. C. and O'Neil E. N. (1959), Kilpatrick (1973), Townend (1973), Wiesen (1973), Braund (1988) 24–68, Jones (1989), Hardie (1990), Tennant (1996), Geue (2017) 53–70, Schmitz (2019) 110–17, Flores Militello (2019) 280–97. On Juvenal and Quintilian the classic study remains: Anderson (1982) 396–486.

1–21   Friedländer argued that this passage was composed later than the rest, as a compliment to the new emperor: he urged that the optimism of the opening lines is undermined by what follows and that the opening lines allude only to poets while the rest of the satire looks at a wide range of literary pursuits. This argument fails on many counts: it fails to appreciate the desperation of the man of letters who has no chance of making a decent living in Rome *unless* the new emperor effects changes: that is the point of *tantum ... solus* in 1–2 (and *posthac* in 18) and it puts the text into a tradition of 'advice to the emperor' which seeks to flatter the ruler into granting what the writer claims is needed. The argument also fails to appreciate the ironic texture of the passage, as shown by Braund ((1988) 30): 'the fact that the poets think it *nec foedum ... nec turpe* (5) to become auctioneers suggests that they have lost all moral sensibility ... and the inclusion of ... lofty-sounding tragedies on mythological themes [auctioned off in line 12] indicates the worthlessness and trashiness of such 'poetry': people would rather sell it than keep it.' Furthermore the passage closes with phrasing from Statius' praise of the maligned emperor Domitian (*Siluae* 5.2.125–7: see Townend (1973) 150) and so renders the hopes of a new age of literary patronage at once suspect since the age of Domitian passed into memory as one of literary repression and even book-burning (cf. e.g. 4.37–8, Tacitus *Agricola* 1–2) although Domitian had been a poet himself (Silius 3.618–21, Statius *Achilleid* 1.14–6, Quintilian 10.1.91) and conferred material benefits on the poets Martial (2.91–2) and Statius (*Siluae* 3.1.61–4).

1.   **Caesar**: the name simply refers to the ruling emperor: J. refers (6.407–8) to a comet which has been dated to January 117 and so it is most probable that this poem postdates the accession of Hadrian (who arrived in Rome in 118), while the word *spes* suggests that the poem is early in the new regime. Otherwise the argument is inconclusive: Trajan (who ruled from 98–117)

was praised by Pliny (*Panegyric* 47) as a patron of rhetoric and philosophy (cf. *Epistles* 3.18) while Hadrian (117–38) was renowned for his passion for all things Greek and founded the Athenaeum (see *OCD* s.v. 'Athenaeum') as a centre to promote Greek rhetoric (Aurelius Victor *de Caesaribus* 14) which may (or may not) have been to J.'s taste, given his contempt for the way Rome was taken over by all things Greek (3.60–1: 'I cannot stand a Hellenised Rome'). Hadrian did however write poetry himself and was described as fluent in both languages (Eutropius 8.7.2) and 'the intellectual emperor' (Syme (1991) 103–9). *studium* means essentially the exercise of attention to something and in particular the pursuit of intellectual activity in general (*OLD* s.v. 'studium' 7, Pliny *Panegyric* 47.1) and literature in particular: the emperor's adviser on literary matters was known as *a studiis* (Suetonius *Claudius* 28, *OLD* s.v. 'studium' 7c). The laudatory tone of this opening line is as much a pious hope and recommendation as a statement of fact – a hope which the remainder of the poem will show is rooted in miserable reality. The collocation of *spes et ratio* recalls Catullus 64.186 (where the terms are reversed) and Cicero *Paradoxa Stoicorum* 2.17.5, *ad Herennium* 1.18.3. *spes* is common at the start of a new regime – cf. *OLD* s.v. 'spes' 5 and *spes magis arridet* (Calpurnius Siculus 4.31: 'hope smiles all the more') said of the accession of Nero – but the intertextual references here to Calpurnius reinforce Townend's idea that this opening is a 'forceful burlesque, providing a devastating send-up of the literary scene of whichever emperor is in fact the satirist's target.' (Townend (1973) 150). *ratio* has the rhetorical sense of **justification** (*OLD* s.v. 'ratio' 5c: cf. 6.223, 14.39) or 'motive' (cf. 4.20, 6.95). *tantum* is in the limiting sense of 'only' as at 1.1, 7.81, 8.31–2, 10.80, reinforced by *solus* at the start of line 2.

2   An elegant line, with the adjectives and the nouns paired at either end around the deictic pronoun *hac*. The *Camenae* were originally the goddesses of a spring just near the porta Capena in Rome (Livy 1.21.3) and (on the analogy of the Greek Muses drinking the waters of Hippocrene) became identified with the **Muses** (the nine female deities of the arts: see Clio in line 7): Livius Andronicus (3rd century BC) uses the term *Camena* for the Greek word for 'Muse' in the first line of his translation of Homer's *Odyssey*: cf. also 3.16, Lucilius 1064W, Horace *Satires* 1.10.45, *Odes* 2.16.38, 3.4.21, *Epistles* 1.19.5, *Carmen Saeculare* 62. **times**: *tempestas* literally means 'storm' but is often used as simply meaning 'time' or 'season' as at 4.140, 6.25–6: in this context of turbulent times the word's original sense is also present, and the pathos of the line is further enhanced by the juxtaposition

of *solus … tristes* which augments the image of depressed Muses (picked up again in *esuriens* (7)) with only Caesar for support. *respicio* here carries the sense of 'look out for' or 'show concern for' (*OLD* s.v. 'respicio' 8) as at Virgil *Aeneid* 4.275 but the word also connotes 'care about' at 7.141.

3–6 Impoverished poets resort to degrading occupations to stay alive, the three occupations placed at the start and end of lines for emphasis. The point is amplified by the pleonasm of *celebres notique*, the conative verb *temptarent* (*OLD* s.v. 'tempto' 7b) showing that they may not even succeed in their efforts, and the chiastic ordering of *balneolum Gabiis Romae…furnos* which juxtaposes the locations while framing the line with the humble workplaces. Romans enjoyed going to the baths (cf. 7.178n.) and some money could be made by hiring a **bath-house** and then charging bathers to use it (cf. 6.447, 7.233, Cicero *pro Caelio* 62, Balsdon (1969) 27, Griffin (1985) 88–89): here the poor poet can only hire a 'small' place, as is shown by the diminutive form *balneolum*. Martial (3.44.12–13) and Horace (*Satires* 1.4.74–6) tell us that poets even recited in the public baths (and Horace comments on the pleasant acoustic of the enclosed space) which makes the bath-house an appealing prospect for a poet. *furnos* refers to **bake-houses** – paired with *balnea* as examples of hot places at Horace *Epistles* 1.11.13 – which produced fast food which could be sold on to the public for a profit: see Beard (2008) 170–77. **Gabii** was famously deserted (Horace *Epistles* 1.11.7) and simple (3.192, 6.56), but had received an aqueduct from Hadrian (*C.I.L.* 14.2797) and so must have had a sizeable population.

5–6 The third lowly occupation is that of **auctioneer** (*praeco*) which presumably suited the poet who will have been used to declaiming his verses. Auctioneers were barred from public office (cf. Hinard (1976)) and J.'s language here shows that the profession was despised – but Martial (5.56: cf. Petronius 46) rates auctioneering as a better prospect for money-making than poetry and J. (3.157) places the 'son of an auctioneer' in the equestrian rows of the theatre. Line 5 is framed by the subjunctive verbs and *praecones* is enjambed for emphasis after the pleonastic wording of *foedum … nec turpe*.

6–7 **Aganippe** was a spring in Boeotia which was sacred to the Muses who were thought to live there: cf. Virgil *Eclogues* 10.12: her Greek name is here used in the Greek form of the genitive case, and ending the hexameter with the four-syllable name gives the impression of archaic epic (cf. *Melanippes* at 8.229, *Ganymedem* at 9.22). Line 7 is bathetic with the prosaic **salerooms** (*atria*) coming after the high register of *desertis Aganippes / uallibus*, the crude term **famished** (*esuriens*) to describe the Muse and the image of her scuttling away from her haunt (*migraret*). The anthropomorphic imagery in *esuriens* reminds us of the poet's riff on the young gods at 13.40–1: it is in fact the poet who is hungry but transferring the epithet to his Muse makes for an irreverent image. **Clio** was later regarded as the Muse of history rather than poetry: but J. is happy to use the names interchangeably (as with Calliope at 4.34, but unlike Terpsichore at 7.35). Her name (deriving from the Greek for 'renown' (κλέος)) is sardonic here as this poet's renown is now his disgrace (*foedum ... turpe*): cf. Horace *Odes* 1.12.2 with Mayer (2012) *ad loc.* **salerooms**: *atria* here connotes the room used in a public building for auctions (*OLD* s.v. 'atrium' 3a: cf. Cicero *de Leg. Ag*.1.7) and there may be a light suggestion of a statue of the Muse coming in to be auctioned off. The primary image here is the familiar topos of divine beings leaving human company in disgust and moving back to the heavens: cf. Hesiod *Works and Days* 176–201, Aratus *Phaenomena*, 96–136, Catullus 64.384–408 (with Godwin (1995) 173–5), Ovid *Metamorphoses* 1.149–50. Here, however, the speaker makes Clio travel not back to her divine abode but *in atria*, once again giving a satirical spin to the traditional mythological motif.

8–9 **Pieria** was a grove near Mount Olympus which was said to be the birthplace of the Muses (Hesiod *Theogony* 52–3, *Works and Days* 1): they were often (e.g. 4.36, Lucretius 1.926, Propertius 2.10.12, Virgil *Eclogues* 3.85, Ovid *Amores* 1.1.6) called *Pierides* as a result. The adjective 'Pierian' came to mean 'of the Muses' as at 7.60, Lucretius 1.946, Propertius 2.13.5, Horace *Odes* 3.4.40, *Ars Poetica* 405: Martial 9.84.3 has the same phrase *Pieria ... in umbra*. **shade:** *umbra* here alludes metonymically to the sheltering grove (*OLD* s.v. 'umbra' 3b: cf. 7.173, 4.6, Catullus 64.41). **penny**: the *quadrans* was a coin equivalent to one quarter of one *as* and so represented the coin of least value in Rome (Horace *Satires* 2.3.93, Petronius 43.1, Martial 2.44.9, 7.10.12) as well as being the standard fee for a male to enter the baths (6.447, Cicero *pro Caelio* 62). The verb *ostendatur* is enjambed for effect – the poet is not even 'shown' this tiny coin, let alone given it – and juxtaposed with *ames* as the poet is urged to (feign) instant love on (not) being shown any cash. The mss reading is disputed: Φ reads *arca* presumably drawing on Martial 2.44.9, but other mss read *umbra*.

9 **Machaera** must have been the name of a well-known auctioneer, but the name is significant as the Greek word μάχαιρα ('a short sword' or 'knife') probably alludes to the practice of *sectio* (*OLD* s.v. 'sectio' 2) which involved buying up confiscated goods at auction and then selling them on for profit – a

practice akin to asset-stripping which Cicero despised in Antony (*Philippics* 2.64) and which incurred public odium. Having to **get to like** such a name was therefore difficult. *uictus* means both 'nourishment' and also **lifestyle** (*OLD* s.v. 'uictus' 2): the starving (*esuriens* 7) poet will need to love the name if he is to receive the food.

10 **selling ... sells**: the line is framed by the verb *uendas ... uendit*, the repetition enacting the repeated transactions, and the auction is elevated with the heroic term *commissa* (*OLD* s.v. 'committo' 5: cf. 5.29) suggesting that the business is one of aggressive conflict. *potius* normally indicates a preference but here the word shows that the poor poet must sell whatever is there, regardless of his feelings: and the list which follows is one of embarrassingly slim pickings.

11 **bystanders**: *stantibus* (from *sto*) refers to the Romans 'standing' in the auction-room bidding for the goods. The four items up for auction are listed in asyndeton: for this device cf. 1.65, 85–6 and especially 10.64 where the bronze busts of Sejanus are melted down into a series of objects ('basins, washpots, a frying pan, chamber pots'). *oenophorum* is a Greek term (οἰνοφόρον) for a **wine-jar**: cf. 6.426, Lucilius 132W, Persius 5.140, Martial 6.89.6. The word here, as at Horace *Satires* 1.6.109, 'combines epic length and resonance with humdrum satirical subject-matter' (Gowers (2012) 244). *tripedes* may refer to the humble **three-legged** table (Horace *Satires* 1.3.13, Ovid *Metamorphoses* 8.661) a three-legged bed (Martial 12.32.11) or stool (*OLD* s.v. 'tripes'). *armaria* are **cupboards** used to hold gold (Cicero *pro Caelio* 52) or precious objects (Petronius 29) and books (Pliny *Epistles* 2.17.8) while a *cista* (a **trunk** large enough to hold a man at 6.44) is also used to hold books at 3.206: this leads naturally onto the titles of texts listed in the following line, suggesting that the book-cases are being sold off with the contents still in them.

12 **Paccius** is a wealthy victim of legacy-hunters at 12.99 and a doctor at Martial 14.78: the name is found also at Cicero *ad Atticum* 4.16, Livy 10.38.6, 27.15, Tacitus *Annals* 13.36, 15.12, but nowhere else is it given to a poet, and it is even possible that Paccius was the owner of the text rather than its author. **Faustus** is also not known as a poet and the name (meaning 'lucky') is certainly ironic here. Hardie ((1990) 161–2) suggests that 'Paccius' here forms a pastiche amalgamation of two famous writers of Roman drama Pacuvius and Accius. The titles of two of the dramas may be significant: **Alcithoe** was one of the daughters of Minyas who denied the divinity of Dionysus and were turned into bats (Ovid *Metamorphoses*

4.1–40, 390–415), while **Tereus** (as depicted in Sophocles' lost play of that name and Ovid *Metamorphoses* 6.424–674: cf. 7.92, 6.644) raped his sister-in-law Philomela and then cut out her tongue to enforce her silence: both tales thus involve the imposition of silence on those who wish to speak and so are apt in this case of discarded poetry. **Thebes** was deemed to be the most ancient Greek site and was the home of many Greek tragic legends such as those of Oedipus and the Seven against Thebes, and Roman poets (such as Statius (7.83)) and dramatists continued the legends: Pacuvius for instance wrote a *Pentheus*, Accius an *Antigone,* a *Bacchae* and a *Thebais*, Seneca an *Oedipus*. This line has been seen as a bathetic ending to the catalogue of goods for auction which undercuts the message of the passage by showing the 'worthlessness and trashiness of such 'poetry': people would rather sell it than keep it' (Braund (1988) 30: cf. Wiesen (1973) 469).

13–14 **I saw it**: in an age lacking forensic science the testimony of witnesses was crucial and such testimony could be bought: poets who are gifted speakers would make excellent perjurers, especially since they made their living from spinning falsehoods in their poetry. J. elsewhere (16.29–34) tells us how hard it is to persuade a witness to offer such testimony against praetorian soldiers and how much easier to find a false witness against a civilian. *satius* (cf. 8.196, Lucretius 5.1127, Virgil *Aeneid* 10.59) is the comparative form of *satis* and means **preferable** (*OLD* s.v. 'satis' 7): it is also found in colloquial Latin (e.g. Plautus *Epidicus* 60, Terence *Andria* 307, Petronius 61.4). *sub iudice* is commonly taken to mean 'under <the authority of> a judge' (*OLD* s.v. 'sub' 15b: cf. 4.12, 15.26n., Persius 5.80) but as Brink ((1971) 167) points out on Horace *Ars Poetica* 78, *sub iudice* 'only sounds legal' and is 'a poeticism': the preposition *sub* has some sense of the witness physically 'under' the **eye** of authority. The repetition of *uidi* ... *uidisti* reminds us that *uidi* was the legal formula of a witness: cf. 16.30, Persius 1.120.

14–16 **knights**: *equites* were wealthy men (whose property exceeded 400,000 sesterces (cf. 7.139n., 14.323–4n., Pliny *Ep.* 1.19) who engaged in trade rather than in politics: see *OCD* s.v. 'Equites'. They had also been used as legal judges in Roman history and so the connection of thought here is deliberate. The usual designation of these men was *equites Romani*: J. here surprises us with his phrase *equites Asiani* referring to them as *arrivistes* from eastern provinces who have now made enough money to qualify as *equites* (cf. *CAH* xi.836–7). Such men were also discredited as lying witnesses by Cicero (*pro Flacco* 60–61) and the clumsy rhythm of the final four-syllabled word *Asiani* enacts the speaker's contempt. The Roman province of Asia was situated in the west of modern Turkey and was a source of great wealth and great military strife in earlier Roman history. *faciant* is a jussive subjunctive, neatly juxtaposed with the indicative *uidisti*: some read it as going with *quamquam* in line 15, and while *quamquam* commonly takes the subjunctive in J. (cf. 10.34, 12.25, 15.30) and the postponement of *quamquam* is also found at 6.198–9, line 15 is probably an interpolation (see next note).

15 This line is suspect, not least because the scansion *Bĭthyni* is unparalleled in Latin verse (contrast e.g. 10.162, 15.1, Catullus 10.7, Horace *Odes* 1.35.7, *Epistles* 1.6.33, Manilius 4.761, Ovid *Amores* 3.6.25, Martial 2.26.3, 6.50.5). Attempts to emend include Markland's *equites Bithyni et* and Hermann's transposition of *Asiani* in 14 with *Bithyni* in 15. Courtney plausibly argues that the line began as a gloss and was then clumsily filled out to become a complete line. **Cappadocia** (in the east of modern Turkey) was rendered a full province of Rome by the emperor Tiberius (Suetonius *Tiberius* 37.4) and was the home of the mysterious werewolf in Petronius (63.5) as well as being a major source of slaves for Rome (cf. Cicero *post Red.* 14, Persius 6.77, Petronius 69).

16 The *gallica* was a low **shoe** – something like a flip-flop – which protected the sole of the foot but left the rest of the foot bare (cf. Cicero *Philippics* 2.76, Aulus Gellius 13.21–2): the unusual word was easily corrupted to Φ's reading *Gallia*, as *noua Gallia* would refer to nearby Galatia. The joke here is that these *equites* still bore on their ankles the marks of the fetters worn when they were slaves: for feet giving away a man's servile origin cf. 1.111. **betrayed**: *traducit* has the metaphorical sense (*OLD* s.v. 'traduco' 4b) of 'exposes to ridicule/scorn' as at 2.159, 8.17, 11.31, Martial 1.53.3 and it is significant that it only took **one** (*altera*) shoe to do this. The line is neatly composed with a central verb framed by pairs of words: adjectives at the front and nouns juxtaposed at the end enacting the physical closeness of the shoe and the ankle.

17 **unworthy of his intellect:** *studiis* (picking up *studiorum* from line 1) is juxtaposed with *indignum* for emphasis. The line-ending *ferre laborem* is found in didactic (Lucretius 5.1214) and epic (e.g. Virgil *Aeneid* 12.635) and the poetic phrasing looks forward to the high register of 18–19 (see next n.). The short final syllable of *nemŏ* is common in J. (the one exception being 14.207 where see n.) but not so elsewhere: see *OLD* s.v. 'nemo', Horace *Satires* 1.1.1, 1.3.68, Persius 1.3).

18–9   The imagery is flowery and exemplifies what it describes. The metaphor of 'weaving' (*nectit*) in poetic composition is as old as Pindar (*Olympian* 6.86–7 ('weaving a varied hymn for spearmen'), fr. 179 ('I weave a varied headband') and is found also in Horace (*Odes* 1.26.7–8), the *Laus Pisonis* 163–5 and Ovid (*Ex Ponto* 4.2.30). **melodious**: *canoris* (from *cano*) recreates the common topos of poetry as 'song' (e.g. Virgil *Aeneid* 1.1, Horace *Odes* 1.32.4, *Epistles* 2.2.76, *Ars Poetica* 322, Statius *Siluae* 1.2.3) and is taken with *modis* which here means 'rhythms' or metrical patterns (*OLD* s.v. 'modus' 7) or simply 'music' (*OLD* s.v. 8b, Horace *Odes* 2.1.40) and the phrase is reminiscent of Virgil *Aeneid* 7.699–701 where it is used of swans in a simile comparing them to soldiers who 'sang their king'. **verbal utterance**: *eloquium uocale* is pleonastic – how can *eloquium* be other than *uocale*? For the noun cf. 7.139, 10.114, 10.118. The high register of the phrasing is brought down to earth with the bathetic final phrase: **chewing laurel** was the mark of the Delphic priestess of Apollo who would eat laurel before uttering her prophecies in a trance (cf. Dodds (1973) 73) and the motif was used by poets who claimed Apolline inspiration (Tibullus 2.5.63–4, Ovid *Ex Ponto* 2.5.67); but the final crude verb *momordit* is fully in J.'s bathetic style (cf. 2.10, 6.80–81, Watson and Watson (2014) 18+n.88) and is here relegated in *hysteron proteron* to the end of the line for surprise: we expect a loftier verb such as *capessit* (Valerius Flaccus 4.548).

20   **To work … young men**: the literary pastiche continues as the speaker invites younger poets to meet the needs of the new emperor: for the poet as an older man addressing younger people cf. Horace *Odes* 3.1.3–4 and for the colloquial phrase *hoc agite* see *OLD* s.v. 'ago' 22 and cf. 7.48, Seneca *de Beneficiis* 3.36.2, *HF* 104, Plautus *Pseudolus* 152. The whole couplet is close to Statius *Siluae* 5.2.125 *ergo age, nam magni ducis indulgentia pulsat* ('come now, for the generosity of the leader is driving us on').

20–21   The final sentence is a resounding piece of rhetoric: three verbs form a tricolon crescendo, *et stĭmŭ/lat uos* has a syncopated rhythm to suggest the act of pushing the youth into action, while line 21 forms the sort of poetic elegance which is itself the sort of poetry being sought. *materiam … sibi* here refers to poetic **material** or even 'copy' which will praise the emperor: see *OLD* s.v. 'materia' 6 and cf. Cicero *Orator* 119, Horace *Ars Poetica* 38, Ovid *Amores* 1.1.2, *Rem. Amoris* 387, *Tristia* 2.1.70. Others take it as referring to the poets themselves ('objects for his favour' (Ramsay) 'talent' (Green)). **kindness of our leader**: *ducis indulgentia* is a periphrastic way of saying *dux indulgens*: the use of the abstract noun is not uncommon (cf.

ducis clementia at Statius *Siluae* 3.4.73 and *ducis indulgentia* at Suetonius *Julius Caesar* 69.1). *indulgentia* 'had become a technical term for imperial favour' (Courtney, citing Syme (1958) 755–56) and Hadrian even stamped the word *indulgentia* on his coins. Its sense here of 'imperial patronage' is paralleled at Tacitus *Dialogus* 9: Pliny (*Panegyric* 21.4, 69.6) states that Trajan displayed it in abundance.

22–35   The appeal for imperial help is now justified as the speaker pleads poverty: rich patrons are too stingy to give anything more than verbal support to the struggling writer.

22–3   **fortunes**: *rerum* here means 'wealth' or 'livelihood' (*OLD* s.c. 'res' 1) and the enjambed *praesidia* (*OLD* s.v. 'praesidium' 1c) is strikingly prosaic (see Nisbet and Hubbard (1970) on Horace *Odes* 1.1.2).

23   '**parchment** of the **yellow** page' means the 'page made from yellow parchment.' The word *tabula* or *tabella* often referred to a wooden frame enclosing 'pages' which had a surface layer of wax on one side which could be erased and re-used *ad infinitum* (see *OLD* s.v. 'tabula' 6, 'tabella' 6, Fordyce (1961) on Catullus 42.5, Paoli (1990) 182)) but it is clear from Martial 14.7 (and *OLD* s.v. 'tabula' 6b) that the word also denoted (as here) a parchment page in a codex which could (like the wax *tabulae*) be erased and rewritten (Fordyce (1961) on Catullus 22.5, Horace *Satires* 2.3.1–2, Brink (1971) on Horace *Ars Poetica* 388–9, Kißel (1990) on Persius 3.10): see Winsbury (2009) 15–26 for details of the whole business of book production. The yellow colour may be the result of a process of dying the sheepskin from which the parchment was made. Parchment was more expensive than the more common papyrus and the phrase here suggests a poet who overspends on materials in the futile expectation of fortune which never comes.

24   **filled up**: *membrana* is singular and so *impletur* must be right: a scribe may have amended this to *implentur* because he thought *membrana* was neuter plural. The passive verb here is uncomplimentary about the poetry, implying that 'making poems is merely a matter of the parchment being filled' (Geue (2017) 57). *lignorum* is partitive genitive with *aliquid*.

25   The **husband of Venus** alludes to the god of fire Vulcan (Hephaestus in Greek) and hence means (by metonymy) 'fire': this sort of mythological allusion (cf. Catullus 36.7–8) indicates the style of the poetry being burned. Telesinus (here addressed in apostrophe) is not known: a Lucceius Telesinus was consul in AD 66 and banished for his philosophy by Domitian (Tacitus *Annals* 16.14, Dio 63.1). **donate**: *dona* (the singular imperative of *dono*) is witty: giving one's poetry to a patron (in the expectation of something in

return) was common, but in this case the 'patron' is the fire and the result is the destruction of the poems: there is also a light allusion to the 'gifts of the Muses and of Venus' at Catullus 68.10.

26   **bookworm**: *tinea* is a destructive grub or maggot (cf. Petronius 78.2, Pliny *NH* 27.52): for its appetite for books cf. Martial 6.61.7 ('intellectuals feed *tineas*'), Statius *Siluae* 4.9.10. The peremptory imperatives *claude* ... *pertunde* continue the point from *dona* – he can burn the poetry or else just lock it away and let it be eaten by grubs. J. elsewhere (3.207) has books being eaten by mice as a sign of poverty. The 'p' and 't' alliteration of *positos pertunde* suggests the gnawing of the grubs and the juxtaposition of *claude ... positos* reinforces the image of 'locking away' the texts.

27   **you wretch ... battles**: this dactylic line is rhythmically expressive of the urgency of the words. The sentiment is drawn from Virgil *Eclogues* 3.12–13 via Calpurnius Siculus 4.23 and Martial 9.73.9. As Rudd ((1976) 93–94) has shown, the word *calamos* in Virgil means 'arrows', in Calpurnius it means 'pipes' and in Martial (and here in J.) it means 'pens': the intertextual reference recreates the act of poetic composition at the same time as it rejects it. The hypallage of *uigilata proelia* is striking and itself poetic: the poet has stayed awake at night composing epic verse involving battles and then transfers the lack of sleep to the subject-matter as at Statius *Thebaid* 12.811. Composing poetry in the hours of darkness is something of a topos: cf. 1.51, 7.99, Lucretius 1.142, Martial 8.3.17–8, Horace *Epistles* 2.1.112–3, *Ars Poetica* 269, Ovid *Ars Am.* 2.285, 3.412, Callimachus *Epigrams* 27.4. At the opening of the first satire (1.1–14) J. expressed disdain for bombastic epic and it is possible to read this passage as expressing similar contempt.

28   **lofty ... tiny**: note the oxymoron of *parua sublimia* (cf. 3.207) and alliteration of *carmina cella* and the elegant pairing of adjectives and nouns in chiastic order: the poet again recreates the style of the poetry to which he is referring. *cella* is the room of a gladiator (6.O10) a prostitute (6.122) or a poet (Martial 8.14).

29   **Ivy** was the foliage of Bacchus/Dionysus who was a god of poetry (see 7.60n., Horace *Odes* 1.1.29, *Epistles* 1.19.3–4, Virgil *Eclogues* 7.25: cf. *thyrsum* at 6.70, 7.60, *bacchamur* at 6.636, Nisbet and Hubbard (1978) 314–317) and busts of poets could be decorated with it (cf. Ovid *Tristia* 1.7.1–2, Persius *prol.* 5)). Busts of writers were placed in libraries: Pliny *NH* 35.9–10, Suetonius *Tiberius* 70.2, *Caligula* 34.2. The *imago* is **skinny** as the poet himself has been starving.

30   **hope**: *spes* picks up the opening words of this poem and *nulla ulterior*

makes the same point as *tantum* did in line 1. *ulterior* here (as at 1.147, 4.20, 9.38, 15.118, Virgil *Aeneid* 12.938: *OLD* s.v. 'ulterior' 5) has the sense of 'additional, further': 9.38 recalls this line closely. **rich miser**: the figure of the *diues auarus* is common in mime (Gellius 10.17.3) and satire: cf. 14.107–331, Horace *Satires* 1.1.28–107, 2.3.85–57, Persius 5.132–41, 6.75–80. The *auarus* (**miser**) recurs at 9.38–42 and the speaker warns the new provincial governor to set limits to his *auaritia* (8.89) and laments (1.88) the 'gaping pockets of greed' prevalent in contemporary Rome, a greed which is to blame for other crimes such as sexual immorality (1.37–41, 1.55–7, 1.77), marital coldness (6.141), disregard for the laws (14.178, cf. Aeschylus *Agamemnon* 382) and bad parenting (14.123–209). The insatiability of the greedy man is proverbial (see Otto (1890) s.v. 'auarus', Horace *Epistles* 1.2.56 (*semper auarus eget* ('the miser is always poor')), *Odes* 2.2, 3.16.28) and cf. the depiction of the mental disorder of ἀπληστία ('insatiability') at e.g. Lucretius 3.1003–10, Horace (*Satires* 2.2.146–54 where it is seen in medical terms). The verb *didicit* here is interesting: the rich man started out thinking he had to provide money but then **learned** that words were cheaper.
31   A heavily spondaic line as the rich man indulges his ponderous judgement – undercut by the enjambed opening of 32. *tantum* again (cf. 7.1, 7.81) means 'only' and is emphasised with anaphora at the start of the line and after the caesura. The thought is close to cf. 1.74 ('honesty is praised – and freezes') and there may also be a memory of Cicero's judgement (*ad Fam.* 11.20.1) that the young Octavian should be *laudandum ... ornandum, tollendum* ('praised, honoured and then discarded'). Tacitus similarly (*Dialogus* 9.1) speaks of the 'empty and unprofitable praise' which poets seek (cf. also Martial 5.16.10–11).
32   **Juno's bird** was the peacock whose tail was seen as a wonderful specimen (Cicero *de Finibus* 3.18.12, Lucretius 2.502, Ovid *Ars Am.* 1.627, *Metamorphoses* 15.385 ('Juno's bird which bears the stars on its tail')) even on the dinner table (1.143, Horace *Satires* 1.2.116, 2.2.23): the bird was proverbially proud of this (see Otto (1890) s.v. 'pauo'). The judgement of children is worthless (cf. 2.152, 10.167, Catullus 17.11–12) and here (as suggested by Stramaglia (2008) 140) the children may be coaxing the bird to show off its feathers for their amusement – rather like the patron who gets the poet to show his own 'feathers'.
32–3   The poet cannot make a living by his poetry – and the speaker will later (53–87) urge that he cannot write decent poetry without financial security – but he is trapped as he is too old to learn a new trade (cf. Seneca

de Tranquillitate 2.6) and so resents his craft. The alternative ways of making a living listed here (seafaring as a merchant, fighting in the army (or as a gladiator), and agriculture) all require youthful vigour. The imagery in *defluit aetas* is striking: time 'flows' like a river (*OLD* s.v. 'fluo' 9) and the liquid imagery leads nicely to the Greek loan-word *pelagi*: but here the motif of decline (*OLD* s.v. 'defluo' 5d) is to the fore. Note also the effective use of nouns to stand for the activities which involve them: the **sea** for seafaring, the **helmet** for military life (but also for gladiatorial combat: cf. 11.5–6) and the **mattock** for agriculture.

34–5 **boredom**: the mental torpor of old age affects even intellectuals, but the couplet expressing distaste for poetry is itself a finely wrought pair of lines: **boredom**: *taedia* comes after too much of a good thing (11.207) or at being kept waiting too long (16.44): here it **invades** the heart (*subeunt*: cf. 14.202, Virgil *Aeneid* 10.824). The sibilance, polysyndeton, and enjambement of *seque suamque/ Terpsichoren* is pleasing. **detests**: *odit* is a powerful verb and J. may be recalling Ovid *Tristia* 2.13: cf. also 3.214, 6.272, 451, 510, 9.96, 15.71, Propertius 1.1.5. The final juxtaposition (and personification of old age) as *facunda et nuda* shows the stark dilemma: however eloquent (*facunda*) he is, the old man is metaphorically **stripped bare** (i.e. destitute). Terpsichore was the **Muse** of dancing and lyric poetry and is well chosen here as Wiesen ((1973) 473) points out: 'Terpsichore is … the least likely inspirer of an aged, unsuccessful, disgusted poet. This ever-youthful spirit of graceful movement strikes the reader as a brilliantly inappropriate symbol of the useless writings of a thread-bare old man. Her presence here seems to represent the gap between the poet's hopes and the grim reality of his actual situation'. *facundus* is a term applied by Martial (7.91.1) to Juvenal himself and *facundia* was valued in poets (cf. Horace *Ars Poetica* 41, 184, 217, Statius *Siluae* 2.1.114, Martial 14.185.1), while *nuda* brings out both the poverty (cf. 3.210, 5.163), the defenceless state (cf. 6.O12, 8.205, 15.54) and the coldness of old age (cf. 10.217–8). For *et* meaning 'and yet' cf. 7.124n.

36 **Listen now**: the imperative *accipe* is a common term in didactic poetry (Lucretius 1.269, 4.722, Manilius 3.386, 4.443, Ovid *Remedia Amoris* 292, *Fasti* 1.115, Virgil *Aeneid* 6.136) and reinforces the poet's pose of superior knowledge. There is ironic force in the word *artes* (**tricks**): the primary meaning (*OLD* s.v. 'ars' 1) of the word is 'art' or 'craftsmanship' (cf. 8.224, 11.100, 14.34), but here the term denotes 'wile, stratagem' (*OLD* s.v. 'ars' 3: cf. 1.123, 4.101–2, 6.595; we thus have the stingy patron using *artes*

to withhold rewards owed to *artes*. For *confero* with the sense 'giving' or 'bestowing' cf. 1.106, 14.223, *OLD* s.v. 'confero' 5.

37   The enjambement helps to create a balanced couplet, with the stingy patron framed by terms relating to the arts. **cultivate**: *colis* often denotes the worship of a deity (1.115, 4.61, 14.103, 15.2, 15.38, *OLD* s.v. 'colo' 6) but here (and only here in J.) has the sense of 'cultivate the friendship of' (cf. Ovid *Amores* 3.4.45, Sallust *Jugurtha* 10.8, *OLD* s.v. 'colo' 7) which ironically sets the patron in ironic comparison with the deities mentioned later in 37. **Apollo** was the patron god of poets: cf. Ovid *Amores* 1.15.35–6, *Ars Am.* 2.493–4, Horace *Odes* 1.31.1–2, *Ars Poetica* 407. The **Muses and Apollo** are from earliest times regarded as the source of epic poetry and lyre-playing, and occasionally the Muses were seen as parents of poets (Hesiod *Theogony* 94–5: see West (1966) *ad loc.*). J.'s phrasing here has made commentators speculate that it refers to a specific building: Augustus dedicated a library in the temple of Apollo on the Palatine Hill and his wife Livia later dedicated another library on the Palatine (the so-called 'new temple') which seems to have been dedicated to the Muses (Martial 12.3.7). It is conceivable that J. envisages the poet leaving the library to court his patron in the city, but the point being made is not dependent on topography: the poet is exchanging the traditional gods associated with poetry for the new 'god' which is his patron, and the style of line 37 is itself suitably epic in form and register to suggest the poetic world which the man and his gods inhabit.

38   **produces verses**: *uersus facere* is a common enough phrase for the practice of writing poetry (cf. Lucilius *frag.incert.*1294, Cicero *de Divinatione* 2.116, Sallust *Cat.* 25.5, Horace *Satires* 1.10.25, *Epistles* 2.2.52, Tacitus *Dialogus* 11.2.1, Pliny *Letters* 1.16.5) and merely suggests the act of writing without any comment on the quality of the poems: the pretension of the patron is spelled out in his delusion that he **defers only to Homer** – solely because of Homer's greater antiquity. Homer was credited with the authorship of the *Iliad* and the *Odyssey*, the earliest works of Greek literature which we possess and the inspiration for all ancient epic poetry which came after. Tellingly, line 38 is framed by the two poets (*ipse ... Homero*) who are being compared: the denigration of pompous poets is something which J. has been attacking from the opening of Satire 1 (17–18).

39   **thousand years**: Homer's dates are notoriously unknown, but J. would have dated Homer according to an authority such as Herodotus (2.53) and so would have placed the poet around 850 BC: this would put Homer roughly a **thousand** years before this satire.

39–40　ablaze for the sweetness of public renown: the phrase is again parodistic of the overblown style. The nearest parallel for the mixed metaphor of *dulcedine succensus* is Pliny *Letters* 8.14.3: J. uses *dulcedine* below at line 84 with reference to the sweetness of poetry, while fire imagery is relatively common to denote the heat of passion (e.g. 1.45 (anger), 6.129 (lust)). **give a recitation**: the first *recitationes* in Rome (see Seneca *Controuersiae* 4.2) were organised by C. Asinius Pollio (76 BC–AD 4), who spent the booty he won in Illyria on building the first public library in the city, although we also hear of public readings in Greece (see *OCD* s.v. 'recitatio'). Writers would read their new work aloud: that such readings could be tedious is made clear by Juvenal (1.1–13) and Persius (1.15–18). It is clear that clients of a rich patron who dabbled in literature would be expected to attend the patron's *recitatio* and members of the audience might well show their distaste noisily as described in Pliny (*Letters* 1.13.2). For **public renown** as the objective of such a *recitatio* cf. Maternus in Tacitus (*Dialogus* 11.2) who compares it to forensic oratory as a way to become famous. For more information on the *recitatio* see Winsbury (2009) 95–110, Dalzell (1955).

40–47　J.'s account of the *recitatio* is supported by Aper's equally scathing version (Tacitus *Dialogus* 9): 'he is forced actually to beg and canvass for people who will condescend to be his hearers, and even this costs him. He gets the loan of a house, fits up a room, hires benches, and scatters programmes. Even if his reading is a complete success, all the glory is (as it were) cut short in the bloom and the flower, and does not come to any real and substantial fruit'.

40　shoddy: most manuscripts read *Maculonis* or *maculonus*, suggesting that 'Maculo' was the name of an owner of a run-down house which was sufficiently well-known to J.'s readers: modern editors prefer to print Heinrich's conjecture *maculosas* – a word more commonly applied to clothing than buildings (cf. e.g. Cicero *Philippics* 2.73, Virgil *Aeneid* 1.323) but which generally indicates mottled staining (e.g. of skin as at Suetonius *Augustus* 80.1, *Nero* 51.1) which could well apply to damp staining the walls. **lets you have**: *commodare* generally suggests that the service is provided free of charge (cf. Catullus 10.26), and the following lines show that this sort of house would not attract rent anyway.

41　out in the sticks, all chained up: the house is not conveniently in the city (cf. Martial 3.58.51 'should this place be called countryside or a 'far-off house' (*domus longe*)?'). *ferrata* means 'coated in iron' and suggests that the venue is bolted and secured owing to its lack of use (cf. 3.303–4). *longe* is taken by *OLD* (s.v. 'longe' 3a) and Courtney to mean 'for a long time' but the more dominant sense of 'set afar off' suits the context better. **ordered ... service**: *seruire iubetur* personifies the house as a reluctant slave.

42 **pigs**: the manuscripts read *sollicitas ... portas* (literally 'anxious gates' and explained by Courtney as 'gates of a city fearing attack') which builds on the imagery of *ferrata* and has the whole building likened to a fortress. Jessen conjectured that *portas*, while being possible, was a corruption of *porcas* caused by the proximity of *ianua* and that the true reading was the auditory image of the unused door squealing like pigs. *sollicitas* agrees more readily with pigs than gates, and the grotesque image is fully in J.'s style.

43 **freedmen ... claque**: the patron packs the audience with his freedmen: *recitationes* were seen as opportunities for critical and hostile assessment of one's work and the wealthy writer would wish to ensure support rather than heckling. The men were seated on the ends of the rows presumably to deter others from walking out and also to spread the applause widely rather than having it all concentrated in one group.

44 **claque**: *comitum* here refers to the troupe of clients (cf. 1.46, 3.284, 6.353, *OLD* s.v. 'comes' 2) who would accompany the patron. When formed into a theatrical or literary claque these were known in Rome as Σοφοκλεῖς as they constantly shouted σοφῶς ('bravo!'): the patron positions their **loud voices** as these are the main reason for the men being there.

45 **princes**: the word *rex* had a pejorative tone in political circles ever since the expulsion of the last king of the city (Tarquinius Superbus) in 510BC but was used for 'the great man' in relation to his clients (cf. 5.14, Horace *Epistles* 1.7.37, 17.43, *OLD* s.v. 'rex' 8). *quanti* is a genitive of price (see 178n.).

45–47 J. supplies an inventory of the costs incurred both in money and also in terms of the cumbersome furniture to be supplied and removed – a list similar to that of Tacitus (quoted above 40–47n.) *subsellia* are the **benches** for the main part of the audience to sit on, while *cathedrae* (καθέδραι) are **thrones** – soft individual chairs (cf. 6.91) placed in front of the benches in what J. calls the *orchestra* (ὀρχήστρα) as in the Greek theatre – a place reserved for the most important guests (see *OLD* s.v. 'orchestra' b). Raked seating was rigged up behind the benches with **scaffolding** (*tigilla* were load-bearing beams used to support doors, houses etc: see *OLD* s.v. 'tigillum') and the elevation is well shown in the verb *pendent*: the **gallery** consisted of *anabathra* (ἄναβαθρα: 'raised seats'). The patron will not supply the goods nor defray the cost of hiring them: both the scaffolding and the *cathedrae*

are rented and J. spells this out with variation of phrasing (*conducto …
reportandis*). The effort involved in erecting all this furniture is evoked in
the spondaic rhythm of *et quae conducto pendent … reportandis*.

48–49 and yet we: J. elsewhere (1.1–14) distances himself (as confined to
the audience rather than being on the platform) from such *recitationes*, but
here he is one of them (*nos*) and his style is itself illustrative of the poetic
form he is using and shows that as a poet he deserves to be heard. *agimus*
is well chosen: as well as meaning 'do' (*OLD* s.v. 'ago' 19) it also indicates
putting on a show (cf. 8.186, *OLD* s.v. 'ago' 25, 26) and so suits this literary
charade. For the imagery of ploughing dust and/or sand as a metaphor for
pointless activity see Propertius 2.11.2, Ovid, *Heroides* 5.115, *ex Ponto*
4.2.16, Otto (1890) s.v. 'harena' 4.

J. lends extra force to the phrasing by the enjambement of *ducimus* and the
repetitive use of 1st person plural verbs (*ducimus … uersamus*) to show the
protracted labour, and by the use of the transferred epithet *sterili* (applied
here to the plough rather than the barren land itself). *tenui* is probably a
literary allusion: see 80n.

50–52 if you … escaped: writing is a condition rather than a choice, J.
suggests, and his language is again poetically self-fulfilling with the powerful
imagery of the noose (*laqueo*), the medical terms (*insanabile … cacoethes*)
and the elegiac tone of sickness and old age to end (*aegro … senescit*). The
text of these lines is disputed and line 51 has been deleted by several editors.
Courtney suggests that J. contradicts himself ('first (all) who try to give up
poetry are unable to do so, then (an anticlimax) many are unable to do so…')
but nowhere does J. actually say that it is impossible to escape the noose,
only that the noose will grip you and <u>many</u> find it inescapable. Housman
suggested excising *laqueo … mali* which leaves the imagery simpler ('if
you try to escape, then you are held by an incurable itch for writing…') and
Courtney neatly explains the interpolation as being a scribe's mistaken gloss
(*consuetudo mali*) on the unfamiliar term *cacoethes* being expanded to fill
up the lines (see Nisbet (1995) 245), but I am reluctant to lose the powerful
imagery here. *laqueo* provides the simple picture of the **noose** used as a
means of execution or a trap for animals or people (10.314, 13.244, *OLD*
s.v. 'laqueus' 1b,c, 2a) and even suggests the poet's dismissive 'go hang
yourself' to his craft (cf. 10.53). *ambitioso* combines the primary sense
(*OLD* s.v. 'ambitiosus' 1) of 'clinging, binding' (cf. Horace *Odes* 1.36.20) –
which fits the image of the rope – with the personal sense of 'eager for glory
or praise' (*OLD* s.v. 'ambitiosus' 4) which is a transferred epithet from the

poet to his metaphorical noose; the phrase encircles the main verb *tenet* as the noose encircles the poet.

52 **cancer**: *cacoethes* (κακόηθες) is a medical term for a malignant tumour (Celsus (5.28.2) and Pliny (e.g. *N.H.* 22.149, 23.95)), used only here in Latin poetry: the Greek adjective means 'malignant' at Hippocrates *Aphorisms* 6.4. For the metaphorical use of this sort of terminology to describe compulsive and self-destructive behaviour cf. the use of *ulcus* (Lucretius 4.1068, Martial 11.60.2) of sexual desire: J.'s choice of *senescit* here recalls Lucretius' imagery of how the 'sore becomes chronic' (*ulcus ... inueterascit*). **old ... sick**: for the combination of old age and sickness see 10.217–28. This malignancy may be incurable (*insanabile* 51) but it does not kill at once, condemning the sufferer to endure a painful old age. The language is obviously overblown for the 'sickness' of being a writer and the irony here is that J., in complaining of his malady, is also illustrating it.

53–55 J. now moves on to the material conditions necessary for the production of real poetry and the need for adequate wealth and comfort. J. describes the **poet of genius** in a tricolon crescendo of imagery drawn from coinage: a) *cui non sit publica uena* (b) *qui nihil expositum soleat deducere* (c) *nec qui communi feriat carmen triuiale moneta*. In all three elements the emphasis is on exclusivity and avoidance of the common (*non publica ... nihil expositum ... nec communi ... triuiale*). Many ancient poets claimed originality in similar fashion – see for instance Lucretius 4.1–28 and Horace *Odes* 3.30.13–14 – and the language here harks back to his condemnation of the hackneyed retailing of derivative epic tales (1.1–14: cf. Virgil *Georgics* 3.4–8.

53 **poet of genius**: the poet is distinguished both by the term *uates* (used of the divinely inspired bard (see 89n., *OLD* s.v. 'uates' 2) and then by the adjective *egregium* (from *ex* + *grex*: literally 'outside the flock') which puts him in a higher order even among other *uates*. The definition of poetic genius and its essential originality was something which preoccupied Roman poets: see e.g. Horace *Satires* 1.4.40–44. The metaphor in *uena* is from mining, as at Horace *Odes* 2.18.10, *Ars Poetica* 409, Catullus 66.49 or (less likely) from a common stream of water (*OLD* s.v. 'uena' 5): the metaphorical use of the word here indicates 'a supply or store of talent and ability that may be drawn upon' (*OLD* s.v. 'uena' 7).

54 **turning out**: *deducere* is a common metaphor from spinning used in literary matters (*OLD* s.v. 'deduco' 4b) but also has the less common sense of smelting ore into refined metal (*Codex Iustinianus* 11.10.1: cf. *OLD* s.v. 'deduco' 12d) which suits this context better as the intermediate stage

between mining (*uena*) and coining (*moneta*). **commonplace**: *expositum* commonly means 'trite', deriving from *expono* and so suggesting 'laid out in public view' or 'in wide circulation'.

55   knock out … mint: the final stage of the poetic minting process is spelled out with the strong verb *feriat* (used for 'striking' a coin: see *OLD* s.v. 'ferio' 5) and the term *moneta* for the die which imprints the iconography on the face of the coin (*OLD* s.v. 'moneta' 3) and so shows the end-product. The sense is also assisted by the expressive alliteration of <u>c</u>ommuni … <u>c</u>armen as the coin is beaten out. The temple of Juno Moneta was the site of the Roman mint. *triuiale* derives from *triuium* ('place where three roads meet') and so means 'appropriate to the street-corner' and hence 'public' (cf. Virgil *Eclogues* 3.26–7, Horace *Satires* 1.9.59). Street-corners are places of gossip and unimportant badinage as at 6.412, Horace *Satires* 2.6.50, Otto (1890) s.v. 'triuium', and are also a byword for the lowest of the low (cf. Phaedrus 1.27.11, Horace *Ars Poetica* 245, Cicero *pro Murena* 13.4) and the site of promiscuity in dogs (Lucretius 4.1203) and even people (Propertius 4.7.19).

56 cannot point out: the rarity of this sort of poet is emphasised in modesty – J. makes no claims to such status for himself – and also reinforces his thoughts (1.1–14) that there are simply no original poets in his contemporary Rome. For *sentio* as 'I imagine' used of one who is unable to see directly what is being described cf. Cicero *Orator* 23.

57–9   no anxiety … completely free: the thought is that one cannot write great poetry in a state of anxiety or unhappiness: cf. Ovid *Tristia* 1.1.39–43, 5.12.3–4. Others argued that the poet will not be concerned with luxury or wealth so long as he has the Epicurean 'little which is enough' and that wealth is an enemy of talent rather than its cause: see Epicurus *Vatican Sayings* 25 and cf. Virgil *Georgics* 2.461–74, Horace *Odes* 2.18, 3.1.17–48, Tibullus 1 (Propertius 3.2.11–16 gives the topos a more poetical twist). The poet here is described with two negative terms (*carens … impatiens*) and two positive terms (*cupidus … aptus*). The subject of the verb and referent of all four terms is *animus* – a term which covers his heart and his emotions (*OLD* s.v. 'animus' 9) as well as his intellectual and creative mind (*OLD* s.v. 'animus' 5).

57   anxiety … bitterness: the line is framed by the key terms *anxietate* and *acerbi* and the busy mental agitation of the poet is well conveyed in the dactylic rhythm of the line.

58   free of all: *impatiens* has the sense 'unable to tolerate' from *in* + *patior*. The juxtaposition of this word with the positive *cupidus* increases the emphasis on the poet's emotional drives rather than his mental powers.

58–59   woods … springs: the poet is depicted as a lover of the pastoral landscape if only as an escape from the disturbing noise of the city: Horace generalises thus at *Epistles* 2.2.77 ('the whole chorus of writers loves the grove and runs from the city'): see also Tacitus *Dialogus* 9.6, 12.1, Pliny *Epistles* 1.6.2, 9.10.2. J. elsewhere (3.164–314) laments the misery and stress involved in being poor in Rome, although the quality of his verse in that passage goes against his argument here that peace and tranquillity are essential for poetic composition. The language here is carefully chosen: the poet needs to have the desire (*cupidus*) if he is to be fit (*aptus*) to drink from the spring of the Muses, who supply the talent only to those who show the enthusiasm. The overflowing of poetic inspiration is suggested by the enjambement of lines 58–9 and the elevated poetic register being sought is itself exemplified in the recondite word *Aonidum* (see next note).

59   Muses: the Aones were a people of Boeotia – the region of Greece where the Muses dwelt on Mount Helicon: thus *Aonides* comes to mean 'the Muses'. This sort of learned allusion is common in serious poetry especially in the case of names (see e.g. Catullus 64.287, 68.112) and 'Aonian' had been used for the Muses before (Virgil *Georgics* 3. 11, Propertius 1.2.28, 3.3.42, Ovid *Amores* 1.1.12).

59–61   The reader assumes that the subject of the verb *potest* is the poor would-be poet, and it is only later that we realise that the subject is **poverty** personified, the noun emphasised in enjambement and at once expanded and defined as *aeris inops* (**lacks the money**).

59   An elegant line, framed by the typical places haunted by Muses (*fontibus … antro*), and running into line 60 with the emphatic *Pierio. sub* here means 'under the shelter of' as at Horace *Odes* 1.5.3, Virgil *Georgics* 4.152, Statius *Thebaid* 10.821. **sing**: *cantare* is often used of the act of composing or reciting poetry, even when such poetry may not have been actually sung to music: cf. 10.178, 11.180, Horace *Odes* 3.1.4, Propertius 2.1.3, *OLD* s.v. 'canto' 2.

60   Pierian: see 7.8n.: J. uses two learned allusions for the Muses in as many lines. The **thyrsus** was properly the wand of Dionysus/Bacchus, waved with inspired frenzy by his devotees (e.g. Catullus 64.256, Ovid *Metamorphoses* 3.542) and feared as a powerful instrument of divine madness (Horace *Odes* 2.19.8): its links with poetic inspiration are also clear (Lucretius 1.922–3, Ovid *Tristia* 4.1.43–4), and poetic inspiration was seen in the ancient world as a form of divine madness which connected Bacchus and the Muses (Plato

Phaedrus 245a ('this type of madness comes from the Muses ... it rouses the soul to Bacchic frenzy')). The verb *contingere* is well-chosen: it means principally to touch (*OLD* s.v. 'contingo' 1) suggesting that the poor poet cannot even make contact with the inspiration he needs: but it is also the word used by Lucretius (1.947=4.22) to describe the process of 'smearing' his material with the 'sweet honey of the Muses'.

61–2   After the high poetry of lines 58–60, J. brings the matter bathetically down to earth with stark facts of **poverty** and **money** and the register of his language also collapses from the poetic heights to mundane reality. **Poverty** (*paupertas*) is sometimes (6.295, Horace *Odes* 3.2.1–3) idealised but J. generally views it as **unhappy**: see 3.152, 6.357–9, 14.236.

   money which the body needs: the phrasing is provocative as money in itself is not of direct use to the body, and J. is perhaps hinting at the Epicurean stance that wealth is of no benefit to the body (Lucretius 5.1427–9), especially considering his very Lucretian phrase *nocte dieque* used when the poet is indulging in scathing rebuke of the search for pleasure or power (cf. Lucretius 2.12, 3.62).

62   **Horace ... "euhoe"**: the poet Horace (65–8 BC) used the Bacchic shout *euhoe* in the course of a poem in which he claimed direct knowledge of Bacchus (*Odes* 2.19.5–7). **stuffed full of food**: *satur* is a double joke: it neatly alludes to Horace's self-portrayal (e.g. *Epistles* 1.15) as one who enjoys good food and of course it also plays on the generic word *satura* (satire) which is precisely what this poem consists of.

63   **genius**: *ingenium* is 'talent' or 'inspiration', often (e.g. Ovid *Amores* 3.1.25, Quintilian 2.20) paired with *materia* (subject matter) as the twin components of poetic composition.

63–4   **distressed**: the enjambed verb *uexant* is deliberate: the poet's hearts are to 'harass' themselves with poetry alone, whereas in fact poverty (61) is 'harassing' them and making poetry impossible. The language continues to be highly stylised and imitative of the poetry being described: instead of 'Apollo and Dionysus' the poet says '**the masters of Cirrha and Nysa**' in an allusive manner beloved of epic (e.g. Statius *Thebaid* 4.383) and especially of poetry about gods (cf. Catullus 35.14): gods are often invoked as 'ruling' over their areas (e.g. Homer *Iliad* 1.37–8, Horace *Odes* 1.3.1). **Cirrha** was a port near to Delphi – which was the prophetic seat of the god Apollo (cf. 13.79, Martial 1.76.11) – and **Nysa** was the mountain where the young Dionysus was tended by the nymphs (*Homeric Hymn* 1.8–9, Dodds (1960) 146). The final verb *feruntur* is close in sense (and sound) to the

Greek verb φέρονται in its sense of 'to be swept along by' (LSJ s.v. 'φέρω' B1: cf. e.g. Homer *Odyssey* 9.82, 10.54).

65   The subject of the verbs is finally revealed as **your hearts** which can only have room for one *cura* if they are to write poetry.

66   The clause (*opus <est>* + genitive + infinitives) here means exactly what it says: 'to behold (all these things) is the work/task/product of a great mind, one not troubled...'. The infinitive phrase defines the nature of the task as at Ovid *Metamorphoses* 2.411 (*non erat huius opus lanam mollire trahendo* ('it was not the task/work of this girl to soften wool by combing'), where we also see the possessive genitive *huius* with *opus*. This is preferable to giving *opus* the sense of 'there is need of' (*OLD* s.v. 'opus' 12e: cf. Propertius 2.10.12) as is found in some translations. **blanket:** *lodix* is a rare word found in verse only here, 6.195 and Martial 14.152.1 and the language of the end of the line mirrors the drop in poetic register attendant on the state of mind.

67–8   **distressed**: the poet's mind ought to be *attonitus* in the sense of 'inspired' (Horace *Odes* 3.19.14, Tibullus 1.9.47) by an encounter with the divine (*OLD* s.v. 'attonitus' 3: cf. e.g. Virgil *Aeneid* 3.172, 4.282, 7.580, Livy 2.12.13, Lucan 1.616, Statius *Thebaid* 3.580) but is instead *attonitus* with high anxiety (*OLD* s.v. 'attonitus' 2: cf. 4.146, 8.239, 13.194, 14.306, Seneca *Troades* 442, 736, *Epistles* 110.5). The word is stressed in enjambement and the line ends with the encounter with the divine which is the proper business of poetic minds. **chariots, horses**: *currus et equos* connotes the world of epic battles, juxtaposed in verse as in life (cf. Tibullus 2.1.87, Virgil *Aeneid* 1.156, Horace *Odes* 1.34.8). To see **features of gods** was a rare privilege enjoyed by Argonauts (Catullus 64.16–7) and early races (Catullus 64. 384–6) but lost along with human virtue (see 7.6–7n.).

68   The idyllic mood of line 67 is shattered with the introduction of the **Fury** – delayed for effect to the end of the line. The *Erinys* (cf. 13.51–2n.) were the avenging spirits which persecuted murderers, especially those who have murdered their own kin, and who carried out curses (see *OCD* s.v. 'Erinyes') and drove men mad (cf. 6.29). Their formidable appearance is enhanced by flaming torches (Cicero *de Legibus* 1.40) – such as were seen in a terrifying vision by the matricidal Nero (Suetonius *Nero* 34.4) – or even flaming hair (Seneca *Hercules Furens* 87): a sight such as to make any poet *attonitus*. The **Rutulian** was Turnus, who was maddened by the Fury Allecto into a passion for battle to recover his bride Lavinia from Aeneas as narrated by Virgil (*Aeneid* 7.445–66). Here as elsewhere (1.162, 12.105, 15.65–7:

see 7.234–6) J. assumes close knowledge of Virgil's *Aeneid. confundat*
is a generic subjunctive with *qualis* ('the sort of Fury to confound': *NLS*
§155–8). The word order is itself poetic, with the object of *aspicere* (*Erinyn*)
understood from the nominative at the end of the line, where it is the subject
of its relative clause: for similar usage involving *qualis* cf. 15.65.

69–70   It has been suggested that *puer* here alludes to the handsome **slave-
boy** ('Alexander'), allegedly (Suetonius *Life of Vergil* 9) given to the poet
by Asinius Pollio and the inspiration for 'Alexis' in his second *Eclogue*:
for discussion see Jenkyns (1998) 7–9 and note how the Virgilian texts
referred to here are from the *Aeneid* which came long after *Eclogue* 2.
Martial (5.16.12 cf. also 8.56.11–12, 8.73.9–10) is close to this passage
in his assertion that 'men of old were content with praise (*laude*), when
the smallest gift to a poet was an Alexis'. J. here may simply mean 'a
slave' as at 5.61, 7.133, 9.64, 10.216, 11.59, 11.146, 11.154, 12.83: and J.
elsewhere (3.166–7) refers to the cost of maintaining one's *hospitium* and
slaves. **acceptable accommodation**: *tolerabile hospitium* is an understated
reference to Virgil's 'house at Rome on the Esquiline close to the gardens of
Maecenas' (Suetonius *Virgil* 13). The imperfect subjunctives in the unreal
conditionals (*desset...caderent ...gemeret*) imply that the events are felt
as being contemporaneous (*NLS* §199), a trope often used of writers and
their works (cf. 1.9–11, 7.62). Allecto had **snakes** in her **hair** which Virgil
(*Aeneid* 7.447: cf. Ovid *Metamorphoses* 4.801, Statius *Thebaid* 11.494)
calls *hydri* and she 'raised up' (*erexit* (Virgil *Aeneid* 7.450)) two of these: J.
deflates this by having **all** (*omnes*) the snakes **fall from** (*caderent*) her, with
pleasing assonance of *crinibus hydri*.

71   **unheard**: *surdus* usually means 'deaf' (e.g. 9.150, 13.249) but here
means 'silent' (cf. 13.194, *OLD* s.v. 'surdus' 4): *graue* is an adverbial
accusative. *bucina* is an epic term for the **trumpet** or horn (cf. 14.152, Virgil
Aeneid 7.519, Lucan 2.689, Silius 15.48) and the phrase here alludes to the
massive trumpet-blast which Allecto produced (Virgil *Aeneid* 7.511–22);
note how the emphatic alliteration of *gemeret graue* enacts the sound.

71–8   The speaker argues that we demand that modern poets be as good as the
great writers of the past but do not give them the financial support they need:
rich patrons plead poverty but their lavish lifestyle refutes this. A strong point,
where the poet includes himself (*poscimus*) among the guilty and where the
strong verb followed by the finger-jabbing final monosyllables (*ut sit*) show
more force than expected: the complaint is not new, and ancient Greek poets
were also said to sell their equipment to survive (Aristophanes *Wasps* 1313).

72 **Rubrenus Lappa** is otherwise unknown as a poet: his name is given in full, in a spondaic rhythm which imparts ironic importance to this impoverished writer. **tragedians**: the *coturnus* (taken from Greek κόθορνος) was a loose boot worn by tragic actors in the theatre: it had the convenience of being wearable on either foot and was built up to add height to the actor (see Watson and Watson (2014) on 6.506) – which adds point to the comparative *minor* here. For its metonymic use to mean 'tragedy' cf. 6.634, 15.29, Ovid *Amores* 1.15.15, *Tristia* 2.1.393, Horace *Odes* 2.1.12, *Satires* 1.5.64.

73 **Atreus** was the cuckolded arch-enemy of his brother Thyestes and father of Agamemnon and Menelaus. His vengeful act of serving up the dead bodies of Thyestes' children to their father in a banquet was notorious in tragedy both Greek and Roman (Boyle (2017) lxix–lxxviii): Ennius composed a *Thyestes*, and Lucius Accius' *Atreus* of 140 BC was still popular in the age of Augustus (Horace *Epistles* 2.1.55–62), while Virgil's friend Lucius Varius Rufus composed a *Thyestes* (performed in 29 BC) which was praised over a century later by Quintilian (10.1.98) and Tacitus (*Dialogus* 12.6). Of this play the only surviving words would fit well into the mouth of J.'s poet here: *iam fero infandissima: iam facere cogor* ('now I bear things most unspeakable: now I am compelled to do this'). The tale was seen by Ovid (*ex Ponto* 4.16.31) as critical of tyranny and Seneca's *Thyestes* (composed during the reign of Nero) was no doubt a brave move since an earlier play (*Atreus*) by Mamercus Aemilius Scaurus in AD 34 had occasioned its author's execution by the emperor Tiberius (Dio 58.24.3–5). J.'s choice of Atreus here may be related to this: a play which could occasion the death of its author is probably better pawned than performed and the reference may cast a shadow on the praise of the new emperor's patronage as proclaimed in lines 1–3. The humour here is of incongruity ('King Atreus taking these mundane items to the pawn-shop' Braund (1988) 59) enhanced by the trope of awarding agency to the tragic hero of the play to express the passive vulnerability of the playwright as well as the simple substitution of play for its author – a trope which he continues in lines 87 and 92 (cf. also 1.4–6). The items being pawned are also significant both as objects pertaining to the food and warmth which the poet lacks and also as relevant to Atreus: **plates** (*alueolos* is the diminutive of *alueos*: cf. 5.88) could have been used to serve up his cannibalistic feast as well as being staple kitchen ware (Columella *de Re Rustica* 8.5.13, Livy 28.45.17), while a **cloak** (*laena*) could be kingly garb (cf. 3.283, Virgil *Aeneid* 4.262, Persius 1.32, Martial 8.59.10, Cicero *Brutus* 56, Kißel (1990) 157–58) as well as being something

a poor poet would wear (5.131, Varro *de Lingua Latina* 5.133 (a *laena* is 'as good as two togas'), Martial 12.36.2, 14.138).

74–75 Numitor was a king of Alba Longa and the grandfather of Romulus and Remus by being father to the Vestal virgin Rhea Silvia who gave birth to them (Livy 1.3.10, Virgil *Aeneid* 6.768) and the name is found among the Italian enemies of Aeneas (*Aeneid* 10.342). The person bearing it here clearly falls into the category of *diues auarus* (30: 'rich miser') whose 'poverty' is selective. The language is powerful: there is elaborate chiasmus of *non habet … quod mittat amico … Quintillae quod donet habet,* the adjective *infelix* is ironic (cf. 10.169) as he pleads poverty to his *amico* while having money for his *amica* (cf. Martial 9.2 for the same accusation) and the distinction is further enhanced by the difference between money being handed over in person (*donet*) to a mistress but not even sent (*mittat*) by third-parties to a man he calls 'friend' (*amico*). Note also the asyndeton between the lines which throws emphasis on the contrast of *amico/Quintillae* and the anaphora of *quod mittat … quod donet.* **Quintilla** is the name of this man's mistress: no woman of this name is found in extant Latin. **client**: *amicus* (literally 'friend') means here 'person (supposed to be) enjoying your patronage' merging with the near-synonym *cliens* (e.g. Cicero *Verrines* 2.4.140, *Laus Pisonis* 118–9).

75–78 lion: pets such as dogs and birds were commonplace in Roman households (see 8.34–7n. and cf. e.g. Catullus 2, Petronius 64, Martial 7.87), but more exotic beasts were clearly only affordable for the wealthy: see 14.246–7n., Seneca *de Ira* 2.31.5, Balsdon (1969) 151. The emperor Domitian kept a tame lion (Statius *Siluae* 2.5) as did the later emperors Caracalla (Dio Cassius 79.7 tells us that the lion shared the man's bed and dinner table) and Elagabalus (SHA *Heliogabalus* 25.1) while Tiberius kept a snake (Suetonius *Tiberius* 72.2). Buying a lion which had already been tamed (*iam domitum*) would presumably cost more than buying a wild one from an animal importer. Lions had long been regarded as the beasts which accompanied gods (Lucretius 2.600–605), their skin the garb of heroes such as Hercules (Aristophanes *Frogs* 46, Seneca *Hercules Furens* 1151) and the notion was even entertained of using them in warfare (Lucretius 5.1310–1322): they were imported in great numbers for the arena (Pliny *NH* 8.53) and Mark Antony was the first to use them to draw chariots (Pliny *NH* 8.55: cf. Cicero *Philippics* 2. 58, Plutarch *Antony* 9).

75–6 did not lack: the litotes of *nec defuit* tartly recalls *non habet* of line 74 and *unde* (literally 'from where') is common with verbs of 'having' to indicate the source of one's wealth: cf. Ovid *Rem. Amoris* 749, Petronius

45.6 (*et habet unde* ('he has the wherewithal')), *OLD* s.v. 'unde' 10. Here the difference is one of expensive physical needs: the amount of meat required for the lion is expressed in the expansive spondaic phrase *multa pascendum carne*.

77 **costs**: *constat* (*OLD* s.v. 'consto' 11: cf. 6.365, 626, 7.45, 188, 14.258) takes an ablative of price (*leuiori ... sumptu*). *leuiori* is preferred to *leuiore* for metrical convenience (cf. *minori* (13.48), AG § 120–121). *belua* commonly denotes a **beast** of abnormal size (cf. 4.121 (a turbot) 10.158, 11.126, 12.104 (elephant)) and is here juxtaposed in oxymoron with *leuiori* and aptly with *sumptu*.

78 **supposedly**: *nimirum* is sarcastic, as at 2.104, 10.248, 14.54, Horace *Satires* 2.2.106, Tacitus *Histories* 1.33. The notion that poets eat more than animals is turned into the grotesque image of their intestines holding more food as at Horace *Satires* 1.1.46: for *capio* meaning 'to contain' cf. 11.171, 197, *OLD* s.v. 'capio' 25. *intestinum* is often used to arouse disgust in the reader, as with the woman vomiting at 6.429 (cf. Petronius 66) and the crow pecking out guts at Catullus 108.6.

79–81 Three epic poets who all died young: the first of them enjoyed fame and fortune, the latter two had only the fame. M. Annaeus Lucanus (AD 39–65) was born in Spain to a wealthy (equestrian) father and was the grandson of Seneca the elder and nephew of Seneca the younger: unlike many poets he remained wealthy (Tacitus *Annals* 16.17). He received a good education with the Stoic teacher Cornutus (who was the mentor of the satirist Persius) and enjoyed the patronage of the emperor Nero, winning a prize in AD 60 for a poem in praise of Nero at the Neronian games. His most significant poetic composition was his 10-book epic on the Civil War between Pompey and Julius Caesar – a text which sees the birth of the principate through Stoic regret for the loss of republican liberty. The poet fell out of favour with Nero and was banned from public speaking: he then joined the Pisonian conspiracy in AD 65 and was forced to commit suicide by opening his veins, reciting his own poetry as he died (Tacitus *Annals* 15.70). He died rich – hence the reference here to his expensive tomb – unlike the other two poets mentioned in 80. The language of *contentus fama iaceat* is that of funerary epitaph, in this case contrasting the blessed state of the dead Lucan (whose literary fame is as secure as was his livelihood) over against the precarious life of Serranus and Saleius (who will be poor despite their fame): cf. 10.288, Lucretius 3.904–8, *OLD* s.v. 'iaceo' 6b, Lattimore (1962) 241–43. This also makes sense of the 'marble gardens' as denoting his marble tomb set in a garden landscape (called a *cepotaphium* (κηποτάφιον) cf. Petronius 71) and possibly adorned with marble images of vegetation (see Ronnick (1996)). Quintilian (10.1.89) mentions a promising poet called **Serranus** who died young and Martial claims (4.37.3) that he is owed a lot of money by one of this name. **Saleius** Bassus is described by Secundus in Tacitus (*Dialogus* 5.2) as 'best of men and most refined (*absolutissimum*) of poets' (but cf. Martial 5.53 for a different view): he was given 500,000 sesterces by the emperor Vespasian (Tacitus *Dialogus* 9.2) but Suetonius (*Vespasian* 17–8) tells us that Vespasian would give that sum every year to 'needy ex-consuls' and so this one-off gift was perhaps less unusual than it might seem. He died young (Quintilian 10.1.90). **famished**: *tenui* is a literary pun: on the one hand it means 'poor' (cf. 3.163, 8.120, 13.7) or physically 'thin' (6.259, 10.269, 15.101, Catullus 89.1: cf. *macra* at 7.29 above), but on the other it may allude to the literary quality of speech which is 'plain' or 'free of ornament' (*OLD* s.v. 'tenuis' 12) and especially the 'fine' poetic texture of Callimachus (see Horace *Odes* 2.16.37–8, 20.1–2 (with Harrison (2017) 238), *Epistles* 2.1.225).

81   The sentence ends with a finely constructed line with anaphora of *gloria* in emphatic positions, a rhetorical question, assonance of 'a' and alliteration of 'q'. *tantum* means 'all that one gets': cf. 7.1n. The future tense of *erit* shows that J. is thinking of the current generation of poets rather than the men named in 79–80 but also conveys the point that these poets who died young all have glory but this will be of no use to them now that they are dead, a thought which goes back to Homer's Achilles (*Iliad* 9.320).

82–87   Publius Papinius **Statius** (c. AD 45–96) was the author of the epic poem *Thebaid* which told the saga of the Theban civil wars following the death of Oedipus (see 7.12n.) as well as an (unfinished) epic on the legend of Achilles (*Achilleid*) and a collection of occasional poetry (*Siluae*). He was very much a court poet of the emperor Domitian: he won 1st prize at the Alban Games in 90 (*Siluae* 3.5.28–9) with a poem *On the War in Germany* (which J. parodies at 4.72–118), but failed to win at the Capitoline Games that year (*Siluae* 3.5.31–3). J. caricatures this court poet as a starving writer forced to produce libretti for pantomime actors such as Paris, even though such libretti were also written by wealthy poets such as Lucan and we have no reason to think that Statius was poor. Paris (cf. Martial 11.13) was a favourite of Domitian until his execution in AD 83 after the emperor's wife became infatuated with him (Suetonius *Domitian* 3, Dio 67.3: for the infatuation of well-born Roman ladies for such *pantomimi* cf.

6.63–75, Franklin (1987) 99): Paris was also the name of the seducer of
the Spartan queen Helen in the sage of Troy, which adds extra resonance to
87. *pantomimi* commonly performed female roles such as Agaue, Pelopea,
Philomela and Leda (6.63). Agaue was prominent in Theban legend as a
daughter of Cadmus and Harmonia and the mother of Pentheus, who (in
a frenzy brought on by Bacchus) tore her son to pieces. The role would be
challenging and exciting for any actor to perform, and the poet of the *Thebaid*
would naturally write Theban legends; J. elsewhere (6.72) refers to the role
of Agaue's sister Autonoe. **virginal**: *intactam* would not easily describe the
married mother of a king and clearly refers to the part itself ('unperformed')
rather than the character, although the oxymoronic juxtaposition of *intactam
Paridi* ('virgin' brought close to the sex-crazed seducer (see Wiesen (1973)
477, Braund (1988) 60)) is also effective.

82–86   The long opening sentence is framed by two passive verbs and
the imagery here suggests that the poem is a prostitute being offered to the
general public (*uulgi*) by the pimp/poet who uses his talents to push his
wares. The **lovely voice** (*uocem iucundam*) and singing (*carmen*) suggest
the serenade, especially since *amicae* looks like a noun ('girlfriend') but
turns out to be adjectival. The girl/poem will make the whole city **happy**
(*laetam*) and the poet agrees a time to meet (*promisitque diem*) which
recalls the promise of a night of love-making as at Tibullus 2.6.49, Ovid *Ars
Am.* 2.523, *Rem. Am.* 400, Propertius 2.17.1. The end-result is sweetness
(*dulcedine*) and desire (*libidine*). Jones (1982) suggests that *fregit subsellia*
is also figurative for the common topos of the woodwork of the bed being
broken by the energetic love-making, but the phrase may simply refer to the
lively audience reception of a thundering declamation (cf. 1.13).

88–90   **Military** service had always been a key element in Roman political
life and it was expected that young men would serve as officers as part of
the typical male career path (see *OCD* s.v. '*cursus honorum*'). Legionary
officers (*tribuni*) were awarded the rank of *equites* (and allowed to wear
the **gold ring** of that rank: cf. 1.28, 11.42–3n., 11.128–9n.) so long as they
served for six months (*OLD* s.v. 'semestris' 1b, Pliny *Epistles* 4.4): the
emperor Claudius appointed honorary tribunes who received the rank of
tribune despite having never served as such (Suetonius *Claudius* 25) and
this 'six-month tribunate' was granted to the poet Martial (3.95.9–10). The
general point made in 88 is repeated with more vivid detail in 89 and then
the shocking conclusion is drawn with epigrammatic wit in 90.

88   **honours**: *honorem* here has the specific sense of 'high office' (*OLD*

s.v. 'honor' 5: cf. 11.87, Horace *Odes* 1.1.8) while *largitur* has the sense of
lavishes as at Horace *Epistles* 2.1.15 (*largimur honores*), Tacitus *Histories*
4.39: *multis* exaggerates the power of Paris and also diminishes the honour
which is being shared amongst **many**.

89   The *semenstre aurum* is the 'gold <ring conferred after serving for> six
months': the shortening of the phrase mirrors the shortening of the service
and the **gold ring** envelops the fingers verbally as well as in real life, a
device known as 'iconic word order' (see Mayer (2012) 86 on Horace *Odes*
1.5.1). A gold ring was the sign of equestrian and senatorial status (see
7.140n.). *uates* is an elevated term for a **poet**, suggesting 'priest' as well
as bard (cf. 13.188, Virgil *Aeneid* 6.12, Horace *Odes* 1.31.2 (with Nisbet
and Hubbard (1970) *ad loc.*), *OLD* s.v. 'uates' 2) and also suggesting the
poet's self-importance (1.18, 7.93, Persius 5.1, Ovid *Amores* 1.1.6, Tacitus
Dialogus 9), helped by the spondaic rhythm of *semenstri uatum*.

90   **An actor ... do not**: the futile process of seeking office is brought
out by the heavy monosyllables of *quod non dant*: the ease with which
the *histrio* confers power is conveyed in the snappy dactylic phrase *dabit
histrio*, where the polyptoton *dant..dabit* reinforces the effect. *histrio* could
denote any form of **actor** but was also used for the *pantomimus* (*OLD* s.v.
'histrio' b): the shame here is that such high distinction could be conferred
by a man whose profession ought to render him disgraced (*infamis*): see
Edwards (1997) 78–81.

90–91   The low-life **actor** is juxtaposed for contrast with the aristocratic
families of Rome and the addressee is mocked with the finger-jabbing
anaphora of *tu*. The **Camerini** were a patrician branch of the *gens Sulpicia*
(see 8.37–8n.) while **Barea** Soranus was a nobleman executed by Nero
(3.116, Tacitus *Annals* 16.21–33). *curas* here has the sense of '**cultivate**
(a person)' (*OLD* s.v. 'curo' 5) and mention of the *magna atria* (cf. Martial
3.38.11) suggests the morning *salutatio* in which wealthy and powerful
men would open their doors for a 'greeting' (1.127–34, 3.126–30, 5.19–21,
10.90, *OCD* s.v. 'salutatio', Balsdon (1969) 21–24). The application of the
personal *curas* to the inanimate *atria* mocks the futility of the exercise.

92   An elegant chiastic line: note the simple central verb *facit* and the
framing of the line with the titles of officers, as well as the use (cf. 7.73)
of the titles of literary works to stand for the performers who brought
them to the stage (cf. 7.151n.). **Pelopea** was incestuously raped by her
father Thyestes (see 7.73n.) while **Philomela** was raped by her brother-in-
law Tereus (7.12n.) who then cut out her tongue to prevent her speaking

of his crime. **Prefects … tribunes**: the title *praefectus cohortis* (cf. 1.58) was given to the equestrian commanders of auxiliary cavalry detachments: the aspiring young man could then become a *tribunus militum* in charge of a cavalry cohort of 1000 (or as part of a Roman legion), before reaching the summit of the *tres militiae* as a *praefectus alae* or *praefectus equitum*, after which he would enter the civil service as a *procurator* (see *OCD* s.v. 'procurator', *CAH* xi. 335, Watson (1969) 24–25). The statement that these passive women could be deemed able to create powerful offices of state is a barbed piece of satire and the ancient *Life* of the poet stated confidently that lines 90–92 were responsible for Juvenal being sent into exile (discussed at e.g. Highet (1954) 23–31, Courtney (2013) 5–7, Schmitz (2019) 39–41). More importantly, it is ironic that the military epic *Thebaid* (feminised as an *amicae*) is not enough to gain military promotion and such offices are conferred by men dressed up as Greek women (Geue (2017) 62).

93 This line was deleted by Markland as being an interpolation (see Courtney (1975) 158). The jussive second-person subjunctive *inuideas* is paralleled at 14.38 (and cf. Virgil *Aeneid* 6.109, K-S II.§47.6c) but J. does not elsewhere use *haud/haut* with verbs but only with adjectives and adverbs (e.g. 3.164, 6.7). Furthermore the thought is odd – after saying that the wretched poet starves unless he sells scripts to the stage, he then tells us not to envy such a poet – although it is always possible that the speaker is thus being characterised as incoherent. The alliterative metaphor of *pulpita pascunt* is however quite pleasing (cf. 9.136) as is the incongruity of a *uates* (see 53n., 89n.) being dependent on his makeshift staging (cf. 6.78).

94–5 A catalogue of famous patrons of poets from the past thrown out in a series of rhetorical questions with anaphora of *quis*. C. Cilnius **Maecenas** was an intimate of the emperor Augustus and patron of Virgil (cf. e.g. *Georgics* 1.2), Horace (*Odes* 1.1) and Varius (*laus Pisonis* 238–9): see *OCD* s.v. 'Maecenas, Gaius'. Martial (8.56.5) makes a similar point to J.: 'there will be no shortage of Virgils if only there are Maecenases'. C. **Proculeius** was also a friend of Augustus and brother-in-law of Maecenas, praised by Horace (*Odes* 2.2.5: see Nisbet and Hubbard (1978) 40). Paulus **Fabius** Maximus and Marcus Aurelius **Cotta** Maximus Messalinus (5.109) were patrons of Ovid: Fabius was addressed (*ex Ponto* 3.3.2) as 'star of the Fabian family': while Maximus Cotta is addressed from exile frequently (e.g. *ex Ponto* 2.8.2, 3.2.1, 3.5.6). Cn. Cornelius **Lentulus** Gaetulicus (see 8.9n.) is mentioned among the illustrious *literati* by Pliny (*Epistles* 5.3.5) but J. may be thinking of P. Cornelius Lentulus Spinther – whom Cicero (*post*

Reditum in Senatu 8) credits for his return from exile in 57BC – in this context of writers having their lives saved. *iterum ... alter* both express the same thought ('another Cotta, a second Lentulus'): cf. Cicero *Philippics* 13.1, Virgil *Aeneid* 10.26–8.

96–7   In those times: the speaker idealises the patronage of the past (as does Pliny (*Epistles* 3.21.3)), in language which he will recall at 9.27–8. The poetic ability is contained with the appropriate *par ... pretium* and the sense of public generosity is stressed with the final word *multis* in a phrase reminiscent of Ovid (*Ars Am.* 1.159). The nostalgic tone of 96 is enhanced by the repetition of *tum ... tunc* and the juxtaposition of the key terms *ingenio pretium*, and the point is then spelt out in the humdrum but equally nostalgic details of line 97: as Roland Mayer comments (*per e-litteras*): ' "Back then" it was advantageous for the poet to deprive himself of everyday pleasures – such as getting to bed at a reasonable hour and enjoying a drink – since study and writing in seclusion through the night, and even excessive abstinence during a holiday season, would still pay dividends.' Paleness – which is mostly associated with illness (2.50, 10.229, 15.101) and fear (1.43, 7.115, 10.82, 13,223) – is associated with poets (Persius *prologue* 4, 1.26, Martial 7.4, Horace *Epistles* 1.19.17–18) and intellectuals (Persius 3.85, 5.62, Aristophanes *Clouds* 103) presumably because they are sleep-deprived from burning the midnight oil (see 7.27n.). **December** 17th–23rd was when the Romans celebrated the Saturnalia (Balsdon (1969) 124–6) which was a byword for alcoholic excess (cf. Horace *Satires* 2.3.4–5, Statius *Siluae* 1.6.5). The language of 96 recalls 1.151 where the poet asks 'where will talent (*ingenium*) equal to (*par*) the subject matter come from?': this intertextual reference suggests (Geue (2017) 62) that the phrase here is 'a false contrast then and now ... where both merit and reward are evenly matched (at zero)'.

98–105   After discussing writers of poetry the speaker moves on to writers of history: the sequence is natural given the ancient discussion of the relative merits of the two (Aristotle *Poetics* 1451, Horace *Epistles* 2.1.245–56, Quintilian 10.1.31 ('history is close to poetry and is as it were poetry in prose')). The new section is again (as at 139 and 215–16) introduced with a fiery rhetorical question. This section is short because Roman writers of history were rarely poor men and it would have been difficult to have presented them in the 'starving artist' pose which he has used for poets. Prose history was mostly written by wealthy and powerful men who had the education and the leisure to give their own account of their life and times:

we know of political autobiographies by men such as Aemilius Scaurus, Lutatius Catulus (Cicero *Brutus* 112, 132), who wrote in Latin, and memoirs of the dictator Sulla composed in Greek. Cicero, who declined the idea of writing history as it demanded an investment of time which he did not have (*de Legibus* 1.9), wrote to the historian Lucceius (*ad Fam.* 5.12) asking him to write up his consulship in a monograph; and some of the eminent prose-writers (such as Pliny and Tacitus) needed no financial support as they had earned their wealth in the law (e.g. Pliny the Younger) or in politics (e.g. Sallust, Asinius Pollio, Tacitus). It was taken as axiomatic in many quarters that only a man experienced in public life would have the authority to write about matters of state and Livy was a rare instance of a full-time historian (see Walsh (1961) 20–21).

In this section, then, instead of describing poverty the speaker focuses on the excessive work which goes into the writing of history and the consequent expense of paper, which chimes with other ancient views: Pliny remarks (*Epistles* 5.8.12) that writing history would be *onerosa* and Catullus (1.7) describes the history of Nepos as 'scholarly and hard work' (*doctis ... et laboriosis*). The speaker's point is enhanced and enacted with the sequence of: *millensima ... omnibus ... crescit multa ... ingens* and the paragraph ends with a contrast between the audience for a considered and lengthy historical tome on the one hand and the hearing of topical daily news on the other: a disparaging view of the reception of serious prose which finds many echoes in more recent times. Here the speaker degrades history to being a matter of writing-by-numbers with the language of mechanical accumulation of facts (*ingens rerum numerus*) as the pages simply grow (*crescit*) of their own accord, eating up papyrus with no creative input from an author who is simply obeying the command (*iubet*) of the generic rules (*operum lex*) to produce what will be a sterile harvest from the excavated earth (103). Any sympathy occasioned by the plea for just rewards in 104 is at once undercut with the harsh (mis)judgement of the anonymous troll at 105.

98–9 **hard work**: *labor* can mean 'labour' in childbirth (*OLD* s.v. labor' 6b) which makes *fecundior* ('more fertile') an apt description – cf. *fecunda labores* at Statius *Siluae* 3.3.123 – and the theme of fertility looks forward primarily to the agricultural metaphors of 103. The elongated enjambed expression *historiarum/ scriptores* is itself suggestive of the enormous length of these books. Note here the chiasmus and syllepsis of *plus temporis atque olei plus*: the reference to **oil** refers to working by night – a practice common among poets (see 7.27n.) but here assumed as common amongst prose writers too. The phrase 'to waste effort and oil' was proverbial (see Otto (1890) s.v. 'oleum' 3, Cicero *ad Atticum* 2.17.1): for *perit* in the sense of 'is wasted' cf. 1.18 (*periturae*), 7.222, 7.225, Martial 2.1.4, Pliny *Epistles* 7.2.1. *historia* (transliterated from the Greek ἱστορία) was taught by *grammatici* (7.231, Quintilian 1.8.18–21) and written up for public consumption (cf. e.g. 2.103, 10.175, Horace *Odes* 2.12.10).

100–101   page: each sheet (*pagina*) of papyrus was glued to the ones on either side of it to make up the *uolumen* (scroll) which was the normal form of the book in ancient Rome until it was replaced by the *codex* (Winsbury (2009) 15–26). There were roughly 200 pages in each scroll and so 1000 pages would make a text in 5 books – although the number (like *centum* at 113) is obviously not exact and simply indicates a vast number as at 3.8 ('a thousand dangers in the street') 12.46 ('a thousand plates'), 14.12 ('a thousand teachers') 16.43–4 ('a thousand exasperations, a thousand delays'). *millensimus* is the ordinal from *mille* (see *OLD* s.v. '-esimus'). *surgit* (as at Ovid *Amores* 1.1.17) suggests that the scroll was laid with pages in portrait rather than landscape mode – so that the pages 'rose up' as the scroll was unwound – while *nullo… modo* is similar to *sine modo* (*OLD* s.v. 'modus' 6c: cf. Plautus *Amphitruo* 806, Sallust *BJ* 41.9, Livy 8.38.13) in the sense of 'without restraint'. *damnosa* indicates **ruinous** (cf. *OLD* 'damnum', 'damnosus') expense (such as that of gambling at 14.4, Persius 3.49, Martial 14.18: drinking at Horace *Satires* 2.8.34, and desire at Horace *Epistles* 2.1.107). **Papyrus** was not itself so expensive (Winsbury (2009) 19–20: texts were normally written only on one side of the papyrus which also suggests the cheapness of the material) but any raw material in these gigantic quantities will rack up the cost (cf. Martial 13.1.3).

102   number … rule: the two reasons for historiographical length are the abundance of material (*ingens rerum numerus*) and the demands of the genre (*operum lex*). The former point is enacted by the abundance of eight accented words in the line, five of which clash with the metrical ictus: and the noun *res* commonly refers to the content of histories (e.g. Sallust *Histories* fr.1.1, Livy *praefatio* 1, Tacitus *Histories* 1.1, *Annals* 1.1.2: the emperor Augustus composed his own autobiographical *Res Gestae*) and the noun here as elsewhere means virtually 'history' (*OLD* s.v. 'res' 7b). **massive**: *ingens* is a common word (x18) in J. and even more common in Virgil: in literary matters it is often pejorative, being used of the bloated text *Telephus* at 1.4 and of a monstrous history at Seneca *Epistles* 95.2. The classic example of a massive history is Livy's *ab urbe condita* in 142 books;

but Livy himself was aware (31.1.1–5) of the ever-growing wealth of facts to be discussed. *operum lex* must mean something like 'the conventions of the genre': see Brink (1971) on Horace *Ars Poetica* 135. For the notion of generic rules cf. 6.635, Horace *Satires* 2.1.2, Quintilian 10.2.22, Cicero *Orator* 198, *de Oratore* 2.62, Pindar *Nemean* 4.3, Keane (2006) 75–84. *operum* (rather than the singular *operis*) is probably placed to mirror *rerum*, as Courtney suggests.

103–4 **what ... what ... who**: the speaker produces a tricolon crescendo of rhetorical questions (*quae ... quis ... quis?*) involving an agricultural metaphor of crops and ploughed earth which at once expresses and also trumps the tedious recitation of facts which the previous lines have explored. The figurative use of *seges* is common (Catullus 48.6, Horace *Epistles* 1.7.21, Virgil *Aeneid* 12.663 (with Tarrant (2012*) ad loc.*), Otto (1890) s.v. 'seges') but is apt here in the context of the papyrus plant whose harvesting will yield no profit. *inde* here means 'from that source' (*OLD* s.v. 'inde' 8) as at (e.g.) 1.168, 3.236, 6.62, 7.220, 9.28. *terrae ... apertae* (literally 'opened earth') refers to ploughed land as producing a 'crop' which is worthless, recalling a similar metaphor for the writing process at 7.48–9 (see n.): cf. Power (2010) 143.

104 **historian**: *historicus* refers to one engaged in historical research (*OLD* s.v. 'historicus²') found only here in extant verse satire but common in prose (e.g. Petronius 118.6, Seneca *Apoc.* 1.2). **gazette**: *acta legenti* ('to one reading the *acta*') refers here to the *acta diurna* or gazette of public events (*OCD* s.v. 'acta', *OLD* s.v. 'actum' 3) said to have been instituted by Julius Caesar (Suetonius *Julius Caesar* 20) which was acknowledged as a source by Tacitus (*Annals* 3.3, 12.24) and published throughout the empire (Tacitus *Annals* 16.22): J. refers to this also at 2.136, 9.84–5. Petronius' Trimalchio has such a gigantic household that his accountant (*actuarius*) reads aloud his *acta* at dinner (*Satyricon* 53). Commentators assume that the point here is that such reading would be done for nothing by a slave and so the historian gets even less than the slave. Notice the polyptoton of *dabit...daret*.

105 **'But they...**: any sympathy for the poorly-paid writer is at once quashed with this anonymous interjection. The public image of writers was often unflattering: prose writers tended to be men of leisure (see 7.98–105n. and cf. Sallust *B.J.* 4.3) and poets too shunned the city for the peace of the country (7.58–9n.) as suggested here by *umbra*. Poets present themselves as men of relative inertia (cf. Quintilian 10.3.22–24, Ovid *Amores* 1.9.41–2, 1.15.1–2, Virgil *Georgics* 4.564, Pindar *Olympian* 2.90) and this line closely

recalls Horace *Epistles* 2.2.78 (*cliens Bacchi somno gaudentis et umbra*). The *lectus* here is a **couch** for study and reflection as well as writing (*OLD* s.v. 'lectus²' 1c: cf. Persius 1.52–3, Horace *Satires* 1.4.133–4, Cicero *de Oratore* 3.17, Pliny *Epistles* 5.5.5, Ovid *Tristia* 1.11.37–8, Seneca *Epistles* 72.2).

106–49 'Line I05 forms the transition from the inactive to the active intellectuals.' (Wiesen (1973) 479). After dismissing the rewards of effete ivory-tower literature, the speaker now turns to the highly engaged and energetic world of the orator. The pickings are again slim, and (as with the previous genres) there is the strong subtext here that the reason for this is the quality of the work as much as the meanness of the public: it is significant that the term used is the more pejorative *causidicus* (see 106n. and cf. Martyn (1964) 122) rather than *orator* – a distinction made by Cicero (*de Oratore* 1.202), Quintilian (12.1.25, who calls the former 'a voice for hire ... a legal attorney who has his uses') and Tacitus (*Dialogus* 1.1) – where Tacitus similarly refuted the notion that oratory would rise to its former glory after the assassination of Domitian in 96 (cf. 4.153). As Syme ((1958) 115) caustically put it: 'there was no cure or remedy, since eloquence itself was obsolete.'

106 **barristers**: *causidici* are 'case-pleaders' (cf. 1.32, 6.439, 10.121, 15.111, Martial 1.97.1, Seneca *Apoc.* 7.5, 12.2, 12.3.28, Cicero *de Oratore* 1.46). Martial (4.8.2) describes them as *raucos* and Lucretius (4.966) has a sketch of *causidici* dreaming that they are in court pleading cases, while the obnoxious Echion in Petronius (46) wishes his son to train to become a *causidicus* as he thinks (probably rightly) that this is a trade (like that of barber or auctioneer) with a guaranteed income at least in the low-level legal work carried out all over the empire (cf. Martial 5.16 and for the evidence see Crook (1995) 172–97). This is complicated by the fact that the *lex Cincia* of 204 BC forbade the giving of gifts above certain amounts (Powell (1988) 124), since Roman tradition saw assisting another man in court as part of the system of *clientela* (Dionysus of Halicarnassus 2.10.1, Gelzer (1967) 63–64). The law was not observed, despite Augustus trying to revive it in 17 BC (Dio 54.18.2). A great debate on the issue in the reign of Claudius (Tacitus *Annals* 11.5, 7) ended with a compromise that 'gifts' up to 10,000 sesterces were permitted – a limit which the senate banned after his death. Nero revived and expanded the remit of the law (Tacitus *Annals* 13.42, Suetonius *Nero* 17) and Pliny (*Epistles* 5.4, 5.9, 5.13) tells us that in his time there was a ban on all forms of haggling over money in advance of

the case (Crook (1967) 90–91). As in the case of doctors, there was a natural feeling that taking bribes for helping others was unethical (see e.g. Lane Fox (2020) 105–106), while accepting that the labourer is worthy of his expenses (Quintilian 12.7.8–12). The language of this line both describes and evokes the *causidicus* at work, using terms which he would use: *ciuilia* (*OLD* s.v. 'ciuilis' 3c), in contrast to *ignauum* in 105, is applied to *officia* in a positive way by Cicero (*de Finibus* 3.64, *de Officiis* 1.122), Livy (1.35), Quintilian (2.4.27), Pliny (4.24.3, 6.32.1), Suetonius (*Tiberius* 8.1); and the peremptory singular imperative *dic* is fully in the manner of the lawyer at work (e.g. Cicero *Verrines* 2.1.143), as is the 'c' alliteration.

107 **duties**: *officia* (emphasised by enjambement) stresses that the lawyer presents his trade as a public duty and his self-importance is enhanced by the fat bundle of briefs. *libelli* were scrolls containing statements of the legal case, usually produced by the plaintiff: cf. 6.244, Quintilian 6.2.5, 12.8.5, *OLD* s.v. 'libellus' 3d. Here they are held together in a large bundle (*fasce*) and personified as his *comites* – a term which often indicates *clientes* ('friends of slender means' cf. *OLD* s.v. 'comes' 2) as at 1.46, 1.119, 3.284, 6.353, 7.44, 7.142.

108–9 They make a **big sound** generally, but especially (*praecipue*, enjambed for emphasis) when a creditor can hear them, presumably to demonstrate that they are good to repay the loan. *magna* (an adverbial accusative) picks up *magno* from 107. For discussion of this passage see Freeman (1984) 344–346.

109–110 A new potential client appears who is going to need a lawyer to pursue a debt in court. *nomen* here means a **debt** (*OLD* s.v. 'nomen' 23, Petronius 53.10, 117.8) as the debtor's name was entered into a **book** (*codice*). This individual has a lot of business (as *grandi* makes clear: cf. 10.71) and is more keen (*acrior*) than the simple creditor, not least because repayment is in doubt (*dubium*: cf. 116, 8.263, 10.82, 11.181). **tapped ... flank**: *tetigit latus* may simply mean 'prod in the side' but there may be a sexual innuendo lurking: *latus* is used of the genital area (Adams (1982) 49, 90: Catullus 6.13, *Priapea* 83.45, Petronius 130.8) and *tango* is often used of sexual congress (Adams (1982) 185–86): it is tempting to think that J. chose this vocabulary for suggestive purposes (see also next note).

111–12 Line 111 is almost a 'golden line' (in which a central verb is framed by matching pairs of adjectives and nouns in AAVNN format) which again enacts the overblown style being described. The imagery is grotesque, with lungs being likened to 'hollow bellows' (*OLD* s.v. 'follis' 3: cf. 10.61,

Persius 5.11, Horace *Satires* 1.4.19–21) breathing **measureless falsehoods**. *conspuiturque sinus* (**and his bosom is spattered**) has been explained since the ancient scholia as referring to the apotropaic act of spitting into the chest to 'placate Nemesis for their boasting' (Courtney, citing Otto (1890) s.v. 'sinus' 3) or to avert the evil eye with a show of modesty (Theocritus 6.39 with Gow (1950) *ad loc.,* Persius 2.31–4, Tibullus 1.2.98, Petronius 74.13): failure to do so shows a want of due humility (Petronius 74.13, Pliny *NH* 28.36: the Greek proverb (*Paroem. Graec.* 1.245) stated that ' "he does not spit into his lap" is said of boastful types.') and so here the lawyer is both acknowledging and apologising for his big talk. Sexual innuendo may also be present in this sentence – *follis* means 'scrotum' at 6.373b (cf. 14.281n., Adams (1982) 75), *sinus* is used often of the vagina (Adams (1982) 90–1 citing Tibullus 1.8.36, Ovid *Fasti* 5.256) and spitting three times was a magical means of gaining sexual potency in Petronius 131.5 – adding a light sprinkling of obscenity to the meaning here. Equally plausible is the simple reading that the lawyer's excited delivery causes him to spit down his toga.

112–114 The speaker contrasts the puny earnings of the lawyer with the massive wealth enjoyed by popular entertainers: in this case the charioteers who rode in the Circus Maximus, a type of contrast which the poet repeats at the very end of the poem (see 7.243n.). This trope – that men of intelligence go hungry while the heroes of the mindless mob or common criminals enjoy untold riches – is a common theme in satire and epigram: cf. Martial 4.67, 10.74.5–6, 10.76. **real**: *ueram* is emphasised by position and by juxtaposition with *deprendere* (which commonly means to discover hidden truths as at 4.142, 6.285, 6.640, 9.3, 9.18–9) as the speaker shows that (whatever the boasting lawyer may claim) the true figure is derisory. **earnings**: the metaphor of harvest (the primary meaning of *messem*) recalls line 103.

113   **estates**: *patrimonium* originally means 'inheritance' but comes to refer to one's entire wealth (cf. 1.138, 10.13, 14.116). **hundred**: *centum* (as *millensima* above: see 100–1n.) is not intended to be an exact figure: cf. 3.229, 8.85, Persius 1.29, 5.1–2, Horace *Satires* 2.6.33. The final two feet of 113 are filled with the one ponderous word *causidicorum* (stressed with the bucolic diaeresis preceding it: cf. 7.123) which enacts the weighty number of lawyers on this side of the scale. Only two things are being compared here but the Latin *ălĭă* is needed because the more correct form *āltĕrā* would not scan. The imagery of weighing one thing against another as if on a pair of scales is formed with the contrast of *hinc* and *parte alia* (cf. 6.437 (*inde ... alia parte in trutina*)): *pars* here is a spatial metaphor (cf. *OLD* s.v. 'pars' 12).

114   There were four firms of charioteers, represented by the colours red, white, blue, green: see 11.198n., Cameron (1976) for the background. The name *Lacerta* (**Lizard**) is 'an excellent name for a quick mover' (Nisbet (1995) 289) and the name of a charioteer C. Annius Lacerta is found on a lamp (*C.I.L.*15.6250), although 'Lizard' might be a stage-name. It is tempting to wonder whether this Lizard started out riding for the Greens; and there is certainly an oxymoron in this Lizard being 'red'.

115–118   The speaker moves into vivid narrative mode, describing the courtroom scene in the present tense with the lawyer addressed in the second person singular (*surgis ... rumpe ... tibi*) for dramatic effect. The scene is closely modelled on Ovid *Metamorphoses* 13.1–2 where the debate over who should inherit the armour of the dead Achilles begins:

> *consedere duces et uulgi stante corona*
> *surgit ad hos clipei dominus septemplicis Aiax*

> ('the generals sat down and with a ring of the crowd standing around/
>   there rose to face them the master of the seven-fold shield Ajax').

J. echoes this with his repetition of *consedere duces ... surgis ... Aiax*: but any sense that the lawyer here is being elevated to epic status is unfounded, although such elevation may be being focalised in the mind of the big-talking lawyer himself. For one thing, Ajax was to lose the debate to the clever talker Ulysses/Odysseus, and in the aftermath of his humiliation he went mad and ended up taking his life (see 10.84n.): secondly, this is a pale imitation of Ajax, with *pallidus* hinting strongly at the speaker's anxiety (as Ovid (*Met.* 13.74) states) – cf. 7.96–7n., 1.43, 10.82, 11.48, 13.223 – and thirdly Ajax became a byword for the heroic disaster, dramatised by Livius Andronicus, Pacuvius and Accius and lightly referred to as an example of murderous violence by Ovid (*Amores* 1.7.7–8) and travestied in Petronius (59).

116   **contested liberty**: the action *pro libertate* refers presumably to the so-called *liberalis causa* (Crook (1967) 58–59), used to ascertain whether a person was enslaved or free. In a slave-owning society with few obvious distinguishing features to differentiate between classes there was always the possibility of people being enslaved unjustly (by pirates for instance) and then reasserting their freedom (a common dénouement of comedies such as Plautus *Curculio*): infants exposed at birth by free parents could be brought up as slaves without legally losing their free status, slaves who should have been freed on the death of their master could be retained illegally by his

heir, while runaway slaves who set up as free men could be unmasked and reclaimed by their former masters. The situation was fraught with challenges – not least the difficulty of backing up claims in a society with little documentary evidence – and much would depend on the oratory of the *causidicus* whose efforts are well conveyed here. The singular noun *iudice* could be taken to indicate that the case was heard before one judge but the term may be used for the collective body known as a *decuria* of judges (*OLD* s.v. 'decuria' 2: cf. Suetonius *Augustus* 29.3, Tacitus *Annals* 14.20). These judges were not known for their intelligence in rural areas (Quintilian 4.2.45), which gives **peasant** (*bubulco*) a point: the word *bubulcus* simply denotes a cowherd in agricultural writers (Cato *de Agri Cultura* 5.6, Varro *Res Rusticae* 1.18.1, Columella *de Re Rustica* 1.9.2) and elsewhere (11.151, Cicero *de Diuinatione* 1.57, Ovid *Tristia* 3.12.30, Petronius 39.6, Seneca *Epistles* 47.15, Martial 10.7.5), but the pejorative tone of the word when applied in enjambed oxymoron to a *iudex* relies on the topos that country people are unsophisticated and crude in thought and deed (cf. e.g. the use of *rusticus* at 14.25n., *OLD* s.v. 'rusticus' 5,6,7, Ovid *Amores* 2.8.3 (in sexual matters), Horace *Satires* 1.3.31 (in haircuts)): for a different (idealised) view of the countryside in satire see Braund (1989).

117–8 **You poor man … staircase**: a fine sentence to show the contrast between the extreme effort and the paltry rewards, a contrast found also at 10.167. The physical language of 117 has sexual undertones (cf. 111–2): *miser* is sometimes applied (e.g. 6.643, Lucretius 4.1076, 4.1159, Horace *Odes* 1.5.12) to the lovesick, while the choice of *rumpe ... tensum* may allude to Horace (*Satires* 1.2.118) *malis tentigine rumpi* ('would you prefer to burst with sexual arousal?'): *rumpo* is often used in sexual contexts such as *Priapea* 23.5, 33.5, Catullus 11.20, 80–7. The liver (*iecur*) was regarded as the seat of passions such as anger (1.45, 6.648, Horace *Odes* 1.13.3–4, *Satires* 1.9.66) or sexual lust (Lucretius 3.984–994, Horace *Odes* 1.25.13–15, 4.1.12) and *lasso* can well describe the resulting sexual exhaustion (6.130). **Palms** (*palmae*) were the prize of victory in chariot racing (e.g. Ovid *Amores* 3.2.82) and success in the courts was also recognised with palm-branches stuck on the door of the house (Martial 7.28.5–6). This impecunious barrister clearly has no front door as he lives in an upstairs room and so pins them on his shared staircase: *scalarum gloria* is juxtaposed in oxymoron to show the meagreness of the 'glory'.

119–120 **price**: since barristers were not supposed to receive fees (7.106n.) they were rewarded with 'gifts' such as described here (cf. also Martial 4.46,

12.72, Persius 3.73–6). *petasunculus* (only found here) is the diminutive of *petaso* – a Gallic word for a **shoulder** of **pork** (Martial 13.55). Pork was the meat of poorer folk in Rome (see 11.82n., Ovid *Fasti* 6.169–82, Balsdon (1969) 53, Gowers (1993) 69–75 *OCD* s.v. 'food and drink'), here dried (*siccus*) to make it last longer (cf. 11.82): this diminutive portion of poor food is indeed small reward. The final monosyllables *et uas* create a sense of expectation which the enjambed noun *pelamydum* disappoints: Pliny (*NH* 9.47) tells us that **tunny fish** (*pelamys*, πηλαμύς, *thynnus uulgaris*) in spring were called 'mudfish' (from πηλός) and the word is less appetising than its near-synonym *cordyla* (Martial 11.52.7, Pliny *NH* 32.146): for fish given to lawyers in containers cf. Persius 3.76. *bulbi* are some form of the **onion** family (included by Martial (4.46.110) in gifts to a lawyer): they were seen as healthy food (Petronius 130.7) and also regarded as sexual stimulants (Columella 10.105–6, Martial 3.75.3–4, 13.34, Pliny *NH* 20.105, Aristophanes *Ecclesiazusai* 1091–2): Pliny (*NH* 19.93–4) describes *bulbi* being used in medicine and mentions the one named after Epimenides ('narrower foliage and less harsh') which may be lurking behind J.'s use of *epimenia* here. **monthly ... Moors**: the appositional phrase *Maurorum epimenia* works as descriptive – these *bulbi* were rationed out to African slaves – as well as faux-epic description complete with pompous use of the Greek term ἐπιμήνια (which means '[monthly] rations' from the word for 'month' (μήν)). As Stramaglia notes ((2008) 176), the satire is accentuated by the 'contrast of the mediocrity of the gift and the elevated style with which it is described.' *Maurus* properly denotes a 'Moor' from Mauretania but often simply means 'African' (3.79, 6.337, 10.148, 11.125, 14.196): such men are mentioned as household slaves (5.53, Martial 6.39.6). *bulbi* were grown in Africa (Pliny *NH* 19.95, Ovid *Rem. Amoris* 797) amongst other places: the point is that the lawyer is degraded by being fed with slave-fodder.

121 **brought down**: the prefix *de-* shows that the wine being given was brought downstream and so indicates wine from Sabinum and Etruria – as opposed to quality wines from Greece and Campania which were brought upstream from the port at Ostia (cf. 5.89) – and is enough to damn the quality. **flagons**: a *lagona* (λάγυνος) was a thin-necked bottle which was clearly portable (cf. 5.29, 8.162, 12.60, 14.271, Persius 3.92–3) and contrasted with the large static storage-jar (*dolium*) at Seneca *Epistles* 118.15: five of these make up a poor reward for four whole sessions of legal striving and the use of the appositional phrase *quinque lagonae* makes the quantitative

assessment a further judgement on the gift, adding the insult of meagreness to the injury of the poor wine.

122   **spoken**: *ago* here (and at 125, 143) means 'to plead in court' (*OLD* s.v. 'ago' 44): a man pleading in court was termed an *actor* (Horace *Ars Poetica* 369–70, *OLD* s.v. 'actor' 4) and the abstract noun *actio* was used of the legal proceedings themselves (*OLD* s.v. 'actio' 6) – in this case the lawyer has had to conduct four such *actiones* to earn his five bottles. **gold coin**: a gold *aureus* was worth 25 denarii (=100 sesterces): it is hard to conjecture the current value of such coins but an unskilled labourer could earn 1000 sesterces (=10 *aurei*) in a year, a soldier in Julius Casear's army would earn 900 sesterces per year with free food, and a gladiator could be given a purse of 500 sesterces for one fight (see 7.243n.). *contigit* has the serendipitous sense of 'receive by chance' (*OLD* s.v. 'contingo' 8: cf. 5.164, 6.49, 6.217, 6.564, 8.28, 13.7, 14.184) and so sets up the sketch of the lucky stroke of fortune (the *aureus*) followed by immediate disappointment (*cadunt partes*).

123   The line (like 113) ends with a five-syllable word, in this case the Greek word *pragmaticorum* (from πραγματικός: cf. Cicero *de Oratore* 1.45.59, Quintilian 12.3.4, Martial 12.72.5–6). These were **solicitors** or legal attorneys (*iuris consulti*) who studied the law, advised the *causidicus* (who was often not trained in the law) on the legal details but did not speak in court: Horace draws the distinction clearly between the man who 'sharpens his tongue' for courtroom pleading and the one who 'gives advice on law' (*Epistles* 1.3.23–4: cf. *Satires* 1.1.9–10, Crook (1967) 88–92, Crook (1995) 149–50). **take their share**: *cado* has the meaning 'be deducted' (*OLD* s.v. 'cado' 27) but retains a hint of its primary sense of 'falling down'. *partes ex foedere pragmaticorum* effectively juxtaposes legal terms: the share (*partes* cf.1.41) of the money belonging to the *pragmaticorum* has been agreed in a contract (*foedere*).

124   **Aemilius**: the *gens Aemilia* was one of the most distinguished strands of the Roman aristocracy (with 21 entries in *OCD*: see 8.3n., 8.9n.) and the name is stressed at the start of a line which concludes with the humble *nos*. The impersonal verb *licet* indicates what is allowed and refers to the limit of 10,000 sesterces placed on lawyer's earnings by Claudius in his revision of the *lex Cincia* (see 7.106n.): this was a considerable sum when contrasted with the meagre list of groceries offered in lines 119–21, and the strong future indicative verb *dabitur* asserts the certainty of the nobleman's earnings. The manuscript reading *et* was corrected to *at* by Ruperti but this is not needed: *et* can mean 'and yet' (as at 1.93, 7.35, 13.91, KS II. §154.6,

OLD s.v. 'et' 14). The inelegant rhythm (with clash of ictus and accent in *át meliús nos*) at the end of this line undercuts the speaker's claim to have spoken better and also indicates spluttering indignation.

125–8 **Why?**: potential clients are impressed by the show of wealth. Nothing succeeds like excess, and this vignette gives us the trappings of ancestral fame and fortune in the form of statues – imagery which becomes sardonic at the end, where it is clear that the former glory is now neglected.

125–6 The **bronze** statue in his hall displays the ancestor riding his triumphal horse-drawn **chariot** as at 8.3, 8.143–4 – a distinction which has to date back to republican times since under the empire citizens were not awarded triumphs. The wealth is shown in the material used (bronze), and the size of the statuary is suggested by the enjambed *alti/quadriiuges* whose expansive phrasing (and lack of 3rd foot caesura) enacts what it describes. **four-horse**: *quadriiuges* is a lofty word (cf. e.g. Ennius *Andromache* fr.92W, Virgil *Aeneid* 10.571, 12.162, Manilius 5.3, Ovid *Metamorphoses* 2.168, 9.272, Silius 4.439) which well suits the family pride of the man – as does the plural form *uestibulis* for the singular (cf. Statius *Thebaid* 1.386–7 and cf. the plural form *atria* at 14.65).

126–8 Some of the details are unclear in these lines (see Alexander (1947), Killeen (1969), Eden (1985) 343–45), but the gist is that the statue displays Aemilius sitting on horseback in military pose – a heroic image undercut by that final word *lusca*. Martial (9.68.6) mentions a similar equestrian statue of a lawyer and the imagery here suggests that our lawyer is as indomitable a fighter as the cavalryman. Eden (1985) suggests that these lines are spoken by the same interlocutor who spoke 124 – which is not implausible but which would demand that we ignore the signs of physical neglect in the statue (or else read these lines as sneering from a disgruntled observer who might as well be the satirist himself). The vignette is an epic action-shot: *bellator* (*equus*) is a **warhorse** (*OLD* s.v. 'bellator' 2b) at Ovid *Metamorphoses* 15.368, Virgil *Georgics* 2.145, *Aeneid* 10.891, 11.89 (modelled possibly on πολεμισταί ἵπποι at Theocritus 15.51–2): the choice of this word (from *bellum* ('war')), stressed by position and enjambed juxtaposition with *feroci* sets the heroic scene, as does the verb *minatur*. The **spear** (*OLD* s.v. 'hastile' 2: cf. Virgil *Aeneid* 9.402, 11.561) is **curved**: in real life this might indicate brandishing the weapon but on a statue it simply looks as if the weight of the (larger) spear-head has over time weakened the shaft and caused it to droop. The speaker creates epic jingles of *minatur...meditatur* and also *minatur...eminus* as well as focalising the mental state of anticipation in threatening and **planning his battles** (*proelia*:

for the phrase cf. 4.112) and the urgency is stressed with the ellipsis of *hastile* *<torquere> minatur*. Line 128 unravels this heroic action: the warrior is in fact only a statue (cf. 8.53, 11.141 for the same effect) and he is lacking an eye (*lusca*). There were notable one-eyed leaders in the ancient world – e.g. Hannibal (see 10.158n.) Sertorius (*OCD* s.v. 'Sertorius, Quintus', Plutarch *Sertorius* 1.2), Antigonus and Philip of Macedon, father of Alexander the Great (cf. 12.47n.) – but the point here is that the statue has lost one of its 'eyes' which would have been formed of a coloured stone which would easily fall out. The contrast of the pompous self-presentation and the grim reality in statues is something which J. will return to at 8.4–5. *statua...lusca* is most easily understood as an ablative absolute construction rather than as a local ablative in the sense of 'in his one-eyed statue'.

129–133   The speaker presents a lengthy tricolon crescendo of aspiring lawyers doomed to bankruptcy if they emulate Aemilius. A certain **Pedo** is named as a writer by Ovid (*Ex Ponto* 4.16.6) and Martial (1.Pr.12, 2.77.5, 5.5.6) but is otherwise unknown, while **Matho** is described as a *causidicus* at 1.30–33 and a 'bigmouth' at 11.34. **Tongilius** is frequently addressed in Martial as a crook (3.52) and a glutton (2.40): Martial also (2.40.7) describes Tongilius visiting the baths on doctor's orders.

129   The demise of the three men increases in degree: **goes bankrupt** (*OLD* s.v. 'conturbo' 3: cf. 14.94n., Catullus 5.11, Petronius 38.16, 81.5) is followed by **fails** (*deficit*: 11.199): the word means 'runs out (of resources)' at 3.311, 12.69, Horace *Satires* 2.1.13 and is often applied to money (e.g. 11.38, Horace *Epistles* 1.4.11) as here. **the end**: *exitus* (literally 'way out') here connotes metaphorically the 'fated death' (cf. 7.204, 10.127, 10.159, 10.271, 11.39, Virgil *Aeneid* 2.554, Horace *Odes* 3.6.6, 3.29.29, *OLD* s.v. 'exitus' 4) or more specifically 'way of dying' (6.33).

130   The **rhinoceros** was known to the Romans not least because it was shown in the arena (Balsdon (1969) 303–304) as part of the beast-hunt (*uenatio*) which could precede gladiatorial combat (see Martial *Spectacula* 9, 22) or else exhibited as a speciality (Suetonius *Augustus* 43.4). Taken literally, the Latin states that Tongilius takes a (real) rhinoceros into the baths (and *lutulenta* would suggest that the beast showers his fellow-bathers with mud): most modern commentators read *rhinocerote* as standing for the rhinoceros-horn which was used as an oil-flask (see Martial 14.52) and taken into the baths (see 3.263, 11.158n.) for use in washing (*lauari*), but the superficial literal sense of the lines adds to the manic tone: Tongilius' extravagance means that his 'horn' is from a larger beast – and it is a big

specimen (*magno*) of a rhinoceros – and the expansive phrasing (which fills most of the line) enacts the oversize object.

131–2   The swarming **mob** of Tongilius' *clientes* fills the lines as it fills the baths and the forum: and the aggressive nature of the man is stressed with the insistent verbs *uexat* (cf. 1.100) and *premit* (a verb which connotes strangulation at 14.221 and drowning at 14.296 and which fits well the choking of the bearers with a heavy pole). The *clientes* are **muddy** (*lutulenta*) from walking the streets with him (cf. 3.247, Horace *Epistles* 2.2.75, Martial 12.26.8). The litter-chair (*lectica*) was carried by *lecticarii* who supported the poles (*OLD* s.v. 'asser' 3, Suetonius *Caligula* 58.3, Catullus 10.20) from which it was suspended: here the singular is used for the plural (as at Martial 9.22.9), while *longo* suggests that this litter was such as to require six (cf. Martial 6.77.10) or eight (cf. 7.141–2, Martial 6.84.1) or even a crowd (cf. Seneca *Epistles* 31.10) of bearers, although Naevolus (9.142) would be content with just two: Petronius (28.4) has Trimalchio carried in a litter from the baths to his dinner, and J. elsewhere (1.32) describes Matho (7.129) 'filling up his new litter all by himself'. *Maedi* were a tribe from Thrace (Livy 26.25, Thucydides 2.98): an inscription (*C.I.L.* 6.6310) records them being used as litter-bearers.

133   **to buy**: the future participle *empturus* conveys the sense of intention as at 1.44, 6.313, 14.314. The shopping list is certainly expensive and delivered in hasty asyndeton: Martial (11.70.7–10) has his own take on this trope with a list of items to be sold: 'silver-plate, tables, *murrina*, land, house … to avoid selling slave-boys'. *pueros* here means **slave-boys** as at 5.61, 6.151, 6.272, 7.69, 10.216, 11.59, 11.146, Petronius 54.5, *OLD* s.v. 'puer' 5: for the mechanics of slave-selling see Harris (1980). *argentum* was **silver**-plate: see 1.76, 3.220, 6.355, 8.123, 9.141, 11.41, 12.43, 14.62n. **myrrhine vessels**: *murrina* (cf. 6.156) were vessels 'made of fluorspar and … hugely expensive (Pliny *NH* 37.18–22, Seneca *Ben.* 7.9.3, Martial 3.26.2) … myrrhine vessels were valued for their variegated colours and their smell (Pliny *NH* 37.22)' (Watson and Watson (2014) 123). **villas** were estates both urban and rural (see *OCD* s.v. 'villa', Balsdon (1969) 193–210, Dewar (2014) 5–15) and J. elsewhere (1.94, 10.225, 14.86–95n., 14.140–1, 14.275) satirises the craze for acquiring ever more of them.

134   **purple … guarantor**: the clothing metaphorically 'stands as a guarantor' (*OLD* s.v. 'spondeo' 2) in the sense that it persuades others to give him money either as loans or as paid work. The *stlatta* was a 'broad ship' (the rare word (cited in Ennius (*Annales* 177W)) derives possibly from *lātus* ('broad': so *OLD*: cf. *stlis* (=*lis*) and *stlocus* (=*locus*): see Gellius 10.25.5). The adjectival form has been taken to mean 'imported' or 'smuggled in' (Stramaglia (2008) 183) or else metaphorically 'deceptive' (which is how the ancient scholia read it). Griffith ((1969) 381–2) temptingly explains the term as alluding to the 'piratical way' (*piraticus mos*) of haggling for high fees which Quintilian (12.7.11) deplores in orators – on a par with the haggling of pirates for ransoms for their hostages.

134–6 **Tyrian** purple was the designer-label of royalty and a byword for dangerous excess in the ancient world (1.27, 12.38–9n., 14.187–8): the emperor Nero (Suetonius *Nero* 32.3) banned the use of 'amethyst and Tyrian colour' in clothing. **crimson garb**: amethyst was a shade of purple 'formed by mixing the juice of the purple fish with that of another shell-fish, the *bucinum*' (Duff): see Pliny *NH* 9.135.3. For *amethystina* <*uestimenta*> cf. Martial 1.96.7, 2.57.2–6. There is a typically Juvenalian outrage here as this stuff of royalty now 'sells' a barrister in the sense of 'gets him paid work' (cf. Horace *Epistles* 2.1.74 for this use of *uendo*). **it pays him**: *conuenit illi* picks up *est illis...utile* from 135: 10.347–8 also links these two terms. For *conuenit* in the sense of 'it suits them' cf. Horace *Satires* 2.4.71, Ovid *Amores* 1.9.3.

135 This line (omitted in one manuscript) has been condemned by some editors as an interpolation: there is nothing in it which is not covered in 134 and 136. Deleting it would however remove the fine chiastic five-word phrase *purpura uendunt/ causidicum uendunt amethystina* which is itself enacting the sort of rhetoric which the speaker would use.

137 **racket ... appearance**: the phrasing shows the auditory and visual display: *strepitu* is a good choice of word because on the one hand the lawyer is making a lot of noise (108, 111) and on the other the mob is crowding the baths (131), while *facie* shows that the wealth is but skin-deep and is just theatre to drum up custom: for this superficial sense of *facies* cf. 6.143, 10.157. *census* (see 13.7n.) means the registered property on which assessment was made to put each man into the right property-band: as shorthand simply for 'wealth' it is common: see e.g. 3.140, 6.362, 10.13, 11.23, 14.176, 14.227, 14.304, 14.317.

138 **Spendthrift Rome** did set limits to what lawyers could earn (see 7.106n., 7.124n.) but not to what they could spend, which explains the lawyers' need for ruinous expenditure in a vicious circle of the need to impress and the quest for the money to finance this: cf. Seneca *Epistles* 50.3. This marks a contrast to the good old days when *par ingenio pretium*

(96) – nowadays the expense is vastly in excess of the genius – and also looks ahead to lines 139–149. *prodiga Roma* is personified, as often in the moralists: cf. 2.39, 3.165, 3.182, 4.38, 8.243–4.

139–49 The speaker rounds off this section with a summary of the argument and a string of examples to support it.

139 **Do we trust...?**: the new section is again (as at 98 and 215–16) introduced with a fiery rhetorical question. *fidimus* is an indicative verb – not 'should we trust?' but 'do we trust?' – pointing to the sad state of affairs in Rome rather than suggesting a course of action. Marcus Tullius **Cicero** (106–43 BC: see *OCD* s.v. 'Tullius Cicero, Marcus') was a great orator and statesman of the late Republic and a byword for political and oratorical excellence (cf. 7.214, Martial 3.38.3): J. elsewhere (10.114–126) uses him as an example of fine oratory causing untimely death, while at 8.231–244 Cicero is the low-born genius who saw off the noble thug Catiline. Cicero was of equestrian family (see 8.237–8n.) which meant that he possessed in excess of 400,000 sesterces: 200 sesterces would represent a trifle to such a man (0.001% of the annual fees sought by other barristers according to Martial 8.16.2). Cicero here is placed for emphasis in the centre of the line, starting with an indignant rhetorical question and ending with assonant *nemo ducentos* and showing the sort of language which the man himself might have used (cf. 10.122 for Cicero's use of assonance in his poetry). This line sharply shows the divergence of our main manuscripts. The reading of Φ is: *ut redeant ueteres Ciceroni nemo* ('were the ancients to return, nobody [would give] to Cicero...') whereas P reads *fidimus eloquio? Ciceroni nemo...* ('Do we trust eloquence? Nobody [would give] to Cicero...'). As Housman ((1931) xxv) notes, 'there is no ground for calling one lection interpolated rather than the other: we cannot be sure which Juvenal wrote: we cannot even be sure that he wrote either.' The late (5th–6th century AD) Latin grammarian Priscian (3.329), and most modern editors (including Housman) read *fidimus eloquio*. Martial 11.5.5 has *si redeant ueteres* in similar vein and some editors regard this as the source of the variant reading.

140 **these days**: the word *nunc* placed for emphasis at the start of the line shows what the speaker is referring to present-times in a counterfactual conditional – the 'vivid' perfect tense of the conditional subjunctives *dederit...fulserit* has present force (Woodcock *NLS* §198) as at 1.105, 2.24, 6.651, 8.30, 10.321 – to argue that even Cicero would not now receive work if he were not seen to be rich: for wealth as the symbol of respectability cf. 3.140–4. A gold **ring** is the symbol of status amongst senators and equites

(7.89, 11.42–3, 11.128–9n., Martial 8.5, Statius *Siluae* 3.3.143–5) and flaunted by *nouveau-riches* (cf. 1. 28, Petronius 32.3) and vulgar plutocrats (Seneca *N.Q.* 7.31.2): Quintilian (11.3.142) urges would-be lawyers not to overdo their ostentation in this regard. This lawyer proves his wealth by the colour of his ring (*fulserit* suggests that it is gold rather than iron) and its massive size (*ingens* is stressed at the end of the line and the sentence).

141–3   looks at: *respicit* has the sense of 'checks to see' (cf. 3.268, 6.115, 8.91). The inventory of visible wealth begins with chiasmus juxtaposing the key numbers (*serui/ octo decem comites*) and has a pleasing scattering of people in front and behind him (*post...ante*) with litter-bearing slaves and toga-wearing free men spread over the lines (in ABAB sequence) encircling the main man (*te*): the slaves are there to carry the litter-chair (cf. 7.131–2n.) while the 'companions' are free-born *clientes* who walk in front of the rich man while he is being carried in his litter-chair as at 1.96, 3.127, Martial 2.57.5–6, 9.100.3, Tacitus *Dialogus* 6.4. The **toga** is the garb worn by a man of citizen status (cf. 10.8, 16.8n.) while a *sella* was a form of **litter-chair** often used by women (1.120–126, 6.353, Tacitus *Annals* 14.4.3) or emperors (Suetonius *Otho* 6.3, Tacitus *Histories* 1.27). *an* here introduces the indirect question as at 6.387, 6.567, 6.591, 7.162, 13.203, 15.89, (*NLS* §182.5).

143–5   plead: *agebat* (cf. 122n.) is repeated in the same position in consecutive lines (cf. *egit* in 5.147–8), mirroring the rhetoric being described, as does the anaphora of *quam ... quam* in 144–5. **Paulus** may allude to the successful lawyer Aemilius Paulus (mentioned at 7.124: cf. 8.21n. for other branches of the family), while **Gallus** is a common enough *cognomen* in Roman families (e.g. the poet Cornelius Gallus): the name may be used to point forward to the mention of Gaul as the source of oratorical education in 148. **Basilus** is not a common name (another man of the same name occurs at 10.222) and may be a sardonic choice here as the Greek word βασιλεύς means 'king' and was a byword for wealth and privilege in the case of the King of Persia (LSJ s.v. 'βασιλεύς' III).

144   rented: *conducere* means 'to hire' as at 3.652, 6.381. **Sardonyx** is a precious stone used to enhance the allure of rings (see 13.139n., Watson and Watson (2014) on 6.382) by rendering them much more expensive (Martial 10. 87.14) and glamorous (Pliny *NH* 37.85: see further Kißel (1990) on Persius 1.16). The prominence of the stone is brought out by its prominent position at the start of the line. *pluris* is a genitive of price (cf. 7.44, 7.178n., 11.16, 14.201, *NLS* §87.iv). *Gallus* is the reading of all modern editors: Φ has *Cossus*, influenced by 8.21.

145 Eloquence ... clothing: a fine generalising epigram (cf. e.g. 1.74, 2.47, 3.152–3, 10.18, 10.297–8, 11.208) to summarise the point being made as a sad reflection on modern life (close in spirit and language to Petronius 83.10 (*sola pruinosis horret facundia pannis* ('eloquence alone shivers in cold clothing'))): Courtney points out that the sentiment conflicts with that of 8.47. Note the juxtaposition of words here: the high-register *facundia* joined to the bathetic *panno* (*OLD* s.v. 'pannus' 2a) and the key adjectives *rara ... tenui*: *rarus* means primarily 'rare, infrequent' (e.g. 7.228) but also 'loosely woven' (*OLD* s.v. 'rarus' 1b) as of clothing – which intensifies the juxtaposed *tenui* whose primary meaning here is 'thin' (of cloth as at 6.259) but which can also mean 'plain' as describing oratory (*OLD* s.v. 'tenuis' 12) and so blends into the world of *facundia*.

146 Speakers in court used a variety of means to elicit pity from the judges in the ancient world (see Winterbottom (2004) 219–23), the most blatant being the introduction into the court of weeping family members (cf. 15.134–7nn.) who will be adversely affected if the case is lost: e.g. Cicero *pro Caelio* 4.2, *Verrines* 1.93, Quintilian 6.1.30, Aristophanes *Wasps* 568, 976–8, Lysias 20.34, Andocides 1.148–9, Demosthenes 19.310, 21.99, Plato *Apology* 34c. **mother**: Cicero (*pro Cluentio* 195) comments that 'many have forgiven the misdeeds of the children out of pity for the parents' and the figure of the **weeping mother** is a topos in ancient literature (e.g. Homer *Iliad* 1.413–427, Virgil *Aeneid* 9.473–502).

147 make do with: *ferat* has the sense of 'endure' a person as at 1.139, 2.24, 3.60–61, 5.163–4, 6.30, 6.166, 6.651 (*OLD* s.v. 'fero' 20a). The point is made counterintuitive by the juxtaposition with *bene dicentem* which has concessive force ('for all his fine speaking') – a description which is undercut by the off-beat rhythm of *accipiat te* which hints that Basilus has a lot to learn.

148–9 Gaul was known to be a centre of oratorical education: cf. 7.214, 15.111n.. The young Agricola (Tacitus *Agricola* 4) received his oratorical and philosophical education at Massilia (Marseilles) – a place which Strabo tells us (4.179–81) was the Romans' preferred choice for educating the young, outranking even Athens. Milo found it to be a highly agreeable place of exile (Dio 40.54): cf. Cicero *pro Flacco* 63, Tacitus *Annals* 4.44.3. The emperor Caligula (Suetonius *Caligula* 20) held contests of oratory in Lugdunum (Lyon) as mentioned at 1.44, and most of the speakers in Tacitus *Dialogus* come from Gaul (Tacitus *Dialogus* 10.2): on this whole topic see

Clarke (1953) 145–46, Bonner (1977) 157–58, Mayor (1886–89) on 15.111.
Africa in general (and Carthage in particular) were similarly known as a
home of oratorical schools (Clarke (1977) 145, Marrou (1956) 294) and
produced many distinguished speakers as well as writers such as Apuleius,
Arnobius, Augustine, Lactantius and the emperor Septimius Severus: this
great tradition is here traduced (as Martyn ((1964) 122) comments) by
being reduced to 'a wet-nurse to molly-coddle the *infantes* of the provincial
schools of rhetoric' with the use of the diminutive *nutricula* (cf. Horace
Epistles 1.4.8). The style of these lines is itself oratorical, with repeated
enjambement of the place-names, a metaphor in *nutricula*, a sonorous five-
syllable word to end 148 and the striking financial phrase *mercedem ponere
linguae* (see *OLD* s.v. 'pono' 14 and cf. Martial 11.31.21, Horace *Satires*
2.3.23, Virgil *Aeneid* 6.611) suggesting that the orator is going to invest
finance in his tongue: for this metaphorical use of *lingua* cf. 10.10–11,
Persius 5.25, Horace *Odes* 3.12.3, Aristophanes *Clouds* 424, *Frogs* 892. The
terminology is however pejorative: 'both *lingua* (9.119, 121 and 3.63) and
merces (1. 42; 3. 15; 5. 13; 6. 33; 8.246, 14.164, 14.273 and 7.157–8, 7.l75,
7.228) have mean, if not servile or vulgar associations' (Martyn (1964) 123
n.1). The section on oratory ends appropriately with an oratorical use of the
word 'tongue'.
150–214   The new section is again (as at 98, 139, 215–16) introduced
with a fiery rhetorical question. Teachers of rhetoric (it is argued) have a
poor life, enduring a tedious method of work and struggling to receive any
money for it: they do not even get the respect which teachers in former
times enjoyed. Education in ancient Rome fell into three rough stages: the
ludi magister ('school master') taught elementary reading and writing to
children from about 7 years: then (aged about 12) the pupil went into the
school of the *grammaticus* (as described in 216–243) for instruction in
language and poetry: finally (aged about 15) he came into the hands of the
rhetor (see *OCD* s.v. 'Education, Roman', Marrou (1956) 265–91, Bonner
(1977)). *declamatio* was a key element in Roman higher education: the two
most popular exercises were the *suasoria* (in which the pupil composed a
speech advising a historical figure such as Hannibal or Sulla on the best
course of action: cf. 1.16–17, Quintilian 2.1.2–3, Bonner (1949) 277–87)
and the *controuersia* (in which a fictitious legal case was discussed): our
main evidence on these exercises comes from the reminiscences of the
Elder Seneca (*OCD* s.v. 'Annaeus Seneca (1), Lucius') who recreated his
recollections of *Suasoriae* and *Controuersiae*: a convenient selection of

sources is translated at Russell and Winterbottom (1972) 344–371 and the whole practice is mocked at Tacitus *Dialogus* 35. This passage is itself a piece of *declamatio* and is studded with undercurrents of irony and self-refuting points, as Braund ((1988) 63–66) makes clear: for one thing, the teacher of *declamatio* ought to be well-placed to use his own oratory in pursuit of fees through the courts, as mentioned at 168–170, although it was observed in antiquity that the 'academic' rhetorician was often out of his depth in a real court of law: see Bonner (1949) 73.

150   **iron-clad heart**: *ferrea pectora* is the sort of rhetoric which the teacher is imparting: cf. Quintilian 12.26. The adjective *ferreus* here (as at 1.31) denotes 'untiring' (*OLD* s.v. 'ferreus' 4c, Livy 39.40.11, Virgil *Georgics* 2.44 (itself modelled on Homer's χάλκεον ἦτορ ('heart of bronze') at *Iliad* 2.490). We know of no teacher named **Vettius**.

151   The class verbally **slays** the **tyrants** as they engage in the stock rhetorical argument for doing so: this is a similar metaphor to 7.73, 7.92 where again literary work is credited with physical power. *numerosa* is usually understood as 'numerous' (cf. 10.105: Quintilian comments on the 'crowd of pupils' (10.5.21)): a large class of students might offer more chance of fees for the poor teacher, but if so many pupils fail to pay up then the bad situation is even worse as the workload is greater with no reward. Wiesen ((1971) 507) argues strongly that *numerosa* can refer to 'the rhythmical quality of artistic prose' (*OLD* s.v. 'numerosus' 5) citing Cicero's discussion (*Orator* 166. 180, 210, 219, 226) of *numerosa oratio* which is distinct from poetry but still marked by rhythmic subtlety: and *numerosus* is used to describe the poet Horace (Ovid *Tristia* 4.10.49) and so might also describe a whole class of students. The florid 'Asiatic' style of oratory is song-like in its enjoyment of rhythms (Cicero *Orator* 27, 57: cf. Quintilian 8.3.76) and it is hard to believe that J. chose this word for 'large' without also intending some interplay with the sense 'musical in rhythm': see next note on *cantabit*. Killing tyrants was a stock topic (10.113) deriving from the Greek tradition since the celebration of Harmodius and Aristogeiton who slew the Athenian tyrant Hipparchus in 514 BC. This could be a dangerous topic to practise in a world of paranoid rulers: Carinas Secundus was exiled for it (Dio 59.20) and Maternus was executed by Domitian (Dio 67.12).

152–3   The lines stress the repetitive tedium with the instant replay of text in *modo legerat ... perferet* (cf. 9.96 for the pluperfect tense with *modo*), the repetition of *eadem ... eadem ... isdem* and also by the addition of the otiose verb *perferet* to draw out the apparent action: *perferet atque cantabit* means *perferet cantans.* What seems to be happening here is that the students read their texts through (sitting down) until they had memorised them and then stood up to declaim to their teacher. Romans would commonly read aloud even to themselves and so the room would be buzzing with the noise of all these pupils even when they were not actually declaiming. It is plausible that the purpose of standing up when declaiming was to speak from memory, with hands free to add gestures (Quintilian 1.11.14). A passage from the *Colloquia of the Hermeneumata pseudodositheana* (*CGL* III, 381. 20–57, edited now by Dickey ((2012) 227–8) first shows the student rehearsing for his recitation, and then jumping up to do the actual recitation: the student learns to present the *uersus ad numerum* ('lines in rhythm') which reinforces the use here of both *numerosa* in 151 and *uersibus* in 153: for *uersus* as prose rather than verse cf. Horace *Satires* 2.5.52–3, Gellius 9.15.10. There is a contrast here between *legerat* (reading to oneself) and *cantabit* (declaiming to others: see Allen (1972) 1–5). *cantabit* is not complimentary: the sense of *canto* is extravagant 'sing-song' delivery of prose at Tacitus *Dialogus* 26.3 (cf. Pliny *Epistles* 2.14.12–3): cf. the derogatory use of *decanto* at Horace *Odes* 1.33.3, *Epistles* 1.1.64, Cicero *de Finibus* 4.10, *recinunt* at Horace *Epistles* 1.1.55 and *cantilenam* at Cicero *de Oratore* 1.105. J. enacts the student clumsily rising to his feet in the bumpy rhythm of the end of the line.

153 **perform**: *perferre* means 'to go through a formula' as in sport (6.261) or in a religious setting (6.392, *OLD* s.v. 'perfero' 5b). The subject of the verbs in lines 152–3 could be *classis*, if there were any evidence for simultaneous choral reading in class. It is more plausible to see the subject of *legerat* as each individual pupil – which also extends the exercise *ad nauseam* for the teacher.

154 *crambe* is **cabbage** (Pliny *NH* 20.79: transliterated from Greek κράμβη) while *repeto* denotes 'rehashing' food. The Greek proverb δὶς κράμβη θάνατος – 'cabbage done twice is death' – reminds us of the dangers of reheating food in an era without refrigeration: Quintilian (2.4.28) uses similar imagery (of recycled arguments as being like rehashed food), but J.'s stark metaphor of *occidit crambe repetita* is brilliant, playing both on the physical danger of rehashed food and the metaphorical 'death' of the tyrant (and the teacher: cf. Horace *Ars Poetica* 475). J. elsewhere (14.129–30) mocks the miser who recycles 'yesterday's stew in September' and the emperor Tiberius used to rehash old food (Suetonius *Tiberius* 34) 'to encourage public thrift'. J. also adds focalised pathos in *miseros* and ends the line and the sentence with the sardonic *magistros* – these 'masters' are not in control of their own fate (cf. 14.246–7 for the same trope).

155–7 Four indirect questions convey the details of the curriculum – only to be contrasted bluntly with the matter of payment (*mercedem soluere*).

155 **gloss**: *color* is a technical term in rhetoric (Greek χρῶμα) for oratorical 'spin': it has a special sense of 'defence ploy' which would be needed especially in cases which were difficult to defend (Quintilian 4.2.100, 12.1.33) such as when one was caught *in flagrante delicto* (cf. 6.279–80), but here probably refers more generally to the overall tone and style to be adopted by the student (as at Cicero *de Oratore* 3.199, Quintilian 6.3.107, 110). This better suits *causae genus*: cf. Quintilian 3.9.6. Ancient oratory fell into different genres: forensic (i.e. legal) speeches, political speeches and epideictic oratory ('showcase' speeches such as those of the sophist Gorgias): here the term *causae genus* is more specifically referring to whether the student was to handle a prosecution or defence, and whether the case was open-and-shut or involved complex issues of law and morality. 155–6 **key-point**: *quaestio* means 'issue' or 'matter to be resolved' (Quintilian 3.11.2, *OLD* s.v. 'quaestio' 6) and the phrase *summa quaestio* therefore 'the point on which the case turns' – something which Quintilian (3.11.2) calls the 'hinge' (*cardo* 5.12.3, 12.8.2, *OLD* s.v. 'cardo' 6) – and the student has to find this so as to frame the argument around it. Words are weapons in adversarial oratory and success also depended on anticipating the counter-arguments of the opposition (and knowing how to combat them) – an exercise known as *anteoccupatio*: see Cicero *de Oratore* 3.205, Quintilian 5.13.44. The counter-arguments are characterised here vividly with the aggressive metaphor of **arrows** (*sagittae*) and military language is not uncommon in forensic contexts: cf. e.g. 6.449–50 (spears), 7.173 (battle), 16.47, Pliny *Epistles* 6.12.2 (arena of words) Cicero *Part. Or.* 14 (spears), Tacitus *Dialogus* 5.5 (armour), 10 (battles) and see Watson and Watson (2014) 221, Mayer (2001) 101–2. The reading *forte* of Φ makes little sense but was no doubt early and caused other scribes to emend *diuersa* (to e.g. *diuersae* agreeing with *sagittae*) to fit. P (and modern editors) read *diuersa parte* (as at 13.136): for this sense of *diuersus* see *OLD* s.v. 'diuersus' 7). The sense of the ablative case as meaning 'from the opposing side' (with or without prepositions) is common in poetry and also known in prose: see *NLS* §42 (2).

157 An elegant line, with the generalised contrast of *omnes ... nemo* (at the end of each half of the line) and the balanced pair of infinitives (*nosse ... soluere*). Education in the ancient world was not free and teachers naturally complain when they are not paid: cf. 7.228, Ovid *Fasti* 3.829. Suetonius

(*Gram.* 9) tells us (*Epistles* 2.1.70) of Horace's teacher 'flogger' Orbilius who taught with 'greater fame than salary', wrote a book on the folly of being a teacher, lived in a garret – and yet survived to be almost 100. St Augustine (*Confessions* 5.22) tells of his pupils leaving his class just before the end of a term when fees were due to be paid in arrears (see Bonner (1977) 146–48 and cf. *Greek Anthology* 3.174). Illustrious teachers of rhetoric known as 'sophists' (cf. 167 below) in 5th century Athens enjoyed far higher rates of pay: a sophist such as Prodicus of Ceos charged 50 drachmas for a single lecture in an age when one drachma was the standard daily wage of a working man (Plato *Cratylus* 384b: see Harrison (1964) 190–1 n.44 for further reff. and Kerferd (1981) 25–28). For the pejorative use of *mercedem* see 7.148–9n.

158   **asking**: *appellare* means 'to ask for money' (9.64, Cicero *Phil.* 2.29.71, Martial 7.92.3, Seneca *de Beneficiis* 4.39.2, *Epistles* 21.11, *OLD* s.v. 'appello²' 5) and the indignation of the question is enhanced by the lack of any question-word and the scornful echoing of *mercedem*. *scio* (literally 'I know') here has the sense 'I have learned' put into the mouth of the pupil: the sophist Protagoras once had to prosecute a student for his fees and argued that he would get his money either because he won the case or else because by losing the case he would refute the charge of having taught the student nothing: the student argued conversely that if he lost the case it would prove his point that he had learned nothing from his teacher (Gellius 5.10). The juxtaposition of *scio culpa docentis* is pointed and enacts the instant judgement made and the response to it: for the teacher being blamed for a failure to learn cf. Quintilian 2.10.3.

158–166   J. puts an indignant speech into the mouth of the teachers, blaming the poor quality of the learner (160) and also blaming the tedious quality of the material used. The speakers use the jargon of their trade (*arguitur ... deliberat ... stipulare*) and rattle off the content of the speeches with weary sarcasm, undermining their own point by their jaundiced view of the student and their admission of just how dull the curriculum is. Other authors (Tacitus *Dialogus* 28.2, Petronius 58.13–14) take a similarly dim view of the talents of teachers.

159–60   **I suppose**: *scilicet* introduces an ironic point as at 5.76, 6.239, 6.635, 14.156, *OLD* s.v. 'scilicet' 4. The speakers are not necessarily assuming here that the 'mind' is in the chest (as stated by Pliny *NH* 11.182 *ibi mens habitat* ('that is where the mind lives') and Lucretius 3.136–42, Persius 2.53) rather than in the head (as assumed at 6.49, 14.57, 15.23: the issue is discussed by Cicero (*Tusc. Disp.* 1.19)). The Romans used a range of bodily areas as the site of human emotions (e.g. the liver at 1.45, 6.648, Horace *Satires* 1.9.66, bone-marrow (*medullas*) at 14.215–6, Watson (2003) on Horace *Epode* 5.37: the heart area (*praecordia*) at 13.181n., 14.35, *OLD* s.v. 'praecordia' 3) and the teachers here are complaining rather of a lack of excitement in the student, whose lack of brains is elsewhere stated in *Arcadico*. The heart-beat (*salit*) would be obvious evidence of excitement: Persius (3.111) has similar language to this (cf. also Plautus *Casina* 414, *Cist.* 551, Seneca *Thyestes* 756). The phrasing here has a further purpose, however: *laeuae* ('left-hand') means more than simply the side where the heart is, but has the sense of 'stupid' or 'maladroit' like the Greek σκαιός (LSJ s.v. III) in passages like Persius 2.53–4, Virgil *Eclogues* 1.16 (=*Aeneid* 2.54), Horace *Ars Poetica* 301, Statius *Thebaid* 2.16–17; or even 'harmful' (6.495, 14.228, *OLD* s.v. 5). The noun *mamilla* is also unnecessarily vivid (cf. 13.163 where the obese infant is being smothered by an even more obese *mamilla*) and more often denotes the breast of a female (e.g. 6.401, 6.491, 12.74) than a male as here, thus adding a touch of effeminacy to the image. *Arcadico* literally indicates a person from the Arcadian region of Greece – an idyllic landscape to some (e.g. Virgil *Eclogues* 10.26, *Georgics* 3.392, Horace *Odes* 4.12.9–12) but also the home of donkeys (Persius 3.9) which adds to the sense of 'stupid' here: like *bubulco* (7.116n.) and *rusticus* (6.66, 14.25n.) the word indicates a boorish lack of sophistication.

160–1   The clumsy rhythm (with clash of ictus and accent) at the end of 160 well evokes the clumsy youth. Regular recitations were arranged where students could demonstrate their oratory to their parents, as line 166 suggests: cf. Persius 3.45–7, Quintilian 10.5.21, 2.18.1–2. Opinion is divided on whether *sexta quaque* is to be read as 'every sixth day' (counting inclusively) or 'every fifth day' (counting exclusively): at 14.105–6 *septima quaeque ... lux* (referring to the Jewish Sabbath) must mean 'every seventh day' and I have translated accordingly.

161   **Hannibal** was famously *dirus* (Horace *Odes* 3.6.36, 4.4.42 Quintilian 8.2.10) as were Carthage and the Punic Wars (Lucan 4.788–90) but the speech itself is *dirus* to the teacher (cf. 151 for a similar trope). Hannibal was a standard topic for the *suasoria* (cf. 10.166–7, [Cicero] *Rhet. ad Herennium* 3.2) not least because the Punic Wars had been such a razor's edge of Roman history (cf. e.g. Lucretius 3.833–7, Horace *Odes* 3.6.33–8). The imagery of *caput implet* is medical (congestion of the head as at Galen 8.205.7–9, or else inhaling of vapours to soothe the head as at Celsus 3.18.8–9, 4.2.7) but

here has the negative sense of causing headaches. The teacher once again (cf. 7.154) is focalised as wretched (*miserum*).

162 pondering: *deliberat* is a technical term – the elder Seneca's *Suasoriae* always begin with this verb introducing the topic (e.g. *Suasoria* 3: 'Agamemnon *deliberat* whether to sacrifice Iphigenia': cf. Quintilian 3.8.19) – and the *suasoria* belonged to the *deliberatiuum genus* of speech-making ([Cicero] *ad Herennium* 1.2, *de Inuentione* 1.7, Quintilian 3.8.6).

162–4 The speakers mention two classic topics for the 'Hannibal' *suasoria*. **Cannae** in Apulia was the site of Hannibal's great victory over the Romans in 216 BC (referenced also at 2.155, 10.165, 11.200). Hannibal failed to capitalise on his victory by marching at once on Rome (here simply called *Urbem* as at 1.111, 2.162, 3.22, 8.118, 8.250, 16.25) as advised by his cavalry chief Maharbal who is said to have promised that 'on the fifth day your dinner will be cooked on the Capitol' (Aulus Gellius 10.25, Livy 22.51). When Hannibal answered that this was too good to be true, Maharbal replied that Hannibal 'knew how to conquer, but not how to use victory'. Five years later in 211 Hannibal again came within sight of Rome and was faced by a Roman army at the Colline Gate (cf. 6.290–1). Two days of torrential rain made battle impossible and Hannibal again withdrew, saying that he had missed taking Rome twice, once due to lack of decision and once due to lack of luck, while his men regarded the storm as providential (Livy 26.11, Silius Italicus *Punica* 12.646–728, 13.15–20).

163 storm-clouds and thunderbolts: the phrase is reminiscent of Silius' account of the incident (12.611). *nimbos et fulmina* are two of the forces of nature which are seen as divine in origin (Cicero *de Natura Deorum* 2.14, Lucretius 6.253–6, Virgil *Georgics* 1.328–9, *Aeneid* 6.590, Ovid *Amores* 2.1.15) and *cautus* suggests 'god-fearing' in this context while also describing sensible behaviour when facing storms (as at Horace *Odes* 2.10.3). The preposition *a* here denotes time rather than space (cf. 7.196, *OLD* s.v. 'ab, abs, a' 13b).

164 wheel round: the same verb *circumagat* is used by Silius (12.663): for the sense here cf. Livy 3.8.8, *OLD* s.v. 'circumago' 5. The verb often indicates indecisive confusion: cf. 9.81, Tacitus *Histories* 3.73.6. The preposition *a* in this line shows causality ('wet from'): *OLD* s.v. 'ab, abs, a' 15.

165–6 give: the teacher's 'offer to pay money to be relieved of his obligations underlines the tedium of his task and detracts from our sympathy' (Braund (1988) 64). The juxtaposition of *stipulare et protinus accipe* enacts the instant payment offered (cf. 13.39–40n.) and the language is legal and precise (*OLD* s.v. 'stipulor'). The present indicative *do* has deliberative force (cf. 3.296, Catullus 1.1, *NLS* §172, Courtney on 4.130) and the monosyllabic ending to these lines indicates impatience. The reader has to understand *totiens* as implying a correlative ('as often <as I listen to him>').

166–7 **This is what**: J. surprises the reader in revealing that lines 158–66 have been spoken in chorus by a group of teachers: the unison voicing of the complaint mirrors the tedious repetitious exercises which the students perform (152–4). The pleonastic bombast of the teachers' complaint (*uno conclamant ore*) is contrasted with the silence (*silent* 169) of their professional duties: the juxtaposition *plures uno* brings out the point that these so-called experts are univocally tedious and predictable, while the phrasing *uno ore* is epic (Virgil *Aeneid* 11.132, 12.837) and also parallel to a similar Greek expression (Aristophanes *Knights* 670, Plato *Politicus* 364a, *Laws* 634e, Otto (1890) s.v. 'os' 4) which is apt for these teachers with the pretentiously Greek title of *sophistae*. The original 'sophists' were travelling teachers of rhetoric and philosophy who converged on Athens in the late 5th century BC (see *OCD* s.v. 'sophists', Kerferd (1981)) but the term was used by and of practitioners of rhetoric in the later Roman Empire who formed what became known as the 'second sophistic' (see *OCD* s.c. 'Second Sophistic', Bowersock (1969), *CAH* xi.900–907) which has been shown to be of great influence on J. (Uden (2015) 54–57, 129–135).

167–170 These lines illustrate the rhetorical nature of what the *sophistae* did: note the jingle of *ore sophistae* ~ *-ore relicto* in 167–8, *uenena silent ... malus ... maritus*, the striking metaphor of *silent*, the enacting juxtaposition of *mortaria caecos* and the tricolon crescendo of the three *controuersiae* in 169–70 ((1) *fusa ... silent* (2) *malus ... maritus* and (3) *et ... caecos*).

168 **real court-cases**: the term *ueras lites* (as contrasted with the artificial legal cases in the schools: cf. Tacitus *Dialogus* 31) has been understood as either prosecuting the parents who refused to pay the fees (as bemoaned in 157) or else abandoning the life of the ivory-tower teacher for the real work of the *causidicus*. J. has already (106–49) detailed the poor working condition of the *causidicus* and the advice to the men to seek retirement (171–3) would fit the latter: but the immediate urgency of the case is prompted by the former. **rapist**: the figure of the *raptor* (Adams (1982) 175) was common in the *controuersia* and was used in colourful cases such as Seneca *Controuersiae* 1.5, where a man abused two women on one day: the law stated that the rapist should either marry the girl or else be put to death, so what if one woman opted for marriage and the other for his execution?

169   **Poison** also plays a regular part (Quintilian 7.2.11) in the *controuersia* and the phrase here suggests the narrative of Seneca *Controuersia* 7.3 where a son (who has been disinherited and reprieved three times) is found by his father mixing poison: the youth says he intended to kill himself with it and pours it away but is accused of parricide. Here the poisons themselves are personified as being 'silent'. The classic **thankless husband** of Seneca *Controuersia* 2.5 divorced his wife even after she had denied under torture knowing anything about his intentions to kill a tyrant.

170   **preparations**: drugs were commonly mixed up in a pestle (*mortarium*: cf. Celsus 5.24.2, Pliny *NH* 33.103) and the word for the vessel here is used for its contents, with *mortaria* juxtaposed with *caecos* in verse as in life. *iam* is to be taken with *ueteres*, indicating that the blindness is 'by now' of long standing and the patient old (cf. 3.206, 6.215, 8.153): weakness of vision (presbyopia) is a natural symptom in the elderly (10.227–8) – and while some thought this was the punishment of a vengeful deity (13.93n. Ovid *Ex Ponto* 1.1.51–4) as was claimed in the case of Tiresias in myth (Ovid *Metamorphoses* 3.334–5) and Pheros in history (Herodotus 2.111), the lack of spectacles would naturally make many older people visually impaired. It is hard to imagine how cures for blindness could ever form part of a declamation unless (as Courtney suggests) J. is thinking of the case of a blind husband whose wife gave him a drug which restored his sight: when he later divorced her he was liable to legal action for his ingratitude. Blindness (of a son who lost his sight rescuing his father from a fire) also features in a lengthy speech of Quintilian (*Declamationes Maiores* 2 Prol.1).

171–2   **retirement**: the image is of the gladiator who on retiring from the arena was presented with the wooden sword (Horace *Epistles* 1.1.2, Martial 3.36.10, Ovid *Tristia* 4.8.23–4, Otto (1890) s.v. 'rudis'): here the teacher, who as a student no doubt offered advice on retirement to the historical figure of Sulla in a *suasoria* (1.15–16), is being given similar advice by the speaker, with *consilia* stressed in enjambement. The metaphor of 'walking a different path of life' is rhetorical and not uncommon in ancient literature: cf. 10.363–4, 14.121–2, Horace *Epistles* 1.18.103, Cicero *de Lege Agraria* 1.27.9, Lucretius 2.10, Fowler (2002) 59–61. *ergŏ* (as here) is the usual scansion in J. but contrast *ergō* at 9.82, Virgil *Georgics* 2.293, *Aeneid* 4.102, Ovid *Amores* 1.15.31, Horace *Satires* 1.10.7, 2.3.192, 2.5.101, *Ars Poetica* 304, *OLD* s.v. 'ergō²'.

173   **shades ... fight**: the line is framed by the binary opposites of the courtroom fray (*ad pugnam*) and the shady retreat of academia (*umbra*).

The imagery here is vivid: the *rhetor* is pictured leaving the safe shade (*umbra*) for the heat of the sun (reflecting the fact that the courts were held in the Forum in the full heat of the sun (Seneca *Contr.* 3.pr.13, Quintilian 11.3.27)) and joining battle like a gladiator (*pugnam*: cf. 7.156 *sagittae*, 16.47n., Pliny *Epistles* 6.12.2). The distinction between battle (forensic) and shade (academic) goes back to Cicero (*de Oratore* 1.157) and lasted to J.'s own day (Statius *Siluae* 5.2.103–6, Tacitus *Dialogus* 10.5). *descendit* is a military image of leaving the tower for the battlefield (*pugnam*) below (*OLD* s.v. 'descendo' 3) as well as being factually accurate in view of 'the low-lying situation of the Forum' (Courtney). The elevation of the academic, raised up above the real world below, is a common image of superiority (Lucretius 2.8–12, Statius *Siluae* 2.2.131–2), while *umbra* (common in describing the writer's detachment from the world (cf. 7.8, 7.105)) was also a sign of feebleness in the shade-seeking man (Balsdon (1969) 136–144) and could be disparaging as at Quintilian 1.2.18, Seneca *de Beneficiis* 4.2.1, Petronius 2.4 (see Schmeling (2011) 6).

174–5   **token**: the *tessera frumentaria* was a token given to a fixed number of Roman citizens which could be exchanged for a ration of corn (see Virlouvet (1995), *OCD* s.v. 'food supply (Roman)', 'tessera'). Feeding the urban poor (the 'bread' of 'bread and circuses' (10.81n.)) had been a divisive issue ever since Gaius Gracchus had first attempted in 123BC to sell corn at subsidised prices – Julius Caesar halved the number of recipients, for instance (Suetonius *Julius Caesar* 41) – and continued to be so under the emperors: Suetonius (*Augustus* 40, 42) tells us that Augustus tried (without success) to amend the system of distribution. The *rhetor* here buys a *tessera* from somebody else perhaps because (being recently arrived in Rome) he is not yet enfranchised and has no *domicilium* (Virlouvet (1995) 241 n.239). These *tesserae* gave access to games (and even brothels) as well as food, and could be bought and sold and even given away by the wealthy (Suetonius *Nero* 11.4, *Domitian* 4.5, Petronius 81.4, Martial 8.78.10). The language here is extreme: the sum of money is mocked with the diminutive *summula* (cf. Seneca *Epistles* 77.8, Apuleius *Metamorphoses* 10.19, 11.28), while the *tessera* is mocked as *uilis* (cheap): some take *uilis* as genitive with *frumenti* (and Persius (5.74–5) talks of a man 'getting mouldy grain for a little token' suggesting that the corn being doled was not of good quality) but given that the *tessera* is as much as this man's pay can afford to buy, it seems sensible to take it as nominative.

175   **lavish**: *lautus* (from *lauatus*: literally 'washed') is common in the sense

of 'sumptuous' (*OLD* s.v. 'lautus' 3) or 'elegant' of food and people (cf. 177 below and 1.67, 3.221, 11.1, 11.140, 14.13, 14.257, Petronius 26, Persius 6.23, Martial 1.99.3, 11.31.20) and repeated in 177: it is sarcastic here in describing the *summula*. For the pejorative tone of *merces* see 7.148–9n.

175–7 **Chrysogonus** and **Pollio** (cf. Martial 4.61.9) were both famous *citharoedi* – men who sang to the accompaniment of the *cithara* (a form of lyre): cf. 6.76, 7.212, 8.198, 10.211. J. elsewhere claims that Chrysogonus (6.74) and Pollio (6.387–8) were also in sexual demand from shameless women admirers – and Chrysonogus was explicitly contrasted (6.75) on this score with Quintilian – but the point here is that their fees for teaching students outstripped those of the *rhetor*. The size of the fees is made clear by the specific claim that Pollio taught the sons of *lautorum* (see previous n.) who alone could afford them, and also by the anaphora of *quanti* (with variation of the metrical stress) expressing open-mouthed astonishment. Music – at least choral singing in religious settings (cf. Horace *Carmen Saeculare* 6, *Odes* 4.6.31, Catullus 34.2) – formed part of the education of the rich (Bonner (1977) 44, Marrou (1956) 248) although a feeling persisted that music and dancing were unmanly (Cicero *Catilinarians* 2.23, Seneca *Controuersiae* 1 pr.8, Nepos *Epaminondas* 1.2) and unsavoury even for girls (cf. Sallust *Cat.* 25.2) and certainly for emperors to perform in public (see 8.220, 224–30, Tacitus *Annals* 13.3). The contrast of the huge sums paid to musicians as against derisory payment to the *rhetor* is made also at Martial 5.56: and Suetonius (*Vespasian* 18–9) tells us that Vespasian gave 200,000 sesterces each to two *citharoedi* but only half of that to *rhetores*. The sentence structure here of imperative (*tempta*) followed by a strong future indicative *scindes* turns a conditional sentence into an assertive statement (cf. 1.155, 10.147–8) although the reading *scindes* (conjectured by Jahn and found in some late mss.) is not certain and the early gloss on the word (*diuidens*) suggests that the reading of our main mss *scindens* may be correct.

177 **Theodorus** of Gadara taught the emperor Tiberius (Suetonius *Tiberius* 57) and founded his own school of *Theodorei* (Quintilian 3.1.18) in rivalry to the *Apollodorei* of his contemporary Apollodorus of Pergamum: there is no evidence that this Theodorus wrote a manual (unlike his rival who composed one which was 'dry as dust' according to ps-Longinus (*on the Sublime* 19)) and it may be that J. is thinking of the handbook of the much earlier Theodorus of Byzantium (5th–4th centuries BC: see Cicero *Brutus* 48: for the handbook (referred to as τέχνη (=*artem*)) see Aristotle *Rhetoric* 2.23.28, Quintilian 3.1.11). *ars* is a standard term for a technical

handbook as in the cases of the *ars poetica* of Horace or the *ars amatoria* of Ovid: see 6.452, *OLD* s.v. 'ars' 9b. *scindes* has been taken by most to mean 'tear up' (as at 3.254, Martial 9.73.9, Horace *Odes* 1.17.27, *OLD* s.v. 'scindo' 5) but Griffith ((1969) 583–85) suggests that the speaker may mean 'subdivide' whereby the music teacher simply teaches the florid 'musical side of rhetorical delivery', leaving the drudge of a *rhetor* to teach all the less entertaining stuff. This is possible but it is hard to believe that the Roman reader would not understand the verb in its more violent sense.

178–88   The speaker contrasts the lavish expenditure of the *paterfamilias* on his own estate and comfort as against the paltry fees paid for his son's education. J. later (14.86–95) mocks the folly of building ever bigger and better villas, and the pointless expense on real estate was a constant theme of the ancient moralist (see Nisbet and Hubbard (1978) 288–89 and cf. e.g. Lucretius 2.24–8 (with Fowler (2002) 92–96), Horace *Odes* 2.15, 2.18, 3.1.33–40).

178   **bathrooms**: public baths were popular with all classes in Rome (cf. 7.3–6n., 6.374–5, 7.130–131, 11.156–7n., *OCD* s.v. 'baths', Balsdon (1969) 26–32) but J. here is thinking of baths installed in private villas – such as the one in which the wealthy Seneca eventually took his life (Tacitus *Annals* 15.64.5) – which were the epitome of luxury and privilege in villas belonging to a Pliny (*Epistles* 2.17.11), a Cicero (*ad Atticum* 13.29.1), a Scipio (Seneca *Epistles* 86, who comments that it was humble by the standards of his own day) or (in fiction) a Trimalchio (Petronius 27–8). **Six hundred** is a common way of denoting an unfeasibly large number (e.g. Plautus *Aulularia* 320, Petronius 56.10, Martial 6.59.2: see *OLD* s.v. 'sescenti' 2) and 600,000 is much more than the 350,000 which Fronto's baths were going to cost (Gellius 19.10.1–4). Latin uses the ablative case to express a price (*sescentis* here: cf. 7.77) 'with which' one buys something, but also a genitive of description with words such as *tanti, quanti, pluris* and *minoris* (see AG §417c: cf. 4.25, 7.45, 7.144, 7.187, 11.16, 14.201, KS ii.§86.3). A *porticus* was a colonnade used for walking during hot or rainy weather (cf. 14.66n., Pliny *Epistles* 5.17.4) but which in the case of the super-rich would be large enough to exercise animals (cf. 4.5–6, Martial 12.50) or to display statues of ancestors (6.162–3, Pliny *NH* 34.17) and to receive guests (14.64–7). The *porticus* was supported by columns (Lucretius 4.426, Vitruvius 5.1.5) and Nero's opulent 'golden house' had a *porticus* one mile long with three sets of columns (Suetonius *Nero* 31.1). There is no main verb in *balnea ... pluit*, expressive of the indignation of the speaker.

179–81   **may ride**: the passive use of *gesto* indicates 'taking a ride' (*OLD* s.v. 'gesto' 3, Martial 7.76.4, Pliny *Epistles* 9.36.5. **calm**: *serenum* is an adjective implying 'weather' as at 13.228. The priorities of the 'master' are eloquently mocked: the sardonic rhetorical question *anne...recenti?*, the framing of line 180 with two key words (*expectet* is not something the wealthy man in a hurry would do, and *recenti* vividly depicts the fresh wet mud which would be more of a nuisance than dried old dirt), the scornful plosive sibilance in *expectet spargatue*, the immersion of the *iumenta* inside the phrase *luto ... recenti* and the assonance of *-menta recenti*. The colonnade was not immune to mud and other pollutants (see 14.64–6nn.): street mud was inevitable in ancient Rome (see 7.131–2n.) but the pretentious obsession with keeping draught-animals – *iumenta* are mules, horses and oxen (*OLD* s.v. 'iumentum') – clean is shown as absurd in the oxymoron of *mundae...mulae* and the surprise ending of line 181. The **mule** was much used in Rome for pulling carriages of all kinds (e.g. 3.316–7) and 'muleteer' was a common occupation for men (even adopted by a man of consular rank according to 8.148–62). Mules of the right pedigree and quality (cf. Petronius 38.4, Pliny *NH* 8.174) could be very expensive (one cost more than a house according to Martial 3.62.6) and the expenditure reached to their feet: Nero's mules had silver shoes (Suetonius *Nero* 30) while those of his wife Poppaea had shoes of gold (Pliny *NH* 33.140), which helps to explain *nitet* here. *hīc* means 'in this place' and is repeated for emphasis. *anne* (as at 4.78, 7.199, 10.207, 15.122) introduces a question indicating surprise or indignation: see *OLD* s.v. 'an²' 1.

182–3   **dining-room**: the *cenatio* had enormous importance in the house as it was the place where dinner-guests were entertained (and impressed). The one depicted here had height (*longis ... surgat*), elegance of design with expensive columns, and the optimum aspect to catch winter sunlight. The lavish dining-room has a long history in ancient literature from Alcinous' banqueting chamber in Homer (*Odyssey* 7.100–103) to Petronius' description of Trimalchio's feast. The use of marble **columns** and flooring is a stock feature of the wealthy household: cf. 1.12–13, 6.430, 11.175, 14.89–90, 14.307–8n., Propertius 3.2.11, Ovid *Metamorphoses* 2.1, Tibullus 3.3.13, Pliny *NH* 36.59. Marble (see *OCD* s.v. 'marble') was quarried in Italy and imported from Greece and Africa by Augustus, who famously claimed to 'have found Rome a city of brick and left it a city of marble' (Suetonius *Augustus* 28.3.3). Yellow **Numidian** marble was highly prized (Pliny *NH* 5.22, 36.49, Seneca *Epistles* 115.9, Horace *Odes* 2.18.4 with

Nisbet-Hubbard (1978) 294)). The extended genitive plural *Numidarum* (from *Numida* ('a Numidian')) helps to create the imagery of the lengthy columns.

183 rise up and catch: *surgat* and *rapiat* are jussive subjunctives focalising the wishes of the rich father. The whole line is a display of the wizardry of Roman building: the juxtaposition of *cenatio solem* enacts the desired effect of placing the room and the sun together, *algentem ... solem* is an oxymoronic pathetic fallacy which well marks the aesthetic finesse of this *bon viveur* while also showing his impatience with any compromise of his comfort, while *rapiat* (for the more neutral word *excipere* as at Horace *Odes* 2.15.16) adds urgency and violence to what is essentially a matter of interior design but also lightly hints at the witches' trick of interfering with the path of heavenly bodies (e.g. Apollonius Rhodius *Argonautica* 3.531–3, Virgil *Aeneid* 4.489, Tibullus 1.2.43, Propertius 1.1.19–24) and turns the tables on the notoriously *rapidus/rapax* sun (cf. e.g. Catullus 66.3, Virgil *Georgics* 1.92, 424, 2.321, Lucretius 5.397, Calpurnius Siculus 1.10, Horace *Odes* 2.9.12, Lucan 10.260). The aspect of the dining-room was important to builders (e.g. Pliny *Epistles* 2.17.10, 12, 15, Varro *Res Rusticae* 1.13.7, Nisbet and Hubbard (1978) 250) and some people had four dining rooms, one for each season of the year (Vitruvius 6.4.1–2: cf. Petronius 77.4). Nero (of course) went one better with his circular dining room whose ceiling rotated like the heavens (Suetonius *Nero* 31).

184–5 someone to ... dishes: this was the job of the *structor* (5.120–3, 11.136–41n.) as in the exceptional case of the 'zodiac dinner' of Trimalchio (Petronius 35.2), while the *cocus* **flavours the food** in the kitchen. No matter how much has been spent on the building, the master will still have enough money for staff: a *structor* and a *cocus*, placed here in inverse order of function but in ascending order of price. The language is again expressive of the luxury depicted: *pulmentaria* are condiments added to a dish such as meat or fish (*pulmentum*) to enhance its flavour (cf. Horace *Satires* 2.2.20 'get your *pulmentaria* by sweat' (i.e. 'hunger makes food taste better')): cf. Persius 3.102, Lucilius 1032–3W. *condio* is to 'give flavour to' food (such as mushrooms at 14.8) and is what one does to *pulmentaria* (Columella 11.3.57). Petronius (70.12) speaks of a *cocus* who 'had just made a goose out of pork and stank of *condimentis*'. The manipulation of flavour was the mark of the best cooks and such men were expensive (cf. Pliny *NH* 9.67, Livy 39.6, Petronius 38, Seneca *Epistles* 95.23, Balsdon (1969) 51–52, Gowers (1993) 50–51). *quanticumque* is a genitive of value (7.178n.) and the verb ('costs') is left to be understood. The indicative verbs *componit* and *condit* are surprising and were 'corrected' to relative final subjunctives in some mss., but here add to the factuality of the statement so that *qui ... componit* simply means 'a *structor*': cf. 9.146, 11.130–1.

186–7   **will suffice**: the contrast between the massive outlay on cooks (and other providers of pleasure) and the pittance given to a 'counsellor' (συμβούλῳ) had already been made by the Cynic philosopher Crates (Diogenes Laertius 6.86) and J. here brings the point home by naming the Spanish orator Quintilian (1st century AD) who was Professor of Rhetoric under Vespasian, possibly the teacher of the younger Pliny (Pliny *Epistles* 2.14.9), a distinguished practising barrister, and the author of the massively influential *Institutio Oratoria*. His image as somewhat stuffy in views and manner (6.75, Martial 2.90) is unfair to him and may be born of envy at his financial success which was far in excess of the two thousand sesterces mentioned here. In fact Quintilian received 100,000 sesterces a year for his post as professor of rhetoric (Suetonius *Vespasian* 18) as well as his fees from the parents of students. The name occupies the final two feet of line 186 in mock grandeur (cf. 3.229, 6.71, 6.338, 6.373, 8.3, 10.151, 10.182n., 10.362) and the juxtaposition of *sumptus sestertia* and then *multum duo* is oxymoronic to highlight the contrast between the outlays. The phrase *ut multum* probably means **a considerable sum** (*OLD* s.v. 'ut' 10: cf. Martial 10.11.6). The future tense of *sufficient* is not 'gnomic' (as suggested by Courtney) but focalises the thoughts of parents planning their finances.

187–8   **son**: The speaker regards education as lower than all other priorities in the parent's mind, with *filius* here standing for 'the son['s education]' but making the statement stronger by the stark placing of the boy as an item to be paid for. J. discusses education as a vital part of parenting in Satire 14.

188–9   **In that case…**: having brought Quintilian in (as at 6.280) as the typical teacher of rhetoric, the speaker now concedes that he is highly untypical in being rich. The passage, far from showing 'the weakness of Juvenal's argument' (Courtney), in fact shows the strength of J.'s literary ability. For one thing, Quintilian is the exception which proves the rule, and for another the introduction of the unnamed interlocutor brings in a dramatic touch which enlivens the passage. The interjection is metrically inelegant, with clash of ictus and accent in *unde igitur tot*, and colloquial in style: for *unde* indicating the source of wealth cf. 7.75–6n., Petronius 45.6, *OLD* s.v. 'unde' 10. *saltus* denotes a landed estate (*OLD* s.v. 'saltus²' 3) and commonly indicated abundant wealth: see Catullus 114, 115, Horace *Odes* 2.3.17.

189–90   **cases**: *exemplum* is a term used in rhetoric for a paradigmatic case to illustrate a point (see 8.184, 13.1n.) or an instance of behaviour useful as a role-model (cf. 14.32, 14.322). Here the word has its more neutral sense of 'case' or 'example' as at 10. 247, but the rhetorical flavour of the sentence is enhanced by the term *transi* ('pass over' or 'ignore': see *OLD* s.v. 'transeo' 12c and cf. 3.114, Martial 10.59.1, Seneca *Dial.* 7.27.1, Quintilian 10.1.57).

190–4   **fortunate**: the speaker attributes Quintilian's wealth to luck and riffs on the theme of luck in a parody of the Stoic argument that the wise man (*sapiens*) is perfect as he will have the knowledge to practise all the virtues – an argument which earlier satirists had mocked (Lucilius 1189–90W, Varro *Men.* 245B: cf. Cicero *pro Murena* 61) and which Horace had also sent up in his *Satires* (1.3.124–33, 2.7) and *Epistles* (1.1.106–8: the word *perfrixit* in 194 clearly recalls Horace *Epistles* 1.1.108). The argument here is that Quintilian was rich not because he was a teacher but simply because he was lucky – and readers may recall that his luck was largely to be favoured by a series of capricious emperors with a sinecure (Anderson (1982) 401–402, Wiesen (1973) 481). *felix* (εὐδαίμων) often denotes being 'enviably well-off' or 'prosperous' in a physical sense (cf. 9.135, 16.1, 16.59n.: see also its opposite *infelix* at 3.152, 6.258, 6.491, 7.74) but also has a more philosophical sense of 'contented', 'serene' as at 3.312, 10.248, 13.21, 14.21, 14.312, Horace *Satires* 1.1.12, Virgil *Georgics* 2.490, *Aeneid* 6.669. J.'s speaker here produces what he imagines to be a version of Stoic language to explain the presence of physical advantages which the true Stoic would regard as accidental trivia to which the virtuous wise man is indifferent. Braund ((1988) 65) comments on the way the sarcasm of the whole passage (190–202) is enhanced by the alliteration of 'f' which was regarded as a harsh sound in Latin (Quintilian 12.10.29–9). *felix* throughout these lines is an adjective used as a noun ('a lucky man') understanding *est* – only to be interrupted with a new verbal phrase in 192 in asyndeton. Deleting line 192 (as suggested by Jahn) would cause us to lose some vivid imagery (see 192n.) and a better solution (adopted by Willis and Braund) is that of Reeve ((1971) 328) who argued that '*nobilis* and *generosus* are meant to elucidate *nigrae lunam subtexit alutae*, *sapiens* and *appositam* to fill out the metre' and who therefore excised *sapiens ... appositam*.

190   **handsome and energetic**: beauty and vitality are enviable qualities which are innate rather than acquired: beauty as a quality which people pray for in their children is discussed at 10.289–345. Being *acer* is seen as inborn in discussion of animals (especially used of dogs (e.g. Horace *Epodes* 12.9,

Virgil *Georgics* 3.405) but also lions (Lucretius 5.862), boars (Virgil *Eclogues* 10.56), wolves (Horace *Epodes* 12.25) and horses (Lucretius 4.420, Ovid *Metamorphoses* 3.704) and also races of people (Virgil *Georgics* 2.167) as well as individuals, where it can connote intelligence (Cicero *Orator* 172 Quintilian 8.3.24), courage (Lucretius 1.69) and aggressive disposition (Horace *Odes* 1.2.39, *OLD* s.v. 'acer²' 9).

191 wise: being *sapiens* is more often a response to *fortuna* than an instance of it: the philosopher Democritus shows *fortuna* the middle finger at 10.52–3, *fortuna* is dismissed by the speaker at 10.365–6 (=14.315–6), and *sapientia* is the 'conqueror of fortune' (13.20). *sapientia* (as 'correct thinking' which an individual may exercise to deal with the vicissitudes of life) is a key component of Stoic ethics: cf. Seneca *Epistles* 71.30, *Oedipus* 86, *Dial.* 2.15.3.5, Manilius *Astronomica* 1.797. Being **noble and well-born** (here given the inflated double definition of *nobilis et generosus*) is a matter of chance and the ways in which this chance plays out in later life is the subject of much of Satire 8.

192 black shoe: patricians and senators displayed their status by their footwear: they wore high-soled shoes (*OLD* s.v. 'mulleus') with a crescent-shaped piece of ivory sewn to the instep, and four black leather thongs (*alutae* here) attaching to their legs (cf. Horace *Satires* 1.6.27–8, Martial 2.29.7–8, Statius *Siluae* 5.2.27–8, Paoli (1990) 105). There is an effective 'black-white' oxymoron here of *nigrae lunam* and suitably solemn spondaic rhythm.

193–4 orator … javelin … sings: ascribing excellence in oratory, athletics and singing to pure chance seems to leave little room for the teacher (such as a Quintilian) to improve matters. J. may be reasoning either that amongst a multitude of great performers it is only the lucky ones who make it to the top or else that people lucky enough to be born with natural talent into patrician houses are more likely to receive the education needed to make the most of their abilities. The *iaculum* was a **javelin** or spear which was thrown in athletic competition and training on the *Campus Martius* (cf. Horace *Odes* 1.8.12, Ovid *Ars Am.* 3.383, Golden (2004) 91, Balsdon (1969) 161): *maximus* can be taken with either (or indeed both) of the nouns surrounding it (the ἀπὸ κοινοῦ construction). Having a good singing voice is a matter of innate talent but also a source of good fortune for the successful singer who gains both financially and sexually from it (see e.g. 6.73–7). The mss. reading *et si* has been amended to *et nisi* by Courtney (and printed by Braund) and *et ni* by Weidner but this is to dilute the language: for one thing, it forces the phrase to be too close to Horace *Epistles* 1.1.108 and it also makes the point tediously obvious ('he sings well unless he has a cold'): far better to read J. as saying 'he sings well even when he has a cold' which increases the almost superhuman power of this *felix* individual (and which is better served by Eden's ((1985) 346) conjecture *etsi*). Horace (*Satires* 1.3.129–30) had already made a similar point in reference to the Stoic *sapiens* (who is the best of singers even when he is silent): for the inhibiting effect of a cold on the voice cf. Martial 3.18.1.

194–6   Our lives (and deaths) are mapped out by the **stars** at the time of our birth: cf. 9.32–37, 10.129, 10.313, 16.4. Interest in astrology was huge in the ancient world (as seen in works such as Manilius' *Astronomica*) and it was regarded as serious science rather than superstition (see Watson and Watson (2014) on 6.553–6). Petronius' Trimalchio has a 'zodiac dish' as part of his banquet and pronounces on astrological matters with pseudo-authority (*Satyricon* 35, 39) and astrology was seen as dangerous enough to have astrologers expelled from Rome periodically (see 6.562–4) especially if they predicted the death or downfall of the emperor (see Tacitus *Annals* 3.22): Tacitus describes (*Histories* 1.22) astrologers as 'a race of men treacherous to the powerful, quick to deceive the hopeful, a race which in our society will always be banned and will always also be retained' and such men were indeed banished in 33BC, AD 17 (Tacitus *Annals* 2.32.3), AD 52 (Tacitus *Annals* 12.52.3) and again thereafter (see Cramer (1951)). Augustus was impressed by the astrologer Theogenes who fell at his feet in homage of his future (Suetonius *Augustus* 94.12). See further *OCD* s.v. 'astrology', Cramer (1954), Barton (1994). Elsewhere (6.553–591) J. explores the female addiction to astrology and fortune-telling and Persius (5.47–51) expresses something of the Stoic belief in determinism as shown in astrology. *distat* is impersonal here (as at Horace *Epistles* 1.17.44, *Satires* 2.3.210, *OLD* s.v. 'disto' 4).

195   **stars**: the word *sidera* is stressed in enjambement and there is an effective jingle of *excipiant ~ incipientem*. J. uses the correct jargon here: *excipere* is the right word for 'taking under one's protection' in the astrological sense (*OLD* s.v. 'excipio' 7, cf. Manilius *Astronomica* 2.833, 3.187: J. uses the word with a play on this sense at 16.3), while *modo primos* (and *adhuc* in 196) indicate that the precise moment of birth is crucial to determining the horoscope.

196   The **wailing** infant fills the line with vivid imagery of sound and colour and the final word (*rubentem*) rhymes with *incipientem* on the previous line in an enactment of the repeated cries. *a matre* has temporal

sense (meaning 'direct from the mother' in the sense of 'new-born') as *a Cannis* in 163. **wailing**: *uagitus* is onomatopoeic for the yelling of a new-born (offering further evidence that Romans pronounced the consonantal 'u' as a 'w' rather than as a 'v': see Gellius 16.17). The vivid description of the 'reddish, squalling, newborn baby' (Wiesen (1973) 481) no doubt adds to the mockery of Quintilian (whose good fortune is being described) but *adhuc* is vital for the point (see previous n.).

197   **Fortune**: *Fortuna* (*OLD* s.v. 'fortuna' 3) is here personified as a capricious Lady Luck – a deity which the poet elsewhere (10.365–6 (=14.315–6): cf. 10.52–3) rejects – in line with common ancient thought (see 13.86–88n.) on the mutability of life (10.73) in which Fortune (in a spirit of mischief (*improba* 6.605)) acts as the 'lady who favours the undeserving' (Pliny *NH* 2.22: cf. 3.38–40, 6.605–9, 9.148–50, Valerius Maximus 6.9.7, Apuleius *Met.* 7.2, Ammianus 14.11.30) and turns rags to riches (and/or *vice versa*: 10.285–6, 12.29, 15.95–6). The dictator Sulla (whose cognomen was *Felix*) erected a temple to Fortuna at Praeneste (14.10n.) and a lucky man could be called a 'child of fortune' (Otto (1890) s.v. 'fortuna' 10): Horace himself was so described (*Satires* 2.6.49), and Oedipus (risen to being a king after being abandoned at birth) calls himself 'a child of fortune – she who gives good things' (Sophocles *Oedipus Tyrannus* 1080–1: see Finglass (2018) 490 for further reff.). Elsewhere (6.287, 8.75, 11.176, 13.10, 14.113, 14.328, 16.34) *fortuna* is used for the end-result of this process. The speaker is probably thinking still of Quintilian who received *consularia ornamenta* from Domitian (Ausonius *Grat. Act.* 31) after acting as tutor to the emperor's two great-nephews. Note here the rhetorical use of chiasmus and polyptoton in *rhetore consul ... consule rhetor* and the anaphora of *uolet fies ... uolet ... fiet* (cf. Manilius 4.46–9) which enacts the process of reversal in verbal form.

198   **consul ... teacher**: if attaining the consulship is seen as advancement, then going from the consulship to becoming a teacher is downward social mobility. J. may be thinking of Lucius Valerius Licinianus, a praetor (not, as J. states, consul) who was banished by Domitian for having sexual contact with a Vestal Virgin: he went on to set up a rhetorical school in Sicily where he began a class saying 'Fortune, what games you play! for you turn senators into professors and professors into senators' (Pliny *Epistles* 4.11.1: see *OCD* s.v. 'Valerius Licinianus, Lucius').

199   Publius **Ventidius** Bassus (*OCD* s.v. 'Ventidius, Publius') came to Rome as a prisoner of war in the triumphal procession of Pompeius Strabo in 89BC but after serving with Caesar in Gaul became consul in 43BC and

in November 38 BC was given a triumph after defeating the Parthians. He had been a muleteer (Cicero *ad Fam.* 10.18.3, Gellius 15.4: cf. 8.148): for more discussion see Syme (1958b) and cf. Valerius Maximus 6.9.9, Velleius 2.65.3, Pliny *NH* 7.135. Servius **Tullius** was an even more extreme case of the mutability of fortune: this son of a slave-girl ended up being the sixth (and 'last good' (8.259–60)) king of Rome. For further discussion see Nisbet and Hubbard (1970) on Horace *Odes* 1.35.2. The language (with repeated rhetorical questions and the ellipsis of main verbs) is itself highly rhetorical, in keeping with the character of the speaker.

199–200 **Does this show anything other than...**: the reductive assertion is couched in an indignant question, with line 200 framed by key words *sidus* and *fati*, with oxymoronic juxtaposition of *sidus occulti* (opposing the brightness of the star to the obscurity of fate). The power of fate is astonishing because of the reversals of fortune which it creates and the phrasing recalls Statius *Thebaid* 9.180.

201 **Destiny ... captives**: a powerful summary statement with a confident future indicative *dabunt* (cf. 90, 10.349), reverses the order of 199 in a chiasmus (captive–slave–slave–captive) and throws *seruis regna* into oxymoronic juxtaposition.

202 The **crow** or raven (*coruus corax*, κόραξ) was the epitome of blackness (Petronius 43, Martial 3.43.2, Otto (1890) s.v. 'coruus' 1: see Thompson (1936) 91–95) and even used by Lucretius to explain his atomic theory (2.822–5): 'white crow' therefore signifies a thing of extreme rarity (cf. *Anth.Pal.*11.417.4) although Aristotle allows for some crows to turn white in certain climatic conditions (*Hist. Anim.* 3.12 (519a6)). If J. regards the white crow as an impossibility then 'rarer than a non-existent thing' amounts to a preposterous degree of rarity (cf. 6.165 and cf. also Otto (1890) s.v. 'auis' 2).

203 The *cathedra* (καθέδρα) denoted the **professor's chair** (cf. 7.223) and the adjectives *uanae* (cf. 8.15n., 13.137, 14.211) and especially the strong metaphor *sterilis* (used literally at 2.140, 6.596, 7.49, 10.145, metaphorically at 12.97, Martial 1.76.14) underline the point of the whole section – that teaching is unprofitable and pointless. The rarity of the *felix* man in 202 is contrasted with the multitude (*multos*) who do not prosper. *paenituit* is impersonal, taking an accusative of the person affected and a genitive of the source of the regret.

204–5 **Thrasymachus** must have been a rhetorician: he had the same name as the sophist of 5th century BC Greece (*OCD* s.v. 'Thrasymachus', Guthrie (1971) 294–98, Kerferd (1981) 120–23) who plays a major role in the first book of Plato's *Republic* and whose aggrieved temperament is fitting here. The scholiast comments that this man 'died by hanging' but this cannot be verified. The tribrach *Thrăsy̆măchus* could not be used in a hexameter and so J. adopts the Greek flexibility of saying θράσος interchangeably with θάρσος to lengthen the first syllable of the name. **Secundus Carrinas** was banished by Caligula for a rhetorical exercise attacking tyranny (Dio 59.20.6). The man mentioned with his name by Tacitus (*Annals* 15.45.2) is probably the son of this individual.

205–6   The speaker addresses **Athens** itself in the rhetorical device of apostrophe. The referent of *hunc* is unclear and it is very difficult to read of an Athenian being given **hemlock** by the state without thinking of Socrates (469–399 BC) who was thus executed there (see 13.185–7n.). Hemlock is termed *gelidas* because it is said by ancient sources (e.g. Aristophanes *Frogs* 124–6, Nicander *Alexipharmaca* 186–94, Plato *Phaedo* 117e4–118a4) to cause progressive paralysis from the extremities (see Sullivan (2001)) and this is a common descriptor: cf. Ovid *Amores* 3.7.13, Pliny *NH* 25.151. Romans tended to use the plural *cicutae* rather than the singular 'possibly because the hemlock plant has a multiplicity of fibrous roots' (Watson (2003) 132). *ausae* is a strong verb in the circumstances: Athens saw him in need of food and **had the nerve to** give him – hemlock to eat. Socrates was of course not a teacher of rhetoric and distanced himself repeatedly from the sophists whom he likened to prostitutes (Xenophon *Memorabilia* 1.6.13): Plato (*Apology* 31c1–4) even has Socrates use his poverty (πενίαν: cf. *inopem* here) as a witness to the fact that he charged no fees.

207–14   The section concludes with a sharp and idealised contrast between the ancient tradition of mutual respect between student and teacher and the current lack of it.

207–8   **May the gods**: the topos of 'let the earth lie light on their graves' (*sit tibi terra leuis*, as at *C.I.L.* 1.1214, 6.10096, 8.10660, 14.1731) is a cliché on tombstones (see Lattimore (1962) 65–73) and often found also in literature (Persius 1.37, Propertius 1.17.24, Euripides *Alcestis* 463–4, *Helen* 852–3, Meleager *Anth. Pal.* 7.461: for the fear on which it is based cf. Lucretius 3.893). Here the language is interesting: the usual prayer is for the earth to be light on the body or its remains (e.g. Ovid *Amores* 3.1.68) and the ancient understanding (from Homer *Iliad* 1.3–5 onwards) was that bodies remain in/on the earth while their 'shades' (*umbrae*) go to Hades (cf. 1.9, 2.157, 8.65, 10.258, 13.52). The usual formula asks for the earth to be 'light' (*leuis*) but J. here uses the adjective *tenuem* which more commonly describes *umbrae* (e.g. Propertius 2.12.20, 3.9.29, [Tibullus] 3.2.9, Virgil *Georgics* 4.472, *Aeneid* 10.636, Ovid *Ars Am.* 3.723). *sine pondere* acts as another adjective explaining *tenuem*, leaving the line to end with a juxtaposition of the apparently impossible 'earth without weight.' Understand a verb such as *dent* in 207.

208   **blooming crocuses**: after the *adynaton* figure of 'weightless' earth in 207, this line continues the fantasy with the touching image of flowers and eternal spring: the conventional image of death being found even in an idyllic landscape (*et in Arcadia ego*) is here inverted into an idyllic landscape being found even in the funeral urn, as flowers grow from the ashes (as at Persius 1.40). Romans decorated their tombs with images of flowers and/ or with actual flowers (see Petronius 71.6, Suetonius *Augustus* 18: people decorated the tomb of the late emperor Nero with 'spring and summer flowers' (Suetonius *Nero* 57: cf. *crocos...uer* here)). The emphasis on **spring** is conveyed in the particular (*crocos*) and the general (*uer*): *spirantes* most obviously means 'sweet-smelling' (*OLD* s.v. 'spiro' 4a: cf. Virgil *Aeneid* 1.403–4) and the crocus was much used for its scent in the theatre (Lucretius 2.416, Horace *Epistles* 2.1.79). The word also keeps its primary meaning of 'living, breathing' and frames the line with *uer* to reinforce the paradox of life in death.

209   **since those men**: a heavily spondaic line asserting a thundering moral sentiment (recalled at 239), with an idealised and focalised description of the parent as *sancti* (cf. Virgil *Aeneid* 5.80, Statius *Thebaid* 4.465, *Siluae* 2.1.82) and the teacher elevated to the parental role (as also asserted by Quintilian 2.2.4, 2.9.1 and required in the Hippocratic *Oath* (see Lloyd (2003) 74–75, Lane Fox (2020) 79–80) of medical teachers and their students). Elsewhere in J. teachers are described more cynically: see 7.215–43n., 10.224n. and note how the term 'Socratic' at 2.10 implies a teacher's unhealthy passion for his students under the guise of disinterested education.

210–12   The example chosen to illustrate the principle is taken from mythology: the warrior **Achilles** was taught music by the centaur Chiron. Centaurs (*OCD* s.v. 'centaurs') were generally a lawless breed of man-horse hybrids (renowned for drunken misbehaviour and sexual assault (e.g. at the wedding of Pirithous and Hippodamia and in the assault of Deianeira by Nessus (Sophocles *Trachiniae* 560–565)). The centaur Chiron however was the civilised exception, being of different parentage from the other centaurs (Watson (2004) 431) and known for his knowledge of medicine (Homer *Iliad* 4.217–9) and his innate moral rectitude (Homer *Iliad* 11.831–2, Ovid *Fasti* 5.384, Horace *Epodes* 13.11) which made him ideal to be the teacher of Achilles, the healer Asclepius and the hero Jason (Pindar *Pythian* 3.63–7, *Nemean* 3.53–5, Quintilian 1.10.30): he also makes a very fine wedding-guest (Catullus 64.278–84). The image of the Greek warrior who would go on to terrify the Trojans being nervous of the **cane** is drawn from Ovid *Ars Am.* 1.11–16 and here the irony is brought out by the juxtaposed detail of *metuens uirgae iam grandis*: Statius (*Siluae* 5.3.193–4) asserts that Chiron civilised his pupil's rough taste for military music with something sweeter. It is noteworthy that the poet does not need to name the teacher in this case since his distinguishing **tail** (*cauda*) is enough to identify him.

210 **cane**: corporal punishment was obviously common in ancient education (cf. 1.15 and see Bonner (1977) 143–5) and Horace (*Epistles* 2.1.70–1) tells us of his teacher whom he names 'whacker' (*plagosum*) Orbilius. The practice was opposed by Seneca (*de Clementia* 1.16) and Quintilian (1.3.14–17) and the logic here whereby beaten pupils learn to beat their teachers is inescapable. The genitive case of *uirgae* after *metuens* (cf. (e.g.) 5.154, Cicero *Post Reditum* 4.5, Virgil *Aeneid* 5.716, Horace *Odes* 3.19.16, *Satires* 2.2.110) may be because *metuens* has the nature here of a noun ('one who is fearful of').

211 **in his father's mountains** (*patriis in montibus*) locates the teaching in Achilles' birthplace at the foot of Mt Pelion in Thessaly: Homer tells us (*Iliad* 16.144–5) that Achilles' great spear had been a gift 'from the peak of Pelion' to his father from Chiron 'to be a cause of death to heroes' which compares ironically with the *uirga* being wielded here. The Homeric Achilles is seen singing to the lyre at *Iliad* 9.186–7 and both the imperfect tense of *cantabat* and the bumpy and inelegant rhythm of *et cŭĭ/ non tunc* (with excessive clash of ictus and accent) shows the incompetent student at work. For the term *citharoedes* see 7.175–7n. *cui* (here dissyllabic as at 3.49) is a dative of (dis)advantage as the tail could not elicit a laugh 'from him'. *tunc* is possibly concessive (**even then** (when a fully grown man)).

212 **tail**: there may be a reference in *cauda* to the childish trick of tying a tail to a person without their knowledge, as mentioned at Horace *Satires* 2.3.51–3, and there may also be a sexual innuendo as *cauda* is used elsewhere for 'penis' (*OLD* s.v. 'cauda' 2, Horace *Satires* 1.2.45, 2.7.49, Adams (1982) 36–7, cf. German *Schwanz*) and centaurs were (like their near-cousins the Satyrs) highly sexed. Ferguson plausibly suggests that the 'c', 't', 'd', and 'g' sounds in this line suggest tittering. For the vivid use of the imperfect subjunctive *eliceret*: cf. 7.69–70n, *NLS* §199.

213 **Rufus** is a teacher who is otherwise unknown, specified here amongst

an unnamed crowd of other victims: the effect is to stress that the problem of indiscipline is widespread. **flogged**: *caedit* is a strong verb (cf. 2.13 (surgery), 11.141 (carving meat), 13.194 (torture) as well as 6.483–4 (where (as here) it means 'flogging': *OLD* s.v. 'caedo' 1) whose meaning can go so far as murder (6.48, 6.447, 8.156 *OLD* s.v. 'caedo' 3). The ironic reversal whereby teachers are beaten by their pupils (cf. Plautus *Bacch.* 152–5, 440–448, Cicero *de Republica* 1.43.67) is another instance of the topsy-turvy world which J. delights in describing: cf. e.g. 14.331 (where the emperor obeyed his freedman instead of vice versa), 13.63n., 16.51–60n.

214   **Cicero of the Allobroges**: the soubriquet is puzzling: it may be an insult – the man is a provincial nobody who thinks he is Cicero – or even a compliment (*totiens* seems pointless unless it is showing a contrast between what the students said and what they did: see Reeve (1983) 32, Braund (1988) 219–20: for the textual issues see Nisbet (1995) 247–48). The **Allobroges** were an important tribe in Gaul (see 8.13n., *OCD* s.v. 'Allobroges') who helped Cicero to bring down Catiline (Tempest (2011) 96–7): and Gaul was an important centre of rhetorical education: see 1.44, 7.148n., 15.111, Tacitus *Dialogus* 10.2, *Agricola* 4. For the use of a proper name and a geographical term in a soubriquet cf. 4.38, 5.59, Cicero *pro Caelio* 18, M. Caelius Rufus *Orationes* 26.1.

215–43   The poem concludes with the lowest rung of the educational ladder, the humble *grammaticus* teaching younger boys literature (Homer, Virgil and Horace in particular) and imparting the correct use of words by means of the grammatical handbook (*ars grammatica*): see Cicero *de Oratore* 1.42.187, Quintilian 1.2.14, Bonner (1977) 189–249, Marrou (1956) 274–83. The numbers of children being educated in this way were only a small proportion of the population (see Hopkins (1978) 77) as Rome had nothing like modern systems of state education and some of the teaching was also done by Greek slaves. Teaching was regarded as the province of 'slaves, freedmen and non-entities' (Marrou (1956) 268) and Tacitus (*Annals* 3.66) tells us with amazement that a former school-teacher (Junius Otho) was raised to the senate by Sejanus (cf. 7.197) and managed 'by his shameless behaviour almost to bring further disgrace to his lowly start in life'. Teachers were furthermore often regarded as morally suspect: see 10.224n., Petronius 85–7, Quintilian 2.2.14–15. What dignity the teacher ought to have is exploded by his having to share his fees with slaves (218–9), to haggle for money like a market-trader (221), to put in more hours than the lowliest workers (222–4) in smelly sooty rooms (225–7) and to go to court to get his fee (228–9). Despite all this the parents demand of him that he be perfect in his knowledge and expertise (230–6) and he ends up being little more than a policeman of their furtive sexual fumblings (239–41: Rudd (1976) 106).

215–6   *gremium* (literally a lap or bosom as at 2.120, 3.176) is used here for a **pocket** (cf. 14.327, Livy 26.15, Apuleius *Met.* 11.20, Petronius 128.6.6, *OLD* s.v. 'gremium' 2) but keeps some sense of the literal meaning in this quasi-parental childcare (cf. Quintilian 2.4.15). **Celadus** was an otherwise unknown teacher: his name is that of a freedman (Suetonius *Augustus* 67) and in Greek (κέλαδος) indicates a loud clear voice. Quintus Remmius **Palaemon** (Quintilian 1.4.20) lived in the 1st century AD and may have taught both Persius and Quintilian, being seen as pre-eminent among teachers of his day (he is here termed *docti*) with an income of 400,000 sesterces and a lavish and louche lifestyle to match (Suetonius *Gram.*23 is scathing in his judgement: Pliny *NH* 14.49–51 tells of his vineyard which made a huge profit when sold to Seneca). His grammatical textbook is mentioned at 6.452, [Cicero] *Rhetorica ad Herennium* 4.12.17 and he may also have composed poetry (Martial 2.86.11). The sequence of short syllables (and the bucolic diaeresis) at the end of 216 suggests impatience and indignation.

217   **whatever it is**: the *grammaticus* earned a maximum of 80% of the fees payable to a *rhetor*, according to the edict of Diocletian (7.70–1), and J. has already told us (7.174–7, 186–7) that *rhetores* earned little. *grammatici* could often be poor (cf. 10.115–6, Horace *Satires* 1.6.75, Ovid *Fasti* 3.829, Marrou (1956) 267): Pliny (*Epistles* 4.13) suggests that in some places teachers were paid from public funds but also argues that parents would be unwilling to spend more than the minimum on teachers (cf. Theophrastus *Characters* 30.14) and is willing to make up the shortfall to secure a good teacher. There are also counter-examples: Gibson ((2020) 42 +n.90) discusses a teacher called P. Atilius Septicianus who left his estate to his home town (*C.I.L.* 5.5278) and other *grammatici* received *ornamenta decurionalia* at Verona (*C.I.L.* 5.3433) and Beneventum (*C.I.L.* 9.1654) which suggests that they enjoyed local status and respect. The issue was clouded by the Roman distaste for regarding the liberal arts as in any way a 'trade' and the issue of fees as somewhat sordid (Crook (1967) 203–5): for fuller discussion see Bonner (1977) 146–54. *quodcumque est* is a dismissive assessment as at Catullus 1.9, Ovid *Heroides* 4.3, *Metamorphoses* 10.405, *ex Ponto* 1.1.14.

218   **bodyguard**: the *discipuli custos* was the *paedagogus* – a slave whose job it was to escort the child to and from school, carrying his satchel (10.117), and also to ensure that the child behaved properly (Martial 10.62.10) and

came to no physical or moral harm: cf. 10.303, Horace *Ars Poetica* 161–5, Martial 9.27.11, 11.39, Quintilian 6.1.41, Pliny *Epistles* 3.3.3–4, Petronius 94.2, Bonner (1977) 37–46. Such a slave might also learn from the lessons and end up becoming a *grammaticus* himself, as did Palaemon (Suetonius *Gram.* 23) but J.'s description of the slave as a **numbskull** dismisses any intellectual potential. The moral protection of the child was also entrusted to the slave, despite fears of paedophilia: see 10.224n., Horace *Satires* 1.6.81–4 (with Gowers (2012) ad loc.), the 'Pergamene Youth' tale (Petronius (85–7), Quintilian 1.2.4: indeed Plutarch (*de Educ. Lib.* 7) says that the worst slaves do this job. **ungracious**: *acoenŏnŏētus* is a Greek word (ἀκοινονόητος) found only in Roman writers: it means 'boorish', 'lacking in savoir-faire (*sensus communis*)' (LSJ, citing Cicero *ad Atticum* 6.3.7, Gellius 12.12 and the present passage: the variant reading *acoenonetus* (ἀκοινώνητος – ‹one who will not share' as in Pliny *Epistles* 3.9.8) makes little sense here). The polysyllabic word at the end of a hexameter is used often when the word is Greek (e.g. 8.103, 8.229, 9.22, 9.64, 10.325, 10.362, 12.101, 13.122, 197, 14.20, 252, Virgil *Aeneid* 11.69), less so when the name or word is Latin (e.g. 1.112, 13.42, 14.41). For the use of *sensus communis* cf. 8.73–4. The verb *praemordet* (literally 'takes a bite from the edge of') is a striking metaphor. **219 cashier**: the *dispensator* was an important household slave who kept family accounts and disbursed fees: cf. 1.91, Martial 5.42.5, 6.73.2, Suetonius *Augustus* 67, Petronius 29–30, Crook (1967) 187–88. **breaks a bit off**: *frangit* (*OLD* s.v. 'frango' 3d) is a strong verb (usually denoting destruction as at 7.27, 10.60, 11.102, 15.9n.) and the clash of ictus and accent (*frang/it sibi*) adds to the sense of violence. Teachers complained of salary deductions also at *Anth. Pal* 9.174.4–8. Palaemon here is chosen as a typical *grammaticus* (rather as Quintilian is named as the typical *rhetor* at 7.186 and 6.75). **Give in**: the apostrophe to **Palaemon**, stressed by the bucolic diaeresis and the enjambement into what becomes a massive sentence (219–227) begins with a pair of peremptory imperatives (*cede …patere*: cf. Lucan 8.750 for the pairing) and goes on to harangue this teacher (almost as a teacher might harangue his pupils) into submission.

220 *inde* (cf. 7.103n., 123) here means 'from the fee'. Once again the clumsy rhythm of the line, with excessive clash of ictus and accent, indicates importunate indignation.

221 like the … mattress: Palaemon himself started out learning the weaver's trade and later invested in the sale of clothing (Suetonius *Gram.* 23) which makes the analogy here pertinent. **street-seller**: an *institor* was not a prestigious occupation and such men were known for loose living and moral turpitude: cf. Horace *Odes* 3.6.30 (with Nisbet and Rudd (2004) 109), *Epodes* 17.20 (with Watson (2004) 553), Ovid *Ars Am.* 1.421, *Remedia Amoris* 306, Seneca *Epistles* 52.15, 56.2. Quintilian (8.3.12) also coined the term 'the *institor* of eloquence' for the venal orator. The textiles here are low-end products: the *teges* was a rough **mat** made from 'hemp, flax, rushes, palms and bulrushes' (Varro *Res Rust.* 1.22) which could make a bed for venal or illicit sex (as at 6.118, Martial 6.39.4) or a beggar's mat (5.8, 9.139–40, Martial 11.32.2), while the *cadurcum* was a **mattress** or bed-quilt (cf. 6.537) made by the Cadurci – a people of Aquitania (Pliny *NH* 19.13). The hawking of the items is conveyed in the advertising tones of the adjectives: the *teges* will keep the user warm in winter (*hibernae*) while the *cadurcum* is attractively 'pure white' (with a hint at the snowy (*OLD* s.v. 'niueus' 1,3,4) weather from which it will also protect the user).

222–3   Lower your fee, just **so long as** (*dummodo non*: cf. Ovid *Ex Ponto* 1.1.14, KS 2.447 §222) you do not lose all the fee which you have earned for working since midnight. **lose**: *pereat* here has the sense of 'go to nothing' as at 3.124, 4.56, 7.174 and the subject is the work defined in the noun-clause *quod ... sedisti*. J. is (of course) exaggerating: classes began before dawn (Ovid *Amores* 1.13.17, Martial 9.59.9, 9.68) but not at **midnight** – which may here be a focalisation of how early the hour appeared to the weary teacher (as to the weary teenager at 14.190n.).

223   The focalisation continues: the spondaic *sēdīstī quā* and the framing of the line with verbs of 'sitting' both suggest the lengthy process. The teacher sat on his *cathedra* (7.203n.) while the pupils stood (226).

223–4   Note here the rhetorical anaphora of *qua nemo ... qua nemo*. The **smith** (*faber*) was a 'craftsman' of some kind (cf. 8.175, 14.116, 15.168) who might spend less time in fact sitting than the teacher does: the weaver is alluded to with a complete line describing the work involved – the carding of wool with the **slanting metal frame**. The language is descriptive and specific, with the use of the weaver's comb (*pecten lanarius*) to 'bring down' (for *deducere* in this context cf. Catullus 64.312) the wool: for details of the processes involved in both industries see *CAH* xi. 750–4. *solet* (Scholte) makes better immediate sense than the mss. reading *docet* but see Stramaglia (2008) 220–221 for a defence of the mss. reading.

225–6   *dummodo non pereat* is repeated from 222. **lamps**: each pupil has his own *lucerna*: the speaker makes this point for several reasons: to continue the theme of working from the middle of the night, to introduce the olfactory imagery of *olfecisse*, and to explain the quantity of soot befouling the texts in 227.

226–7 Flaccus … Virgil: Jenkyns ((1982) 178–9) well describes how the use of the poets' names for the texts of their works forces us to see 'those noble Augustans discloured and covered with smuts.' The use of the name for the text of the work is another example of the 'personification' trope in this poem (cf. 92, 160–1, Rudd (1976) 111–14). The two poets Publius **Vergilius** Maro (70–19 BC) and Quintus Horatius **Flaccus** (65–8 BC) were (along with the Greek epic poet Homer) the standard literary fare of the *grammaticus*: Quintilian (1.8.5–6: cf. 10.1.85–6) outlines the range of texts to be studied, starting from Homer and Virgil: the teacher would read the text aloud and comment on it while the boys followed the text in their own copies (Quintilian 2.5.4). Horace foresaw this befalling his own text (*Epistles* 1.20.17–18) and tells us that his own education was similar (*Epistles* 2.2.42). These same Roman poets were seen earlier (7.62–71) as living the dream in circumstances of material comfort and intellectual inspiration: their teacher is now shown suffering the opposite of this and even the poets themselves share his disgrace in their sooty shabbiness: cf. 6.131–2 for the grime generated by lamp-smoke. There was also a tradition in antiquity (Donatus *Life of Virgil* 8) that Virgil was 'dark in complexion' which may add further point to the line. The language is expressive with variation of vocabulary (*decolor … nigro*), with intensifying *totus* and the strong verb *haereret* for the soot 'clinging', with assonance of *nigro fuligo* and with the framing of line 227 with the names of the poets. Some commentators have seen the poets' names here as referring to busts rather than books (cf. 8.8n. for the effect of smoke on statues).

228–9 investigation: a *cognitio* (cf. 6.485, 16.18, *OLD* s.v. 'cognitio' 3, *OCD* s.v. 'law and procedure, Roman') was a court hearing conducted by a magistrate – in this case a *tribunus plebis* – who 'tried' the civil case (*OLD* s.c. 'cognosco' 4: cf. Ulpian *Digest* 50.13.1). The office of **tribune** gained in status under the empire and they had amassed almost consular power by J.'s time (cf. 11.7, *Digest* 1.2.2.34) especially in judicial matters (see Tacitus *Annals* 13.28 for attempts to restrict this), although how this worked in practice is not clear. **pay**: the key word *merces* (cf. 7.149, 157–8, 175) is emphasised before the caesura and the statement ('most teachers go to law') is couched in the litotes *rara…quae non*: the verb *egere* is commonly associated with poverty (e.g. 7.62) and its use here to mean 'require' adds to the theme of indigence.

229–236 you: the speaker now addresses the audience as real or potential

parents with a strong imperative *imponite* (cf. 237 *exigite*) and a 'hammering series of anaphoras' (Stramaglia (2008) 222) as they launch ever more strident indirect commands at the teacher.

229   **conditions**: the teacher is going to law (228–9), but here the parents are told to impose *leges* on him. **harsh**: *saeuus* is elsewhere (7.151, 8.223, 10.307) used of tyrants, of harsh punishment (13.196), murder (4.109–10, 15.17) and wild animals (13.170, 15.164), while *imponite* has the obvious sense of compulsion (*OLD* s.v. 'impono' 11, Virgil *Aeneid* 6.852) and even a sexual sense of 'forcing animals to mate' as at 6.334 (Adams (1982) 207).

230   A line which is as spondaic as a hexameter can be, expressive of the weight of linguistic rules to be laid upon the teacher – who is here ironically called a *praeceptor* when he is the one being given instructions. **command**: *regula* here means 'rule' (*OLD* s.v. 2, cf. Quintilian 1.5.1, 1.7.1, Petronius 2.7, Seneca *Epistles* 114) and was apparently a favourite word of the grammarian Palaemon: the phrase equates to what J. elsewhere (6.453) refers to as the *lex et ratio loquendi* but also carries tones of moral laws (cf. Persius 4.12, 5.38, Martial 11.2.3) which looks forward to 237. **unfailing**: *constet* has the sense of 'to remain fixed' (*OLD* s.v. 'consto' 6) and also 'to be correct' (*OLD* s.v. 10b: cf. 6.166).

231   **stories**: the school curriculum included explication of texts in prose (Cicero *de Oratore* 1.187, Quintilian 1.2.14, 1.8.18–1.9.1) although Seneca (*Epistles* 88.3) suggests that historians were extra to the core curriculum: see Bonner (1977) 239. The questions put to the teacher in lines 234–6 are drawn from epic poetry rather than what we would term 'history' and the term here refers to what Suetonius (*Tiberius* 70.3) called *notitia historiae fabularis* or 'knowledge of mythology'. The writings of historians and mythographers were voluminous (7.99–102) and so the requirement that the teacher know all of them (*omnes* – emphasised at the end of the line) is a herculean task, especially given the stated remark of Quintilian (1.8.21) that it is a sign of a good teacher *not* to know everything: contrast the tediously erudite woman at 6.450 who 'knows all the historians'. Here the stress and the urgency of the demand is enhanced by the asyndeton and by the juxtaposition of *historias auctores*: *omnes* (taken ἀπὸ κοινοῦ with both nouns) comes as an added demand. *legat* has been suspected by Nisbet ((1995) 248) who suggests emending to *ut sciat* (cf. 6.450).

232   **nails and toes**: the Latin conveys the idiomatic sense of 'know it like the back of your hand' (Otto (1890) s.v. 'digitus' 2 lists only this passage): for similar expressions see *domus* at 1.7, Cicero *ad Q.Fratrem* 1.1.45 and

Otto (1890) s.vv. 'nomen' 1, 'domus' 4. Braund ((1988) 67) comments that this 'mundane image of familiarity 'suggests how casually the parents make such an imposssible demand.' The expression here is probably a hendiadys for 'toenails'.

232–3   to name: The hyperbaton of *ut ... dicat* allows the speaker to place the verb *dicat* immediately before the questions to be answered in 234, while *forte rogatus* (suggesting the random nature of the inquiry) shows that the teacher is always expected to be on duty. *thermae* were public **hot baths**, with lecture-rooms and libraries as well as gymnasia and baths, whereas *Phoebi balnea* indicates a private **bath-house** (cf. 7.3–6n.) owned by the named *balneator* Phoebus. The name suggests that he was a rich Greek freedman but also sets up further irony: Phoebus was the name of the god Apollo in Greek mythology and this teacher who intended to relax at 'Phoebus' is instead quizzed on mythological matters in the street. There may also be a slight reference to Horace *Satire* 1.9.78 where 'Apollo' saved the poet from the pest who attached himself as he walked down the street: in this case the teacher is no doubt wishing that 'Phoebus' Apollo will give him refuge from *his* street-encounter. For private baths with named proprietors cf. Persius 5.126, Martial 1.59.3, 11.52.4, Balsdon (1967) 27.

233–5   name: *dicat* here (as at 214) has the sense of 'put a name to', whereas at 235 the meaning is 'give an exact number of'. Riddling questions of this kind (*quaestiones*, ζήτηματα) fascinated the Romans: the emperor Tiberius (Suetonius *Tiberius* 70) would ask *grammatici* such questions as 'what song did the Sirens sing?' and Hadrian also did the same (*SHA* 1.16.8, 20.2): cf. e.g. Suetonius *Gram.* 11, *Tiberius* 56, Quintilian 1.2.14, Bonner (1977) 239–40. Such minute attention to unnecessary detail is mocked by Seneca *Epistles* 88.37, Philippus *Anth. Pal.*11.321, Gellius 14.6. The four questions listed here are all taken from Virgil's *Aeneid*: **Anchises** was the father of Aeneas and the ancient commentators named his nurse as Tisiphone but this has no independent corroboration. **Anchemolus** was an Italian who fought under Turnus and incestuously slept with his stepmother (*Aeneid* 10.388–9) whom Servius (*ad loc.*) calls Casperia: see Harrison (1991) 272–73. The request for the **native land** as well as one's name is standard when asking for somebody's identity in ancient epic (e.g. Homer *Odyssey* 1.170) and the phrase *nomen patriamque* is taken straight from Virgil (*Aeneid* 11.249). Line 234 (framed by the nurse and the stepmother) is an unusual line, being made up entirely of nouns and proper nouns.

235–6   Acestes was a Trojan man of 'ripe years' (*aeui maturus*) but we are nowhere told in the *Aeneid* his exact age. He was the king of the city of Segesta in Sicily who entertained Aeneas and his men on their journey from Troy to Italy in Virgil *Aeneid* 5: as they left he gave them an indeterminate number of **jars** of wine (Virgil *Aeneid* 1.195–6): and the juxtaposition of *Siculi Phrygibus* brings out the closeness of the friendship. An *urna* holds 24 *sextarii* (about 13.6 litres) and was a common container for wine: cf. 6.426, 12.44, 15.25. *annis* here is ablative of extent of time: cf. 6.183, 10.239, 11.53, 11.72, Seneca *Apoc.* 6.1.4, KS II.§79 Anm. 12.

237   **demand**: *exigite* is another strong verb (cf. 6.35, 10.314, 13.36), repeated in anaphora in the following line. **characters**: these parents expect the teacher to provide moral education (cf. Quintilian 1.2.2–5, 2.2.3–4, 2.2.14–15, Pliny *Epistles* 3.3.3, Seneca *Contr.* 4.pr.11): their naive view of the children's pliant and docile nature (which will be exploded with the sordid reality of 240–1) is focalised with *teneros* and with the analogy from the plastic arts. The imagery of the child's character as clay to be moulded throws the entire responsibility for the child's future character onto the teacher and/or parents – an assumption which lies behind *Satire* 14 – and recalls the tale of early man being moulded from clay by Prometheus (see 14.34–5n.). The imagery of 'moulding' the character is found at Plato *Republic* 377c and cf. Persius 3.23–4, 5.39–40, Pliny *Epistles* 7.9.11, Statius *Achilleid* 1.332–4, Horace *Ars Poetica* 163. Here (as at Ovid *Met.*10.284) the detail of the thumb adds an extra touch of vividness, to be spelled out in the following line. **tender**: *tener* is used by itself to denote children at 14.215 although more commonly in J. it denotes effeminacy and sexual loucheness (e.g. 1.22, 6.O24, 6.383, 6.548, 8.16n., 9.46, 12.39): here the qualifier *ceu* adds an epic touch to the image (cf. 10.231, Lucretius 3.456, Virgil *Georgics* 4.499, *Aeneid* 2.516).

238   **Wax** was used for portraiture as will be explored in the following poem (8.19–20n.: cf. Martial 7.44.2, Ovid *Rem. Am.* 723).

239–241 The reality of moral education is sordid and consists chiefly in deterring gross sexual habits. The teacher who was to be *in loco parentis* (209–210) is to be the *pater* of the group. *ipsius* goes grammatically with *coetus* and this has troubled commentators who would prefer an *ipse* going with *pater* (cf. 8.138); the point here may be that *ipse* can mean 'the master' (*OLD* s.v. 'ipse' 12: cf. 1.33, 5.30, 5.114, Horace *Satires* 2.8.23, Petronius 29.8) and so *ipsius coetus* suggests that the children are in fact the master: there is also a sexual undertone to the word *coetus* (Adams (1982) 178–9).

239–41   **playing dirty games**: the poet manages to allude to the sexual games without using primary obscenities. Playing (*ludant*) is what one expects of children (e.g. 14.168) but the word also has the sense of sexual 'fooling around' (e.g. 6.O1, Catullus 61.204, Ovid *Ars Am.* 2.389, Petronius 127.10, *OLD* s.v. 'ludo' 4 (cf. LSJ s.v. 'παίζω' 5)) especially by the young (Catullus 68.17, Horace *Epistles* 1.14.36: cf. 8.163–4). **dirty**: the games are *turpia* – a term of strong disapproval (e.g. 2.9, 2.71, 6.97, 6.241, 7.5, 8.165, 14.41) – but *uicibus* is somewhat vague and the specific nature of the act is only revealed in 241. **doing it**: *facio* can be used as a euphemism for sexual activity: cf. Ovid *Amores* 3.4.4, Lucretius 4.1195, Petronius 45.8, 87, Adams (1982) 204, Henderson (1991) 158 (ποιεῖν), Martial 1.46.1. **taking turns**: *uicibus* (= *in uices* as at 6.311, Pliny *NH* 7.15) must mean 'one by one' as opposed to all together: Adams ((1982) 166 n.2) thinks the boys took it in turns to be *pedicator* but even the most shameless pupils would baulk at this and furtive masturbation is probably envisaged here. The scene is focalised through the eyes of the teacher who needs to keep a vigilant eye (*obseruare*) on their hands (*manus*) – which presumably disappear from view – and then deduces what they are doing from the eyes and the movement (*oculosque trementes*), with the participle *trementes* to be taken ἀπὸ κοινοῦ with both *manus* and *oculos*. *finis* has the sense here of 'orgasm' (*OLD* s.v. 'finis' 14, Martial 9.69.1, Adams (1982) 143n.1). The effect of orgasm on the eyes is also seen at Persius 1.18 (cf. [Aristotle] *Probl.* 4.32.880b8).

242–3 **That's your job**: the unnamed parents interject here with bluntness (for similar interjections cf. 3.153–8, 8.44–6, 13.84–5, 14.153–5: this is preferable to the reading *curas* addressed to the teacher by the speaker). Fees were paid either at year-end (*cum..annus*: cf. Suetonius *Gram.*17) after the Quinquatria in March (cf. 10.115) or else monthly (Horace *Satires* 1.6.75, Palladas *Anth. Pal.* 9.174) – and always in arrears. **victorious fighter**: the poem ends with the contrast between the annual salary of the teacher and the fee paid for one day's work to a *uictor*, and the nature of this *uictor* is much disputed (see Bonner (1977) 150–52). Davey (1971) argues that it refers to the teacher who has won his lawsuit (228–9) and so is awarded the cash by the people sitting in judgement: if so this would throw the emphasis on the year-long wait to secure the payment (cf. 16.42–3). More appealing is the suggestion that *uictori* refers to a winning charioteer (such as the 'Lizard' at 7.114) or (better still) a gladiator (so Clarke (1973)) who did receive five gold pieces (=500 sesterces) if they were free men (or 400 sesterces if slaves) from the *editor* of the games, as evidenced by Suetonius *Claudius* 21.5. The lavish fees payable to men in the arena were a source of comment (e.g. Martial 4.67. 10.74.5–6) as was the fact that they also attracted considerable adulation from women (6.81–113). *postulat* is the *mot juste* for the mob yelling for what they wanted in the arena: cf. Suetonius *Caligula* 30.2, *Claudius* 21.5, Tacitus *Hist.* 1.32: Seneca (*Epistles* 7.4) alludes to a gladiatorial event called the *par postulaticium* which seems to have been held after the advertised events and consisted of audience requests.

SATIRE VIII

Satire 8 has attracted a range of comments from critics:

'This new J. is clearly a Nihilist with an acute sense of humour'

Braund (2004) 321

'Juvenal's Eighth Satire abandons the mood of pure *indignatio* in his early satires and provides a new moral atmosphere which has been described as more hopeful and positive'

Fredericks (1971) 111

'A curious poem, astringent and sour'

Highet (1954) 116

'Juvenal's poem is not so much a panegyric of plebeian merit as a lament for the decline of aristocratic *uirtus*'

Syme (1939) 490

All discussions of the poem have to accommodate the issue of the *persona* being adopted and projected by the speaker, remembering that the speaker is a performer who is not under oath to tell the truth and is out to be read and enjoyed as literature rather than a pamphleteer for social reform. Braund's seminal study ((1988) 122) branded the speaker a 'pseudo-moralist rather than a moralist' (cf. Vessey (1973) for a similar judgement) and argues this from the tone and the choice of material: it is all very well to lambast the effete *jeunesse dorée* but the details of self-depilation (16), the comparison of Rubellius to a castrated Herm (52–5), the envious mention of oysters and perfume-baths (85–6) all indicate prurient anger rather than detached disapproval. The advice on provinces is undercut with cynicism – the provincials are now too poor to be worth robbing (95–112) anyway – and the fuss he makes about a Lateranus driving his own cart and then going to the tavern says as much about the speaker's inverted snobbery as it does about Lateranus. The speaker affects outrage at aristocrats appearing on stage and in the arena – but if we are all equal, as the coda (269–75) urges, then why does their pedigree matter and why should they not perform alongside other men? The absurd remark that Nero's worst crime was his acting (220–224) blows up the argument that the inner man is more important than superficial exteriors of birth. This is all literary satire, affecting a pose of moral *indignatio* which is undercut by the irony and the artifice of its execution.

The speaker's viewpoint is close to that of the cynic who bursts open the bubble of pretension and gets to the raw humanity underneath – we are all descended from the lowest classes in Romulus' asylum (275) or from the primeval mud in Prometheus' hands (see 133n. and cf. 4.133, 6.13): no blood is blue blood and nothing is left except the scope for eminence in individual achievement. What matters in the end? Not family, pedigree, trappings of authority and power, but only goodness (24–5, 79–84): the argument is similar to that of *Satire* 10, where there is a similar rejection of superficial 'goods' in favour of personal health and happiness (10.356–64: 'the one and only path to a happy life is through *uirtutem*' (364) reminds us of 8.20 ('the one and only nobility is *uirtus*').

This poem also looks back to the earlier satires, re-echoing the *indignatio* of Satires 1–5 with an underlying challenge to his so-called betters – just who do they think they are? The argument is an old one: people of 'noble blood' claim to be superior to others and entitled to deference but their behaviour is worse than that of their so-called inferiors. The idea of *noblesse oblige* – that 'nobles' ought to behave better than the rest of society to earn their privilege – had been around at least since Sarpedon enunciated the idea in Homer (*Iliad* 12. 310–321), and the point that noble blood does not confer real superiority was explored to good effect in Euripides *Electra* (see especially 367–385, where the noble Orestes is baffled by the nobility of the peasant who has married his sister: a man who is too deferential to consummate their marriage as she is of royal blood). J. finds abundant evidence of upper-class men behaving badly and his stance is in some ways the familiar one of the underdog of the earlier poems who has as much right as his so-called betters to respect and dignity. Fredericks ((1971) 118) puts it well: 'the satirist, straightforward fellow that he is, proposes a simple morality of *uirtus* (ethical virtue, not military valor), *mores* (morals, not *mos maiorum*), and *bona animi* (not wealth, *bona*)'.

The argument is not new, then, and the material of J.'s argument is not original either but was something of a stock topic in the rhetorical schools (see Braund (1988) 77–91, 122–29): the low-born general Marius (see 245–53n.), for example, on taking up the command against Jugurtha which nobler men had mishandled, makes a rousing speech (Sallust *Bellum Jugurthinum* 85) which gives J. many of his best ideas: and Seneca also (*Ep.* 44.5) talks of how 'an entrance hall full of smoky (*fumosis*) portraits does not make a man noble': cf. *fumosos* line 8). The *panegyric of Piso* (of uncertain authorship, praising (probably) the Gaius Calpurnius Piso who mounted a conspiracy against the emperor Nero in AD 65) also seems to lie behind some of J.'s lines, especially lines 2–11: ['Piso, you have in fact got noble birth, but] it is your excellence of character (*uirtus*) which impresses me, and your life is astonishing in all its facets, a life which would have been on a par with nobility (*nobilitas*) if you had not been granted nobility at birth. For what use are entrance halls shored up with portraits and ancestral triumphs (*imaginibus, quid auitis fulta triumphis / atria*), archives full of copious consulships, if a man's way of life is unsteady? If his only source of honour is his birth, then the whole distinction of the family dies in him' (*perit omnis in illo / gentis honos, cuius laus est in origine sola*). Nor was J. the first satirist to venture into this field: Horace (*Satires* 1.6) praises Maecenas for seeing that even a freedman's son like Horace might have more to show than his low birth would lead men to expect, and Persius (*Satire* 4) presents a lively scene of Socrates tearing into the entitled nobleman Alcibiades for his lack of self-knowledge. In J.'s own times the Greek writers of the Second Sophistic such as Dio Chrysostom continued to plough this well-worn furrow (see Uden (2015) 130–33), and Plutarch may have composed a (lost) essay 'On Nobility'.

The whole issue may seem otiose to modern meritocratic ears, but ancient Rome (at least under the Republic) was not generally meritocratic and the ancient world was generally preoccupied with good breeding even when society was operating in what looked more or less like a democracy. The argument between 'nature' (*natura*) and 'nurture' (*cultura*) saw views ranging from the haughty aristocratic views of a Pindar (*Pythian* 8.44–5 'by nature the noble spirit from the fathers is conspicuous in their sons') through the more balanced views of Pericles' funeral speech (Thucydides 2.37), to the scorn of the philosophers who mocked snobbery: Bion of Borysthenes gave a scathing reply to the tyrant Antigonus (Diogenes Laertius 4. 46–7) who asked about his parentage, and Diogenes the Cynic described 'noble birth' as just a 'fig-leaf to cover wickedness' (προσκοσμήματα κακίας: Diogenes Laertius 6.72). Many Romans routinely mocked upstart *nouveaux-riches* in the mime (Cicero *Philippics* 2.65), in satire (e.g. Juvenal 1.26–9, Nasidienus in Horace *Satires* 2.8, Trimalchio in Petronius' *Satyricon*), in scabrous verse (cf. e.g. the wealthy ex-slave who is the target of Horace's 4th *Epode* and cf. Martial 3.82). In the Republican period men who attained the consulship for the first time in their family history were referred to as 'new men' (*noui homines*: see 237n.) and their families were thereafter entitled to be called *nobilis*: men such as the general Marius (157–86 BC) and the orator, statesman and writer Cicero (106–43

BC) attained this distinction in the teeth of social and political opposition where the playing field was hardly level. Under the emperors of course these entitled scions of old republican families were reduced to subservience to the emperor, causing the old social world to be thrown upside down: to begin with, the emperor Augustus created many more *noui homines* which 'diluted' the nobility, and (more importantly) in a world where a capricious emperor like Nero could do as he wished (211–30) the scope for nobles to enjoy their status was inevitably restricted. Gelzer ((1969) 157) suggested that since *nobiles* under the emperors had to be men who had a consul in their family from the republican period, they were a dwindling group: and even though this rule was not strictly true (see Hill (1969)) the families whom Juvenal discusses in this poem were all in fact of great republican renown. 'Few <Republican nobles> survived in Juvenal's day: and they mattered not at all. The Empire had broken their power and their spirit.' (Syme (1939) 490). Gibson ((2020) 115) more positively mentions 'the boost to personal merit over bloodline that Trajan's adoption by Nerva had apparently provided'. This poem thus has a political edge: in an age of emperors the only possible 'nobility' is one of morals rather than *maiores* because all men were rendered equally inferior to the one man at the top: current *nobiles* are at the mercy of emperors (cf. 1.33–5, 4.96–103, 4.150–4) and if they behave like plebeians (8.171–82) that is perhaps because the all-powerful tyrant Nero (211–30) goes even lower. The catalogue of infamy in this poem plots a descending graph from the muleteer consul Lateranus who at least hides his misbehaviour by night (146–82), to a Damasippus (185–199) who appears on stage in full view but wearing a costume, to a Gracchus (199–210) who fights in the arena with his face fully visible to the crowd, to a Nero (211–230) who caps all the above by being a murderer <u>and</u> an actor, to Catiline and Cethegus (231–244) who fought against Rome herself.

Much of this poem is material which J. finds congenial: the good old days contrasted with the contemporary world, the debunking of pretentious aristocrats now reduced to shameful exhibitionists on stage or arena, the seedy world of the night-time *popina* where the noble mixes with lowlifes (158–62), the shameful treatment of Rome's allies abroad. The poet also makes a good job of Romanising the very Greek argumentation, bringing in the language, the history and the intertextual references of his own culture (e.g. 224n.); Uden ((2015) 125) sensitively suggests that he 'decks his *atria* with the textual *imagines* of his predecessors, curating in this poem his own densely packed museum of Roman moralism'.

For discussion of this poem see: Highet (1954) 113–116, Fredericks (1971), Braund (1988) 69–129, Henderson (1997), Dimatteo (2014) 3–12, Uden (2015) 117–45, Geue (2017) 113–129, Schmitz (2019) 117–122.

The poem can be summarised thus:

1–38	Family-trees are worthless now that the old aristocracy behave so badly
39–70	such as Rubellius Blandus
71–86	acceptable behaviour
87–126	provincial governors should restrain their greed
127–41	and that of their staff.
142–82	The consul Lateranus is a disgrace to his famly name without facing criticism
183–210	Aristocrats even go on stage or work as gladiators
211–230	as did the emperor Nero
231–68	but many people of humble origins behave much better
269–75	we are all descended from the shepherds and crooks of Romulus' time.

1–20   The poem begins with eighteen lines of rhetorical questions before giving us a magisterial pronouncement that *nobilitas sola est atque unica uirtus* ('the one and only nobility is virtue' (20)). The poem opens with three (almost equivalent) questions in a rising sequence (*quid faciunt? quid prodest? ... quis fructus?*) and the imagery in the opening lines is of transience and wasting away: in lines 1–2, J. makes metaphors of words whose literal meaning suggests physical weakness: *stemmata* ('garland'), *sanguine* (blood), *uultus* (faces), and in 4–5 the images themselves are stunted and deformed, like the noble families whose fame they celebrate. The big names are rolled out in a parade of aristocratic honour only to be contrasted with the sordid and squalid reality of the lives now being led: and the plural family names (*Aemilianos ... Curios*) give way to singular men who are themselves fractions of their former selves (*minorem ... carentem*). The thrust of the passage is that modern 'nobles' are a disgrace to their noble ancestors: an argument which J. has already enunciated (2.149–70) with similar naming of great families (Curius 2.153~8.4, Scipios 2.154~8.3, 8.11, Fabii alluded to at 2.155, named at 8.13–14) and similar language (2.156 *tot bellorum ~ tot bellatorum* 8.10: *traducimur* 2.159 *~ traducit* 8.17).

1–2   **What use...?:** the poem opens with strong anaphora of *quid* + verb, alliteration of 'p' and effective enjambement into lines 2 and 3. *stemmata*

are **family-trees** and the poet expands this concept with the vivid details of
the two-dimensional wax masks (**painted faces of your ancestors** (*pictos
... uultus / maiorum*)) and the three-dimensional statues of men 'standing
in chariots' and missing parts of their bodies: the classic account of these
objects is Flower (1996) 32–59. We read in Pliny (*NH* 35.6) that in former
times 'faces made from wax were set out each on a separate cabinet, to
provide portraits which could be carried in procession at family funerals
(showing that they were detachable and portable: see Polybius 6.53–4 for
the classic account of Roman funerals and cf. Flower (1996) 91–127): when
a family member died, all the people who had ever been part of <the family>
were present'. The masks seems to have been put on show in the atrium (cf.
Martial 4.40.1, Valerius Maximus 5.8.3, Suetonius *Galba* 2, Flower (1996)
185–222) and were joined into *stemmata* which marked out the relationships
between them (Pliny *NH* 35.6–7), although we possess no archaeological
evidence to show how this was effected. The word *stemma* transliterates the
Greek (στέμμα) which means 'wreath, garland' and it is easy to envisage
the family 'tree' as organic – an image which *uirga* in line 7 and *ramum* at
Persius 3.28 enhances – with the added resonance that Romans decorated
the wax masks with actual garlands on festival occasions (Cicero *pro
Murena* 88): the term *generis tabula* (6) suggests that the *stemma* was at
least sometimes painted on wood or inscribed in stone, with names below
each image. Alternatively the images themselves may have been arranged
into a family tree on the walls of the *atrium*, with perhaps woollen threads
connecting them – but (in that case) we are left wondering what was the
role of the 'cabinets' (*armariis*) which Pliny mentions explicitly. Henderson
asks us to imagine 'concise family trees painted on the walls of the atrium'
with 'lines of *imagines* and rows of busts set out along the same walls'
(Henderson (1997) 19) – which is very much the general impression which
lines 1–18 are seeking to create. We know that *imagines* were important
status symbols: Marius sardonically brags of his low birth and tells us that
he cannot point out *imagines* and triumphs of his ancestors but has plenty
of military experience and that 'these are my *imagines*, this is my nobility,
not left to me in a legacy ... but sought out by my many toils and dangers'
(Sallust *B.J.* 85). Pliny also describes (*NH* 35.7) the written records of
distinguished careers (*monimentis rerum in magistratu gestarum*) being kept
in the 'study' (*tablinum*) of the old Roman house and tells us further that
other *imagines* were displayed outside the house and round the thresholds
(*foris et circa limina*) which were decorated with spoils taken from defeated

enemies. Seneca (*de Beneficiis* 3.28) mocks men who 'display *imagines* in their halls, and put the names of their family in the *atrium*, arranged in a long sequence and woven with the many twists and turns of a genealogical tree – are these men not well-known (*noti*) rather than noble (*nobiles*)?' Family history could of course be dangerous: Nero executed the blind lawyer Cassius Longinus for having kept in his *stemma* the image of the Gaius Cassius who had assassinated Julius Caesar (Suetonius *Nero* 37.1). For more discussion of the stemma see Kißel (1990) 401–2 on Persius 3.28, Corbier (2007) 74–78, Hillner (2003) 138.

quid faciunt (as explained in the immediately following *quid prodest*) is best translated as 'what's the use of?' 'what good are' (cf. 9.34, *OLD* s.v. 'facio'25) but the phrase also has the sense 'what do they achieve?' (cf. 2.166, 8.115, Petronius 14.2.1 (*quid faciunt leges ubi sola pecunia regnat* ('what difference do laws make where money alone rules')) Martial 6.40.4 (*tempora quid faciunt* ('what a difference time makes')) Catullus 66.47 *quid facient crines cum ferro talia cedant*? ('what will hair achieve when such things yield to the blade?')) Persius 2.69 (*quid facit aurum* ('what's the good of gold?')). The phrase might also mean 'what are they up to?' or 'what's their game?' (Henderson (1997) 22) as *quid facit is* ('what is he up to, the man who…') in Catullus 88.1.

Ponticus sounds like a *cognomen ex uirtute* – an honorific name added to commemorate a distinguished military achievement and passed on to one's ancestors, such as we find in (e.g.) Publius Cornelius Scipio 'Africanus' and in men named by Juvenal such as Allobrogicus (8.13), Gaetulicus (8.26), Bithynicus (15.1). In this case it is reasonable to assume that one of Ponticus' ancestors had achieved military glory in Pontus (a province occupying what is now the Black Sea region of Turkey and which, under its king Mithridates VI Eupator (135–63 BC: see Juvenal 10.273, 14.252), had mounted a war against Roman rule which only ended when he was defeated by Pompey in 67 BC). The Ponticus addressed here cannot be identified but a man with that name was banished by Nero (Tacitus *Annals* 14.41) for judicial misbehaviour and Martial is less than complimentary about a man named Ponticus whom he calls 'timid' (2.32), cruel (2.82, 3.60), mean to his guests (4.85), a vain writer (5.63) and an onanist (9.41): J.'s readers may also have been reminded of Horace's ship (*Odes* 1.14) which is a 'pine from Pontus, daughter of a noble forest' (*Pontica pinus / siluae filia nobilis*).

2   **blood-line**: Blood as metaphorical for the family line is common in English ('blue blood') and Latin: see 8. 27, 42, 11.62, Ennius *Annals* 1.108,

Virgil *Aeneid* 5.45 (*genus alto a sanguine diuom* ('a race from the lofty blood of the gods': cf. Horace *Odes* 4.2.14), 6.835 (where *sanguis meus* means 'my child'). The qualifying adjective *longo* (inappropriate for literal blood) spells out the metaphor, and the enjambement has the effect of lengthening the phrase and so enacts the length of the blood-line. *censeo* is to 'evaluate' (*OLD* s.v. 'censeo' 8b) as at 8.74: its cognate noun *census* is common in J. to mean 'family wealth' as at 10.13, 11.23, 13.7, 14.176, 227.

2–3 **painted faces** (*pictos uultus*) presupposes that these images were painted portraits (Corbier ((2007) 76) distinguishes these from the wax masks) – but men 'standing in chariots' suggests triumphal statues as at 7.125–6, Pliny *NH* 35.7: *effigies* in 9 and 22 covers both forms of representation.

3 The heavy spondees mark a mood of grandeur, with the final two feet taken up by a single family name (Martial (5.81.1) uses the same name in the same way) and the plural form of a famous name to indicate 'men like Aemilius' or 'men of the Aemilius clan' is not uncommon: cf. 8.9 (*Lepidis*) 1.109, 2.3 (*Curios* as 8.4, Lucan 7.359), 2.35, 10.108, 11.90–91. The effect is slightly altered by the choice of *Aemilianos*: an adopted son added the suffix *-ianus* to his original gentile name – see *OCD* s.v. 'names, personal, Roman' 8: in this case Scipio Aemilianus was the natural son of Lucius Aemilius Paulus. J.'s choice of the plural form of this name to begin with is pointed: there were few greater men in Roman history than Publius Cornelius Scipio Aemilianus Africanus (185–129 BC), the destroyer of Carthage in 146 BC, a man of military and diplomatic distinction who also enjoyed literary connections (with the satirist Lucilius for instance) or his adoptive father Publius Cornelius Scipio Africanus (236–183 BC) the conqueror of Hannibal at the battle of Zama in 202 BC: the two together are called 'two thunderbolts of war' (*duo fulmina belli*) by Anchises in Virgil (*Aeneid* 6. 842–3).

4–5 **chopped**: J. is thinking of statues which are easily broken. The **Curii** were an ancient patrician family referred to elsewhere (cf. 2.3, 11.78: 2.153–4 (which links Curius with the Scipios as here), Martial 1.24.3) as bastions of ancestral virtue. Manius Curius Dentatus (so called as he was born with teeth already in his infant mouth: see 11.78n.) was censor in 272 BC and the conqueror of Pyrrhus and was famously found cooking turnips when the Samnite embassy called on him (Pliny *NH* 19.87: see further *OCD* s.v. 'Curius Dentatus, Manius'). Marcus Valerius **Corvinus** was military tribune in 349 BC: he acquired his cognomen Corvinus ('raven-man') when he was (allegedly) assisted by a raven in his successful single combat against a Gaul (see *OCD* s.v. 'Valerius Corvus, Marcus'). Servius Sulpicius **Galba** (3 BC–AD 69) was briefly emperor of Rome (he was the first of the four emperors in AD69) and was summed up by Tacitus (*Histories* 1.49) as *omnium consensu capax imperii nisi imperasset* ('a potential emperor by general agreement, if only he had not been made emperor': an opinion echoed by Plutarch *Galba* 29). Suetonius (*Galba* 2) tells us that he claimed to be able to trace his ancestry back to Jupiter and Pasiphae and his family pride was well known (Tacitus *Histories* 1.15.1, 1.49.2: Vespasian 'gave way before the family portraits of Galba' (Tacitus *Histories* 2.76.2)). After his death Galba's severed head was fixed on a pole and abused by a variety of people (Tacitus *Histories* 1.49.1, Plutarch *Galba* 287.2–3, Suetonius *Galba* 20.2) – a good reason for J. here to mock his mutilated image, facially castrated after death as defeated enemies were sometimes treated in life (cf. e.g. Deiphobus in Virgil *Aeneid* 6. 494–7) and showing clearly the gap between his family pride and the degradation of his corpse. He had more illustrious ancestors, most notably P. Sulpicius Galba Maximus who was consul in 211 BC and again in 200 BC: and the family history well shows J.'s point about the degradation of ancestral greatness in vivid and all too real detail with the demise of this recent member of the *gens*. The mutilated statues show former glory now **chopped in half** (*dimidios*): *dimidios* is found in this sense also at 13.95 (where see n.), 15.5, 15.57. Here the diminishing continues throughout: Corvinus lacks arms (see below), Galba lacks **ears and nose** – and his ears were already diminutive (*auricula* is the diminutive form of *auris*). The reading *umerosque* (an accusative of respect) found in P ('smaller with respect to the shoulders', i.e. lacking arms, as Housman read it) makes more sense than the later reading *umeroque* ('smaller by a shoulder', i.e. 'one shoulder missing': one cannot lose a shoulder without also losing an arm, as Nisbet ((1995) 289) points out). The accusative is used in this way also at 6.491, Virgil *Aeneid* 6.495.

6–8   These lines are problematic as they stand in the manuscripts. Line 7 begins *Coruinum posthac*: the repetition of the name from line 5 is almost certainly a scribal error – although it is not true that the 'reference to a capacious family tree does not suit the mention of only one man' (Courtney) if the one man in question is so distinguished – and *posthac* does not make any sense as we talking about the glorious past and not later times. Φ omits line 7 (presumably because the scribe saw the initial word *Coruinum* and thought he had already written it) and so makes *fumosos ... magistros* the object of *iactare*: Guyet and Jachmann deleted lines 6–8 altogether and the sentence certainly gains in power and purpose if the thought moves straight from *nasoque carentem* to *si coram Lepidis male uiuitur*. There are other arguments to be made however for the lines as they stand. Courtney rightly states that *quid prodest* needs a protasis (i.e. *si* in line 9) but this is not obviously so: cf. Lucan 1.669 (*et superos quid prodest poscere finem?*), 9.828, Ovid *Ex Ponto* 2.6.11–12, Seneca *Epistles* 94.25.1, 104.8.3. Furthermore, *quid prodest* is repeated in varied form in *quis fructus* (line 6) and the expected protasis follows on after both at line 9 and so at the very least we need to remove any strong punctuation after line 5. Courtney dismisses as a 'feeble defence' the point that *Lepidis* goes neatly with the previous line as M. Aemilius Lepidus was *magister equitum* of Julius Caesar but this is not fair: J.'s point is that it is no good boasting of distinguished ancestors while behaving badly in front of their images – and here we have a good example of the honour followed by the name of a man who held it. But there is also the suggestion that the distinguished old members of the Lepidus clan are being poorly represented by modern members of the family who are no longer *magistri equitum* (etc) but merely *Lepidis*. The question of whether to retain or delete lines 6–8 will ultimately by decided by the question of whether they are authentically in J.'s style, and this is a subjective judgement which the notes below will seek to assist.

6   **What profit**: *quis fructus?* here means 'what is to be gained' (cf. 7.103, *OLD* s.v. 'fructus' 5) and takes the infinitive sequence *iactare posse* as at Calpurnius *Decl.* 22. *tabula* usually means 'a flat piece of wood' (*OLD* s.v. 'tabula' 1,2) and *generis tabula* has to mean the 'family record' as indicated above with the *pictos uultus* which suggests to many (e.g. Dimatteo (2014) 51, Flower (1996) 40) that the waxen images and the accompanying names were affixed to a wooden 'notice-board', with the familial lines of descent marked by lines (referred to with *uirga* in line 7 and with *lineis* in Pliny *NH* 35.6). *iactare capaci* has suitably ebullient assonance to reinforce the meaning of both words: *iacto* is often used of bragging (Horace *Odes* 1.14.13, *OLD* s.v. 'iacto' 11) or showing off (1.62, Horace *Satires* 1.2.85, *OLD* s.v. 'iacto' 12) while *capax* conveys the sense that this family tree has to be huge (and long) to contain all the big names in it (cf. 1.63, 11.41, Lucretius 6.123).

7   **censor**: *Coruinum* is not impossible but is probably a scribal error (as we are looking for the name of a political distinction rather than another personal name) as is *posthac* which makes no sense here. Of the many suggestions

put forward the best one is probably Harrison's *censorem* (Harrison (2015)) followed by Withof's *posse ac*. A censor in the family-tree is enough to distinguish a family *in perpetuum* and the *gens Fabia* (mentioned by name at 14 and elsewhere) boasted one famous such man (see note on 13–14 below). Housman's suggestion *pontifices* is also worthy of mention. *uirga* literally means a 'twig' or 'branch' and here signifies a metaphorical 'branch' of the family tree (*OLD* s.v. 'uirga' 1d), like *ramus* (Persius 3.28) – although at line 23 it refers to the *fasces* carried by a magistrate. *contingere* has the sense of 'establish kinship with' in Livy 45.7.3, Seneca *Apocolocyntosis* 9.5 Lucan 8.286–7 (see *OLD* s.v. 'contingo' 2b and my note on 11.62). *multus* with a singular noun indicates 'many a' as at 8.104 (*multa ... uirga*).

8   The word **dictator** in Republican times referred to a man chosen to run the city for a maximum of six months in extraordinary circumstances (such as if elections needed to be held, armies needed to be commanded or in the case of civil unrest). The office (see *OCD* s.v. 'dictator') was used in early Roman history (up to 202 BC) as a functional way to solve a crisis, but in the 1st century BC the office was revived and given to Sulla (81BC: see *OCD* s.v. 'Cornelius Sulla Felix, Lucius') and Julius Caesar (49–44 BC: see *OCD* s.v. 'Iulius Caesar, Gaius') for more wholesale reform. On taking up office a dictator would at once appoint a second in command called the 'master of the horse' (*magister equitum*) (see *OCD* s.v. 'magister equitum'). The point here is that any family which could boast men holding either office had to have a long ancestry as the office had been defunct since the demise of the republic. The antiquity is helped by the word *fumosos* (**smoky**) as the images were kept in the atrium which was originally the site of the family hearth 'whose smoke caused the blackening (*ater*) which gave the place its name' (*OCD* s.v. 'houses, Italian': cf. Seneca *Ep.* 44.4, Cicero *in Pisonem* 1, Martial 2.90. 5–8). J. neatly juxtaposes the key 'power' nouns (*dictatore magistros*) at the end of the line.

9   **Lepidi** refers here to a sub-branch of the *gens Aemilia* which boasts eight entries in *OCD* (s.v. 'Aemilius Lepidus') and which held consulships from 187 BC (Marcus) right up to AD 11 (Manius). Marcus Aemilius Lepidus was the dictator Caesar's *magister equitum* in 46–44 BC and was made triumvir (alongside Octavian and Antony) in 43 BC. The last of the line was married to the emperor Caligula's sister and executed by him for his alleged involvement in the conspiracy of the love-poet Cornelius Lentulus Gaetulicus (see *OCD* s.v. 'Cornelius Lentulus Gaetulicus, Cn.', Suetonius *Caligula* 24.3). J. uses the family name *Lepidi* as a byword for distinguished

ancestry also at 6.265 (cf. Cicero *Phil.* 13.8, Lucan 7.583–6). *quo* followed
by a noun in the accusative to mean 'what is the purpose of?' (understanding
something like *quo <prodest habere> effigies*) is found also at 8.142, 14.135,
15.61, Horace *Satires* 1.6.24, *Epistles* 1.5.12, *OLD* s.v. 'quo' 2.

9–10   The phrasing is effective: from the bucolic diaeresis of the last two
feet of 9 (with the monosyllabic *quo* causing a clash of ictus and accent
and so emphasising the question) to the grandiose spondaic phrasing of *tot
bellatorum* and the use of passive verbs (*uiuitur ... luditur*) to contrast the
effete present with the active energy of the men of old (*mouebant*). For the
phrasing of the sentiment *coram ... uiuitur* cf. Valerius Maximus 2.9, Seneca
Ep. 74.6, 97.1 (where the argument is that, *pace* J., wrongdoing 'was never
more openly committed than in the presence of Cato (*coram Catone*)').

9–11   **in the presence of...**: the common trope that the house itself is
a potential witness of its occupants' misbehaviour goes back to Greek
literature (Aeschylus *Agamemnon* 37–8, Euripides *Hippolytus* 418, 1074)
and is found also in Catullus 67 and in oratory (Cicero *pro Cluentio* 15,
pro Caelio 60.7, *Philippics* 2.69.1). It is given a further twist here (and in
Pliny (*NH* 35.7–8)) in the implied pathetic fallacy that inanimate images
are somehow watching the misbehaviour of the living descendants: these
images may have lost parts of themselves (4) but still have eyes to see what
is going on under their gaze.

10   **war-heroes**: *bellator* is an epic word for a fighting man (Virgil *Aeneid*
11.553, 12.614: J. uses it sarcastically of pygmies at 13.168) or a warhorse
(7.127, Virgil *Georgics* 2.145, *Aeneid* 10.891) or the god of war himself
(Virgil *Aeneid* 9.721). J. elsewhere (11.176) calls gambling 'a disgrace' (*alea
turpis*), pairing it with adultery as a social evil: and gambling was certainly
regarded as an evil by the legislators throughout Roman history who only
allowed it to happen during the holiday of the *Saturnalia* (Martial 5.84). The
statutes declared that the penalty for gambling was to be four times the sum
wagered (ps-Asconius on Cicero *Caecil.* 24) and civil rights were withheld
until the offender had paid up (Cicero *Philippics* 2.56), while the praetor
would not chase up gambling debts or offer legal redress to those who ran
gambling dens (*Digest* 11, 5, 1, 2: Crook (1967) 271). The law was difficult
to enforce when emperors themselves were keen on gambling: Suetonius
tells us that Claudius was a gambler as a young man (*Claudius* 5) and as
emperor, and was even said to have written a book on the subject (*Claudius*
33.2); and other emperors were equally keen (see Suetonius *Augustus* 71.1,
Caligula 41–2, *Domitian* 21), with Caligula even gaming during his sister's

funeral (Seneca *Dial.* 17.4–5). J. disapproves of gambling as a waste of time and cash (*damnosa* (14.4): cf. Ovid *Tristia* 2.484) and it is seen, often in association with excessive drinking and sexual promiscuity, as a sign of dissipation by Cicero (*Philippics* 2.67, 3.35, *de Officiis* 3.91, *Catilinarians* 2.23) and Quintilian (*Inst. Or.*2.4.22). It was especially linked with theft and debt as gamblers always need more money than they have (Justinian *Digest* 21.1.1.19.1, Horace *Epistles* 1.18.21–5, *Odes* 3.24.58–64): Sallust tells us firmly that Catiline's supporters were found from 'any debauched man, glutton or gambler who had, with his hand, his belly, or his penis torn up his ancestral fortune' (Sallust *Cat.* 14.2). For the moral disapproval of gambling see Edwards (1993) 190–1 and especially Purcell (1995) 6–16.

pernox means **all night long**: cf. 14.46 (*pernoctantis*) Catullus 88.2 (*peruigilat*). There is disapproval of the inversion of day and night here which continues in the following lines. The word grammatically agrees with *alea* but may be understood as adverbial ('all night long').

11 **Numantini**: *Numantinus* was the unofficial *cognomen* conferred on P. Cornelius Scipio Aemilianus Africanus after he had captured Numantia in Spain in 133 BC (cf. *OCD* s.v. 'Cornelius Scipio Aemilianus Africanus (Numantinus), Publius', Appian 6.98). For the plural form cf. 8.3n.: this name in particular was so used also by Propertius (4.11.29–30) and Pliny (*Epistles* 8.6.2).

11–12 **you** here is probably the impersonal 'one' rather than specifically referring to Ponticus. **only start to sleep**: going to sleep at dawn, when others are starting their day, is (yet) another symptom of the topsy-turvy world which J. uncovers: see Seneca *Epistles* 122.9, *Thyestes* 466–7, Horace *Satires* 1.3.17–18, Martial 1.28 for similar disapproval, although elsewhere the all-night drinking party is regarded as something to be celebrated on a special occasion (e.g. Horace *Epistles* 1.5.9–11, *Odes* 3.8.14–15, 21. 23–4, Plato *Symposium* 223c). The enjambement of *Luciferi* evokes the shock of sudden dawn coming upon the recently ensconced sleeper: **Lucifer** is the morning star, son of Aurora and Cephalus: J. elsewhere (13.158) uses the word to mean simply 'morning'. Moving standards and striking camp is the language of Roman generals on campaign: e.g. Caesar *BG* 1.39.7, Livy 5.6.14, 29.21, Silius *Punica* 12.541.

13–14 **Fabius**: the *gens Fabia* (on which see 11.90–91n. and cf. 8.191) was allegedly descended from Hercules (*in Herculeo ... lare*) and boasted a number of distinguished figures in Roman history. Quintus Fabius Maximus, nephew of Scipio Aemilianus, was consul in 121 BC and was given the cognomen *Allobrogicus* after his defeat of the Gallic tribe the Allobroges in that year. The first triumphal arch (*fornix Fabianus*) was built in his honour (cf. *OCD* s.v. 'Fabius Maximus Allobrogicus, Quintus' and 'Forum Romanum'). The **Great Altar** (*ara maxima*) was built by Hercules (Propertius 4.9.67–8) or in his honour in the Forum Boarium in Rome (Ovid *Fasti* 1.581–2, Virgil *Aeneid* 8.271–2, with Servius *ad loc.*) and was burnt in the great fire of Rome (Tacitus *Annals* 15. 41). This scion of the Fabian gens takes pleasure in his ancestors and in the link with Hercules but is hardly worthy of them: the link with Hercules is sardonic as the hero was famously offered the choice of virtue or pleasure and chose virtue (Xenophon *Memorabilia* 2.1.21–2), whereas his (putative) descendant has clearly chosen pleasure. The same contrast of Herculean virtue versus decadent hedonism is found at 10.361–2, and Hercules had been taken up by the Stoics as the symbol of their ethical code (see e.g. Seneca's *Hercules Furens* (with Bernstein (2017) 65–93) and Galinsky (1972) 101–7) as well as an iconic figure in Virgil's *Aeneid* (8.190–305) and elsewhere (Lucretius 5.22–51, Ovid *ex Ponto* 3.3.98–9). Rubellius Blandus also claims descent from a legendary Greek (Cecrops) at line 46. **house**: *lare* here refers literally to the household god (*Lar*) but is used metonymically for the household itself as at 3.110, 14.20, 15.153: see *OLD* s.v. 'Lar' 2, *OCD* s.v. 'Lares'.

14–18   After less than two lines describing the family history, the poet now spends over four lines exposing the shortcomings of the current generation with a tricolon crescendo introduced by anaphora of *si* (and with effective syncopation of *si cupidus si*).

14–15   It seems that this Fabius has inherited only the worst traits of Hercules and none of the good ones. *cupidus* means **greedy** and was in fact something of which Hercules himself was guilty on occasion – he appears in literature as a glutton (Euripides *Alcestis* 753–4, Aristophanes *Frogs* 62–5, 549–60). *uanus* denotes 'void' or 'pointless' (as at 7.203, 13.137) but here means a **fool** as at 3.159, 14.211 (see *OLD* s.v. 'uanus' 6) and again folly is something which the Hercules of comedy shows on occasion (see e.g. Aristophanes *Frogs* 106–7). **softer**: *mollis* is often used of effeminacy (e.g. 2.47, 6.63, 366, 9.38, Catullus 25.1) and the only instance in which Hercules was said to behave thus was his famous enslavement to Omphale where he was said to wear women's clothes (see *OCD* s.v. 'Omphale', Ovid *Heroides* 9.53–118 and the fragmentary satyr play *Omphale* by Ion of Chios). *quantumuis* is the neuter singular of *quantusuis* used as an adverb ('as *uanus* and *mollior* as you like'): see *OLD* s.v. 'quantusuis' c, KS 2.446 § 221 and cf. Seneca *Apoc.* 9.2, Horace *Epistles* 2.2.39, Seneca *Ep.* 122.17, Suetonius *Caligula* 53.1). **Euganean** is more than an 'ornamental epithet' (Duff and Courtney): the Euganei were a tribe in Venetia in Northern Italy, and their town Altinum (modern Altino, near Venice and described as *Euganeus* by Martial 4.25.4) produced sheep which were famous for their fine soft wool (Martial 14.155). More significantly, the word plays on the Greek noun εὐγένεια ('fine breeding') which is the origin of the name (Pliny *NH* 3.134): the wool clearly shows better breeding than the *mollis* man compared with it.

16–17 smooth ... hairy: J. effectively brings out the contrast between modern artificial smoothness (*tenerum*) and authentic ancestral hairiness (*squalentes*), a contrast also brought out at 8.114–6, 2.11–13, Martial 2.36. Shaggy, unkempt hair was often used as a sign of ruggedness and moral strength (cf. 14.194), while the modern taste for depilation shows the opposite: but hairiness was also seen as a sign of a lack of urbane civilisation (cf. e.g. Catullus 33.7).

16 rubbed smooth: male depilation was vividly stigmatised by Persius (4.35–6), J. (2. 12–13, 9.95) and Martial 2.62, 14.205.1: anal depilation in particular was a target for ridicule in Greek comedy (Aristophanes *Knights* 1368, *Frogs* 423–4, *Acharnians* 119). The degenerate Fabius has his *lumbus* rubbed smooth (*attritus*, from *attero*) as part of his general effeminacy (*mollior*): the *lumbus* was 'a vaguely defined area within which the sexual organs might be situated, but not necessarily coterminous with them' (Adams (1982) 48): cf. 6.O24, 9.59, Persius 1.20, Catullus 16.11, Lucretius 4.1267. This **pumice** stone used was high-quality – Catana (modern Catania, near the volcanic Mt Aetna in Sicily) was famous for its abundant pumice – but the town was also known for its dissolute ways, according to the scholiast who quotes a fragment of Furius Bibaculus ('Oscan old man, boy of Catana, prostitute from Cumae' (*FLP* 194)) to back this up. Cicero notes (*Verr.* 2.3.103, 2.4.50) that its inhabitants were wealthy – and so luxury and therefore *mollitia* were more available to them. Lentulus (a mime-writer under Domitian) composed a mime called *Catinenses* (cited in Tertullian *de Pallio* 4) which mocked a certain Catinensan fighter called Cleomachus ('glory-fighter') for covering with bracelets the bruises left by the boxing glove and also for making the 'coarseness' of his track suit more bearable with some 'finely wrought tissue'. The juxtapositions in line 16 are expressive: *pumice lumbum* (with its powerful assonance) enacts the process and *tenerum attritus* brings out the smoothness of the result before the verb which explains it. *tener* is often used of femininity of appearance: see e.g. 1.22 (a *tener* eunuch) 6.O24 (the *teneris* loins of the pervert), 6.548 (a *tenerum* lover (i.e. 'toyboy')), 9.46 (a catamite) 12.39 (worthy of a *tener* Maecenas – a man known for louche behaviour). Excessive concern with one's appearance is often criticised an unmanly: see e.g. 2.99 (where the emperor Otho is abused for carrying a mirror in his kit), Ovid *Ars Am.* 507–8, Cicero *in Cat.* 2.22, Williams (1999) 31–2, 130–131.

17   **hairy**: the association of venerable elders and/or philosophers with shaggy hair and beards is not uncommon – Cynics and Stoics in particular wore beards and Epictetus even offered to die rather than to lose his beard (*Discourses* 1.2.29: cf. Pliny *Epist.* 1.10.6, Persius 1.133, 4.1, Horace *Satires* 1.3.133, 2.3.35 (where 'to grow the wise beard' means 'to become a philosopher', but simply having the beard did not make one a philosopher according to Gellius 9.2.1–4), Paoli (1990) 110: see also e.g. Appius Claudius Caecus at Cicero *pro Caelio* 33 and cf. Juvenal 5.30, 16.31–2. Hadrian had brought the beard back into fashion either as part of his philhellenism (see *CAH* xi 975, Anderson (1955)) or to cover his own facial blemishes (*HA Hadr* 26.1: for the fashion cf. Dio Chrysostom 36.17). The language is strong: *traducit* is 'to expose to scorn or obloquy' (*OLD* s.v. 'traduco' 4b; cf. 11.31) while *squalentes* is often itself a pejorative term for self-neglect (9.15, 11.80, 15.135) but here denotes rugged masculine unkemptness. The paradox is that the apparent self-neglect of the ancestors was morally superior to the modern fastidious young man, and the point is made more telling with the use of *traducit* (from *trans-duco*) which has the sense of 'leading in triumph' as Roman generals did with their conquered enemies: this modern Fabius only *traducit* his family, unlike the ancestors who *traduxerunt* their foes.

17–18   **poison-dealer**: making, selling and administering poisons feature significantly elsewhere in J.'s account of Rome (e.g. 1.158, 8.219, 9.100, 10.25–6, 13.154, 14.173–4) and was a crime of which the emperor Nero (8.219–220n.) was guilty as he tried to poison his mother Agrippina (Tacitus *Annals* 14.3) and succeeded in poisoning his step-brother Britannicus (Tacitus *Annals* 13.15–16) as well as his aunt Domitia (Suetonius *Nero* 34).

18   **image ... smashed**: the *imago* of a disgraced family-member was not allowed to be displayed in public (Tacitus *Annals* 2.32.3, 3.76) and Pliny (*Ep.* 1.17.3) is astonished that people could even have such *imagines* at home. The verb *frangenda* suggests positive destruction such as happened to the image of Sejanus (10.58–64) and others (Cicero *in Pisonem* 93, Suetonius

Domitian 23, Tacitus *Annals* 3.14, 11.35.2, *Histories* 3.85) and introduces a note of violence which does not sit well with the common reading of this satire as one which eschews *indignatio*. Elsewhere (12.18) J. speaks of breaking up family images as a desperate means of raising money. *funestat* is sardonic – Roman heroes glory in killing their enemies, but this man **pollutes** his family: for the sense of *funestat* cf. Catullus 64.201. Line 18 is a 'golden line' in which the central verb is framed by two adjectival words before it and two nouns after it in a pattern abVAB: J. is perhaps evoking the loss of epic grandeur in the style as well as the content of this line.

19–20   The section concludes with a neat two-line summary of the argument, with effective contrast of the omnipresent (*tota ... ubique*) external symbols over against the singular (*sola ... unica*) form of true *nobilitas*. The lengthy and extravagant decoration of the *atrium* is neatly enacted in the enjambement, the use of the plural *atria*, the cumulative force of *tota ... undique* and the reminder that this family tree is long as well as wide (with *ueteres* telling us that the family line began many years ago). *cerae* (literally 'pieces of wax': see *OLD* s.v. 'cera' 5 and cf. Ovid *Amores* 1.8.65 for the phrasing) refers to the **wax masks** (*imagines*) worn by actors at family funerals and displayed in the *atrium* (see 1–2n.). The resounding conclusion (that the only form of social distinction worth having is that of moral excellence) is enhanced by the chiastic word order of *nobilitas sola ... unica uirtus*. Not all 'nobles' are 'virtuous', but (says J.) all 'virtuous' men are to him 'noble' and this is the only criterion for so describing a man, whatever his origins. The two often are said to co-exist (e.g. 15.113–4, Cicero *Verrines* 2.3.56, *pro Cluentio* 11.10, Tacitus *Agricola* 1.1.4) but can be distinguished as descriptors (Tacitus *Germania* 7.1: kings are chosen for *nobilitas*, but generals for their *uirtus*). *licet* with the subjunctive is concessive ('**even though**' *OLD* s.v. 'licet' 4).

21   Ponticus is urged to imitate the great dead in **behaviour** (*moribus*) and the singular short forms of the names make it clear that these are types rather than specific individuals: the combination of Paulus with Cossus recalls Augustus' remark to the conspirator Lucius Cinna (quoted by Seneca *de Clementia* 1.9.10), that modern aristocrats such as 'Paulus and Fabius Maximus, and the Cossi and the Servilii' were 'men who are a credit to their *imaginibus*'. The choice of names is deliberate (as Henderson notes ((1997) 67–8 with n. 128): 'each of them began as a gentilician *cognomen* but, in a short-lived aristocratic onomastic fashion, relocated as *praenomina*'. The names also belonged to men of both republican and imperial times: Paulus

may refer either to Lucius Aemilius Paulus Macedonicus (who overcame Perseus of Macedon at the battle of Pydna in 168 BC) or else to more recent men such as the Paulus Fabius Maximus (consul 11BC: *OCD* s.v. 'Fabius Maximus, Paullus') who was pontifex and a close friend of the emperor Augustus. Aulus Cornelius **Cossus** won the *spolia opima* in 437 BC after killing Lars Tolumnius in combat (*OCD* s.v. 'Cornelius Cossus, Aulus'), while much later Gnaeus Cornelius Lentulus Cossus defeated the Gaetuli in N. Africa in AD 6 and his family was given the *cognomen* Gaetulicus (see 26 below). The man alluded to here is perhaps more likely to be the later Cossus as he was sent to quell disorder in Pannonia alongside Nero Claudius **Drusus**, one of the two sons of Livia and stepson of the first Roman emperor Augustus: this Drusus fought in Germany (being awarded the cognomen Germanicus) and died there after falling from his horse in 9 BC. Drusus was much lauded in Augustan literature: see especially Horace *Odes* 4.4 and 4.14, which both celebrate his achievements in Germany in hyperbolic terms: Horace at times produces lines which are highly relevant to this poem (e.g. *Odes* 4.4.29–36 'the brave are produced by the brave and the fine: in cattle and horses the mettle (*uirtus*) of the fathers is found and fierce eagles do not produce the timid dove: but training (*doctrina*) promotes inbred power and the cultivation of what is right strengthens hearts. When good practices (*mores*) have ceased, then wrongdoing shames even the well born (*bene nata*)'). The name Drusus (derived from the man who originally slew the chieftain Drausus (Suetonius *Tiberius* 3.2)) was also one which had passed through many generations of political and military distinction in the *gens Liuia* (see e.g. *OCD* s.v. 'Livius Drusus, Marcus') and Virgil (*Aeneid* 6.824) lists a plurality of *Drusos* in the pageant of heroes: Norden ((1957) 329–30) remarks that Virgil's readers will think first of Rome's salvation from disaster thanks to Tiberius' and Drusus' ancestor Gaius Claudius Nero (consul 207 BC: see *OCD* s.v. 'Claudius Nero, Gaius') who defeated Hasdrubal at the Metaurus river, and Horace (*Odes* 4.4.37–72) also moves from praise of the imperial Drusus to his republican counterpart. The heavy spondees of line 21 and the formal future imperative *esto* well evoke the *grauitas* of these distinguished names.

22   *hos* (and *illi* in 23) could refer to the men named in 21 or else could pick up *mores* ('character') from *moribus*: perhaps the ambiguity is conscious, as the men are only to be so prized because of their character, and J. is using the names as exemplars of virtue. *anteponere* is often found in prose in its inseparable form (e.g. Cicero *Verrines* 2.2.97), meaning 'to prefer'

(*OLD* s.v. 'antepono' 3), but such a form would be metrically impossible in hexameters and there may be also a play on *pone* meaning 'behind' (*OLD* s.v. 'pone'). The literal meaning is found at line 228.

23 **let them walk**: after two peremptory second-person imperatives (*esto ... pone*) J. uses a jussive subjunctive *praecedant* in emphatic position at the start of the line, followed by the three pronominal words *ipsas illi te* in juxtaposition. *uirgas* refers here (as at 136: *OLD* s.v. 'uirga' 3a) to the *fasces* (the **rods** which (along with 'axes') were the symbols of consular power carried in front of him by attendants (lictors) as he processed and which symbolised legitimate power granted by the senate and people of Rome (cf. see 8.7, 8.260., 10.78–81n., *OCD* s.v. 'fasces')). J. might easily have written the metrically equivalent *fasces* (as at 260) but *uirgas* recalls *uirga* in 7 and also has more sense of violence as at 8.136 ('breaking *uirgas* on the blood of our allies'), 3.317, 7.210, 8.153, 14.63. Ancestors always precede us in time: these men (or their *mores*) are to **walk** in front of us (*praecedant*) like lictors in a procession. *te consule* (an ablative absolute construction) has temporal and/or conditional force: 'if/when you become consul'.

24–25 **goodness of heart**: the *mores* associated with the great names of line 21 are here summed up as *animi bona* – a common phrase in Latin (e.g. Tacitus *Histories* 1.15.23, Seneca *Ep.* 108.8, *de Beneficiis* 4.8.3, 5.13, Cicero *Tusculan Disputations* 5.51.2) and in Greek (τὰ τῆς ψυχῆς ὑπάρχοντα) for 'things good for the mind/soul' (as opposed to things beneficial to the body) but which here indicates 'goodness of character' (which is good for society as well as for oneself) as at Cicero *de Finibus* 4.17, Nepos *Epaminondas* 3.1, Ovid *Tristia* 1.6.34, [Seneca] *Octavia* 548–9, Tacitus *Histories* 1.15. **first**: *prima* is given appropriate emphasis at the beginning of the line and the sentence. The logic here is one of social necessity: if you deserve a great reputation (*sanctus haberi*) – and the question form of *mereris* makes this word act as the protasis of a conditional – then you must (*debes*) deserve it by your deeds and words (*factis dictisque*). *sanctus* (*OLD* s.v. 'sanctus' 4) has the sense of 'blameless, virtuous' as at 127, 10.298, 13.64 14.68 (applied to the house itself) but also has the meaning of 'enjoying immunity from assault' (most famously of tribunician *sacrosanctitas*: a sense found at 3.109 and coming from *sancire*) and so 'untouchable' or (here) **unimpeachable**. *haberi* here has the common meaning of **to be considered** (*OLD* s.v. 'habeo' 24: cf. 141, 3.272, 10.92). *mihi* is probably (as Ferguson states) an 'ethic' dative ('**I think**': AG § 380, K-S § 76: 8c, pp. 323–4, *NLS* §66, *OLD* s.v. 'ego' c: cf. Horace *Epistles* 1.3.15). **never letting go of**: *tenax* + objective genitive recalls Virgil *Aeneid* 4.188 (*fama* is *tam ficti prauique tenax*) Horace *Odes* 3.3.1 (*iustum et tenacem propositi uirum*) Ovid *Met.* 7.657, 10.405, Persius 5.48 (*tenax ueri*), Seneca *Ep.* 7.6, 66.32, 92.3, Quintilian 11.1.90.

26 J.'s point throughout the poem is that being 'noble' (*procerem*) is a matter of behaviour rather than birth, and so the poet claims to recognise (*agnosco*) such distinction only in those among the aristocracy whose behaviour merits it. *proceres* is listed in *OLD* as a plural noun (cf. 2.121, 3.213, 4.73, 4.144, 7.90) and the singular form *procerem* occurs only here in extant Latin.

26–27 **Gaetulicus** was the cognomen won by Gnaeus Cornelius Lentulus Cossus after defeating the Gaetuli in N. Africa in AD 6 (see 21n.), while **Silanus** denotes a member of the Iunii Silani – a branch of the *gens Iunia* which was one of the oldest Roman families. D. Iunius Silanus Gaetulicus became a member of the distinguished order of Salii (see *OCD* s.v. 'Salii') in AD 63 and was 'presumably a grandson of the victor of the Gaetuli, adopted by a Iunius Silanus' (Courtney). *alio* ('**…or you Silanus – or from whatever other bloodline…**') fits the hymn formula here (cf. Catullus 34.21–2, Macrobius *Sat.* 3.9.10): J. even hints at the use of prayer-formula in which a worshipper addresses a divinity by a series of alternative names (cf. 13.115n.), as at e.g. Horace *Carmen Saeculare* 15–16, *Odes* 3.21.5–6, Euripides *Heracles* 352–355, *Trojan Women* 886–7: see Dimatteo (2014) 68. Many modern editors print Richards' emendation *alto* ('lofty' 'distinguished'), restricting the 'bloodline' to a noble one, but this would weaken the cletic language of the sentence. For *sanguis* as **bloodline** see 2n.

28 **citizen**: the enjambed *ciuis* is something of a surprise but is in fact key to the satirical stance adopted: as Roland Mayer comments (*per e-litteras*), 'J. is insisting that the aristocrat be assessed in 'civilian' terms, not just in accordance with his ancestry. What is 'good character' in a citizen is 'good character' in a nobleman; his nobility is a plus (and makes him *rarus*) but it is not enough on its own.' After the listing of elevated aristocratic names and the adjective *rarus* (**rare**: cf. 6.165, 10.297) we expect something more special than simply a 'citizen' and the theme of popular acclaim in 29 will extend this point that all are called (and able) to be good citizens. **outstanding… to your fatherland**: the phrase *egregius patriae* is recalled later in 14.71–3 ('it is pleasing that you have given the fatherland (*patriae*) and the population a citizen (*ciuem*), but only if you ensure that he is of benefit to his fatherland, useful in the fields and useful in engaging in the activities of war and peace'). **turns out**: *contingere* in line 7 had the sense of 'establish kinship with' but the word often suggests the workings of chance

(cf. 6.49, 6.564, 13.7, *OLD* s.v. 'contingo' 8) which is apt here as people cannot safely predict how their children will behave. *ouanti* (**rejoicing**) evokes images of major figures being cheered on entering the theatre amounts almost to a technical term in this context as an *ouatio* was a minor form of the Roman triumph, awarded to a victorious general who did not fulfil all the requirements of a full triumph (see *OCD* s.v. 'ovatio', Beard (2007) 62–63).

29–30 A virtuous aristocrat is as much of a miracle as a man brought back from the dead: J. uses this form of argument ('as unusual as…' with a list of bizarre examples) also at 13.60–70. **Osiris** was an Egyptian god who was killed by his brother Set but restored to life by his wife/sister Isis and her sister Nephthys: the myth was celebrated in the 'festival of Choiak' (see Apuleius *Met.* 11.27–30) and the ritual persisted well into the 5th century AD (see Rutilius Namatianus *de Reditu* 1.371–6). The annual ceremony recalling the search for (and discovery of) the god's resurrection was called the *heuresis* and we know that worshippers uttered the ritual cry εὑρήκαμεν συγχαίρομεν ('we have found him: we rejoice together'), a cry quoted by Seneca at *Apoc.*13.4 and in his lost work *de Superstitionibus* (cited from there by Augustine *Civ. Dei* 6.10): cf. also Ovid *Met.* 9.693. Plutarch constructed a neoplatonic philosophical interpretation of the myth in his essay *de Iside et Osiride* and many Romans (including the emperor Domitian) were drawn to the Isiac cult – the emperor Commodus even shaved his head and wore white as a devotee – and we have a full account of the cult in Apuleius *Metamorphoses* (11.9–10): see further *OCD* s.v. 'Isis', Beard, North and Price (1998) i. 264–6, ii. 134–7, *CAH* xi. 994–6, Green (1931). Egyptian cults were sufficiently well-known in Rome for their heroes to be used in literature without explanation: cf. 6.529, 12.28, 13.93, Propertius 4.5.34, Lucan 6.363 (Isis), Catullus 74.4, 102.4 (Harpocrates), Ovid *Met.* 9.690, Propertius 3.11.41, Virgil *Aeneid* 8.698 (Anubis): and J.'s use of the term *populus* here suggests more than a small group of eccentrics. J. devoted most of *Satire* 15 to an attack on the beliefs and behaviour of the Egyptians, showing that the curiosity about the Egyptians shown in Herodotus was still alive in imperial Rome. The enjambement of the word *inuento* enacts the time-gap separating the demise and the discovery of Osiris.

30–38 Noblemen who behave badly find their celebrity-status used against them. J. compares this with the sarcastic nicknames sometimes used to mock people and animals for characteristics such as size and colour. The difference between these and the ignoble nobles is (J. implies) that the former have no choice about being black/small/deformed, whereas the latter choose to behave badly. These lines when read today evoke an air of cruel mockery (*caueat lector!*) but are artfully composed and play on mythical and historical themes: see Dimatteo (2009).

30–32 The perfect subjunctive *dixerit* has the same force as the present subjunctive in this potential sentence (**who would call?**): cf. 2.24, 7.140, 10.321, Woodcock *NLS* §119: we have to understand a part of *sum* after *qui*. The contrast of birth and behaviour is well adduced by the parallel adjectives *indignus* and *insignis* beginning lines 31–2, and *generosum* is contrasted with *indignus genere. generosus* (**noble**) indicates being of good family (*genus*) as at 6.124, 7.191, 8.57, 8.224, 14.81. *tantum* has limiting force (**only** <in this and nothing else>) as at 1.1, 7.1, 10.80.

32 The speaker springs the next point on us with the unexpected word *nanum* (**dwarf**). Dwarves were prized as speciality slaves: ps-Longinus *On the Sublime* 44.5 mentions 'cages in which dwarves and pygmies are kept' supporting the idea that such abnormalities were even exhibited to the public (see Friedländer (1968) iv.6 and cf. Suetonius *Augustus* 43.3 for the dwarf Lycius with his Stentorian voice) and kept as possessions: Pliny (*NH* 7.16) tells us that Augustus' grand-daughter Julia had two dwarves Conopas and Andromeda kept as pets (*in deliciis*), although we also hear (Suetonius *Augustus* 83) that Augustus himself did not share the enthusiasm for 'nature's laughing stocks' (*ludibria naturae*). A particular form of dwarf was the 'idiot-dwarf' or *morio* (Greek μωρίων) who acted as a jester at banquets (Pliny *Ep.*9.17): they were expensive to purchase and not such idiots in fact – see Martial 8.13.1, 12.93.3. Dwarf-slaves were indeed given joke names, and the first-person verb *uocamus* implicates the narrator in the practice: besides 'Atlas' here, Propertius (4.8.41–2) mentions one called 'Magnus' ('big man'): cf. how giants were called 'tiny' (Pliny *NH* 7.16.75)) and were part of the general Roman market in human oddities (Plutarch *de Curiositate* 10.520c: cf. 13.167–73n.) **Atlas** could refer either to the mountain (as at 11.24) whose peak was too high to be seen from the ground (Herodotus 4.184) or to the Titan who lives at the world's end and holds up the heavens on his shoulders (13.48, Hesiod *Theogony* 517–20, Propertius 3.22.7, Virgil *Aeneid* 4.481–2). He is a byword for massive size (*maximus Atlas*) in Virgil (*Aeneid* 1.741).

33 *Ethiopia* is loosely used in Latin to refer to the whole of inland central Africa, while also having a more specific reference to a region whose kingdom was Meroe and which corresponds roughly to modern Sudan:

see 10.148–50n.: **Ethiopian** simply means 'black African' here as at 2.23, 6.600 and the juxtaposition *Aethiopem cycnum* is oxymoronic. *Cycnus* (the Greek word (κύκνος) for **swan**) was a name with much mythology behind it (see *OCD* s.v. 'Cycnus'), most notably referring to the son of Poseidon who was strangled by Achilles and transformed into a swan (as narrated in Ovid *Metamorphoses* 12.71–145). The swan is proverbially white (see Otto (1890) s.v. 'cycnus' a and cf. Lucretius 2.824, Virgil *Eclogues* 7.38, Ovid *Tristia* 4.8.1, Martial 3.43.2). At 6.165 J. describes the ideal woman as *rara auis in terris nigroque simillima cycno* ('a rare bird on the earth and most like a black swan': Lucretius also (2.824) used 'black swan' as an example of an impossible phenomenon).

33–4   The ideal girl was *recta* (Catullus 86.2, Propertius 2.34.46), but the unfortunate female here was *prauam extortamque* (**twisted and deformed**). The phrasing here recalls Horace *Satires* 1.3.47–8 ('[the doting father] gives one son the pet name 'knock-kneed' when he has twisted (*distortis*) legs, and the son who finds it hard to balance on his crooked (*prauis*) ankles he calls 'rickety''). *prauus* means 'crooked' in a physical sense (cf. Lucretius 4.513), while *extortus* (the past participle of *extorqueo,* meaning properly 'twisted out of shape <as if from torture>') is a more powerful word than its close relative *distortus* (cf. Seneca *Epistles* 66.43, 104.18, Pliny *Epistles* 8.18.9). This deformed child is sarcastically termed **Europe**, the mythical daughter of the Phoenician King Agenor (in other versions the daughter of Phoenix: see Homer *Iliad* 14. 321–2) whose beauty enticed Jupiter (in the disguise of a bull) to carry her off to Crete where she bore him children: see *OCD* s.v. 'Europa' and cf. Horace *Odes* 3.27.25–76, Ovid *Heroides* 4.55–6, *Ars Am.* 1.323–4, *Metamorphoses* 2.833–75, [Seneca] *Octavia* 766–7.

34–7   From people to animals with the sarcastic naming of household dogs, with variation of vocabulary as the personal verb *uocamus* (32) becomes the impersonal *nomen erit* (36). These dogs – like the *nobiles* with whom they are compared – are **idle** (*pigris*) and have lost their fur due to chronic mange (*scabie uetusta leuibus*). They **lick the rim of a dry lamp** to find something to drink as they cannot find water: and yet they will be given the names of fierce and fearsome cats. Romans used dogs as guards (6.415–18) as well as pets (cf. 6.654, Martial 1.109, Toynbee (1973) 108–22, Toynbee (1948) 34–36): Trimalchio's household has both a fierce guard-dog (a huge beast which itself has the sarcastic name of *Scylax* ('puppy-dog' in Greek)) and a lapdog belonging to his catamite (Petronius 64): see further 5.11, 9.104, 14.64–5n. for dogs as part of Roman everyday life.

34   Canine scabies (also known as sarcoptic **mange**) is caused by the mite
sarcoptes scabiei. The mites cause itching (pruritis), thickening of the skin
and pustules which are either weeping or dry (as noted by Celsus 5.28.16a).
The disease is extremely contagious and was common in ancient times in
sheep as well as dogs: cf. 2.79–80, Virgil *Georgics* 3.299, 3.441. Symptoms
include loss of appetite and weight-loss – which would lead to the lack of
energy shown here (*pigris*) as well as loss of fur (*leuibus*). J. here frames
the disease with the key symptoms, with light recall of earlier images: the
smooth-skinned dogs are like the depilated Fabius in 16, while *uetusta* recalls
the 'long blood-line' of those family-trees (1–2). *uetusta* here indicates that
the disease is chronic – explaining the loss of both fur and energy.
35 Dogs usually lick the faces of people – but the only 'faces' (*ora*) these
useless dogs lick are those of a dried-out lamp. It was proverbial in Greek
that it is a bad idea to let a dog taste guts (Theocritus 10.11) in case the dog
thereafter neglects its duties in pursuit of more guts, and Horace imitates the
Theocritean line at *Satires* 2.5.83 ('a dog will never be scared away from a
greasy hide'): cf. Williams (1959), Otto s.v. 'canis' 11. Here the word *siccae*
is prominent and predicative: note also the alliteration of 'l' appropriate to this
action. The *lucerna* was an oil-lamp (Paoli (1990) 81–82, Beard (2008) 92)
which is elsewhere regarded as smoky and smelly in J. (cf. 6.131, 7.225–6).
36   The ineffectual dogs are sarcastically named after fierce and frightening
cats: the grouping of **leopard, tiger** and **lion** is mirrored at Martial 1.104 and
the list here is striking for its asyndeton. One of the animals in Ovid's 'catalogue
of dogs' belonging to Actaeon is called *tigris* (Ovid *Metamorphoses* 3.217).
Cicero (*de Finibus* 5.38) links lions and dogs together as being animals with
'spirit', while Lucretius (5.862–4) distinguishes the 'savage tribe' of lions
whose survival was ensured by courage from the faithful dogs which owe
their survival to mankind.
36–7   *adhuc* could go with *uiolentius* ('still more violently': KS 2.462–
3, *OLD* s.v. 'adhuc' 7) but here more probably *siquid adhuc* means *aliud*
(**anything else which**: *OLD* s.v. 'adhuc' 8a: cf. 6.502). The word order
suggests the latter, although the prolepsis and hyperbaton could be read as
appropriate in this ironically excited account of wild beasts, enhanced by
the offbeat rhythm of *si quid adhuc est*. *fremat* is a potential subjunctive
('anything which could roar') and the word (and its cognate noun) are
common in the context of raging lions (cf. 14.247, Catullus 63.86, Lucretius
3.296–7, Virgil *Aeneid* 9.341, 12.6–8, Seneca *Dial.* 3.1.6, Statius *Thebaid*
6.599, Silius Italicus 2.684–5). *in terris* (**on the earth**) is common with

general expressions for what can/cannot appear (e.g. 6.165, 10.279, 13.126, Lucretius 1.130).

37–8 **For that reason**: *ergo* points the moral conclusion – these animals are given noble names in sarcasm and so you should make sure that your illustrious name does not in this way (*sic*) become a sarcastic joke. The final phrase is metrically marked with the bucolic diaeresis before *ergo* and the spondaic monosyllables *ne tu sic* and the pair of verbs *cauebis* (**beware**) and *metues* (**be anxious**) amplify the sense of warning: the future indicative tense is used here in imperative form as at 9.101 (see AG §449b2, KS 1.144). The scansion of *ergŏ* is the norm in J. (see 7.171–2n. and cf. (e.g.) 6.175, 9.114). The word is common in didactic poetry (e.g. 45 times in Lucretius, 8 times in Manilius, 21 times in Horace's hexameter poetry) and in Ciceronian rhetoric to point towards conclusions.

The names are once again chosen for their historical resonance rather than as specific allusions to individuals. **Creticus** was the cognomen of Quintus Caecilius Metellus (consul in 69 BC) who conquered Crete in the years after his consulship (Cicero *ad Att.* 1.19.2); his descendant (Q. Caecilius Metellus Creticus Silanus) was consul in AD 7. The *Camerini* belonged to the *gens Sulpicia* (cf. 7.90) and had produced consuls in the distant past (e.g. 500 BC, 461 BC, 393 BC) as well as more recently (Q. Sulpicius Camerinus was consul in AD 9 and Q. Sulpicius Camerinus Peticus was suffect consul in AD 46). These names have an alliterative ring (*cauebis…sic Creticus… Camerinus*) and they clearly evoke the glory of Rome's past, although the last time we met a Creticus in J. (2.65–78) he was denounced as a hypocrite and a dandy. The town of Camerium was also part of Rome's past, having been 'scrubbed from the map of Roman Italy aeons ago' (Henderson ((1997) 71) but still retained as a cognomen of distinction (cf. 7.90) even though (as Syme (1986) 98 tartly puts it) the family of the Camerinus who was consul in AD 9 had had 'no consul since 345 BC'. One Camerinus faced prosecution for cruelty (Tacitus *Annals* 13.52) and was later put to death by a freedman while Nero was away in Greece because he refused to give up the family cognomen *Pythicus* which the emperor had reserved for himself (Dio Cassius 63.18.2: so much for the power of family names). A runaway slave called Geta tried to pass himself off as 'Scribonianus Camerinus' in the reign of Vitellius and was put to death (Tacitus *Histories* 2. 72) while another was an epic poet (Ovid *ex Ponto* 4.16.19).

39–40 **Rubellius Blandus**. Braund ((1988) 231–32) rightly argues that the man named has to be a 'descendant, preferably a son (42 *conciperet*) of

Julia who in AD 33 married Rubellius Blandus' (see Syme (1982)) but it is difficult to find one. There was a famous Rubellius Plautus (Tacitus *Annals* 13.19) but the man referred to here has to be a nonentity for the argument to stand and attempts to see our man as 'really' Plautus fail on that score. He has to belong to the *Drusorum stemma* (40) – and Julia was the daughter of Drusus who was son of emperor Tiberius (cf. 42 for her 'Julian' blood). Rubellius Plautus was 'as related on his mother's side to the divine Augustus as Nero was' (Tacitus *Annals* 13.19: cf. 72 *Nerone propinquo*) and was widely tipped to replace the emperor Nero (Tacitus *Annals* 14. 22) only to end up being butchered in AD 62 by a centurion sent by the emperor (Tacitus *Annals* 14.58–9) and his head sent back to Rome. This man's behaviour and fame would never merit the sentiment of lines 40–46 (Syme (1982) 81): and so scholars have postulated that the marriage of Julia and Blandus produced another forgotten son, brother to Plautus, for whose existence this passage is the main evidence (Syme (1982) 78 n.102). Syme ((1982) 81) allows that our Blandus may be a 'plausible and malignant invention' just as Henderson ((1997) 93) speculates that he may be 'a 'rhetorical figure whose role is to suffer what he bespeaks': he also plausibly suggests that the name may be significant as *rubellus* is a deep red colour and *blandus* means 'attractive, seductive' but Braund ((1988) 232) reminds us that the name may in fact be the sort of antinomy which lines 32–8 have explored: Blandus' alleged arrogant boorishness as described in 44–6 hardly merits the name 'Blushing sweet-talker' without heavy irony. Uden (2015) 121 cogently suggests that Blandus' lack of a biography may be the whole point: 'the man is no more than his name ... having achieved nothing ... to justify his high status.' The poet turns to address the long-dead Blandus with the device known as apostrophe (cf. 95, 171, 185, 231, 1.50, 2.67, 10.166–7, 13. 81, 15.85–6, Homer *Iliad* 16.843, *Odyssey* 14.55) after the catechism-style question of **who have I been warning** (*his ego quem monui?*, where *quem* is the accusative of the interrogative pronoun *quis*) and with the effective juxtaposition of *tecum mihi* marking the direct contact between the two men. *sermo* (**conversation**) is also the word used by Horace for his two books of *Satires* and so there may be a play on that sense here as Blandus is going to be the butt of this satire. Blandus (if he ever existed) is of course long dead and so the speaker can make final judgements on his character and attitudes: this is good protreptic method in speaking to the young Ponticus who has his future before him and so has the power to make choices which would avoid similar things being said of him as are said here of Blandus.

40   *tumes* (*OLD* s.v. 'tumeo' 4) has the metaphorical sense of **puffed up** with conceit as at Tacitus *Histories* 1.16, Horace *Epistles* 1.1.36, Ovid *Metamorphoses* 15.755–6, although elsewhere in J. it has its literal meaning of 'to be swollen' (3.293, 6. 462, 10.309 and cf. the uses of *tumidus* at 2.13, 13.162, 16.11). At 14.282 there is a sexual overtone ('tumescent') which may also be present here and the image is repeated with the different word *inflatum* at 72. The juxtaposition with *alto* (**lofty**: originally the perfect participle of *alo* and so literally meaning 'fed full') enhances the meaning of both words. *Drusorum* (cf. 21n.) refers to the last three of the Julio-Claudian emperors, i.e. Claudius, Caligula and Nero (cf. *Nerone propinquo* in 72).

40–42   *tamquam* introduces a series of counterfactual subjunctive clauses (**as if you have personally done something** <but you haven't> to deserve the title *nobilis* <which you don't> and to arrange for you to be born to a mother of the Julian race <when it was nothing to do with you>'.) See AG§524, *OLD* s.v. 'tamquam' 5.

41   A very prosaic line giving the lie to the 'persuasive sweet-talking' suggested by the name *Blandus* (39–40n.). The emphasis is thrown onto the key term *nobilis*.

42–43   Two alternative mothers are contrasted but the contrast is one of lifestyle as well as pedigree. Blandus' mother was as noble as it was possible to be – the *gens Iulia* was descended from the founder of the Roman race, the Trojan prince Aeneas, whose son was called Iulus and whose descendants were (it was claimed) the men who ruled Rome from 27 BC onwards (see Virgil *Aeneid* 1.286–8, with Austin (1971) *ad loc.* and cf. Lucretius 1.465, Catullus 64.355, Virgil *Aeneid* 3.359). The 'Trojan' origin of blue-blooded Romans is mentioned again at lines 56 and 181. She only needs to flaunt her **glowing** (*fulget*) name to be well off. The low birth of the other (anonymous) woman is proved by her degrading existence of menial work.

42   **glowing**: *fulget* is a powerful metaphor (see *OLD* s.v. 'fulgeo' 3) and the juxtaposition with *sanguine* (for which cf. 2n.) produces a striking image: the nearest parallels are Seneca *Medea* 209 (*quondam nobili fulsi patre* ('once I shone with the nobility of my father')) and Silius Italicus 17.12 (*multa fulgebat imagine auorum* ('shone with the many images of his ancestors')). The verb *fulget* contrasts strongly with *texit* in emphatic final position on the next line.

43   The *agger* (cf. 5.153–5, 6.588, 16.25, *OLD* s.v. 'agger' 2c) was the **embankment** surrounding the city of Rome, built by Servius Tullius (Livy 1.44.3) or Tarquinius Superbus (Pliny *N.H.* 3.67), used as a favourite place

to walk (Horace *Satires* 1.8.15) and connecting the Esquiline to the Colline
Gate (Livy 1.44.3). It deserved the epithet 'windy' (*uentoso*) because of
its height and was known as a place to encounter fortune-tellers (6.588)
and performing monkeys (5.153–5). Weaving was a decent occupation for
noble women (cf. e.g. Lucretia at Livy 57.9) but this one does so out of
necessity and is working **for hire** (*conducta*: cf. Tibullus 1.6.79). There may
be an ironic reference to Helen who walks along the walls of 'windy' Troy
(Homer *Iliad* 3.154) and is seen as a disgrace to her sex and her family even
by herself (*Iliad* 3.180). Blandus despises plebs (44–6) but could easily have
been one but for an accident of birth.

44   **inferiors**: the people are addressed as *humiles* (cf. 3.39, 6.287 (where
humilis fortuna means 'slender means'), 6.414, 9.48, 11.171) which may
have legal status since *honestiores* (senators, *equites* and others of like status)
enjoyed freedom from humiliating punishments denied to the *humiliores*
(*plebs* and slaves): see *CAH* xi. 851–2. The line is framed with the key
antithetical words *uos…nostri*, and the ellipsis of the word *estis* ('you are')
makes the phrase sound like a derisory vocative, glossed with a second
abusive phrase to follow. *uulgus* is a common pejorative term for 'common
people' (cf. 3.36–7, 7.85, 10.51, 10.89, 11.3, 15.29, 126) but these people
are the **lowest section** of that low: *pars ultima* here has the sense of 'the
dregs' as at 6.O12, and the phrasing is reminiscent of Lucan 6.593–4. The
major manuscripts read the third-person verb *inquit* but the correction of
later scribes to *inquis* has been followed by most modern editors, addressing
Rubellius Blandus and so doubling the dialogue form whereby the speaker
addresses Blandus and quotes his address to others. The earlier reading
might be a scribal 'correction' to avoid confusion about who is addressed:
but *inquis* is supported by the second-person verbs addressed by the speaker
to Blandus in 46–8.

45   The insult is extreme. Not knowing one's father is bad enough, but not
knowing one's **fatherland** suggests that the father in question was a slave of
foreign extraction. It was common in Latin to call somebody of low (or no)
birth a *terrae filius* ('son of the earth') as at 4.98, Persius 6.57–9, Petronius
43, Otto (1890) s.v. 'terra' 2.

46   **Cecropid**: Cecrops was a mythical king of Athens and so the
patronymic *Cecropides* declares the oldest pedigree, allowing the speaker
to be able to trace his ancestry back to legendary times (see Otto (1890)
s.v. 'Cecrops'). The phrase is mocking, however: Cecrops was famously
indigenous (αὐτόχθων) to the land of Attica and so was 'earthborn' in a

literal sense: and yet the speaker mocks others for being *humiles* (derived from the word *humus* meaning 'earth'). The name *Cecropides* and the adjectival *Cecropius* came to mean 'Athenian' in Greek (Herodotus 8.44, Aristophanes *Knights* 1055) and 'Greek' in Latin, especially epic (e.g. Virgil *Aeneid* 6.21, Ovid *Ars Am.* 3.457, *Metamorphoses* 6.667, 7.671, *Fasti* 3.81, Statius *Thebaid* 12.570, Silius Italicus 13.484). J. elsewhere (6.187) uses the cognate term *Cecropis* of a noble Athenian woman (cf. *Cecropiam* at 2.92). J. is mocking this Roman for using the Greek term as self-praise (cf. 14 for the use of Greek heroes as ancestors); the following passage will show Roman plebeians excelling in the archetypically Roman skills of oratory, law and military glory while the indolent 'Greek' aristocrat sits idly by. **Long life ... may you**: the speaker wishes Blandus well with a sentiment framed by the two subjunctive verbs (*uiuas...feras*). *uiuas* (literally 'may you live') could have the sense of 'farewell' as at Virgil *Eclogues* 8.58, Horace *Satires* 2.5.110, *Epistles* 6.67, with the more usual generalised *uale* replaced by the specific wish *originis...feras*. It is also used as a toast ('long life to you') at Lucilius 70W: but the primary meaning 'may you live' will be picked up at 55 where Blandus is described as only different from a mutilated statue in that he is a **living statue** (*uiuit imago*).

47 *longa* has temporal significance (**long-lasting**) here as at (e.g.): 6.221, 6.292, 9.16, 10.190, 10.204, 14.158, 14.251, 15.82, 15.96, Catullus 76.13. The word is well chosen here as the ancestry (going back to Cecrops) is itself lengthy (cf. *longo* / *sanguine* line 1) and the poet wishes a long future of joy to match this long past.

47–52 The poet describes three typical professions in which the able poor man can surpass nobles: oratory, legal work and military service. The three are combined as routes to advancement at Livy 39.40.5, Tacitus *Dialogus* 28.7 (see Mayer (2001) *ad loc.*): at 14.191–207 the poet mentions legal work, military service and trade as sources of high income for the son of the ambitious father.

47 **citizen**: *Quiritem* denotes a Roman citizen (cf. *OLD* s.v. 'Quirites' 2, Lucan 2.386) 'especially in contexts in which the poorest and most insignificant Roman is granted the dignity of his status as citizen' (Kißel (1990) on Persius 5.75). The phrasing of Ovid *Ars Am.* 1.7.29 (*minimum de plebe Quiritem*) is close to J.'s language here (cf. also Ovid *Amores* 3.14.9 *Tristia* 2.569).

48–9 **articulate**: *facundum* announces the first category of talented plebeian with its emphatic position and the contrast of the able plebeian and the uneducated (*indocti*) nobleman is pointed. The figure of the 'poor boy turned barrister' can be found also at Tacitus *Dialogus* 8.3, Petronius 46. The most notable man to turn oratory into a route to high office was Cicero as discussed at 243–4 (cf. also 10.114–126); but Cicero is described at 7.139–140 as a man who would not find work in J.'s own day as the highest a lawyer could aspire to was the centumviral courtroom which argued cases of inheritance – unless one wished to make one's name prosecuting the enemies of the (current) emperor (cf. Gibson (2020) 88). The asyndeton and juxtaposition of the verbs *inuenies solet* may evoke the language of the spoken word in full flow, but the 'parataxis is awkward' (Brown (1972) 374) and the sentence would run more smoothly (with pleasing juxtaposition of *inuenies ueniet*) if the whole phrase *solet ... indocti* were deleted as an interpolation.

49–50 legal puzzles: the *iurisconsultus* (see *OLD* s.v. 'consultus²') was a legal expert who could rise to fame and fortune by his legal expertise, defined by Cicero *de Oratore* 1.212 as the man 'who is an expert in the statutes, and in the legal practice observed by private citizens in the state, who is qualified to make rulings on points of law (*respondere*), to initiate legal proceedings (*agere*) and to protect (*cauere*) his client' (see Crook (1967) 25–7, 88). J. elsewhere (4.75–81) mentions the lawyer Plotius Pegasus who rose to the rank of consul and city prefect (but see Syme (1958) 805), but he does not qualify as one who rose from the lowest ranks of society: Horace's Trebatius (*Satires* 2.1) was of equestrian origins. J. appears to distinguish between civil rights (*iuris*) and statutory laws (*legum*) but the terms are often joined in describing the principles of legal practice (cf. Cicero *pro Plancio* 95.9, *de Oratore* 1.48.6, *Orator* 120.5, *de Legibus* 1.17) and Horace describes a man such as this as *iuris legumque peritus* (*Satires* 1.1.9). The two nouns here go with two metaphors for legal intricacy: *nodos* ('knots') is a common enough term in describing verbal and conceptual intricacy (cf. Seneca *Letters* 45.5, 82.19 (*nodos*), Horace *Satires* 2.3.70 (*nodosus*) and cf. the verb *enodo* ('to de-knot') as used in the sense of 'untie complexity' at Cicero *de Legibus* 1.26, *Rhet. ad Herrennium* 2.15, Gellius 3.10), while *aenigmata* was the Greek word for 'riddles', commonly associated with the riddle of the Sphinx (Quintilian *I.O.* 6.3.98, Pliny *N.H.* 34.48, Martial 1.90.9, Sophocles *Oedipus Tyrannus* 393, 1525) but also often used of obscure language (e.g. Cicero *de Oratore* 3.167, Petronius 41.4, Quintilian *I.O.* 8.6.52, Pliny *Epistles* 7.13.1, Aeschylus *Agamemnon* 1112, 1183). **untie**: *soluat* is the *mot juste* for 'untying' knots both literal and also metaphorical as here (*OLD* s.v.

'soluo' 16): similar phrasing (*soluuntur...aenigmata*) is found at Quintilian 8.6.53. In line 49 most mss. read *plebe*, while one (F) reads *gente*. Housman proposes reading *pube*, suggesting that *plebe* was written in error from line 47 and comparing the same corruption at line 256 (and Statius *Thebaid* 1.619) where Φ reads *plebe* but P reads *pube*. This would however remove the key term for 'non-noble birth' which is the whole point of the passage, and his argument that *plebs togata* requires that *ima plebs* must mean 'the plebs who wear a tunic rather than a toga' (cf. Tacitus *Dialogus* 7.16 for the distinction) is not strong. It has been suggested (by Dunbabin (1925) 113 and Courtney, picking up an emendation first proposed by Scriverius in 1705) that the phrase would be improved further with the emendation of *togata* to *togatus*: but again this is not necessary as the use of adjectival *togatus* is common: cf. 1.96, Propertius 4.2.56 (*turba togata*), Virgil *Aeneid* 1.282 (*gentemque togatam*: cf. Statius *Siluae* 1.6.36, Gellius 1.2.4), Livy 45.37 (*contionem togatam*) Seneca *de Beneficiis* 3.26.1 (*togatam ciuitatem*), Martial 2.57.5 (*grex togatus*). The toga was the symbol of the citizen (cf. 7.142–3 and Vout (1996) 215) and the civilian (as opposed to the military man such as will appear in 51 and again at 240: cf. 10.8–9 for the distinction). **51–2** *hinc* means **from this class** (i.e. from the plebeians) as at 2.156 (*OLD* s.v. 'hinc' 1b). The **Euphrates** marked the eastern boundary of the Roman empire as the Rhine marks the northern frontier: for the use of the two frontiers as symbols of the extent of Roman rule and the threat to Roman peace cf. 8.169–70, Virgil *Georgics* 1.509, *Aeneid* 8. 726–7, Statius *Silvae* 5.1.89–90. They are later mentioned as places where Lateranus ought to be headed (169–70, where see notes) and the Euphrates was a familiar destination for military service (cf. e.g. Statius *Silvae* 3.2.136). Trajan campaigned there (see *CAH* xi.308–10, Garzetti (1974) 363–73) in AD 114–116 which may make it topical here. The **Batavian** refers to the German tribe (*Bataui*) living on the Gallic side of the river Rhine who supplied 'men and weapons' to the Romans and 'increased their glory' by service in Britain (Tacitus *Histories* 4.12: see Hassall (1970)). They were members of the emperor's bodyguard but also revolted unsuccessfully against Roman rule in AD 69–70 (Tacitus *Histories* 4.12–37, 54–79, 5.14–26: their defeat was attributed to Domitian (Silius 3.607–8, Josephus *Jewish War* 7.84). The term *Batauus* became synonymous with 'barbaric' (Martial 6.82.6: Lucan (1.431) calls them *truces* ('savage')). Germans were pre-eminent in courage (Tacitus *Germania* 29.1) and deemed to be *ferox* (Tacitus *Histories* 1.59) which makes their subject status beneath the Roman eagles (*domiti*

Bataui/ custodes aquilas) all the more remarkable. The image of an eagle was the military standard of a Roman legion (*OLD* s.v. 'aquila' 2) and here these **eagles** are envisaged as guarding the German tribe, the phrase being juxtaposed with *armis industrius* (**tireless in fighting**) which helps to explain the victory by the energy of the *iuuenis*.

52–3   After the fulsome description of the successful and hard-working plebeians the speaker rounds on his 'noble' addressee with a string of finger-jabbing monosyllables (*at tu/ nil*) before reminding him of his boast at 46, here cut down both by the preceding *nil nisi* (you are 'nothing but' a *Cecropides*) and by the brilliant comparison with a herm.

53   A **Herm** was a small, squat statue of the Greek god Hermes (the Roman god Mercury) which stood outside houses in ancient Athens showing typically a bearded face and a phallos: in 415 these images were defaced (Thucydides 6. 27–9), an act of sacrilege blamed on (oligarchic) men keen to overthrow the democracy (Thucydides 6.27.3) and later attributed to the aristocratic rake Alcibiades (Lysias 12.41–2) which gives the incident possible political connection to the argument of this poem. Herms were already less than full figures – but this one is even more **stunted** (*trunco*) and the obvious way to deface a herm is to remove its phallus (cf. Aristophanes *Lysistrata* 1094) giving a comedic innuendo to the insult. *truncus* also means 'tree-trunk' (as at Horace *Satires* 1.8.1) and Blandus is thus compared to a common image of a blockhead (cf. Catullus 17.18–22). Geue ((2017) 117) suggests that *trunco* may be a reference to Rubellius Plautus who was decapitated (Tacitus *Annals* 14.59: see 39–40n.) for his alleged potential as a replacement for the emperor Nero and so became literally *truncus*.

54–5   The insult continues with what appears to be a compliment giving Blandus one advantage over the herm: the statue has a **marble head**, whereas Blandus is alive – but the final word *imago* shows that this is yet another insult as the speaker alleges that the only part of Blandus which is alive is his *imago* – a thing which is usually inanimate (see 1–2nn.). Uden ((2015) 121–2) well comments: 'that Blandus can be reduced to a 'living bust' is a sign of his indolence and uselessness … he is merely the breathing personification of his ancestral line. That he differs from a Herm only in the head … also suggests the complete stone-like inactivity of the rest of his body (he is even perhaps the end of his line, since he is after all like a mutilated herm). Yet there is significant … ambiguity in the phrase, since in another sense Roman aristocrats were indeed expected to be the living personification of their *imagines* … The ambiguity between these two meanings of *uiuit imago*, both a deprecation of aristocratic listlessness and the statement of a venerable Roman ideal, encapsulates the problem on which *Satire* 8 is focused ... the very emptiness of this contemporary Blandus calls into question the reliability of the past as a guarantor of the present. He is nothing *but* the past, a living bust.' The paradox is enhanced by the swapping of terms: we expect the poet to say that the *imago* is marble while the head is alive.

56 offspring of the Trojans: the speaker mocks the pretensions of the man who claimed to be a Cecropid (46) with the mock-epic phrase *Teucrorum proles*: cf. 42–3n. for the 'Trojan' origin of the Romans and cf. also *Troiugenae* at 181, 1.100, 11.95 and *Troades* at Persius 1.4. *dic mihi* is an indignant imperative as at 6.393. **Tell ... dumb**: line 56 is framed with words for speech and silence (*dic ... muta*), beginning with an arresting imperative.

57 *putet* is a potential subjunctive: not 'who thinks' but **who could think**. **dumb animals**: *animalia muta* is something of a cliché (cf. e.g. Lucretius 5.1087–8, Columella *de Re Rustica* 9.9.2, Horace *Satires* 1.3.99–100, Manilius 2.99, Petronius 140.15, Quintilian 1.2.20, 1.10.7, 5.13.23, Seneca *Dialogi* 3.3.6, 4.26.4, *Epistles* 74.16, 76.26, 90.45, Tacitus *Histories* 4.17) and the adjective stands alone at 15.143 (*a grege mutorum*) to denote animals as distinct from humans (see my note *ad loc.*). The word is however pointed here: Romans such as Rubellius speak of their nobility but do nothing, whereas animals say nothing but prove their worth by their actions. **well-bred**: *generosa* is commonly applied to people (cf. 30–32n.) and here has provocative value when applied to animals, although the word is applied to a foal by Virgil *Georgics* 3.75 and Horace calls a ship a *siluae filia nobilis* at *Odes* 1.14.12. Analogies from the animal world are common in philosophy and satire: J. compares the behaviour of birds/animals and humans also at: 14.74–85, 15.159–64 and cf. (e.g.) Plato *Apology* 20a7, Xenophon *Mem.* 2.7.13–14, Aesop *Fables*, Quintilian 5.11.4, Horace *Epistles* 1.2.64–67, 7.29–33, 14.43, *Satires* 1.90–1 (asses), 2.86–89 (horses) and the extended tale of the town mouse and country mouse in *Satires* 2.6.79–117. The basic argumentation is familiar from J.'s near-contemporaries Quintilian (*I.O.* 5.11.5) as well as Epictetus (fr. 18.6–9) and Dio Chrysostom *Orationes* 15.30–31, but J. injects his own characteristic force into the form.

57 *nempe* introduces a strong assertion whose validity cannot be doubted: cf. 164, 180, 10.110, 185, *OLD* s.v. 'nempe' 1a. *uolucrem* (see *OLD* s.v. 'uolucer' 2a) is from the adjectival *uolucer* here (**swift**) rather than the noun *uolucris* ('bird') and there may be an implicit reference to the myth of the flying horse Pegasus.

58–9   *plurima* agrees with *uictoria* (contrasted with *rara ... uictoria* in 63) and *facili* goes with *palma* as ablative of cause: *uictoria* is the subject of both verbs *feruet* and *exultat*. The rapturous applause is well conveyed with the plosive alliteration of *plurima palma*, the adjective *rauco* (**hoarse** from shouting, applied here in hypallage to the Circus itself as at 9.144 *clamoso ... Circo*) and the pair of verbs *feruet et exultat* – where the length of the phrase enacts the extended applause. *feruet* (**seething**) is a 'heat' metaphor whose basic meaning is 'to boil' and here means 'to be hot with passion' (*OLD* s.v. 'ferueo' 5b: cf. 3.49–50, 5.29) and/or to 'seethe' (11.51), while *exultat* (originally *ex-sultat*) suggests 'leaping with joy' as at 15.87. *feruet et ex(s) ultat* is a direct quotation from Ovid *Metamorphoses* 7. 263 where it describes the boiling and foaming of a pot of magic herbs being used by Medea: Braund (1981) comments well that the use of the Ovid passage invites us to 'see the Circus as a rounded container, analogous to the cauldron', reminding us that similar description of the noisy games is to be found at 11. 197–8. Alternative readings take *palma* as nominative with *plurima* and *feruet* ('many a palm boils': cf. Martial 7.28.6) with the suggestion that *palma* here means 'palm of the hand' being heated in applause: but the following lines (*victoria ... ante alios et primus ... puluis*) make it clear that victory secured by coming first in the race is what is being celebrated and the 'palm' was the symbol of this in contests real (e.g. Petronius 70.13, Lucretius 4.989, Virgil *Aeneid* 5.70, 7.655–6) and metaphorical (6.323, 11.181, Martial 4.23.4, Catullus 62.11) and both in one line (Ovid *Amores* 3.2.82). The sport being watched is chariot-racing which took place in the Circus Maximus, which could hold 250,000 people. The venue attracted capacity crowds (Suetonius *Augustus* 43), and the chariot-races were organised in four 'factions' with the colours: red, green, white and blue.

60   **pedigree**: *nobilis* is a word with a long history in Roman political history (see e.g. Gelzer (1969) 27–40), denoting one whose ancestors have held the position of consul: it is here applied provocatively to horses, with *gramine* standing as the equine equivalent of 'family background' (cf. 27) and with the even more provocative depiction of flight which in humans would be cowardice but which in horses is glorious.

61   **running is clear**: *clarus* also means 'glorious' so that *clara fuga* is oxymoronic, as *fuga* generally means 'desertion' or 'running away' (cf. 2.64, 144, 6.253, 339, 8.206, 10.160, 15.75) which is the opposite of 'glorious'.

To be *ante alios et primus* was the goal of many ancient males (cf. Homer *Iliad* 6.208), while ending up mere dust is something to dread (cf. Propertius 2.13.35, Horace *Odes* 4.7.16), but in this context of horse-racing the *puluis* is the guarantor of glory, emphasised at the end of the line.

62–3 Coryphaeus and **Hirpinus** (Martial 3.63.12) were famous horses in chariot-racing teams. *Coryphaeus* (a Greek word for 'leader' (κορυφαῖος: cf. Herodotus 3.82)) is apt here; the Hirpini lived in Samnium (modern Irpinia) and so *Hirpinus* refers to the geographical origin of the horse. This horse was a well-known winner (*CIL* 6.10069) and is mentioned by Martial (3.63.12): the *bellus homo* Cotilus has access to the best horse 'and he well knows the ancient pedigree of Hirpinus'. The rhythm of the end of 62 with its final monosyllable and clash of ictus and accent suggests the limping sluggish gait of the inferior horse and the pompous phrase *Coryphaei posteritas* (cf. 1.148) is a sardonic way to describe what the poet has just called a *uenale pecus*. *posteritas* is a word for human descendants here applied to animals, while *pecus* is a pejorative term for any group of animals but applied to the first humans in Horace's scathing phrase *mutum et turpe pecus* ('dumb and vile herd' *Satires* 1.3.100). *uenale* makes it clear that these slow horses are to be sold for whatever they will fetch (65–6). The sentence ends with the fine metaphor of the goddess Victory (cf. *OCD* s.v. 'Victoria') sitting on the **yoke** (*iugo*) of the chariot: this goddess was often depicted as winged (cf. *uolucrem* 57) but the closing verb is one of immobility which well suits the horse which does not win the races. *rara* agrees with *Victoria* but has adverbial sense here (**rarely**).

64–5 No ... no: line 64 is framed by the negatives *nil ... nulla* and the sentence uses an asyndetic chiasmus of *maiorum respectus: gratia ... umbrarum*. *respectus* (**regard for**) literally means 'looking back at' (*OLD* s.v. 'respectus' 1) which suits the notion of reviewing past ancestors (*maiorum*: an objective genitive). *umbrarum* refers to the **shades** of the dead ancestors (cf. 2.157, 10.258, 13.52): if *gratia* has its common meanings of 'regard for' or 'favour shown towards somebody' (*OLD* s.v. 'gratia' 1, 4) then *umbrarum* is an objective genitive ('no regard for the ghosts') but Dimatteo ((2014) 96) also suggests that the ghosts may be (not) conferring the favour and so the genitive is subjective: the ambiguity is perhaps intentional.

65–6 A vivid picture of equine weakness: the horses are now passively **told** (*iubentur*) to change their **masters** for **tiny** sums of money, with the key word *exiguis* emphasised in enjambement. *domini mutatio* was the legal term whereby a slave was transferred to another master (cf. Cicero *ad Att.* 12.19.1, 14.14.4, *ad Brutum* 24.1, Seneca *de Beneficiis* 6.1).

66–7　drag ... millstone: the former stars of the race-track are reduced to dragging carriages and turning millstones. **slow-footed**: the compound adjective *segnipedes* – a word which only occurs here in Latin – is in emphatic position and describes both the cause and the effect of the work endured, since even the fastest race-horse would be 'slow-footed' when compelled to pull carts or turn millstones. The compound adjective (cf. *sonipedes* (Accius *Trag* 603) *quadripedes* (Virgil *Aeneid* 3.542), *cornipedes* (Virgil *Aeneid* 7.779)) adds something of an archaic epic tone to the line and the word *nepotes* (more commonly used of human descendants rather than animals) ends the line with similar mock-gravity, especially with the qualifying adjective *digni*. A *raeda* was a 'four-wheeled travelling carriage' (*OLD*: cf. 3.10. 4.118) and the rare word *epiraedium* derives from Gallic (Pliny *NH* 3.123: see Hendry (1999) 299 n.12, Schmidt (1967) 165–6) and may suggest that the glory of the Roman Circus is now abroad in servile labour: certainly the effect of the work is felt on the **worn** neck of the horse. The effect of hard labour on the necks of animals is something of a topos in Roman literature (cf. 14.146, Catullus 64.38, Virgil *Eclogues* 6.50, *Georgics* 3.167) and the subjection of the neck is a common image of slavery (cf. Horace *Satires* 2.7.92, Statius *Achilleid* 1.944) or sacrifice (10.269). Here the juxtaposition of the adjectives *exiguis trito* adds force to both words. Millstones were usually turned by asses rather than horses (Ovid *Ars Am.* 3.290, Plautus *Asinaria* 709, Cato *Agr.* 11.1): cf. Phaedrus *Fab. Appendix* 19 for this scenario of a race-horse being sold to turn the mill. What makes this more pointed is that being sent to work the mill was a punishment for slaves and criminals (Plautus *Pers.* 22, Terence *Andria* 199, Catullus 97.10, Apuleius 9.12, Millar (1984) 126, 129–30) and so the destination is the ultimate in social degradation for people as well as horses. The major manuscripts are both palpably wrong on line 66: *tritoque* (Φ) and *et trito* (P) are both metrically impossible and we have to rely on later mss. for better readings: it may be suspected that scribes saw the postponed connective (*et*) and tried to 'correct' it in the two most obvious ways, either by word order or substitution of a connective (*que*) which commonly goes after a word which it is connecting.

68　And so: *ergo* is a common word when Juvenal is drawing conclusions: see 37–8n. The contrast between what a man is and what he has (in the way of ancestral achievements) is well brought out with the antithetical phrase *te non tua* and the line ends strongly with a clash of ictus and accent and a singular imperative (*da*). *priuum* denotes something which is the property of the individual (cf. Horace *Satires* 2.5.11, *Epistles* 1.1.93) and makes good sense here, although the mss. reading *primum* ('first show me...') is not obviously wrong.

69   could: *possim* is a potential subjunctive after *aliquid* (**something ... which I could chisel**). A *titulus* is a 'commemorative tablet on which details of a person's career etc are inscribed' (*OLD* s.v. 'titulus' 1b), especially used of the listing at the base of a statue of the honours earned: cf. 1.130, 5.110, 6.230, 8.241, 10.143, Horace *Odes* 4.14.4, [Tibullus] 3.7.33). *incīdere* (from *in-caedere*) is the word for chiselling inscriptions (see *OLD* s.v. 'incido' 3).

70   give (and have given): note the polyptoton of *damus ac dedimus* (cf. 3.190), bringing out the ongoing honours being given to the family, and the triple alliteration of 'd' in the line. **those**: *illis* is picked up and explained by the final phrase (*quibus omnia debes*), which recalls Antony's scathing rebuke to the young Octavian as 'one who owes everything to his name' (*qui omnia nomini debes*: Cicero *Philippics* 13.24.14, Syme (1939) 191). The final word is suitably one of obligation (cf. 24), reminding the reader of the *noblesse oblige* theme of this powerful paragraph.

71   We have to understand *sunt* with *haec satis* and the ellipsis enacts the 'cutting off' of the address to the man – Blandus was once a *iuuenem* (see 39–40n.) with his life in front of him. The juxtaposition of *fama superbum* is deliberate: *fama* can mean **reputation** (as at 15.93) and here would have to refer to his arrogant manner – but the word also has the sense of 'glory' (*OLD* s.v. 'fama' 7: cf. 76 below and 6.500, 7.39, 7.79, 10.114, 10.125, 10.140, 11.23, Tacitus *Agricola* 18.7) and the juxtaposition suggests a connection between the pride and the 'renown/reputation'.

72   puffed up ... full: note the expressive pleonasm of *inflatum plenumque*. The image recreates the growth from 'swelling' (*tumes* (40)) to being positively 'full', and *inflatum* (literally 'inflated with air') well evokes the fatuous emptiness of Blandus' self-image. Blandus' connection with Nero was explored at 39–40n.: here it has moral as well as chronological force. **connections**: the adjective *propinquo* stands for the abstract noun, so that (e.g.) *Neronis propinquitate* becomes *Nerone propinquo* (cf. 1.163, 12.127: KS ii. § 138, 766–770, *NLS* 75–6). *plenus* (which can take either the genitive or the ablative (as here: 'filled with')) renders the image grotesque with the suggestion that Blandus is 'stuffed' with his relative Nero.

73–4   A generalisation (qualified slightly by *ferme* (cf. 13.236)) about people in **that income-bracket** – with the key word *fortuna* stressed in enjambement – to explain why the speaker need say no more, with *rarus* here recalling the remarks about the *rarus ciuis* in 27–8. *sensus communis* has to mean something like 'fellow-feeling' or **empathy** as at 15.133, 15.146, Horace *Satires* 1.3.66 (see Thompson (1920), *OLD* s.vv. 'sensus' 6c, 'communis' 5c). *fortuna* (literally 'great wealth') here stands for the people who have it, as at 11.176, Tacitus *Histories* 2.61, *OLD* s.v. 'fortuna' 11b: it carries here the strong sense also of unearned wealth which arrive thanks to chance (*fors*: cf. 7.197–8).

74–6 The speaker sets up a contrast between the family's past (*tuorum*) and the individual's future (*ipse futurae*).

74 assessed: *censeri* (cf. 2n.) is the *mot juste* for the classifying of citizens into their tribes and centuries – a task performed on criteria of citizen status and property (see *OCD* s.v. 'census'): the word also has the wider sense of 'to evaluate the worth of' (*OLD* s.v. 'censeo' 8) which is the primary meaning here.

75–6 I would not: *noluerim* is a perfect potential subjunctive (cf. *crediderim* at 15.21, 2.24, 6.651, *NLS* 90). The genitive case of *futurae laudis* is partitive with *nihil* and the word *laudis* has the sense of 'praiseworthy act' (*OLD* s.v. 'laus' 3b, Virgil *Aeneid* 10.825), picking up *laude* from 74.

76 pathetic: *miserum* contrasts with the positive *laudis* just mentioned; and the instability of the dependence on others is enacted in the double elision of *miser(um) est alior(um) incumbere*, as Dimatteo ((2014) 104) points out. *incumbere* ('to lean on' in the sense of 'to depend') is metaphorical here (*OLD* s.v. 'incumbo' 3b: cf 14.122) but literal at 15.128. The use of the word in building contexts (such as Martial 5.13.5, Statius *Thebaid* 7.44) leads neatly onto the metaphor of the collapsing building. The metaphor of 'leaning on *fama*' is surprising as *fama* is most often depicted as something in motion (e.g. Virgil *Aeneid* 4.666).

77 columns … ruins: the juxtapositions of *collapsa ruant* reinforces the image of collapse and then *tecta columnis* (cf. Martial 2.14.9, 5.13.5) shows the debris which results.

78 vine-shoot: imagery from viticulture is not uncommon in wine-drinking Rome (cf. Catullus 62.48–52): for the practice of 'marrying' the vine to the elm for support cf. 6.150 (with Watson and Watson (2014) *ad loc.*), Virgil *Georgics* 1.2, 2.367, Horace *Epodes* 2.9–10, Pliny *NH* 17.199, Watson (2003) 93, *OCD* s.v. 'wine'. The pathetic fallacy of *desiderat* (**longs for**) is strong (cf. Ovid *Amores* 2.16.41 for a similar usage which is (like this) part of an analogy) and made even stronger by the juxtaposition with *uiduas* (literally 'bereaved') which is itself a common metaphor for the unsupported vine (cf. Catullus 62.49, Horace *Odes* 4.5.30). The connection of thought from the collapsed building (77) to the vine trailing on the ground is natural and pleasing.

79–80 soldier ... guardian ... judge: the speaker lists available aspirations for public service, with neat chiasmus of *bonus miles tutor bonus* and emphasis on the enjambed *integer*. The imperative *esto* is emphasised by its position and its repetition (cf. 5.112–3: at 8.164 the word scans *estō* (as commonly in verse: cf. Catullus 103.2, Horace *Epode* 8.11, *Satires* 1.6.19, Martial 2.88.2, Ovid *Heroides* 20.66) but here has to scan *estŏ* as at Ovid *Tristia* 4.3.72). The virtues of being a good **soldier** are obvious: cf. 8.51–2, 14.72, Horace *Odes* 3.2.1–16. *tutor* indicates a **guardian**, 'appointed to look after the interests of a person incapable of managing his own affairs' (*OLD* s.v. 'tutor'), a role which invited abuse: see 15.135–6n. and cf. 1.46–7, 6.629–30, 10.222–3, Horace *Epistles* 2.1.122–3, Persius 2.12–14 (with Kißel (1990) 304), Crook (1967) 113–16. *arbiter* indicates a form of legal **judge**, especially in cases of land and/or inheritance (Crook (1967) 78, 82) where it was vital for the *arbiter* to be free from bias (see *OLD* s.v. 'integer' 13 and cf. Horace *Odes* 1.22.1, Martial 6.28.6). *idem* here means 'also, at the same time' (*OLD* s.v. 'idem' 8 cf. 10.331).

80–84 The mention of the legal *arbiter* leads neatly to the responsibility of being a truthful **witness** in court. Witnesses were vital in establishing the truth in court in an age which lacked forensic science and photography, and such people were also liable to be bribed or threatened to induce them to lie. The image of the man enduring pain and death in order to do the right thing is a commonplace in philosophy and literature: cf. for instance Regulus who returned to torture and death in Carthage rather than break his word (Horace *Odes* 3.5): and the concept of heroic suicide in preference to disgrace, as seen in legend (e.g. Ajax in Sophocles' *Ajax*) and in history (e.g. Cato Uticensis: see 14.41–3n., Diogenes Laertius 7.130, LS i.428–9, Sandbach (1975) 48–52)) became a Stoic theme (cf. 15.106–8). The language of this passage recalls Horace *Odes* 4.9.50–52, Seneca *Epistles* 66.21 but – while the use of the *topos* of Phalaris may cause the tone to sound hyperbolic and bathetic (Braund (1988) 114, Fredericks (1971) 122) – torture was used in real life. The freedwoman Epicharis, for instance, was tortured (to no avail) by Nero to extract information against the Pisonian conspiracy (Tacitus *Annals* 15.57).

80 *si quando* has the force of **if ever** (*OLD* s.v. 'quando' 4: cf. 3.173, 5.40, 12.23). *cito* is commonly used of 'summoning' a witness (*OLD* s.v.

'cito' 4b, Cicero *pro Quinctio* 37) and *testis* is in apposition with the subject of the verb. *ambiguae* and *incertae* (used together also at Tacitus *Annals* 1.11, Virgil *Aeneid* 8.580) are the key words here as cases where the issue was uncontested would be harder to win by lying: J. elsewhere (16.35–50) explores the plight of the man fighting a legal case against superior odds.

81–2　Phalaris (see *OCD* s.v. 'Phalaris') was the tyrant of Agrigentum in Sicily, famous for torturing his enemies by roasting them in a huge bull-shaped bronze vessel, so that their screams of pain sounded like the bellowing of a bull (cf. Pindar *Pythian* 1.95–6, Persius 3.39, Ovid *Tristia* 3.11.39–44, *Ibis* 437–40). Epicurus was said to have asserted that the wise man could be happy even when he is bring roasted in the bronze bull of Phalaris (see Cicero *in Pisonem* 42, *Tusculan Disputations* 2.7.17, Seneca *Epistles* 66.18) although his extant fragments say something different ('Even when on the rack the wise man is happy … but he will moan and groan' Diogenes Laertius 10.118) and Aristotle (*Nicomachean Ethics* 1153b19) also disputed the general principle. The image of the tyrant and his bull became a *topos* in ancient literature (see Otto (1890) s.v. 'Phalaris').

81　The scansion *rēī* is unusual: *licet* with the subjunctives (*imperet ... dictet*) here (and at 85) has concessive force (**even though**) and the final monosyllables (*ut sis*) suggest the finger-jabbing tyrant.

82　to lie: *falsus* is a common word to describe a lying witness: cf. 14.218 (where the witness sells *periuria*), 16.32. The imagery is vividly drawn, with the fatal **bull** dragged out for use (*admoto ... tauro*) as the tyrant **dictates** (*dictet*) the lies demanded. *Dictare* is a strengthened form of *dicere*, used elsewhere (14.29) of the wicked woman dictating love-letters for her daughter to use: while *admouere* (used of applying torture also at e.g. Horace *Odes* 3.21.13) is elsewhere used of leading live animals (*OLD* s.v. 'admoueo' 2) including bulls (Seneca *Oedipus* 334), thus injecting life into this bronze instrument of torture.

83–4　think it: this point is repeated later on at 195–7. Note here the peremptory imperative (*crede*), the plosive alliteration (*praeferre pudori*) and the marked juxtaposition of *uitam uiuendi*: line 84 is as spondaic as is possible for a hexameter, the weighty syllables bringing out the *grauitas* of the statement. **existence**: the *anima* is the 'soul' or 'life' of the individual (*OLD* s.v. 'anima' 3) which is here preferred to *pudor* (**honour**: cf. 10.329, 11.154, 16.34) in the sense that the witness would prefer to be a living sinner than a dead saint. The phrase *uiuendi ... causas* ('the reasons for living') assumes that life is only worth living when it is lived morally: elsewhere (11.11) J. notes men whose *uiuendi causa* is food and Pliny (Ep. 1.12.3) runs through a range of *uiuendi causae*. The phrasing here is intentionally paradoxical (men are too attached to life to keep reasons for living: cf. Lucretius 3.79–82, where men are so frightened of death that they commit suicide).

85–6   is not alive: *perīt* is the perfect tense (*periit*) of *pereo* (cf. 10.118) and so means 'is <already> dead': the thought is close to Lucretius 3.1045–6 where the man terrified of death is one 'whose life is almost dead already although he lives and sees' (*mortua cui uita est prope iam uiuo atque uidenti*). The theme of the morally bankrupt being as good as dead has a long history in Latin (cf. Plautus *Bacch.* 485, Sallust *Catiline* 2.8) and the idea that life is not worth living under certain conditions underpins J.'s account of old age in 10.188–288, 358–9 and reminds us of Socrates' dictum (Plato *Apology* 38a) that 'the unexamined life is not worth living' (cf. also Sophocles *Oedipus Coloneus* 1692–3, Xenophon *Memorabilia* 4.8.8). *ostrea* are **oysters**, a byword for lavish eating (cf. 4.140–1, 6.302, 11.49, Horace *Satires* 2.2.21–2, 2.4.32, *Epodes* 2.49 (with Watson (2003) 114–15), Martial 3.60.3, Pliny *Ep.*1.15.2, Andrews (1948)). J. increases the opulence here both by postulating a gargantuan number of oysters (*centum*: cf. 7.113) and then specifying that they are the finest quality: Mt. Gaurus was known as a source of fine wine (9.57) and close to 'the best oyster-beds of Baiae and the Lucrine Lake' (Mayor (1888) ii. 19).

86   Gauran ... Cosmus: the poet juxtaposes the 'designer label' names for effect and the line is heavily spondaic and weighty with opulence. **Cosmus** was the most famous maker of perfume at the time (Martial 1.87.1–2, 3.55.1–2) whose significant name (Greek κόσμος ('decoration' whence our word 'cosmetic') was often applied to feminine adornment (cf. Plato *Republic* 373c) was an advertisement for his wares. The poet specifies that the bath is made of **bronze** to bring out the irony that immersion in a bronze vessel of perfume is a living death, while immersion in the bronze bull of Phalaris was a literal death. Once again hyperbole is at work: filling a bath with perfume so that the bather could be totally immersed would cost an enormous sum. *toto* has been explained as adverbial but as Courtney points out could easily be read as agreeing with *aeno* in the sense that once the bather was submerged the 'entire' vessel would be occupied.

87–141   *Provincial government and the scope for bad behaviour*
Rome exercised control over a vast area of the world, divided up into separate 'provinces' governed either by Roman ex-magistrates (consuls and praetors)

or else by 'client-kings' installed from the local population but beholden to Roman power (see *OCD* s.v. 'provincia/province', *CAH* xi. 266–92). The province of Bithynia and Pontus, for instance, was governed by the lawyer and ex-consul Pliny the Younger from AD 110–113 (*CAH* xi.118–123, Gibson (2020) Chapter 8), and his letters are a good source of information on how a province was governed. Corruption by governors, who extorted money and fine goods from the provincials, was a well-documented and chronic problem, despite all the legal strictures: see Brunt (1961) for the situation under the empire and for the procedure in prosecutions. Provincial governors could be tried before the senate in full session, where up to 600 senators could be present and where, 'if convicted, [the defendant] would suffer *infamia* and forfeit his standing as senator' (Gibson (2020) 198). Advice to provincial governors was not a new genre: Cicero wrote a long letter on this precise theme to his brother in Asia (*ad Q.F.* 1.1) and Pliny penned some good advice to Maximus (*Epistles* 8.24), but both of these look back further to the whole Greek tradition of 'advice to the ruler' such as we find in Plato's *Letters* to the rulers of Sicily and Isocrates' speech *To Nicocles*: closer to this satire, Seneca wrote eloquent books of advice to the young emperor Nero on topics such as mercy (*de Clementia*: not a lesson the emperor heeded if lines 211–220 are to be believed).

The speaker here begins with (87–94) the stock themes – curb anger, greed and lust – but (as if realising that such pieties are a waste of breath when delivered to his addressee) then presents a largely cynical argument – that robbing these poor folk is not worth it as they have been cleaned out by earlier governors and might also prove hard to fight now that their luxury has been removed and their bodies and hearts accordingly hardened. This is a massively overstated picture of provinces beaten and stripped into poverty and desperation, which was not the case for many of the provinces in the empire – for a different view see e.g. De Ste Croix (1981) 381–82 – but it contributes to the overall argument of the poem that faded aristocrats such as Ponticus have no morals and need selfish motives to do anything. This therefore amounts to a further satirical criticism.

87   **province**: under the republic, the senate allocated the provinces which outgoing consuls would often move to as soon as their year in office came to an end (although this was not inflexible: Cicero (who was consul in 63 BC) did not go out to govern the province of Cilicia until 51 BC), not least in order to recoup financial losses (incurred during the election campaign) at the expense of the provincials. Under the empire the allocation of provinces

was decided by the emperor. The length of time between year in office and provincial governorship varied: Pliny the Younger for instance was consul in AD 100 and governor of Bithynia/Pontus in AD 110. The words *expectata diu tandem* recall Catullus (62.2) who uses them of the longed-for evening star on a wedding night, and the intertextual reference supports the idea that this governor views the province as a source of pleasure rather than as a dutiful responsibility.

88–9 rein in … moderate … take pity: the speaker barks three orders at Ponticus, with anaphora of *pone*. The motives for provincial misbehaviour are assumed to be anger (*irae*) and avarice (*auaritiae*: cf. 135 *ambitio atque libido*), while the third imperative looks on the **penniless allies** (*inopum sociorum*) and demands **pity** (*miserere*), the clash of ictus and accent suggesting emotion. *frena* (**reins**) is a metaphor from charioteering and horse-riding (cf. Propertius 3.19.3, Horace *Odes* 4.15.10–11 *Epistles* 1.2.62–3) often found in the adjectival form *effrenatus* ('unbridled') used of desire, anger etc. *modum ponere* means to 'set a limit to' (*OLD* s.v. 'modus' 5b, Virgil *Aeneid* 7.129, Horace *Odes* 1.16.2–3): proportionate anger could be seen as the correct response in some situations, but *auaritia* is (by definition) not something which can ever be proportionate. *socii* here refers to Rome's 'allies' who lived in the provinces (*OLD* s.v. 'socius' 4,5: the term primarily means 'partner' (e.g. Tacitus *Annals* 4.2.11, referring to Tiberius' henchman Sejanus)) and so the phrasing here forces the point: 'partners' who are penniless deserve pity or else they are not partners at all, and line 90 expands the point with vivid imagery.

90 you see … empty: an elegant line with repellent sense. Note the second person verb *uides* and the effective juxtaposition of *exsucta medullis*: the imagery of bone-marrow as a life-giving fluid is old (cf. Watson (2003) 214) and having it 'sucked out' is a good metaphor for the stripping of power from the people concerned (cf. Homer *Iliad* 20. 482–2). *uacuus* usually describes the empty vessel rather than the substance removed, and (as Courtney points out) a more straightforward method of expression would be *uacua exsuctis medullis*: the hypallage enhances the vividness of the imagery (as does (e.g.) that at Virgil *Aeneid* 6.268 (see Austin (1977) *ad loc.*)) by suggesting the sucking of the bones and the empty spaces where the marrow used to be. Almost all modern editors read *rerum* (P), dismissing *regum* (Φ) as a simpler 'correction': Braund argues that the word refers to client-kings, but this is to limit the sense of *sociorum* to one sub-group, and *rerum* ensures that we see that the line is metaphorical.

91–2 **Keep an eye on**: the didactic tone continues with the peremptory imperative *respice* (cf. 2.44, 3.268, 5.60, 6.115, 7.141) and the sequence of question words in anaphora: *quid ... quid ... quanta ... quam*. The chiastic order of *moneant leges ... curia mandet* juxtaposes the **laws** and the **senate-house**. The laws here are personified as at 2.37, Pliny *Epistles* 4.23.3, Plato *Crito* 50a7–54d1. The *curia* was the **senate-house** but is often used metonymically for the senate which occupied it (cf. *OLD* s.v. 'curia' 5, Horace *Odes* 2.1.14) and the personification adds to the power of the sentence.

92 **benefits ... condemned**: there is a contrast here of benefits (*praemia*) for good behaviour and punishment for bad. *maneo* is often used of what awaits us in the future (e.g. 4.95, 5.103, 11.39, Catullus 76.5, *OLD* s.v. 'maneo' 4); and Pliny (*Panegyricus* 70.4) specified that the reward awaiting good provincial governors lay in 'the emperor's judgement and support' in an age where imperial favour guaranteed professional success or failure. The wrath of the senate is described in almost divine terms since *fulmen* often denotes the thunderbolt of Jupiter (cf. 3.145, 13.78 (with my note *ad loc.*), Ovid *Tristia* 1.1.72, *OLD* s.v. 'fulmen' 1c) which (allegedly) struck the wicked.

93 Cossutianus **Capito** was a 'flawed and disgusting man who thought he had the right to behave with the same arrogance in the province as he did in the city' (Tacitus *Annals* 13.33). He was condemned for extortion in Cilicia in AD 57 thanks to the relentless efforts of Thrasea Paetus (Tacitus *Annals* 16.21, Quintilian 6.1.14): he later on helped to secure Paetus' death under Nero. The manuscript reading *Numitor* is almost certainly a mistake by a scribe who confused this line with Virgil *Aeneid* 6.768 (*et Capys et Numitor*): **Tutor** is unknown, but both names might be significant as *capitis damnare* means to 'condemn to death' and a corrupt governor called *Tutor* would be sardonic as the word means 'protector, guardian' (cf. 79). *ruerint* picks up *ruant* (77) and denotes here personal ruin (*OLD* s.v. 'ruo' 7, Cicero *Verrines* 5.12, Horace *Odes* 1.2.25).

94 There is irony here: Cilicians were renowned **pirates** (*OCD* s.v. 'piracy': cf. e.g. Caesar *B.C.* 3.110, Cicero *in Verrem* 2.4.21), but these Roman governors outdid even the Cilicians in plundering – the Cilicians themselves: this irony was exploited to the full in Cicero's prosecution of Verres, the corrupt governor of Sicily (e.g. *in Verrem* 2.1.90, 154). *damnatio* picks up *damnante* in the same position in 93: despair at securing justice is a recurrent theme in J. (cf. 1.47–50, 7.106–29, 16.7–34).

95   **Chaerippus** (a Greek name, here addressed in apostrophe (cf. 39–40n.)) must refer to a provincial. The line is framed with key words – the man now possesses only **rags** (*pannis*) and has to hire an **auctioneer** (*praeconem*: cf. 7.6) to raise cash from them (cf. 6.255–8). The difficulty of finding such a man is brought out by the spondaic rhythm of *praeconem Chaeripp-* and the expressive verb *circumspice* which here denotes 'search for' (*OLD* s.v. 'circumspicio' 6b).

96   **Pansa** and **Natta** may well be token *cognomina* belonging to the sort of men who would govern provinces. There was a M. Hirrius Fronto Neratius Pansa who governed Cappadocia from AD 77–79 (see Torelli (1968) 174) but no accusation of corruption attaches to his name: Natta is a name which crops up several times in Latin literature as a filthy man (Horace *Satires* 1.6. 124), a pathic homosexual (Martial 11.72) and a fat and amoral reprobate (Persius 3.31–4) but (again) no evidence of provincial misbehaviour. The strong verbs are placed at key positions before the caesura and at the end of the line and the pronoun *tibi* continues to make the pillaging personal to Chaerippus.

97   **stop speaking up**: *tace* (literally 'be silent!') here means 'stop making accusations' and *iamque ... post omnia <perdita>* shows the provincial persistence finally worn down to nothing by the inordinate protraction of legal proceedings (as at 16.43–7). **madness:** *furor est* + infinitive is also found at 1.92–3, 14.136–7, Martial 2.80.2. *naulum* is a Greek word (ναῦλος) for **fare** and it seems likely that the term suggests both the fare needed to travel to Rome to pursue the case and also the fare given to the boatman of the underworld Charon (cf. 3.265–7, Aristophanes *Frogs* 270, Apuleius *Met.* 6.18.7): *perdere naulum* means 'to waste one's fare' (referring to a pointless journey as at Plutarch *Moralia* 439e).

98–108   J. gives us a contrast of then (*olim*) and now (*nunc*) as he postulates that provincials in the past had enough goods to be able to lose some without too much pain. The speaker is not idealising republican provincial government – they suffered, as *gemitus* and *uulnus* make clear – but is cynically contrasting their former wealth with their current poverty from the point of view of a prospective governor who is going to be wasting his time seeking wealth in the cash-strapped provinces.

98   The clash of ictus and accent in *uulnus erat par* enacts the uneven nature of the evidence. *gemitūs* (the plural form as at 13.11) is a cry of pain as at 6.271, 13.130, Lucretius 4.1015, while *uulnus ... damnorum* is an effective metaphor which hints at the physical punishment which often

accompanied the stealing of property under governors such as Verres (e.g. Cicero *in Verrem* 2.5.161–2).

99   just: *modo* is usually taken with *uictis* to mean 'recently conquered' (cf. 125, 7.152, 9.96, 14.298, 15.119, Petronius 37.3, *OLD* s.v. 'modo¹' 5a) but can also mean 'only' (*OLD* s.v. 'modo¹' 1): simply being **conquered** was a blessed state compared to being conquered and fleeced.

100–104 The speaker exaggerates – not every house was full – and conveys the quantity and quality of goods worth stealing with his asyndetic inventory spread over four lines. The sense of luxury is heightened by the use of Greek terms (*chlamys, conchylia*) and the citing of key names (Parrhasius, Myron, Phidias, Polyclitus, Mentor) who are elsewhere named as the masters of Greek art (cf. e.g. Cicero *Tusc.* 1.4.4, Martial 8.51.1–2).

100–1 Line 100 is metrically awkward, with no strong caesura and only a weak caesura in the 3rd foot, and the rhythm and the enjambement perhaps suggest the breathless excitement of the viewer of this treasure, whose quantity is repeatedly stressed (*plena … omnis … ingens … aceruus*). *stabat* means more than simply 'stood there': it also means to 'cost' (*OLD* s.v. 'sto' 23) and this wealth proved costly to its owners. The image of a **heap of cash** is common in Roman satire: cf. 6.364, 13.10, Horace *Satires* 1.1.44, 51, 2.2.105, 2.5.22, Petronius 37.2 (Fortunata 'measures her cash by the bushel').

101 The items of clothing are in chiastic order. The *chlamys* (χλαμύς) was a Greek **cloak** (similar to the Roman *paludamentum*) worn by common soldiers but also by royalty (e.g. Dido in Virgil *Aeneid* 4.137 and Pallas in *Aeneid* 8.588: cf. Persius 6.46 ('*chlamydes* of kings')) and people of imperial distinction (Agrippina wore a golden *chlamys* in Tacitus *Annals* 12.56): the wealthy Lucullus had five hundred of them, according to Horace (*Epistles* 1.6.40–44). *Spartana* refers to the military Greek city-state Sparta, noted for its austerity but also for producing the finest purple dye (see Pliny *N.H.* 9.127, 35.45, Horace *Odes* 2.18.7, Martial 8.28.9) whose colour was a mark of wealth and distinction (cf. 7.135–6). The *conchylium* was an edible shellfish (Horace *Satires* 2.2.74, Martial 11.52.13) from which purple dye was obtained, so that the plural of the word denoted 'purple garments' (3.81, Suetonius *Caligula* 17.2, *OLD* s.v. 'conchylium' 2c). The Greek island of Cos was famous for its silk textiles (see *OCD* s.v. 'silk') which were the height of feminine fashion (*OLD* s.v. 'Cous' 1b, Propertius 1.2.2, 2.1.6, Horace *Odes* 4.13.13, Griffin (1985) 10) and notorious for their diaphanous quality (cf. Horace *Satires* 1.2.101–2).

102 *Parrhasii tabulis signisque Myronis* is another chiasmus. **Parrhasius**

was a Greek painter from about 400BC, a rival of Zeuxis (Quintilian 12.10.4) and famous also for wearing a purple cloak and a gold wreath (*OCD* s.v. 'Parrhasius') which gives his name added relevance here: Xenophon has him discussing art with Socrates (*Memorabilia* 3.10.1–5). **paintings**: *tabula* denotes a picture painted on a wooden board (*OLD* s.v. 'tabula' 2) while *signum* means a **statue** (110, 3.216, 14.307, *OLD* s.v. 'signum' 12): Verres stole *signa* and *tabulas pictas* from Achaia (Cicero *in Verrem* 1.45). **Myron** was active in the mid-5th century BC and had a great reputation for his bronze sculptures (Pliny *NH* 34.58, Statius *Silvae* 4.6.25-6, Ovid *Ars Am.* 3.219): his work was sought out by the rapacious Verres (Cicero *in Verrem* 2.4.5, 2.4.12, 2.4.93). Myron's image of a cow was especially famous for its verisimilitude (cf. *Greek Anthology* 9.736, Ovid *Ex Ponto* 4.1.34).

103   The line is framed with the key names. **Ivory ... lived**: the speaker is telling of a time when the provinces still possessed works of art, and so *uiuebat* can simply mean 'were there': but the verb also alludes to the skill which made the statues appear to be alive (cf. Virgil *Aeneid* 6.848, Martial 3.35, Petronius 52, Statius *Thebaid* 4.132, *Achilleid* 1.332, *Silvae* 2.2.67, *Greek Anthology* 16.159.1, *OLD* s.v. 'uiuo' 4). **Ivory** was imported for use in sculpture, according to Pausanias (5.12.1) and **Phidias** (who worked in the mid-5th century BC) was renowned for his massive chryselephantine (gold and ivory) statues of Athena and Zeus (see *OCD* s.v. 'Phidias': Quintilian (12.10.9) states that he was the finest Greek sculptor). Hexameter poets (e.g. Propertius 3.9.15, Ovid *ex Ponto* 4.1.32, Statius *Silvae* 2.2.66) used the adjectival form *Phidiacus* as the genitive form of his name would produce a cretic rhythm (*Phīdĭæ*) which cannot fit into a hexameter. *nec non* (*OLD* s.v. 'neque' 10b) began as a colloquialism (as it remained in e.g. Petronius 72.7.4) but became an elevated way of saying 'and' in the hands of Virgil (see Austin (1971) on *Aeneid* 1.707) and his successors (e.g. Ovid *Met.* 2.615, Lucan 3.516, Manilius 1.779, Statius *Thebaid* 5.190, Silius 1.411, Valerius Flaccus 2.664) and even elegists when in epic mode (Propertius 3.1.33). J. uses it seven times, sometimes for mock-epic grandeur (3.204, 9.88) and sometimes simply in the colloquial sense (e.g. 6.282). Here it continues the excited listing of names, enhanced by the bumpy rhythm of the final four-syllable word. **Polyclitus** was also active in the 5th century BC and worked in bronze and marble (*OCD* s.v. 'Polyclitus'): his name is joined with that of Phidias as the leading sculptors of Greece (e.g. Aristotle *Nicomachean Ethics* 6.7 1141a10–11, Cicero *de Finibus* 2.115.4, Quintilian 12.10.8, Martial 10.89.1–2).

104   The poet finds two different ways to say 'many' in *multus…rarae sine* placed in emphatic positions at the start of the line and after the caesura. **works**: *labor* here means 'production' (*OLD* s.v. 'labor²' 4) as at Martial 4.39.5, and the juxtaposition of *multus ubique* brings out the impressive quantity of these statues. For *multus* with a singular noun cf. 8.7n. **Mentor** was a renowned silversmith (Pliny *NH* 33.154) whose works attracted the attention of Verres (Cicero *in Verrem* 2.4.38). Dining tables could be objects of high art and great luxury (see 1.75–6, 11.117–27nn.) and silver was much prized as a medium (cf. 14.62, Musonius fr. 21 p.110 Hense ('couches of ivory and silver')). The name **Mentor** here stands for 'a work made by Mentor' (cf. 12.128n., 14.326, Martial 11.11.5).

105   This line is almost certainly textually corrupt (see (e.g.) Eden (1985)) as it is unmetrical – unless we force the final syllable of *Dolabella* to be scanned long in arsis and then allow a hiatus before *atque*. The first name is probably secure: there were two men called Cn. Cornelius **Dolabella**, both of whom were prosecuted for extortion: one a consul in 81 BC, proconsul in Macedonia and prosecuted unsuccessfully in 77 BC, the other a praetor in 81 BC and governor of Cilicia with Verres on his staff (*OCD* s.v. Cornelius Dolabella, Gnaeus'). A third member of the family (P. Cornelius Dolabella) married Cicero's daughter Tullia and plundered the province of Syria in 44–43 BC. Emending to the plural form *Dolabellae* (with Ruperti) would help the scansion of the line but still leave the hiatus. C. **Antonius** Hybrida was prosecuted in 76 BC for his extortion in Greece but secured the consulship alongside Cicero in 63 BC, went on to govern Macedonia in 62 BC and was condemned for extortion there in 59 BC (Cicero *in Vatinium* 28). *hinc* is odd as there is no contrast being set up between two sources of provincial extortion, and I have printed Knoche's *audax* as preferable to other suggestions (cf. Lucan (5.478)). The line is framed by anaphora of *inde … inde* which enacts the repeated instances of robbery from these provinces.

106   **Verres** was given to stealing works of sacred art such as statues of gods from temples (e.g. Cicero *in Verrem* 2.1.9, 2.5.4, 2.5.188) and so is well described as **impious** (*sacrilegus*: see 13.72, 13.150 and cf. Cicero *in Verrem* 2.1.47). The **tall** ships are also deep (*altis*) in the water as they are weighed down with their heavy freight of plunder.

107   A heavily sardonic line about the 'spoils' of peace. A Roman triumph was a victory procession where the **spoils** of war (*spolia*: cf. *OLD* s.v. 'spolium' 2) would be paraded through the streets – the word is used metaphorically elsewhere (see 6.232 with Watson and Watson (2014) *ad*

loc.) as here, since these allies have not been at war with their conquerors and so the 'triumph' is also not a real procession but a word for the 'victory' itself (*OLD* s.v. 'triumphus' 2b). The preposition *de* (in *de pace*) points to the forces 'defeated' (cf. 15.47, Livy 7.32.17, Tacitus *Annals* 12.20.2) but here the 'enemy' are in fact the so-called 'allies' who have been recently overcome (99) and the 'pacified' peoples are also simplified to the abstract noun 'peace'. We thus have a scathing image of merciless Roman governors celebrating their victory over peace itself. The word *plures* suggests that these men won more triumphs over peaceful peoples than they did over states with which they were at war. *occultă* agrees with *spolia* as the final -*ă* is lengthened by position before the two consonants (*sp-*).

108   *nunc* picks up *olim...tunc* from 98–100 to seal the contrast between 'then' and **these days**. The inventory-style word order of *iuga pauca boum, grex paruus equarum* suggests the way governors viewed the goods available, and *pauca..paruus* is effective variation of vocabulary. *sociis* has been seen as a dative of possession with the series of nouns, understanding <*sunt*> but is more likely to be a dative of disadvantage with the verb *eripietur*, which commonly takes a dative of the person robbed. *iugum* properly denotes the yoke (ζυγόν: cf. 6.208, 8.63, 10.135) which joined the oxen in pairs as they ploughed: it comes to mean a pair of such animals by metonymy (*OLD* s.v. 'iugum' 3: cf. Propertius 3.5.5). Cicero inveighed against Verres' theft of *greges nobilissimarum equarum* ('herds of the finest mares' *in Verrem* 2.2.20). *sociis* is a dative of disadvantage going with *eripietur*.

109   **little estate**: the small size of the estate is brought out by the diminutive *agello*. *armentum* is suitably vague, being applicable to both cattle and horses and so *pater* could refer to either a prize bull or a stallion: without this animal there would be no future animals to steal and so this beast was taken only after the others had gone. **snatched**: *eripietur* is a violent verb (showing the amoral power of the governor) and acquires added force for being framed by the ablative absolute *capto...agello*.

110   *Lares* (cf. 9.137) were the **household gods**, represented by small statues kept in the *aedicula* ('domestic shrine': cf. Petronius 29.8 and see *OCD* s.v. 'Lares', Watson (2003) 122, Beard, North and Price (1998) 2.30–31, 102–103 with images and further bibliography). *signum* makes it clear that J. is referring to the statues of these deities, while *spectabile* shows the discriminating governor who regards some 'gods' as not being worth stealing unless their statues are **worth looking at**. The strong sibilance of the line indicates contempt.

111–2   Manso condemned these lines (followed by many subsequent editors including Clausen and Willis), but the sequence of thought from line 110 to line 113 is then abrupt. Housman objected to the repetition of *etenim sunt ... nam sunt*, but at least one editor (Ferguson) prints the text as it stands and it is always possible that the poet is mocking the speaker's jejune language – and repetition of ideas and vocabulary (*despicias*) is one mark of the ranting speaker. The point being made is one of comparative size: in the 'little temple' (*aedicula* is the diminutive of *aedes* (temple)) there stands a single god (who must be similarly pint-sized), but statues like this are 'in place of' (cf. 6.223, *OLD* s.v. 'pro' 6) 'the exceptional <statues>': these are the biggest (*maxima*) specimens available these days. The repetition of words is varied by chiasmus (*haec sunt ... sunt haec*) and vocabulary (*pro summis ... maxima*) as well as reinforced by spondaic rhythm. To replace *haec etenim sunt* Courtney ((1966) 40) proposed reading *haec retinentes* (as object of *despicias*, in place of *haec etenim sunt*) and Dimatteo (2011) *haec rapientur.*

113–6   The weaker provinces are described in general terms (**unwarlike**: *imbelles*) and then in more specific detail (*unctam ... resinata*). The 'argument' here is that provinces which are addicted to luxury and soft-living are easier to rob and so Ponticus may treat them with contempt (*despicias*), while more manly races would be more of a challenge and be less worth the effort as they do not possess luxurious goods to steal. The effeminacy of eastern lands is a *topos* in ancient literature drawing on the medical writers (Pelling (2019) 19–20) and indulged by the Romans towards the Greeks (3. 93–7, Edwards (1993) 92–97), and the Trojans (Virgil *Aeneid* 4.215) and in fact everyone from the East (cf. Sallust *Cat.* 11.5–6, Seneca *de Ira* 1.11.4, Latham (2012)). The language here is close to that of Martial 10.65 where the Spanish speaker contrasts his own 'hairy legs and cheeks' over against the effeminate Corinthian with his sleek curly hair.

113–4   The speaker speculates (*despicias tu/ forsitan*: cf. 1.150, 5.156, 11.162) on Ponticus' contempt for less manly people and then confirms it with the corrective adverb *merito*. Rhodes was mentioned at 6.295–6 as a source of luxury and 'filthy money', while Corinth was famous for its lavish lifestyle (such as its temple of Aphrodite with one thousand prostitutes (see *OCD* s.v. 'prostitution, sacred')) and loose living (cf. Martial 10.65, 10.68.11, Cicero *de Republica* 2.4.7–8). **oiled**: *unctam* refers to the use of oil on the hair of people at banquets: the attention to hair is part of the standard ammunition used against the effeminate man (see Virgil *Aeneid*

12. 99–100, Ovid *Metamorphoses* 3.555, 5.53 and goes back to Homer: the Trojan Euphorbos is killed by Menelaus and stains his hair and 'love-locks' with blood (*Iliad* 17.51)).

114–5 The speaker has a horror of male depilation (cf. 8.16) although he also sees hirsute bodies as a sign of dissolution (9.12–15) as well as of healthy disregard for effeminate luxury (11.150, 157, 14.194): Seneca (*Epistles* 114.14) draws the line between effeminacy and boorishness in similar terms: 'one plucks his legs, the other not even his armpits'. **resin-smeared**: *resinata* refers to the use of resin to burn off hair (Pliny *NH* 14.123, 29.26, Martial 3.74.4, 12.32.21–2: cf. the use of pumice at 8.16 and pitch at 9.14): the term combined with *iuuentus* forms a 'jocular oxymoron' (Dimatteo (2014) 141) as *iuuentus* is often used of soldiery (e.g. 2.155, Livy 1.9.10, 5.39).

115 *lēuis* means 'smooth' or '**hairless**' (as at 2.12, 3.111, 6.356, 8.35, 9.95, 10.199): the legs are chosen as they would be visible to the observer and the surrealistic image of a whole race of disembodied hairless legs attacking people is striking. *quid facient tibi* here means 'what <harm> will they do to you?': see *OLD* s.v. 'facio' 14b and cf. 2.166, 8.1.

116–7 The poet varies the didactic tone with a gerundive of obligation (*uitanda*) and a simple imperative (*parce*). The provinces are personified: *horrida* (**hairy**) is emphasised by position to contrast with the previous line and the fearsome combination of worthy opponents is reinforced by the juxtaposition of *Hispania Gallicus* followed by the enjambed *Illyricumque*. *axis* often means the 'poles' of the earth and the heavens, or else a specific portion of the earth under its sky as here (*OLD* s.v. 'axis' 5b, cf. 6.470, 14.42). *latus* suggests the 'flank' of the body (see *OLD* s.v. 'latus²' 1–4) and the flank of an army (*OLD* s.v. 5) and so the attention is brought back to the human threat posed by the Illyrians. Gaul was famously divided into three separate parts (Caesar *BG* 1.1.1) and together had a fearsome reputation for bellicosity (e.g. Tacitus *Histories* 3.53.3, Cicero *ad Q. Fratrem* 1.1.27, Virgil *Aeneid* 6.858) as did Spain (Horace *Odes* 4.14.49–50), although J. elsewhere (7.148) writes of Gaul as the 'nurse of barristers' (cf. 15.111n.) suggesting that their aggression was verbal as well as military. Gauls invaded Rome (cf. 11.113, Livy 5.34–5) before being subdued in 191 BC and in more recent times there had been rebellions in Gaul (AD 21 and AD 68). **Illyricum** (roughly the area now covered by Albania, Bosnia/Herzegovina, Croatia and Montenegro) was notoriously rough terrain (Livy 38.17.16) and was a focus of military activity under the Flavian emperors (*CAH* xi. 577–

85), needing a large garrison of seven legions and being a problem province even then (Tacitus *Histories* 1.2, Pliny *Epistles* 3.16.7).

117–8 *messoribus* (**harvesters**) refers to the people of Africa who produced vast amounts of corn for Rome: see 120 *Afros* and cf. 5.118, Horace *Odes* 1.1.9–10. There are two points being made: firstly, the Africans were listed along with Spaniards and Gauls as being 'monstrous and barbarous races' (Cicero *ad Q.F.* 1.1.27) and so not a pushover for the predatory governor: secondly, the Africans ensure the supply of corn which allows the Romans to idle in the Circus and the theatre rather than work for their own food – a sentiment expressed in similar language by Varro *Res Rusticae* 2 *prol.* 3. This hints at the poet's contempt for the idle mob in contrast to their valiant peasant ancestors (cf. 11.196–201 for the games, 14.159–172 for the idealised view of the past: see also Highet (1954) 136). Slightly pejorative verbs frame the line: *saturant* denotes the provision of excessive food (cf. 7.62, 14.166, 15.3, Petronius 46.2, 58.3, Catullus 32.10), and *uacantem* has the sense of 'idle' (1.21, Horace *Odes* 3.18.11, *Epistles* 2.2.95, *OLD* s.v. 'uaco' 7). The **Circus** Maximus hosted chariot-races which were highly popular, as well as beast-hunts, executions and gladiatorial combat (see Paoli (1990) 249–55) – although by J.'s day the fighting had moved to the Colosseum and the Circus was predominantly used for chariot-races. *sc(a)ena* (from the Greek σκηνή) strictly denoted the 'background' scenery behind the performers of a play but commonly came to be used in metonymy for the dramatic performances themselves (cf. 8.220, *OLD* s.v. 'scaena' 3).

119 The Africans are not worth robbing (cf. 108–112) and any interruption to the corn supply would have catastrophic consequences: the phrase *dirae...culpae* (repeated at 13.106) alludes to the famine which could result in Rome. *inde* means 'from that source' (105n.).

120 Marius Priscus was prosecuted by Tacitus and Pliny for extortion in N. Africa in AD 100 (Pliny *Ep.* 2.11) and banished from Rome and Italy: cf. 1.49–50 ('Marius in exile drinks from the afternoon onwards and enjoys the hostility of the gods – but you, province, weep even though you won the case against him') and see Courtney on 1.49 and *CAH* xi.843. **to the bone**: *tenues* (cf. 3.163, 7.80) is proleptic, indicating the end-result of his robbery. *discinxerit* literally means 'unbelted' (*OLD* s.v. 'discingo', Martial 9.101.5) but (as Romans carried money in their belts) bears the metaphorical sense of **stripped** or 'disarmed' here and at Martial 12.29.13–4, Seneca *Epistles* 92.35, Silius *Punica* 7.153. There is almost certainly a joke here, as Courtney points out: Virgil (*Aeneid* 8.724) has Vulcan depict the *discinctos Afros*

('Africans wearing loose robes') on the shield of Aeneas, and *discinctus* can also mean 'undisciplined' (as at Horace *Epodes* 1.34, Persius 3.31) – and so we have the witty point that Priscus (who is *discinctus* in the moral sense) is making the Africans wear loose robes by stealing their belts.

121–2 **strong and desperate**: men of courage and poverty have nothing to lose in fighting back. Line 121 is heavily spondaic and *fortibus et miseris* is stressed by enjambement and the subsequent pause at the caesura. *in primis* is common in didactic literature (e.g. Lucretius 6.536, Virgil *Georgics* 1.338, Manilius 3.618, Vitruvius 5.2.1, Horace *Satires* 2.2.71) and the solemn tone of the sentence feigns moral concern while remaining cynical and sardonic.

122–4 **even if**: *licet* is concessive as at 19. The opening salvo is framed by the key verbs *tollas* and *relinques*, the former a conditional subjunctive, the latter a strong future indicative. The phrase is strengthened by the pleonasm of *omne quod usquam est* (for simple *omne*) followed by the enjambed *auri atque argenti* listing the precious metals. The inventory of armour left to the provincials is a combination of offensive (sword and spear) and defensive (shield and helmet) in chiastic order – and the whole sentence ends with the gnomic three-word summary *spoliatis arma supersunt*. Weapons were not made of gold but horse-trappings could be made of silver (see 11.109n.). Brunt (1975) supports the thesis that Romans did not disarm the provincials: see further Prag (2007) 80–87. 124 was deleted by Lachmann as being superfluous but the argument is strengthened by the polysyndetic list of weaponry: and the final aphorism is fully in Juvenal's style (cf. e.g. 1.74, 2.8, 2.60, 10.25–6, 13.100, 14. 47, 14.224).

125–6 The speaker now sets up a binary contrast between the rhetorical status (*sententia*) of his gnomic statement and its truth (*uerum*), implying that *sententiae* are not (often) true: a contrast between rhetoric and truth which was explored at length in (e.g.) Plato *Gorgias* 454b8–460c6, 463e5–466a3. This ironic metapoetic remark casts doubt on the veracity of the whole passage: cf. 15.69–70n. The **Sibyl** was a prophetess in Cumae who, in some accounts (e.g. Virgil *Aeneid* 3.441–62, 6.45–51) would go into a trance and then make prophetic utterances which were written down by the priests on a leaf (*folium*: see *OCD* s.v. 'Sibyl', Beard, North and Price (1998) vol. 2: 179–83). The authoritative 'gospel truth' of an oracle is a trope found also at Ovid *Ars Am.* 2.541, Cicero *de Republica* 5.1, *de Finibus* 1.7.20 (where Epicurus uttered 'a kind of oracles' in 'succinct and weighty *sententiis*'), Horace *Carmen Saeculare* 5, Otto (1890) s.v. 'Sibylla' 3: but the Sibylline oracles were also in the keeping of the *quindecimuiri sacris faciundis*, a noble priestly college. *modo* means 'just now' (see 8.99n., 9.124, 14.298n., *OLD* s.v. 'modo' 5). The plural verb (*credite*) and pronoun (*uobis*) has the effect of broadening the effect so that the speaker is addressing 'prospective provincial governors' in general as well as Ponticus in particular.

127   Note the striking anaphora of *si*. The *cohors comitum* was the informal **staff** of the provincial governor (cf. 3.47, Catullus 10.10, 13 with Fordyce (1961) 118–9, *OLD* s.v. 'cohors' 5a). A *tribunal* was a platform from which a presiding magistrate would utter his judgements (cf. 10.35): here in metonymy it means the **verdict** itself which could be 'sold' (cf. Ovid *Amores* 1.10.37–40) by a member of his entourage. For the short final syllable of *nemŏ* cf. 7.17n.

128   **long-haired**: *acersecomes* (ἀκερσεκόμης) is used in Homer (*Iliad* 20.39: cf. *Hymn to Apollo* 134) to describe 'long-haired Apollo' and refers here scornfully to a 'slave-lover' (Dimatteo (2014) 153): the poet again uses Greek for scornful effect (as at e.g. 5.121). This effeminate Greek youth reminds us of the long-haired youths in Petronius (27, 97.2) and contrasts strongly with the homely peasant slave idealised at 11. 146–60 (especially 11.149 *tonsi rectique capilli*).

128–30   **wife**: there were some well-known criminal wives of provincial governors such as Plancina, the wife of Cn. Calpurnius Piso, who helped to murder Germanicus (Tacitus *Annals* 2.74–5, 3.15–18, on which see Marshall (1975): cf. also Martial 2.56.1–2). The speaker's misogyny comes to the fore in this vignette of the governor's wife as a **Harpy** with **curved talons** aiming to steal cash throughout **all** (*cuncta*) the towns (and not just some of them), all accentuated with harsh 'c' alliteration. *conuentus* here means **district courts** (*OLD* s.v. 'conuentus' 4, Burton (1975) 92–94, *CAH* xi. 347). Celaeno (whose name in Greek means 'black, dark') was one of the Harpies named in Virgil: he describes (*Aeneid* 3.216–7) them as 'birds with female faces, disgusting droppings, hooked hands (cf. *curuis/unguibus*) and faces always pale with hunger'. *curuis/unguibus* is elsewhere used of the cranes which attack pygmies (13.169–70) and *ire parat raptura* is a threatening combination showing her intention (*parat*) to mount her predatory attack, while *ire parat* is an epic phrase (four occurrences in Virgil's *Aeneid*) which helps to mythologise this monster of greed. *raptura* (from *rapio*) reminds us that the name Harpy comes from the Greek verb ἁρπάζω ('I seize').

131   **Picus** (see *OCD* s.v. 'Picus') was a son of Saturn, father of Faunus (Virgil *Aeneid* 7.48–9) and an early king of Latium. He was transformed into a woodpecker by Circe (Ovid *Metamorphoses* 14. 308–415) which brought

food to Romulus and Remus (Plutarch *Roman Questions* 21) and is used here as a kindly bird to contrast with the winged Harpy of 130. **you may**: *licet* here has its common meaning rather than the concessive meaning of 19, 81. *tum* picks up *si* from 127 and means 'in that case' (*OLD* s.v. 'tum' 5b): *numero a* + ablative is common in Latin for 'to count from' (*OLD* s.v. 'numero' 3b).

132 The **Titans** (children of Earth) included Cronos whose son Jupiter supplanted them as rulers of the world. The Titans fought back unsuccessfully (Hesiod *Theogony* 617–735). *Titanis* is the epic (cf. Ovid *Met.* 6.185, 13.968, 14.376, Valerius Flaccus 7.212) adjectival form: this and the metonymy whereby *pugnam* (literally 'battle') means **phalanx**, hyperbolised with *omnem*, adds epic flavour to the phrase.

133 *ponere inter* has the sense of 'to name amongst' or 'consider a part of' as at 10.358, Horace *Epistles* 2.1.43, 2.34.94 (*OLD* s.v. 'pono' 22b). **Prometheus** was also one of the Titans but was regarded as a saviour of humanity, in that he stole fire from heaven to give to those on earth (15.85–6). According to some legends (see *OCD* s.v. 'Prometheus' and cf. Horace *Odes* 1.16.13–14, Ovid *Met.*1.82–3) he created the first men out of clay, a tale alluded to at 4.133, 6.13: this means that claiming him as an ancestor is something which <u>all</u> humans can do and mocks the 'nobility' of the claimant. In Plato *Protagoras* 320d2–3 the gods fashioned all living things out of a mixture of earth and fire and then instructed Prometheus and his brother Epimetheus to endow them with gifts and talents, a process which left mankind lacking the animals' superior physical attributes of hides, speed, strength etc but having both 'technical cleverness' (ἔντεχνον σοφίαν) and fire (321d2): Prometheus is often seen as being kindly towards mankind (φιλάνθρωπος [Aeschylus] *Prom.*11) but his earlier image in Hesiod was more that of a grinning rogue (*Theogony* 546–7) and even the source of human misery in his misguided efforts to outwit Zeus (see Griffiths (1983) 166–68).

134 Ribbeck deleted this line: the future imperative form (*sumito*: AG § 163b) is not found anywhere else in Juvenal (except *esto* and *memento* and the dubious *tollito* at 9.105 (where see note)) but the meaning 'you may take' (see KS 2.1.§50.4) fits the context here after *licet*. The sentiment is banal after the mythological fireworks of 131–3, and *libro* adds a bathetic ending to the sentence as the addressee is taking his ancestry from literature rather than life.

135 **power ... headlong**: the line well expresses criminal passion, with

the juxtaposition of *praecipitem rapit*, the singular verb followed by two subjects (suggesting that the speaker is thinking aloud) and then the spelling out of the link between desire for political power (*ambitio*) and desire for sex (*libido*). *quod si* is often used in didactic and satirical poetry (e.g. 2.43, Horace *Satires* 1.1.43, *Epistles* 2.1.90 and many times in Lucretius) to introduce an alternative proposition. *rapit* in the sense of 'force into' (*OLD* s.v. 'rapio' 11b: cf. Virgil *Aeneid* 9.211) picks up *raptura* from 130 but adds to the sense of rapidity in *praecipitem*. *ambitio* denotes the aspiration for power and influence (cf. 3.182–3, 7.50, Horace *Satires* 1.4.26, 1.6.52, 129, Cicero *de Officiis* 1.87) while *libido* has both the more general sense of 'overwhelming desire' (as at 7.85) and also specifically sexual lust (4.3, 6.135, 6.318, 6.349, 10.208, 11.174) caused by luxurious living (6.286–300) and exercised frequently by the salacious Verres in Sicily (e.g. Cicero *in Verrem* 2.1.62–7 (with Steel (2004)), 2.1.120, 2.3.77).

136 **rods**: flogging people until the rod broke was a byword for the vicious disciplinarian (such as the centurion in Tacitus (*Annals* 1.23) whose nickname was 'fetch me another <vine-branch> (*cedo alteram*) as the flogger broke his staff on the back of the victim and cf. 247n.). The 'rod' (together with axes: see 23n.) was a symbol of power but was also more than a symbol in provincial government under the Roman republic: see the shocking tale which outraged Gaius Gracchus as told by Gellius (*N.A.* 10.3.5) and cf. Cicero *in Verrem* 2.3.55, 2.3.70, 2.3.143, 2.5.161–2. *sociorum* is again (cf. 89n.) sardonic – is this the way to treat one's friends? – while the choice of *sanguine* (**blood**) for a more predictable word ('back' for example) is perhaps because *sanguis* is a key word in this poem (cf. 2n.) and to enhance the sibilance.

136–7 *si te / delectant* repeats the same phrase from 131–2: Courtney calls the repetition 'careless' but the point is surely the characterisation of this tub-thumping moralist speaker. The axes have been blunted and the lictors exhausted by so much use (cf. 6.484 for the use of *lasso*): J. elsewhere (14.15–24) depicts similar examples of sadistic violence with similar distaste. The axe was used as the instrument of execution in Roman provinces, according to Cicero (e.g. *Verrines* 2.1.7, 2.4.144: cf. 267–8n.).

138–9 **pedigree...oppose**: the paradox – that noble birth ends up being a liability to the nobleman – relies again on the idea of *noblesse oblige* (see introduction to this poem) and is heightened by the enjambed *nobilitas*, the juxtaposition with *claram* and the spondaic rhythm of *ipsorum contra te*. **oppose**: *stare contra* is a military phrase (cf. 3.290, Virgil *Aeneid* 12.565,

Persius 5.96, *OLD* s.v. 'sto' 12a). The end of line 139 superficially means 'exposes your shameful deeds' but the imagery is violent, suggesting a flaming torch applied to the *pudenda* (cf. Aristophanes' *Thesmophoriazusai* 236–42). *pudenda* suggests 'private parts' (*OLD* s.v. 'pudendus' b, Adams (1982) 55) and *facem praeferre* is commonly used in cases of literal torching (e.g. Cicero *in Verrem* 2.4.75, ps-Virgil *Culex* 262, ps-Seneca *Octavia* 594, Tacitus *Annals* 14.30) although it is also used in the metaphorical sense of 'lighting the way to' (Cicero *Cat.* 1.13, Tacitus *Histories* 2.86, *OLD* s.v. 'fax' 1c).

140–1   **Every ... himself**: a fine gnomic couplet to conclude this section. The final word *habetur* (cf. 3.272, 5.111, 8.24, 10.92, 11.1, *OLD* s.b. 'habeo' 24) is important as this is all a matter of image (as is shown by the choice of *conspectius*). *crimen habere* is to **face charges** as at 13.210, Ovid *Remedia Amoris* 328 (*OLD* s.v. 'crimen' 3c), while *animi uitium* denotes here 'moral failings' (Green) as at Cicero *pro Cluentio* 199.6, *de Oratore* 2.339, Ovid *Met.* 5.195, Quintilian 3.7.20, rather than simply errors of judgement (as at Horace *Satires* 2.3.307, Lucretius 4.386). *tanto...quanto* with comparative adjectives are correlative (AG §414a).

142–4   *quo ... te ... si* means **what use are you if** (as is the case)? (cf. 8.9n.) – i.e. 'given your behaviour, are you any use?' *mihi* is the 'ethic dative' meaning **tell me** (cf. 8.24n.). The rhetorical question lists concrete examples of the general point made at 140–1, showing the combination of bad behaviour and ancestral glory. **Wills** were (and are) important legal documents and were often sworn and held in temples (cf. Martial 10.70.7, Tacitus *Annals* 1.8) to add religious sanction to the weight of the law. Forging a will was a crime mentioned elsewhere by J. (e.g. 1.67): the criminal surreptitiously substituted a forged document before sealing it (*signare*): cf. Cicero *pro Cluentio* 41, Sallust *Cat.* 16.2, Livy 39.18, Suetonius *Augustus* 33. The crime was subject to investigation under the terms of the *lex Cornelia* of the dictator Sulla in 81 BC (Pomponius 1.2.2.32, Justinian *Institutes* 4.18.7, Crook (1967) 270) and the emperor Claudius even found himself accused in a case of this kind (Suetonius *Claudius* 9.2). The crime here is amplified by being described as habitual (*solitum*).

143–4   The language and word-order are expressive, referring to ancestry both immediate (*parentis*) and more distant (*auus*) and specifying both public property (*templis*) and also personal items (*statuam*), with the enjambement stressing that this statue was in recognition of victory won (*triumphalem*): the Temple of Mars Ultor contained statues set up by Augustus of Roman generals in triumphal regalia (cf. 1.129). For criminal acts committed in front of one's ancestors cf. 8.11.

144–5 The noble rake sneaks out by night for adulterous liaisons (cf. 11.186–9, Catullus 7.7–8 for the *topos* of adultery taking place by night), with the concealment stressed by the pleonastic juxtaposition of *uelas adoperta*. Line 145 is a 'golden line' (of the form noun – adj. – verb – adj. – noun) ennobling in its style what it is denigrating in its content. *Santonico* refers to the Santones in Gaul who produced clothing (Martial 14.128.1), and the noun *cucullus* derives from Gallic: it denotes a plebeian cap (3.170) used as a convenient disguise for men visiting brothels (Cicero *in Pisonem* 13, Petronius 7.4) or for an empress working in one (6.118: cf. Watson and Watson *ad loc.*) or for men engaging in sordid sexual encounters as here and at Suetonius *Nero* 26, Horace *Satires* 2.7.55.

146–62 The **Lateranus** here referred to is a mystery, although the name itself may be significant as derived from the noun *later* and so meaning 'Bricky' (Henderson (1997) 132). Plautius Lateranus was a colourful character from the era of Claudius and Nero; accused in AD 48 of adultery with Messalina he would have faced execution then but for the merits of his uncle Aulus Plautius who had conquered Britain in AD 43 (Tacitus *Annals* 11.36). He returned to the senate in AD 55 (Tacitus *Annals* 13.11) and was consul designate in AD 65 but never actually took up the office as he was executed for his part in the Pisonian conspiracy: see 10.15–18nn., Tacitus *Annals* 15.49, 15.60. His property was confiscated and given later to the Christian church which has a 'Lateran Cathedral' in Rome. This Lateranus was 'mentally strong and physically huge' (Tacitus *Annals* 15.53) which fits *pinguis* here and it could be urged that the speaker worries less about the 'bad historical mistake' (Courtney) of calling him *consul* (148) – when he never actually took up the role – than he is keen to present the grotesque image of the fat man on wheels rollicking through the streets, as well as playing on his fame (*et ipse*) and the outrage conveyed in the oxymoron of *mulio consul*. The other possible referent is T. Sextius Lateranus who was consul in 94, but he is known neither for fatness nor for adultery and served under Domitian: we would then have to understand 170–1 as referring to Domitian rather than Nero which is possible (cf. 4.38, Martial 11.33, but see Nisbet (1995) 23–4 and 170–1n. below). The offence of which he stands accused is that he drove his own vehicle (cf. *flagellum/sumet* 151–2) instead of being driven (as at e.g. Valerius Maximus 9.11), which is not in itself any kind of crime but may well have attracted disapproval (cf. 1.61–2) – a sensitivity which Lateranus shares as he hides his driving while he is in office. The small-minded speaker is seen as one who gets excited about trivia and gets his facts wrong in his haste to concoct a scandal. The speaker is also overconfident in his predictions of future behaviour, as is shown by the string of future indicative verbs (*sumet ... trepidabit ... adnuet ... soluet et infundet*) in 152–4, and scathing in his innuendo-laden aspersions of 158–62. The passage makes good use of bathos: the stately worship of great gods in fact is the cult of a Gallic horse-god (155–7): and the only ritual he pursues all night long is that of his appetites (158–62).

146   The poet cleverly links the activity with the rank by having him race past his ancestors' tombs: tombs were generally placed outside the city-boundary (*pomerium*) by the roadside (cf. 1.170–1, 5.55, Cicero *de Legibus* 2.58, Petronius 62) and often addressed the 'traveller' who would pass them (see e.g. Lattimore (1962) 230–34, Feldherr (2000) 222). *cineres atque ossa* are juxtaposed in verse as in death.

146–7   The adjectival *uolucer* derives from *uolo* and means **flying**: the enjambement into the next line adds to the sense of speed, while the anaphora *et ipse/ipse* brings out the surprise factor of the man and his activity. *rapitur pinguis* is something of an oxymoron – his carriage should have been slowed down by his girth – and adds to the surprise of *uolucri/ carpento*. The *carpentum* (cf. 9.132) was a two-wheeled carriage pulled by two mules (Paoli (1990) 230 with illustrations).

148   *sufflamen* is a **brake** ('a road-haulier's term' (Eden (1984 (147)): cf. Seneca *Apoc.* 14.16 ('poor Ixion's wheel should one day have the brakes applied (*sufflaminandam*)): the word is used metaphorically at 16.50. The manual brake was needed for places where the vehicle was going downhill and might otherwise harm the mules drawing it. *mulio consul* is one of J.'s oxymoronic compounds, as *praetextatus adulter* in 1.78, *citharoedo principe* (8.198) and *mimus/nobilis* (8.198–9).

149–150   **but ... but**: the mood of shock is enhanced by the anaphora of *sed* and the personification of the moon and stars, with variatio of *uidet ... intendunt oculos* neatly applied: the massive moon would easily 'see' the act but the tiny stars had to **sharpen their eyes** (see *OLD* s.v. 'intendo' 6c) to do so. Having the moon and stars as witnesses is a *topos*: cf. 6.311, Propertius 2.9.41, Virgil *Aeneid* 9.429, Catullus 7.7–8: in Greek it is often the sun-god who sees and tells as at Homer *Odyssey* 8.302. *testes* could be either accusative agreeing with *oculos* or nominative in apposition with *sidera*: the run of the sentence supports the latter.

150–1 **office has finished**: the phrasing assumes that Lateranus completed a year of office as consul (see above on 146–62n.): the term *honoris* (simply meaning his magistracy (*OLD* s.v. 'honor' 5) but also suggesting 'dignity' (*OLD* s.v. 'honor' 6) may be ironic in view of his disreputable behaviour.

151 **bright daylight**: the phrase *clara ... luce* (*OLD* s.v. 'clarus' 2, cf. Livy 23.10.7) picks up *nocte* (149) and shows that Lateranus no longer has to hide his behaviour: *clarus* is also itself a term for 'illustrious, famous' (*OLD* s.v. 8) and so injects a note of irony into this tale of disgrace.

151–4 Lateranus is now shameless, taking the initiative (*prior*) in greeting others and possibly making noise with the whip, his mood of insouciance well conveyed in *numquam trepidabit* (cf. 10.21). The *flagellum* was used for controlling the animals (*OLD* s.v. 'flagellum' 1b, Martial 14.55.1), as is the *uirga* in 153 (cf. *OLD* s.v. 'uirga' 2b: cf. 3.317) – although the latter also recalls the consular rods of office (23).

153 The point of *iam senis* is assumed to be that Romans would regard an old man as 'a stickler for respectability' (Duff) and so regard this greeting by the younger man as a sign of disrespect. *adnuet* means no more than 'indicate greeting' as at 3.318. *prior* has the sense of 'greets him before <the other man can greet him>'.

153–4 Lateranus is now 'groom as well as chauffeur' (Ferguson) with prominent play on words. *maniplus* often means a unit of infantry (*OLD* s.v. 'manipulus' 3) and *soluere* can easily mean to 'disband' (*OLD* s.v. 'soluo' 11b) but the only *maniplos* being freed here are bundles of hay (*OLD* s.v. 'manipulus' 2: the syncopation (*maniplus*) is common: cf. 16.20) while *hordea* refers to the **barley** with which horses were routinely fed (Varro *Res Rusticae* 2.8, Martial 13.11). As with the driving, the serving of food is something the ex-consul will do for himself. *lassis* makes the point that Lateranus is such an energetic muleteer that he exhausts his animals (cf. 8.137).

155–7 The speaker appears to be conceding that Lateranus worships in traditional and respectable ways (*more Numae*) in order to enhance the bathos of line 157.

155 *lanatas* (literally 'woollen females') stands here (since the term was so commonly applied to sheep) for the animals which wore the wool (cf. 12.4n. and 15.11n.): a common form of kenning (cf. 13.232–3n. and West (1978) on Hesiod *Works and Days* 524). Here the juxtaposition with *robum* makes for a pleasing colour-contrast as well as recalling the language of archaic ritual, a theme pursued in *more Numae* in 156. Sheep and cattle were sacrificed to the gods (cf. 12.1–9) and the celebration referred to here is the *Feriae Latinae* (Ogilvie (1981) 83–84) where such animals were offered to Jupiter Latiaris on the *mons Albanus* (Dionysus of Halicarnassus *Roman Antiquities* 4.49).

156 **Numa** was the second king of Rome (715–673 BC) and was credited with creating the framework and the rituals of Roman religion (Livy 1.19–20: cf.*OCD* s.v. 'Pompilius, Numa', Ogilvie (1965) 88–89).

156–7 The poet sets up the expectation that **Jupiter** is the god addressed – but the enjambement adds emphasis to the surprising identity of the god by whom Lateranus really and solely swears in what is thus a pointed snub to Jupiter himself. **Epona** was a Celtic divinity whose name derives from the Celtic for 'horse': she was the goddess of the stable (cf. Apuleius *Metamorphoses* 3.27, Gschlößl (2007), *OCD* s.v. 'Epona'). The **images painted on the stinking stables** are (one assumes) in the mind of Lateranus as he stands before the altar of Jupiter: the muleteer-consul is physically in a place of high state religion but mentally in his smelly stables at home with his images of the goddess. *olidus* (cf. 11.172, Petronius 21.2, Horace *Epistles* 1.5.29) is very pejorative and the spitting 'p' alliteration further expresses contempt.

158 **revisit**: *instaurare* (*OLD* s.v. 'instauro' 1, cf. Cicero *de Haruspicum Responsis* 23) is the verb used for 'repeating' a ritual because an error has been made, as happened in the *Feriae Latinae* on one famous occasion (Livy 40.16.2). Festivals could last **all night** (cf. 15.43n.) and so we expect the line to end with a word for 'ritual' rather than the bathetic word *popinas* which refers to cheap food-shops (see 11.81n.) such as the emperor Nero used to haunt in disguise after dark (Suetonius *Nero* 26, Tacitus *Annals* 13.25 cf. Dio Cassius 62.14, Edwards (1993) 193). J. gives us a garish list of typical customers at 173–6 and cf. Apuleius *Metamorphoses* 8.1 for a similar picture of a well-born youth addicted to *luxuria popinalis*.

159–60 **Phoenician**: *Syrophoenix* denotes a resident of Phoenicia (which was then regarded as a part of Syria: cf. *Gospel of Mark* 7.26): the word is used of a money-grubbing man in Lucilius (540–1W) and a trader in Lucian (*Conc. Deorum* 4). The adjective is repeated in epanalepsis for added indignation and the lines are full of stereotypical descriptions of 'eastern vulgarity' (Fredericks (1971) 127) as we see the host rushing to meet him with indecent haste (*obuius…currit*) and reeking of scent. **perfume**: *amomum* was a 'symbol of leisurely self-indulgence: e.g. … Martial 5.64.3' (Braund 1996) on 4.108), while the point of *assiduo* is that this man wears his scent all day and not solely for the dinner-party where it was expected (cf. Catullus 13. 11–14).

160   runs: *currit* in enjambement stresses the eagerness of the host. The adjective *Idymaea* (referring to Palestine) comes to mean 'Jewish': Virgil *Georgics* 3.12, Martial 2.2.5, Statius *Silvae* 3.3.140, Silius *Punica* 7.456. The **Jewish Gate** probably refers to the Porta Capena which had a settlement of Jews nearby (cf. 3.11–13). J.'s view of Judaism is mostly negative: see 6. 542–9, 14.96–106nn. and cf. Tacitus *Histories* 5.2–5.

161   master and lord: the focalised juxtaposition of *dominum regemque* dramatises the effusive greeting (*salutans*) of the host (*hospitis*) as at Martial 4.83.5 and is of course ironic: a blue-blooded Roman should be 'master' to a Syrian Jew whose province he has conquered, not simply a patron in the man's pub. Housman argued that Latin poetry does not supply a fresh main verb after a repetition of a word in epanalepsis (*Syrophoenix* here) and so suggested that a line had been lost after 160, while Jahn deleted line 160 altogether to avoid the problem: but *salutans* (Leo) makes the sentence run more smoothly (see further Helmbold (1962) 226–27 who proposes *adfectu et*).

162   Cyane is the name of the nymph of the eponymous spring in Sicily (Ovid *Fasti* 4.469, *Met.* 5.425). The name derives from the Greek for 'dark' or 'dark-blue' (κυάνεος) and suggests that the person here named was a dark-haired (or blue-eyed) servant-girl. The Greek term also refers to the 'Clashing Rocks' in the Argonaut saga (see 15.20n. and Martial 11.99.6 for an obscene metaphor derived from this). *lagona* is a Greek term for **bottle** (λάγυνος) domesticated into Latin and used of the cheap kitchenware from Spain which was given to the lower order of dinner-guests (5.29) and contained the rough wine which is the paltry reward for legal success at 7.121. The scholiast and many modern editors assume that Cyane was a prostitute: *lagona* might be a double-entendre for vulva (cf. Adams (1982) 86–8), the 'bottle' is certainly *uenali* and her skirts are already **hitched up** (*succincta*) for action. J. is often effective at conveying such innuendo without using primary obscenities (cf. 1.39–41, 2.10, 3.134, 9.26, Godwin (2016) 12–13), and cheap eating-houses were seen as seedy places (like the *salax taberna* of Catullus 37) associated with prostitution: see Beard (2008) 227–33.

163–7   Someone will excuse: the speaker brings in an *occupatio* in the mouth of an imaginary interlocutor to anticipate the defence for the bad behaviour and then refute it (see Courtney (1980) 31 and cf. 1.150–157,

6.142–3, 161–6, 7.188–80, 10.324–5, 13.174–82, Horace *Satires* 1.1.101–2).
It was a *topos* to be indulgent towards the sins of youth (cf. Cicero *pro Caelio*
39–43 (with Dyck (2013) 124), Horace *Epistles* 1.14.31–6, Plautus *Bacch.*
409–10) and the phrasing here is similar to Martial 4.78.9 (*haec faciant sane
iuuenes*: 'young men would no doubt do this'): the more extreme forms of
this *topos* are in misogynistic attacks on older women trying to behave like
younger women (e.g. Horace *Epodes* 8, *Odes* 1.25, 3.15 (with Nisbet and
Rudd (2004) 191), 4.13, Tibullus 1.6.77–82: cf. Aristophanes *Ecclesiazusae*
877–89). The ancients expected old people to be more sensible than the
young, from Homer's Nestor (*Iliad* 4.310–25) onwards (cf. 13.33, Homer
Iliad 3.108–10) not least because older people are less distracted by physical
passion (cf. Euripides *Phoenissae* 528–30, Plato *Republic* 328–330, Cicero
de Senectute 7.20, *Tusc.* 1.94, Sallust *Cat.* 6.6).

163   The heavily spondaic rhythm here, the alliteration of 'd' and 'c',
the bucolic diaeresis and the two final monosyllables in this line suggest a
rhetorical *gravitas* which J. is going to expose as hollow. *culpa* is commonly
used of allegations of immoral behaviour (e.g. 1.167, 6. 494, 6.540, 7.158,
8.119, 13.106, 14.37, Virgil *Aeneid* 4.172). The first-person plural language
of *fecimus et nos* attempts to establish shared guilt, only for the speaker to
retort with finger-jabbing second-person singular verbs in 164–5.

164–5   *iuuenes* here means 'when we were young'. *esto* is an imperative
conceding the point (**Yes – but**: cf. 79–80n., 6.222, *OLD* s.v. 'sum' 8b) here
scanned as a spondee (see 79–80n.). **did not … any further**: the speaker
could have left it at *desisti*: the enjambed embellishing of the statement adds
rhetorical power, with the suggestion that misbehaviour in adults is a sign
of indulgence. *fouisti errorem* is a paradoxical metaphor: 'cherishing' (*OLD*
s.v. 'foueo' 7b) is not something we associate with wrongdoing and the term
well conveys wilful mischief which chooses to go beyond the naivete of
youth: cf. Cicero *ad Att.* 12.18.1 (*fouebam dolores*), Livy 22.53.4 (*perditam
spem fouere*: cf. Martial 9.48.4), Ovid *Met.* 7.633 (*uota fouebam*), Seneca
68.8 (*fouere morbum*).

165   The line is framed by two strong main verbs and there is a strong
break at the caesura. The final phrase is a *sententia* in J.'s best lapidary style,
with jussive subjunctive of *sit* (and *resecentur* in 166). The sentiment – that
a short period of wrongdoing is excusable – recalls the anecdote of Cato
approving of a young man visiting a brothel but not of excess in doing so
(Gowers (2012) 98) and the phrase *turpiter audes* recalls 6.97.

166   The syllepsis of the *crimina* being **trimmed** with the **first beard** is

excellent (similar phrasing is used with *crimina* by Ovid *Amores* 3.14.20, 27) and *resecentur* turns the generality of *breue sit* in 165 into a vivid image. The first beard was cut and kept as a memento when the youth assumed the *toga uirilis* (see e.g. 3.186, Petronius 29, Suetonius *Caligula* 10, *Nero* 12.4 for the *depositio barbae*). For more on the Roman attitude towards shaving see 14.12n., Paoli (1990) 108–10. J. regards the first beard as the time to cease from youthful folly, while at 14.216–7 it is seen as the entry to adult misbehaviour: allowing the beard to grow was one sign of the philosopher (e.g. Horace *Satires* 2.3.35) although facial growth also was a mark of 'primitive rusticity' (Courtney on 4.103). The line opens with ponderous spondees until the dactylic chopping of the beard at *resecentur*.

167   **make allowances**: the primary sense of *indulgere* is 'to allow a person to have his way' (*OLD* s.v. 'indulgeo' 1) as at 6.282, Cicero *de Legibus* 1.39. Here, with the accusative *ueniam*, it means 'bestow' as at 2.165, 6.384, 13.217, 15.148–9, *OLD* s.v. 'indulgeo' 5: *ueniam* means 'forgiveness' as at 2.19, 63, 6.535, 15.103. The contrast of the *pueris* and *Lateranus* is enhanced by juxtaposition.

167–8   **marches off**: the urgency of Lateranus' journey (*uadit*) is enhanced by the enjambement, while the juxtaposition of *thermarum calices* brings out the simultaneous combination of bathing and drinking. *thermae* (θέρμαι: cf. 7.233, 11.4) were Roman baths, which could contain gymnasia, libraries, gardens and even lecture-halls; they were places of social interaction as well as simply hygiene (*OCD* s.v. 'baths', Balsdon (1969) 26–32, Paoli (1990) 221–27). The object of Lateranus' interest is the drinking establishments which were routinely found in or near them (cf. Seneca *Ep.* 122.6, Martial 12.70) and here the word for the vessel (*calices*) stands by metonymy for the drinking itself (cf. Ovid *Fasti* 3.534, Martial 9.87.1). The *inscripta lintea* here are **awnings** outside the bar painted with advertisements (cf. Seneca *Ep.* 21.10) although *lintea* also means 'towels' such as were used in baths (Petronius 91.1, 95.8) and only *inscripta* confirms the meaning 'awnings': *calices inscriptaque* are juxtaposed to stress that Lateranus' interest in the baths is purely bibulous.

169–70   **ready for**: *maturus* + dative means 'old enough for': cf. 12.7, *OLD* s.v. 'maturus' 5, Virgil *Aeneid* 7.53, Livy 1.3.1. After the generalising term *bello* (**war**) there is an impressive list of places which ought to be his focus, ranging from the far eastern end of the empire to rivers closer to Rome. The rivers of Armenia and Syria are the Tigris and the Euphrates, which were the eastern frontiers of the empire: the Rhine and the Danube make up the other two major river-frontiers (cf. 51n., Tacitus *Annals* 4.5), but all four areas were notorious trouble spots. Trajan had been involved in extensive eastern campaigns which were a 'disastrous failure' (*OCD* s.v. 'Trajan', *CAH* xi.123–8) and the Parthians had earlier proved more than a match for Roman forces, while the German frontier had been the site of the *clades Variana* in AD9 when three legions were wiped out. Telling Lateranus to abandon the baths and go to these rivers is not likely to be appealing to the dissolute youth. The mss. reading *amnibus* has been suspected as a gloss on *Rheno atque Histro* and Markland proposed *finibus* (accepted by Braund).

170–1   secure Nero's safety: defending river-frontiers is hard, but keeping an irrational tyrant in a state of tranquillity is even more challenging and the speaker adds this surprising point in a mood of sardonic bathos. Nisbet ((1995) 23–24) proposes deleting *praestare...aetas* to remove the name Nero and thus allow this passage to refer to the T. Sextius Lateranus who was consul in 94 under the emperor Domitian (but see above 146–62n. for other reasons for favouring the Neronian Lateranus). Nisbet also objects to the idea that an army commander would act like the prefect of the praetorian guard in guarding the emperor personally: but the sentence may refer to keeping the emperor safe from rebellion at the frontiers rather than just in his palace. *securus* (from *se+cura*) denotes 'free from anxiety' and even suggests philosophical detachment (cf. Lucretius 3.211, 3.939 (of death), 5.82, Horace *Satires* 1.5.101 (of the gods) Cicero *de Natura Deorum* 1.53.2, Horace *Odes* 1.26.6 (of the mind)) and Nero would strike many readers as the most difficult emperor to soothe in this way. *praestare* here has the sense 'render' 'cause to be' (*OLD* s.v. 'praesto' 13) as at 6.287, Lucretius 3.214, Horace *Epistles* 1.16.16. *ualet* adds the sense of 'strength' to mere capability (see 13.120n.) and when joined with *aetas* emphasises the physical power of this youth (cf. Ovid *Met.* 15.207) which is currently being dissipated.

171–2   Ostia was the nearest port to Rome and the place from where military commanders would board ship if going abroad by sea. The style is highly rhetorical: there is apostrophe of Caesar (see 39–40n.) and epanalepsis of *mitte ... mitte*, leading up to the bathos of *popina* (see 158n.) at the end of the sentence. The language is formal – Caesar is the generic name for an emperor, the new provincial governor receives his title as *legatus (Augusti pro praetore)* and the adjective *magna* leads us to expect 'army camp' or some such instead of the bathetic *popina*. *missio* was the formal term for the dispatch of an officer (cf. Cicero *Philippics* 7.14) while *quaere* refers to the physical locating of the individual. The *legatum* is verbally as well as physically inside the *magna ... popina*.

173–6   The speaker now lists seven types of individuals who will be Lateranus' drinking companions. Certain occupations and classes of citizen were considered *infames* and suffered restrictions on their legal status: see 1.48, *OCD* s.v. 'infamia', Edwards (1993) 123–26, Crook (1967) 83–85, Bond (2014), Nappa (2013). There was no official list of such occupations but the rogue's gallery assembled in this *popina* would certainly contain some of them and the list also included disgraced provincial governors (Brunt (1961) 196). Some of these men were regarded as polluted and so not allowed to move freely in the city. The list is neatly composed with chiasmus (*percussore iacentem/ permixtum nautis*), polysyndeton (174) and *variatio* (*cum ... inter*).

173   A *percussor* (from *percutio*) was a 'hit-man' or **assassin** (as at Suetonius *Nero* 33.3): the word is prosaic (cf. e.g. Tacitus *Histories* 1.41, Livy 33.28, Petronius 39.11) and only found here in extant Latin poetry. **lying with**: *iacentem* may refer to the Roman tradition of reclining at meals (cf. 1.136, 4.120, 15.43) but *popinae* were hardly formal dinner-parties and the word also has the more dubious sense of being 'in bed with' (as at 4.9, 6.36, 269, 279), as well as 'being ill in bed' (6.580, Pliny *Ep.* 2.20.1) which suits the context of heavy drinking.

174   **sailors**: 'seafaring was a despised profession, practised for the most part by persons of lowly birth (Cicero *de Officiis* 1.150–1, *Verrines* 5.167) ... and of dubious character' (Watson (2003) on Horace *Epode* 17.20, comparing also Horace *Odes* 3.6.29–32). Sailors also appear in J. at 6.101, 12.81–2: Duff states that their presence here suggests that the *popina* is in Ostia rather than in Rome – but see Horace *Satires* 1.5.3–4 where the town of Forum Appii is 'stuffed with *nautis* and stingy inn-keepers'. *permixtum* (see *OLD* s.v. 'permisceo' 2) has the sense of 'promiscuously thrown together': cf. *differtum* with similar sense and force at Horace *Satires* 1.5.4. *furibus ac fugitiuis* makes good use of 'f' alliteration and the offbeat rhythm of the four-syllable word which ends the line adds a jarring note.

175   **executioners**: the *carnifex* or *tortor* was a slave whose job was to punish and even execute other slaves: cf. 6.479–80, 6.O29, 8.175, 13.195 Plautus *Captiui* 597, Lucretius 3.1017. They were regarded as disgusting (Catullus 97.12, Martial 2.61.3–4: Pompey the Great as a young man was given the insulting soubriquet 'teenage executioner' (*adulescentulus carnifex:* Valerius Maximus 6.2.8.21)). **coffin-makers**: the *sandapila* was a common stretcher which would convey a pauper's corpse (Pelling (2016): cf. Martial 2.81.2, 8.75.14, 9.2.12, Suetonius *Domitian* 17.3) while *faber*

denotes a man who works with his hands (cf. 1.54, 7.223, 14.116, 15.168). Both *carnifices* and undertakers were regarded as polluted from having to handle the dead (e.g. Martial 8.76.14–15), who were always buried outside the city-walls (146n.): Petronius provocatively states (*Satyricon* 78.6) that the slave of an undertaker was the highest-born man to attend Trimalchio's dinner and inscriptions from Cumae and Puteoli show that undertakers suffered restrictions on their rights even to enter a town (*CAH* xi. 390–1).

176 A *gallus* was a **eunuch priest** of the Phrygian goddess Cybele or Magna Mater, whose worship was introduced to Rome in 205 BC. J. expresses contempt for such people at 2.110–116, 6.511–6 – a contempt which was not unusual in Rome (see Beard, North and Price (1998) i.96–8 and Beard (1994)). They were famed for their self-castration (Pliny *NH* 35.165, Catullus 63.5–6) and as eunuchs regarded with contempt: see 14.91n., Horace *Epode* 9.13 (with Watson (2013) *ad loc.*) – such men were also assumed to be pathic homosexuals: cf. Plautus *Poenulus* 1317–8, Martial 3.81, 9.2.13–14. The goddess had her own festival in Rome (the *Megalesia* from 4–10 April: see 6. 69) and a temple on the Palatine; but her priests were only allowed out of it on specific days (Dionysus of Halicarnassus 2.19.5) when they took to begging and fortune-telling (6.517–8). The worship of Cybele was accompanied by noisy drums (*tympana*: see 6.515, Catullus 63.8–9, Lucretius 2.618, Varro *Menippeans* 364.2, Virgil *Aeneid* 9.619, Ovid *Ibis* 456, Suetonius *Augustus* 68) and this 'eastern' music was regarded as effeminate and un-Roman (cf. 3.63–5). The poet effectively switches focus from the man to his silent drums: the priest here is lying flat either because he is drunk, as the scholiast suggests, or else to submit to sexual demands (cf. 3.112, 10.224, Catullus 28.9, Apuleius *Met.* 8.29) as suggested by Adams (1982) 192 and Braund (1988) 117 (and hinted at by the scholiast).

177–8 The dinner-party (*conuiuium*) was a vital part of Roman social life: guests reclined on couches (typically three, each seating three guests) and the dishes were served on low tables (see *OCD* s.v. 'conuiuium', Carcopino (1956) 288–90). Bad hosts would discriminate between higher and lower classes of guest (as explored in *Satire* 5, Horace *Satires* 2.8, Martial 3.60, 3.82, 4.68, 6.11, 9.2, Pliny *Ep.* 2.6: see Balsdon (1969) 42–43) even though the dinner-party was also said to be an arena of equality (with the word *cena* punning on the Greek κοινωνία ('shared fellowship'): see Braund (1996) 306). Good hosts (e.g. the emperor Trajan with his *mensa communis* (Pliny *Pan.* 49.5) and Pliny (*Ep.* 2.6.3: cf. Gowers (1993) 26, 212) treated all the same. J. here inverts the *topos* by having Lateranus descend to the level of the inferior types who are in the *popina* and so create 'equality' by slumming it: Lateranus is 'equal' to these lowlifes in his behaviour as in his personality and all the guests are on the same (low) level. The speaker plays on ideas of Stoic equality as expressed by Seneca ('equal freedom (*aequa libertas*) must exist amongst philosophers more than among any other group' (*NQ* 4.3.6) but the phrase *aequa libertas* has serious traction in Roman society: see Wirszubski (1968) 9–15. The poet effectively uses *variatio* on the theme of 'shared equally': *aequa ... communia..non alius... nec remotior* and juxtaposition of *pocula lectus* to reinforce the idea that this 'meal' is dominated by promiscuous drinking such as we find at 6.O14–16, although (again) the surface meaning of *communia* is that all guests drank the same vintage (cf. Martial 4.85).

178   **not ... nor**: the speaker achieves variation again in this matching pair of negative statements: *non ... nec* and then *cuiquam ... ulli* (as at 12.130). *alius* here means 'different' as at 5.52, 10.150 and the enjambement enacts the spatial distancing envisaged. *remotior* has the sense of 'set apart' and the comparative form of the word suggests 'more distant <than is necessary>: cf. e.g. Plautus *Curculio* 276, AG §291, K-S II.2 §225 A19).

179–82   The speaker produces a *reductio ad absurdum*: you would not let your slave behave like that and yet this behaviour is seemly for the so-called nobles. The point is also sardonic as the 'free' man is in fact enslaved to his appetites, a *topos* found in philosophy (e.g. Plato *Gorgias* 492d1–493d4 and the Stoic mantra that 'only the wise man is free' in Cicero *Paradoxa Stoicorum* 5, 33–41, *de finibus* 3.60, Diogenes Laertius 7.121) and satire (e.g. Horace *Satires* 2.7, Persius 5.83–188).

179   **fate gave you**: *sortior* (from *sors*) literally means to 'draw lots for' but often has the sense of 'to be blessed/cursed with' (cf. 6.505, 14.96, Horace *Satires* 1.6.53, *OLD* s.v. 'sortior' 4). *sortitus* here is the concealed protasis of a conditional question, suggesting '<if you were to> acquire', with *facias* supplying the apodosis in a rhetorical question directly fired at Ponticus, leading to the answer in 180 introduced by *nempe* (cf. 57n.) and framed by the key verbs (*quid facias ... mittas*): this sort of catechism-style stichomythia is fully in the poet's didactic manner. Slaves were (understandably) drawn to the *popina*: see 11.81n. and cf. Horace *Epistles* 1.14.21–2.

180   **Lucania ... dungeons**: the errant slave would be sent away from the urban home to the less agreeable *uilla rustica*, a form of punishment also found at Terence *Phormio* 249–50, Horace *Satires* 2.7.117–8, Seneca *de ira* 3.29.1. **Lucania** (see *OCD* s.v. 'Lucania') was known for sheep-farming

(Horace *Epodes* 1.28) and for producing the finest wild boar (Horace *Satires* 2.8.6) and game in the chilly mountain forests, but much of it was worked as *latifundia* by gangs of slaves rather than freeborn farmers (Scullard (1963) 19–22, *CAH* xi.702–6: cf. Seneca *Dial.* 9.2.13, *de Beneficiis* 7.10.5, Plutarch *Tiberius Gracchus* 8.3): an environment conducive to health rather than pleasure. *Tusca* refers to the region of Etruria which was a byword for rural slavery and its discomforts (Martial 9.22.4 'The Etrurian land rings out with countless fetters') although Pliny is more reassuring (*Epistles* 3.19.7). The *ergastulum* was a **dungeon** used for housing slaves in rural estates: see 6.151 (with Watson and Watson (2014) *ad loc.*), 14.24, Livy 7.4.4.

181   **you ... yourselves**: the self-serving attitude is stressed with the polyptoton of *uos ... uobis* and the *noblesse oblige* theme is re-echoed with the grandiose descriptor *Troiugenae* (cf. 42n., 56 (*Teucrorum*), 1.100, 11.95n., Virgil *Aeneid* 8.117, 12.626).

182   **labourer**: a *cerdo* is glossed as an 'artisan' in *OLD* (s.v. 'cerdo'), and is used to refer to a cobbler in Martial (3.16.1, 3.59.1, 3.99.1), but it was a name in Latin or Greek (Κέρδων) given to slaves (Courtney on 4.153, Kißel (1990) on Persius 4.51, Petronius 60). The scholiast glosses the word here as a significant name (from the Greek κέρδος meaning 'profit') but it is more plausible that it is here intended to be a slave's name to produce a trio of names in this line. **Volesus** Valerius came to Rome with Tatius (Dionysus of Halicarnassus 2.46.3) and was probably ancestor to P. Valerius Poplicola who (it was claimed) was consul in 509BC and helped Lucius Junius Brutus to expel the last king of Rome (cf. 4.103) after the rape of Lucretia (Livy 1.58). **Brutus** is clearly a name of great resonance to Romans (see 5.37, 14.43n.) and the juxtaposed combination of the liberators *Volesos Brutumque* is ironic in this context of people enslaved to bodily pleasures. **disgraceful ... honourable**: the final line of this section is framed by a fine oxymoron of *turpia...decebunt*, where the future tense of the final verb amounts to a strong confidence ('is sure to...').

183–210   Many nobles voluntarily appear on stage or in gladiatorial combat, both of which were highly unsuitable occupations for Roman citizens. This section follows on from the preceding passage: Lateranus only made himself at home among *infames* but many other nobles have rendered themselves *infames* by their behaviour.

183–4   **so disgusting ... that**: the construction is a consecutive clause (*adeo ... ut non*) to express the idea that there may always be worse examples of noble misbehaviour even when it seems they can stoop no lower. The

rhetorical question is enhanced by the anaphora of *adeo* and the variation of
foedis … pudendis (on which cf. 139). *exemplum* is a term from rhetoric for
a specific case to illuminate a general argument about behaviour: see 13.1n.,
14.322n.

185   The speaker uses apostrophe again (see 39–40n.) to name and shame
his new addressee, who has spent his wealth and is now reduced to menial
occupations: cf. Catullus' mockery of the 'bankrupt from Formiae' (41.4,
43.5). A **Damasippus** is found in the Iunii and Licinii family and is the name
given to a bankrupt in Horace *Satires* 2.3: but no certain identification can
be made here. The name derives from Greek Δαμασίππος where it means
'tamer of horses'. *locasti* is the short form of *locauisti* with the meaning
'hire out' (*OLD* s.v. 'loco' 7a).

186   **stage**: *sipario* (stressed in enjambement) refers to a 'small curtain or
screen concealing part of the stage and serving as a backcloth to interludes
etc by *mimi*' (*OLD* s.v. 'siparium'). Here the word is metonymic for the
activity of performing mimes, rather like the similar use of *syrma* (tragic
robe) at 15.30 or *coturnus* (actor's boot) at 6.634, 7.72, 15.29. Catullus (cf.
13.111) was a mime-writer (see *OCD* s.v. 'Catullus' (2)), famed for his mimes
Phasma ('The Ghost') and *Laureolus* (mentioned by Suetonius *Caligula*
57.4 as being performed just before Caligula's assassination in AD 41).
Martial (5.30.3) describes him as *facundi* – as J. (13.111) calls him *urbani*.
T. P. Wiseman ((1985) 192–98, 258) argues strongly for the identification
of this Catullus with Valerius Catullus the republican poet, but this cannot
be proved. J. neatly names the two mimes and their author in enjambed
juxtaposition and **noisy** (*clamosum*) picks up the idea of Damasippus using
his voice to earn money (*locasti*). The mime was enormously popular
lowbrow entertainment: see Balsdon (1969) 276–78, *OCD* s.v. 'mime,
Roman', Fantham (1989).

187   It is surprising to find Lentulus (from *lentus* ('slow')) being called
speedy (*uelox*): the noble family of the Cornelii Lentuli occurs several
times in J. (6.80, 7.95). This play concerned the crucifixion of the robber
Laureolus which was (according to Martial *Spect.* 7) performed with a real
crucifixion suffered by a criminal (cf. Coleman (1990) 64) – as proposed for
this Lentulus in line 188.

188   The trope that he **deserved** (*dignus*) a **real** cross is recalled at 15.17
where the Phaeacians are imagined wishing that the braggart Ulysses
were faced with real (*uera*) monsters and so paid for his lies with his life.
Crucifixion was one method of executing non-citizen criminals and slaves

(*OCD* s.v. 'crucifixion': see 13.105n., 14.77n.). *iudice me* contrasts the judgement of the speaker with that of the crass populace in 189.

188–9 **Do not**: the subjunctive *ignoscas* here is a prohibition with *nec* as at 3.302, 9.99: note the polyptoton of *populo populi* as J. turns his focus onto the spectators. The phrase *frons durior* is striking: see 13.241–2n. and cf. 11.204, Persius 5.103–4 (with Kißel *ad loc.*), *OLD* s.v. 'frons' 3b. J. elsewhere (7.243, 11.199–201) describes the spectators at Roman games as loud and unreasonable: here they are lapping up the nobleman's disgrace.

190 **sit**: the audience in the theatre obviously sat down for the performance: the point of *sedet* is that they were content to stay in their seats when they ought perhaps to have risen in protest (*OLD* s.v. 'sedeo' 7): there is also contemptuous sibilance in *sedet et spectat*. A *scurra* was a professional buffoon (a 'republican cultural composite of threatening socialite, tasteless joker and pushy freeloader' (Gowers (2012) on Horace *Satires* 1.1.23–4) mentioned also at 4.31, 13.111 in connection with Catullus the mime-writer. Here J. coins the intensive term *triscurria* (**triple-buffooneries**) on the analogy of *trifur*, *trifurcifer*, τρισκακοδαίμων (Aristophanes *Plutus* 850–2) and the similar usage of *ter* (*OLD* s.v. 'ter' 2b, e.g. *terque quaterque beati* (Virgil *Aeneid* 1.94: cf. Homer *Odyssey* 5.306), *felices ter et amplius* (Horace *Odes* 1.13.17). **Patricians** were properly the descendants of Romulus' first senate (Cicero *Rep.* 2.23, Livy 1.8.7) but the term here indicates noble blood in general as at 1.24, 4.102, 10.332 (where Silius was in fact of plebeian origin but is called 'finest and most handsome of the *gentis patriciae*'). The three families referred to here (Cornelii, Fabii and Aemilli) were in fact patrician.

191 **listen to**: the verb *audit* (matching *spectat* in 190) is enacted in the plosive alliteration of the compound adjective *planipedes*. **barefoot**: mime-actors, unlike tragic performers, wore no footwear (Seneca *Ep.* 8.8). See 13–14n. for the Fabii family: here and in the next line there is a plurality of such aristocrats being exposed to ridicule (note the juxtaposition of *Fabios ridere* as with *Mamercorum alapas* in 192).

192 *alapa* means a 'slap' and so here refers to **slapstick** comedy (cf. 5.171, Martial 5.61.11) such as was commonly found in the 'adultery' mime (cf. 6.42–4, Horace *Satires* 2.7.58–61). The **Mamerci** belonged to the *gens Aemilia* (see 9n.): the original Mamercus was a son of the second king of Rome Numa Pompilius and the Aemilian family claimed him as an ancestor (Ogilvie (1965) 89). *Mamercorum* is here objective genitive.

192–4 **What does it matter…?**: a strong indictment: a rhetorical question (with the dismissive *quid refert* enjambed for effect) with the triple repetition of *uendant ... uendunt ... uendere*, each of which ramps up the argument. The selling is first a transaction (*quanti*), then it is done even without compulsion and finally it is done with no misgivings at all. *quanti* (a genitive of price recalling the fact that Damasippus had 'spent all his wealth' (185)) is appropriate with *uendant* (a subjunctive in indirect question) as 'selling' usually involves a price to be paid – but both words here are metaphorical as the 'price' is one of reputation and the 'selling' is more a matter of 'selling out'. *funera* has been doubted (and emended) but may simply refer to the 'stage-deaths' such as that of the crucified Laureolus as performed by Lentulus (187–88) and looks forward to the binary choice of 'death or stage' posited in 195. Braund ((1988) 104) points out that 'Lateranus' companions in the sleazy bar – assassins, executioners and coffin-makers (173–5) – are associated with death and the nobles who participate in the mime 'die' on stage (187–8, 192)'. The scholiast glosses the word *funera* as meaning *turpitudinis crimina* and Duff accordingly explains the word as meaning 'moral suicide' (cf. 8.85) while a scribe has written *uulnera* over the offending word in the manuscripts P A and U which has been improved on further with Courtney's emendation to *uerbera*. More discussion is to be found at: Quincey (1959), Griffith (1962), Watt (2002), Dimatteo (2014) 209–10.

193　　The emperor Nero was known to have **forced** (*cogente*) members of the senatorial class into acting on the stage: 'he brought onto the stage the descendants of noble families whom poverty had rendered bribable … payment from a man who can command carries the power of an order' (Tacitus *Annals* 14.14–15: cf. Dio Cassius 61.17, Suetonius *Nero* 4). Caligula had similarly forced freeborn men and women into prostitution to raise state revenue (Suetonius *Caligula* 41, Dio 59.28.9–10).

194　　**They have no qualms** (*nec dubitant*: for this sense cf. 1.103, 9.97–9, 12.43) about selling themselves before a praetor – for sport (with *ludis* emphasised at the end of the line and the sentence). *ludi* refers to the main public Roman games (see *OCD* s.v. 'ludi') which were presided over by a praetor (cf. 6.380, 10.36–7, 14.257n.) since the time of Augustus (Dio Cassius 54.2.3, Balsdon (1969) 263). The official is here described as literally looking down on men who were his social equals (or even his superiors) who had degraded themselves to the level of actors. *celsi* may simply be an adjective alluding to the praetor's **lofty** position on his platform (*OLD* s.v. 'celsus' 2b: see Suetonius *Augustus* 44.2) but there is also a strong suggestion of superiority of moral and social position (*OLD* s.v. 'celsus' 3b, 4,5). *ludis* is a locative/temporal ablative ('at the games').

195–7 **execution or ... stage**: the old heroic ideal of death rather than disgrace is here used to denigrate the nobles' willingness to incur shame in public, invoking the trope that in warfare the moral imperative was to die rather than to be seen as a coward, especially if the fighter were noble (e.g. *Iliad* 12. 310–321). The duty to live and die nobly was elevated over any conceivable physical pressure: cf. the tale of Regulus who returned to Carthage to face torture and death rather than break his word (as told by Cicero (*Paradoxa Stoicorum* 2.16 and *de Officiis* 3.97–115: see Morford (2002) 93–94) and Horace (*Odes* 3.5 (cf. Nisbet and Rudd (2004) 80–81)) or the suicide of Cato in preference to living under the rule of Julius Caesar (*OCD* s.v. 'Porcius Cato (2) Marcus'). Seneca (*de Ira* 3.15) argues that suicide is the 'road to freedom' when the wise man is threatened by tyranny, and the line of argument that honour should triumph over expediency is explored and stated by Plato (e.g. *Crito* 50a7–54b2, *Gorgias* 474c4–479e9).
195 *gladios* ('swords') stands here by metonymy for 'execution' as at 10.123. **stage**: for *pulpita* cf. 225, 3.174, 6.78, 7.93, 14.257 (*praetoris pulpita lauti*). There is neat chiasmus (noun – *inde atque hinc* – noun) enacting the even-handed choice.
196–7 The alternatives are loaded on the side of honour (a quick and simple *mortem*) over against the whole of line 197 spelling out the dramatic roles to be played with an abundance of Greek names and words to add to the disgrace. The adultery mime (cf. 192n.) featured a jealous (*zelotypus* is a Greek word (ζηλότυπος): cf. 5.45, 6.278) cuckolded husband which was clearly an embarrassing role to play. **Thymele** was the leading lady of the actor Latinus in Domitian's time (1.36; cf. 6.66, Martial 1.4.5–6). **clown**: *stupidus* was another term from the mime which could be applied to the cuckold but here seems to allude to the role of **clown**. *collega* is a political term (cf. 3.130, 8.253, 11.92, *OLD* s.v. 'collega' 1) here used ironically as this man who ought to be a *collega* to (say) a consul is now *collega* to a clown (*stupidus*).
198 *citharoedo principe* and *mimus nobilis* are a juxtaposed pair of oxymoronic phrases cf. 148n., while the word order also juxtaposes the emperor and the mime-actor, with the word *nobilis* stressed in enjambement. A *citharoedus* (**lyre-player**) sang and accompanied himself on the lyre (*cithara*): cf. 7.212, 10.211, Quintilian 1.12.3. Nero was famed for his activities as a singer, performing at the *ludi iuuenales* in AD59 (Tacitus *Annals* 14.15) and later on (AD65) in the Theatre of Pompey (Tacitus *Annals* 16.4).

199   The *ludus* was the **gladiatorial school**. The theme of the degradation
of noble men and women in the gladiatorial schools is found also at 11.7–8
(men) and 6.82–113 (women). The use of senators and knights in the arena is
well attested (see e.g. Seneca *Epistles* 87.9, Dio 48.43, Suetonius *Augustus*
43) and it is possible that senators and knights chose to work as gladiators
in search of fame and military prowess (see Hopkins (1983) 20–21) rather
than merely out of desperation as stated by Dio (56.25). *et illic* (**there too**)
suggests that the arena was yet another locus of disgrace.

200–1   **disgrace**: *dedecus* is a strong word (at 10.342 it is used of the disgrace
of the emperor's wife marrying another man behind his back), made stronger
by its position at the start of the line. Gladiators fought in different types of
armour (see *OCD* s.v. 'Gladiators, combatants at games'): the *murmillo* and
the Samnite *secutor* (210) wore helmets and carried oblong shields and short
swords, the 'Thracian' had a helmet, a round shield and a short sword (*falce*),
while the light-armed *retiarius* fought only with a net and a trident (*tridentem*)
and with unprotected face: these men were thus recognisable to the crowd (see
nudum uoltum ... agnoscendus in 205–6). This blade is described as *supina*
which is usually taken to mean 'bending backwards' (*OLD* s.v. 'supinus'
4) and so clearly refers to the scimitar-shaped sword of the Thracian. The
gladiatorial fighting of Sempronius Gracchus is described (in similar language:
cf. 2.148 (*retia misit*)) at 2.143–8 after an extended account (2.117–31) of his
homosexual marriage. His status as a Salian priest is alluded to at line 207
(*tunicae*). Dimatteo ((2014) 219) notes that his fighting is conveyed in a priamel
(200–201: *nec ... nec ... aut ... nec ... ecce*).

202–3   The text here is uncertain and many editors follow Hermann in
deleting *sed ... abscondit*. If we follow Guyet and Ruperti in deleting line
202, thus leaving the crucial point that Gracchus does not hide his face and
deleting the jejune *damnat et odit*, we are still left with awkward syntax
as the subject of the participle *pugnantem* suddenly becomes the subject
of a main verb (*abscondit*); but this is not impossible if we punctuate after
201 and thus leave 203 with two strong juxtaposed verbs across the fourth-
foot caesura, showing the negative and the positive ways of identifying this
retiarius. The phrase *damnat et odit* occurs also at Ovid *Tristia* 3.1.8 and cf.
J.'s phrase *ridet et odit* at 15.71: but the connective *sed* seems meaningless
before the repetition of the verb. The unprotected face of the *retiarius* is
also shown in the story (Suetonius *Claudius* 34) of the emperor Claudius
having gladiators who fell down executed, 'especially *retiarii*, so that he
could watch their faces as they died'.

203–5   The *retiarius* threw his **net** to try to ensnare his opponent and then used the **trident** to despatch him. Here the sense of excitement is brought out by the imperative *ecce* (cf. 2.129, 6.511, 12.24), by the atmospheric description of the arm-movements (*uibrata ... dextra*) and by having the failure (*nequiquam*) emphasised in enjambement in 205. Courtney points out that one normally *uibrat* a weapon in the hand and suggests emending to *librata* – but this useless fighter is well characterised as one whose hand is shaking along with the gear it is holding which is just **dangling** (*pendentia*: cf. Catullus 67.21) and which is verbally contained with the *uibrata ... dextra*.

205–6   **crowd**: *spectacula* (literally 'shows') here refers either to the spectators (cf. 11.193) or to their seats (cf. 6.61) and the phrase brings out the public disgrace (cf. Livy 5.42.4). *ad* can take the sense here of 'in front of' (*OLD* s.v. 'ad' 17: cf. 8.225). Seneca, in a famous passage (*Ep.* 7.5.6), remarks on how the crowd wishes to see criminals butchered 'with their naked (*nudis*) chests exposed'. The strong verb *erigit* shows his shameless attitude even when he is running away (*fugit* cf. 2.144) all over (*tota*) the arena. Running away is of course a shameful act in normal circumstances: cf. Virgil *Aeneid* 9. 719 (where *fuga* is linked with 'dark terror') and Horace *Odes* 3.2.13–16. The gerundive *agnoscendus* has the force of an adjective here ('recognisable'): see KS 1.733 (§ 130 An.4).

207–8   **Let's**: the 1st person plural jussive subjunctive *credamus* brings the speaker and his addressee together. The **tunic** is a matter of debate: Suetonius mentions (*Caligula* 30) *retiarii tunicati* but that passage is a tale of weak gladiators who then turn on their victors and kill them and so the tunic may have been part of the simulated weakness: and 2.144 shows that Gracchus had form for this apparel. Gladiators typically fought naked except for the loincloth (*subligaculum*) and Owen (1905) persuasively argues that the tunic distinguished amateur gladiators from their slave fellow-fighters who fought naked: the passage thus shows Gracchus flaunting his shame and doing so with a tunic which is both brightly coloured (*aurea*) and longer (stretching (*se/porrigat*) from the throat (*faucibus*) rather than the shoulders). **high hat**: the *galerus* was a head-covering (Virgil *Aeneid* 7. 688–9, Moretum 122, Statius *Thebaid* 4.303, Suetonius *Nero* 26.1), especially used of the ceremonial cap worn by priests, or a wig (6.120): the term also has been seen as referring to the shoulder-guard worn by a *retiarius* (Watson and Watson (2014) 191) but this sense is difficult to apply here even though the context would seem to call out for it. *spira* is a coil of rope or **ribbon** (*OLD* s.v. 'spira' 1b), and *aurea* is to be taken with *tunicae* (which becomes the subject of *se/porrigat*) rather than with *spira*. *iactetur* can have the sense of 'flaunting' (*OLD* s.v. 'iacto' 12) but here **bouncing** (*OLD* s.v. 'iacto' 7) makes more sense. Much is made (2.125–8) of the fact that Gracchus was one of the priests of Mars known as Salii, who had to be of patrician birth, who wore a *tunica picta* (with a golden stripe in this case) and a distinctive conical felt hat (Dionysus of Halicarnassus 2.70). They were 'famous for their magnificent dinners' (Nisbet and Hubbard (1970) on Horace *Odes* 1.37.2): their name derives from *salire* (to leap) and their energetic ritual dance was well known (Livy 1.20.4. Ovid *Fasti* 3.387–8) and it is tempting both to imagine Gracchus 'leaping' in flight around the arena, and also to suggest that he was wearing his Salian apparel to invite the support of the war-god Mars in his conflict. Not only is this noble man fighting, but he does so bare-faced and so can be recognised (*agnoscendus*): and if the crowd did not recognise his face they could hardly miss his distinctive priestly garb of embroidered tunic and long hat.

209–10   We expect the disgrace to be Gracchus' – but J. tells us that the *secutor* (200–1n.) who was pitted against him was even more embarrassed at having to fight him than Gracchus was to lose (cf. Seneca *Dial.* 1.3.4: 'a gladiator thinks it is a disgrace to be pitted against an inferior'). *omni* here means 'any' rather than 'all'.

211–230   An extended attack on the late emperor Nero who exemplified many of the failings of the aristocracy. As is his stated practice (1.170–1), J. attacks dead rather than living emperors.

211   **free**: the first word is key to what follows, as Romans under Nero would have voted to remove him had they been free to do so. The phrase *libera ... dentur populo suffragia* is strongly reminiscent of phrasing in Canuleius' speech in Livy (4.3) where he is arguing for plebeians to have the right to elect consuls. At 10.77–8 J. blames his fellow citizens for 'selling' their votes (*suffragia*) and now only caring for 'bread and circuses' (10.81).

212   **Seneca ... Nero**: Tacitus reports (*Annals* 15.65) that there were rumours that the members of the Pisonian conspiracy in AD 65 intended to kill Piso after killing Nero and then make **Seneca** emperor since he was a man of moral distinction: the conspiracy failed and Seneca was forced to commit suicide (see 10.15–18n. and Tacitus *Annals* 15.48–74). *perditus* has a range of meanings (see 14.269n.) but here means **beyond help** in the sense of 'crazy' as at 3.73, 5.129–30 (which also has *quis perditus ut…?*), Cicero *Verrines* 1.1.15, Martial 6.64.27, 12.43.6.

213–14 monkey ... snake ... sack: Roman law (Justinian *Digest* 48.9.9.1) stated that anyone who murdered a close relation should be flogged and then executed by being sewn up into a bag with a variety of animals (dog, cock, ape and snake) and drowned in the sea (see *OCD* s.v. 'parricidium', Radin (1920), Cicero *pro Roscio* 62–73). This elaborate punishment was designed, says Cicero (*pro Roscio* 70–1) to deter men from this most abhorrent crime and also to prevent earth, air, fire and water from being polluted by this execrable human being. The choice of animals was based on the notion that they were all ones which attacked their own kin. Augustus exercised clemency in this respect (Suetonius *Augustus* 33.1) but Claudius was fond of enforcing it (Seneca *de Clementia* 1.23.1 tells us that he sewed more men into the sack than all the previous ages before him). Nero was deemed to deserve this punishment (Suetonius *Nero* 45.2, Dio 61.16) because of all the relatives he had killed (see below) and J. indulges the paradox that he deserved to be executed more than once with the anaphora of *una ... unus ... unus*. J. mentions the snake and the ape (omitting the cock and the dog) to create contemptuous sibilance in line 214.

215–17 Agamemnon's son: Orestes, like Nero, killed his mother (Clytemnestra), but did so to avenge her murder of his father Agamemnon. This was a tale narrated in tragedy both Greek (Aeschylus *Oresteia*, Sophocles *Electra* and Euripides *Electra* and *Orestes*) and Roman (Ennius (*Eumenides*), Accius (*Agamemnonidae, Atreus*), Aemilius Scaurus (*Atreus*), Pomponius Secundus (*Atreus*), Seneca (*Agamemnon*)) and is alluded to also at (e.g.) 14.284–5, 16.25–7, Horace *Satires* 2.3.132–41, Virgil *Aeneid* 4. 471–3, Persius 3.118. The dilemma (of how the young man could resolve the ethical quandary of conflicting duty towards his parents) was a stock topic of the rhetorical schools (cf. e.g. Cicero *de Inuentione* 1.18–19, Quintilian 3.11.4–6: J. was himself a product of this sort of rhetorical education (1.15–17)). The language of ancient epic and tragedy is well conveyed here with the patronymic *Agamemnonidae* (cf. *Cecropides* (46), *Aeacidae* (270), *Tydides* (15.66)) and with the archaic-sounding clash of ictus and accent in *causa facit rem*: the literary nature of the analogy is also pointed as Nero was himself a singer and musician, as J. will point out in 220–1.

215–216 equal ... very different: *par* is emphasised at the start of 215, only to be corrected by *dissimilem* in the same stressed position in 216. The language in the second half of 215 is all legal: *crimen* can mean either 'accusation' (*OLD* s.v. 'crimen' 1: cf. 4.15, 8.128, 8.141, 9.110, 13.210) or 'crime' (*OLD* s.v. 4: cf. 1.75, 1.167, 6.23, 6.219, 6.294, 8.166), while *causa*, which often means a legal 'case' (e.g. 2.51, 6.242) here has the legal meaning 'motive' (as at 6.202, 8.84: *OLD* s.v. 'causa' 7a) and *rem* has the technical sense of 'legal case' (*OLD* s.v. 'res' 11: cf. 15.94).

216   *ille* refers to **Orestes**, who acted on orders from the god Apollo according to Aeschylus (*Eumenides* 622–4), Euripides (*Orestes* 416) and Sophocles (*Electra* 32–7 (where see Finglass (2007) *ad loc.*)), although Dover ((1974) 180–4) points out that it would be taken for granted in Greek thought that a man would seek to avenge his father's murder. In Aeschylus' *Choephoroi* 900–2 the decisive order to obey the gods is given by the hitherto unspeaking actor playing Pylades (cf. 16.26n.) which heightens the force of the divine command. Cicero (*pro Roscio Amerino* 66–7) reports the matter as J. does here.

217   J. follows Homer (*Odyssey* 4. 529–35, 11.409–11) and Seneca (*Agamemnon* 875–907) and Sophocles (*Electra* 203: see Finglass (2007) 159–60) in having Agamemnon slain **at a banquet**: Aeschylus (*Agam*emnon 1108–9, *Choephoroi* 491, *Eumenides* 631–5) and Euripides (*Electra* 157–8, *Orestes* 367) have the king murdered in his bath: see Seaford (1984). *caesi* (from *caedo*) is a strong word, often used of slaughtering sacrificial animals (6.48, 6.447, 8.156) or for punishing slaves (6.483–4) or pupils (7.213) or carving meat (11.141) or for the metaphorical 'flogging' of a guilty conscience (13.194). *pocula* (literally 'drinking cups' as at 8.177) is here used to signify the drinking session (*OLD* s.v. 'poculum' 2b, Propertius 2.15.48): the phrase *inter pocula* means 'while drinking' as at Persius 1.30, Virgil *Georgics* 2.383, Propertius 3.10.21 (cf. *inter uina* at Persius 3.100, Horace *Odes* 3.6.26). The phrase here reinforces the point that Agamemnon was at a disadvantage owing to drink, like the drunken Ombites at 15.47–8, and so his murder was a cowardly act.

218–9   Line 218 is framed with the key naming words, both of them heavy-sounding molossi (three heavy syllables in succession) and ending the line with a fifth-foot spondee and four long syllables. **Electra** was one of the sisters of Orestes (along with Iphigenia and Chrysothemis) – cf. Horace *Satires* 2.3.139–41 for the thought here – while his **Spartan wife** was Hermione, the child of Helen and Menelaus (king of Sparta). Nero had his step-sister wife Octavia (child of Claudius and Messalina and subject of the ps-Senecan drama *Octavia*) executed on a trumped-up charge of adultery (Tacitus *Annals* 14.60–4, Dio 62.13.1) and he also executed Antonia (daughter of Claudius by his second wife Paetina (Suetonius *Claudius* 27.1) on a charge of conspiracy (Suetonius *Nero* 35.4). He was also said to have kicked his wife Poppaea to death when she was pregnant by him after she scolded him for coming home late (Suetonius *Nero* 35.3: see however Mayer (1982)). The vocabulary is expressive: *iugulo* (literally 'throat') suggests the execution of Octavia who had her veins cut and bled to death (Tacitus *Annals* 14.64) while *se polluit* hints at the pollution (μίασμα) of killing blood relations – a danger which Orestes did incur in killing his mother but not with regard to a sister or a wife. *coniugii* (literally 'marriage union') here stands for *coniugis* ('wife').

219–20 *aconitum* was a lethal **poison** derived from the plant of the same name (known in English as 'monk's hood' or 'wolf's bane') which is a subspecies of the buttercup and which causes death (by a variety of gastrointestinal and cardiac effects) and which was thought to be undetectable in food or wine. J. mentions it several times as the poison of choice (cf. 1.158, 6.639, 10.25) and *miscuit* alludes to its mode of preparation (as at 1.70, 14.174). The plural *aconita* here denotes 'doses of poison' (see AG§100b). Nero tried to poison his mother Agrippina and succeeded in poisoning his stepbrother Britannicus (Tacitus *Annals* 13.15–18): his stepfather Claudius was also poisoned with a dish of mushrooms by Nero's mother Agrippina (5.146–8, 6.620–23, Tacitus *Annals* 12.66–7, Pliny *NH* 22.92, Dio 60.34.2–3).

220 **sang ... Orestes**: the monstrous catalogue of infamy reaches a climax with the artistic 'crimes' of singing the part of Orestes on stage (see Suetonius *Nero* 21.3 ('amongst other things Nero sang the role of Orestes the mother-killer'), Dio 63.9.4) and writing (poor) poetry. The mss. reading *Orestes* made sense ('Orestes never sang on the stage') but is greatly improved by Weidner's emendation *Oresten* ('Orestes never sang *Orestes* on the stage'): see Jones (1972). Subrius Flavus, when facing execution for his part in the Pisonian conspiracy, included 'acting' alongside homicide as damning character-traits of the emperor – a view which made him also damn Piso himself (Tacitus *Annals* 15.65–67). Nero's singing was seen as adding insult to injury by traditional Romans such as Subrius: see 223n. and Courtney (2013) 23, 336).

221 The popular account has Nero 'fiddling while Rome burned' in the great fire of AD64: ancient rumour (Tacitus *Annals* 15.39, Suetonius *Nero* 38.2, Dio 62.18.1) had it that he was reciting from his Greek work 'The Capture of Troy' (ἅλωσις Ἰλίου) in full costume. The term *Troica* here refers to his epic poem on Troy (Dio 62.29) which took the Trojan prince Paris as its hero and which he recited in public the following year (Tacitus *Annals*

16.4, Suetonius *Nero* 10). The critique is both specific – that the emperor shamed his office by indulging his feeble talent in public – and also part of the general critique of otiose epics as detailed in 1.1–14. Nero's poetic activity is well documented: Martial (8.70.8) calls him *docti* ('learned') and cf. Tacitus *Annals* 13.3, 14.16, 15.49, Suetonius *Nero* 10, Griffin (1984) 160–63.

221–3   J. names some key players in the transfer of power from Nero to Galba: Gaius Julius **Vindex** was governor of parts of Gaul and led a revolt against Nero in AD68, backing Servius Sulpicius **Galba** for the throne: this revolt was put down (with Vindex killed in battle) by Lucius **Verginius** Rufus (consul AD 63 and governor of Germany in 68: see Tacitus *Histories* 1.51) who seems to have been loyal to Nero at that stage. Verginius was himself offered the throne and turned it down, but later went along with the accession of Galba and served as Nerva's consular colleague in AD 97. He was celebrated as a man of great civic duty and courage and his funeral oration in AD 97 was given by the historian Tacitus (Pliny *Epistles* 2.1: see Levick (1985)). J. gives most prominence here to Verginius as he was the most high-minded and principled of the three – although Vindex was also a critic of Nero's singing (Dio 63.22, Suetonius *Nero* 41.1). The closeness of Vindex and Galba is reinforced by the juxtaposition of their names.

223   This line was deleted by Knoche as being overblown in stating that his poetic work (however bad) could not rank among the aspects of his 'cruel and savage tyranny' which merited vengeance. This is perhaps to miss the element of affront felt by traditional Romans at such (to them) outrageous imperial behaviour – affront which could tip people over the edge into open rebellion and tyrannicide as happened in the case of the emperor Caligula who teased and mocked the praetorian Cassius Chaerea (Suetonius *Caligula* 56.2, Dio 59.29.2) and ended up being assassinated by him. The language here is strong: *crudus* here (cf. *OLD* s.v. 'crudus' 7) means 'wild, savage' but primarily means 'raw, crude' (as at 1.143, 11.76, 15.83) and would be a term which Nero (with his pretensions to artistic sophistication) would have found most offensive. The term *tyrannis* is Greek (cf. 261, 10.113) and looks ahead to the reinvention of Nero on the Greek stage in the following lines.

224   **These ... emperor**: this rhetorical line is framed by *haec opera ... artes* with striking anaphora of *haec ... hae*, and the sardonic use of *generosi* (cf. 6.124, 14.81n.) and *artes* (recalling his famous dying words *qualis artifex pereo* ('what an artist dies with me' Suetonius *Nero* 49)). The line also recalls Anchises' instructions to the Romans (Virgil *Aeneid* 6.851–3) to

exercise fair government as their distinctive *artes* (see Schmitz (2019) 121).
225   pleasure ... foul: the juxtaposition of *gaudentis foedo* well evokes
the perversity of Nero's acts. Nero's voice was said to be feeble and 'dusky'
in quality (cf. Suetonius *Nero* 20: contrast his own opinion of it at Tacitus
Annals 15.33) but *foedo* here refers rather to the disgrace of his singing on
foreign stages (cf. 2.82, 4.14, 6.132, 7.5, 8.183, 14.44 for this use of *foedus*).
See 195n. for *pulpita*.
226   prostituting: *prostitui* is a strong metaphor (cf. Horace *Epistles*
1.20.2: 1.47, 3.65, 6.123, 9.24 use it literally) made stronger by its enjambed
position and building on the Roman assumption that actors were as bad
as prostitutes in that they hired out their bodies for pleasure (see Edwards
(1993) 128, Edwards (1997) 78–85, Keane (2003) 260–61), they induced
sexual pleasure in their female audience-members (6.60–75, Petronius
126) and they were of indeterminate gender (3.95–7). *Graeae* rather than
Graecae is the more archaic and poetic term for 'Greek' (see 10.138n.,
11.100n., 15.110) and better suits the poetic context. *apium* is the name
given to 'a number of species of plants including celery ... **parsley**' (*OLD*
s.v. 'apium') and made up the garland worn by the singing shepherd Linus in
Virgil *Eclogues* 6.68 or worn at symposia (Horace *Odes* 1.36.15–6, 2.7.23–
5, 4.11.2–3: cf. Anacreon 410–2, Theocritus 3.22–3). Dio (63.21) tells us
that Nero won 1,808 crowns in his triumphant tour of Greece in AD 66–67
(cf. Suetonius *Nero* 22.3–24.1) when he also claimed to liberate Greece (cf.
Gallivan (1973)).
227   trophies: the phrase is sardonic as *insignia* more commonly denotes
the marks of military success (*OLD* s.v. 'insigne' 2a, Tacitus *Annals* 1.72,
Virgil *Aeneid* 8.683, 11.334).
228   Nero was born Lucius **Domitius** Ahenobarbus and only changed
his name (to Tiberius Claudius Nero Caesar) when he was adopted by his
stepfather Claudius. The two branches of the *gens Domitia* go back to a
Lucius Domitius (Suetonius *Nero* 1.1, Syme (1970) 33) and Nero was also
said (Tacitus *Annals* 13.10) to have erected a statue of his birth-father Cn.
Domitius which may be one of the *effigies* referred to here: for the paternal
line of Nero see Griffin (1984) 20–23. **Thyestes** was a tragic character
whose children were killed and served to him as food by his brother Atreus
(father of Agamemnon: cf. 7.73). His tale was well-known in the ancient
world (see Boyle (2017) lxix–lxxviii) and memorably dramatised by Seneca
(*Thyestes*). The role was one of those played by Nero (Dio 63.9.4, 63.23.6).
229   The *insignia uocis* (227) are now itemised as clothing, a mask and a

lyre. For the tragic *syrma* (a long trailing **robe** worn by actors) see 15.30n.
mask: *personam* recalls how Suetonius tells us (*Nero* 21.3 cf. Dio 63.9.4–5)
that Nero sang 'wearing the tragic mask' (*personatus*). Male actors would
obviously need to wear a mask to impersonate female characters (see Watson
and Watson (2014) on 6.70) such as Antigone or Melanippe. **Antigone** was
one of the daughters of Oedipus and Jocasta: she defied king Creon's edict
not to bury her brother Polynices (as dramatised in Sophocles *Antigone*)
and Nero himself is said (Philostratus *Life of Apollonius* 4.39.2) to have
composed a tragedy on the same theme. **Melanippe** was the daughter of
Aeolus whose father blinded her when he discovered that she had given
birth to twins by Poseidon and then imprisoned her, ordering her babies to
be exposed. The tale was the subject of two (lost) plays by Euripides. For the
polysyllabic word (here *Melanippes*) at the end of a hexameter cf. 7.218n.

230   **colossus**: Nero had a huge bronze statue of himself erected in his
'Golden House' (Suetonius *Nero* 31, Pliny *NH* 34.18.45) but this one is
marble. Nero did in fact have his prize for lyre-playing taken to the feet of
the statue of Augustus (Suetonius *Nero* 12).

231–68   Epilogue: a series of thumbnail sketches – moving back in time
from Cicero to the foundation of the city – of cases where so-called lesser
men have outshone their 'betters'.

231–244   The Catilinarian conspiracy (as reported by Cicero and Sallust)
demonstrates that nobly born men may behave badly and be surpassed by
men of low birth. The patrician Lucius Sergius Catilina had a successful
career and was praetor in 68 BC, but failed in his bid to be elected consul for
63 (despite enjoying the support of Caesar and Crassus). He stood again for
the following year but failed again and, facing bankruptcy, plotted a coup
with a group of fellow-conspirators which included C. Cornelius Cethegus.
The coup was thwarted by one of the consuls of the year, the *nouus homo*
Marcus Tullius Cicero, and Catiline died fighting in battle in 62 BC (see
OCD s.v. 'Sergius Catilina, Lucius'). Cicero bathed in the glory of defeating
Catiline, was given the title of *pater patriae* (244) and even composed a
poem 'On my consulship' which contained the line *o fortunatam natam me
consule Romam* ('fortunate Rome, born in my consulship') which J. roundly
mocks at 10.122. Later on Cicero's enemies exiled him for having these
Roman citizens executed without trial. J. elsewhere uses (2.27, 10.287–8)
the pairing of Catiline and Cethegus: he sees Catiline as a byword for a
wicked man at 14.41. Catiline passes into literature as a villain – he finds a
place on the shield of Aeneas where he is depicted in Tartarus, 'hanging on a

threatening rock, trembling at the faces of the Furies' (Virgil *Aeneid* 8.668) and cf. Lucan 2.541, Martial 5.69.4, 9.70.2. For more judicious assessment of the conspiracy and its aims see Dyck (2008) 7–10.

231 J. opens his paragraph with apostrophe to the dead **Catiline** (see 39–40n.) contained in a rhetorical question – a device echoing the famous opening of Cicero's 1st *Catilinarian Oration* (*quo usque tandem abutere, Catilina, patientia nostra?* ('For how long will you continue, Catiline, to abuse our patience?). *natalibus* here denotes 'parentage' or 'origins' (*OLD* s.v. 'natalis²' 7: cf. 6.323, Tacitus *Agricola* 6.1, *Laus Pisonis* 12).

232 **elevated**: *sublimius* is a word with rich aesthetic overtones ('sublime' as at 7.28, Horace *Epistles* 1.12.15) but here as elsewhere (*OLD* s.v. 'sublimis' 8) is used to allude to social elevation. The line ends with clash of ictus and accent (*árma ta/mén uos*) which enacts the sudden violence referred to.

232–3 The proposed **night-time** attack on the city was described by Plutarch (*Cicero* 18) and referred to by Cicero (*Cat.* 3.15, 4.13) and Sallust (*Cat.* 43.2): the verbal combination of 'fire and sword' is something of a commonplace (cf. e.g. Livy 2.10.4, Cicero *Phil.* 13.47, Seneca *Ep.*7.4): and the speaker adds a religious dimension with *templis* – a motif straight out of Cicero's denunciation of Catiline (e.g. *Cat.* 1.12.2, 3.2, 3.22, 4.2). *parastis* is the shortened form of the perfect tense *parauistis* and is the reading of Φ: many modern editors have followed the later reading *paratis* which leads on to the historic present tenses of 236–9.

234 The assumption is that **arson** was the behaviour expected of Gauls, with an added xenophobic sneer at their barbarian trousers (*bracatorum*) – a sneer made at Narbonese Gauls (Cicero *in Pisonem* 53.13), Parthians (Propertius 3.4.17) and Getae (Ovid *Tristia* 4.6.47). The **Senones** were a tribe in Gaul who sacked and burned Rome on the 19th July 390 BC (Livy 5.35, Tacitus *Annals* 15.41)): Lucan (1.254) lists them along with the German Cimbri (see 249) as threats to Rome, and Silius (4.160, 6.555) describes them as 'unspeakable' (*infandi*). *minores* (**offspring**: *OLD* s.v. 'minor²' 3c: cf. 1.148, Virgil *Aeneid* 8.268) also carries a denigratory sense ('inferior') which adds to the mockery of these would-be assassins.

235 The language and sentiment is similar to that of 213–4. The **shirt of pain** (*tunica molesta*) was a garment smeared with pitch which was set on fire to cremate the wearer while he was still alive: Coleman ((1990) 60) tells us that this was used as part of the 'fatal charade' form of execution which re-enacted the death of Hercules who died when he wore the 'shirt of Nessus' given to him by his unwitting wife Deianeira: see also Martial 4.

86. 8, 10.25. 5, Plato *Gorgias* 473c, Seneca *Ep.* 14. 5. The point here is that these would-be fire-raisers (*flammas* 233) would deserve a fiery death.

236   There were two consuls in the year 63 BC but the singular here echoes Cicero's own words (*Cat.* 1.2 *consul uidet*): later on he allows his colleague Antonius into the action (2.27: *consules uigilantes*). *uigilo* means 'to be awake' and looks back to *nocturna* in 233 as well as recalling the specific night of November 63 when Catiline's men planned to assault Cicero in his own home early in the morning, only to find the consul ready to bar their way (Sallust *Cat.* 27–8, Cicero *Cat* 1.8–10, 2.6): the verb also alludes ironically to the current *nobiles* who also stay awake to gamble (see 9–10). **standards**: *uexillum* means originally a military ensign (as at 2.101, 10.156) but here as elsewhere (*OLD* s.v. 'uexillum' 3) is used metonymically for a detachment of troops (Livy 8.8.8, Tacitus *Histories* 1.31, *Annals* 2.52). Here the word adds alliterative force and also raises the register of language to full-blown military assault rather than small-scale thuggery.

237–8   Cicero came from **Arpinum**, a hill-town in the Liris valley about 70 miles distant from Rome which enjoyed full citizenship as a *municipium* (Livy 38.36, Cicero *pro Planco* 20) – i.e. a self-governing town in Italy which was bound by rights and duties to Rome (see *OCD* s.v. 'municipium'): see also 245n. The words indicating low-birth – a sequence of ironic 'titles' – accumulate here: *nouus ... ignobilis ... municipalis*: *nouus* denotes a *nouus homo* (**new man** – a man who is the first in his family to reach the consulship), *ignobilis* simply means 'of low birth' (*OLD* s.v. 'ignobilis' 3: cf. 4.104) while *municipalis* often has the pejorative sense of 'provincial' (as at 3.34, Tacitus *Annals* 4.3.4). Plutarch (*Cicero* 1.1) tells us that Cicero was brought up in a fuller's shop but was determined to make his name famous; his mother Helvia was said to have been well-born (γεγονέναι καλῶς) but his father was of unknown pedigree and Dio (46.4–5) regarded his father as low-born. *modo Romae* has the sense of 'only just arrived in Rome' or *parvenu* (see 2.73, 2.160, 4.77, 7.152, 8.99, *OLD* s.v. 'modo' 5 for this sense of *modo*: elsewhere (1.111) J. is rude about ex-slaves recently arrived in Rome). A Roman qualified as an *eques* ('knight') by owning property in excess of 400,000 *sesterces* (see 14.323–4n., *OCD* s.v. 'equites') and the class as a whole did not engage directly in politics just as the senators were not supposed to engage directly in trade.

238–9   **helmeted**: Roman forces carried helmets and only put them on when in sight of the enemy (cf. 1.169, Caesar *BG* 2.21.5): *galeatum* shows the imminent threat posed by Catiline, while *ubique* (as *omni* in 239) adds the point that the enemy were **everywhere**. *praesidium* was a word used sixteen times by Cicero himself in his *Catilinarian Orations* (e.g. *Cat.* 1.1) of his defensive measures and is here given prominence by its position. *attonitis* (cf. 4.77, 7.67, 13.194n., 14.306, *OLD* s.v. 'attonitus' 2) refers to the citizens and adds to the praise of Cicero – while all around were losing their heads, he tirelessly secured their defence, and the threat faced was on the epic scale of being **thunderstruck**. Rome famously had seven hills (cf. e.g. Martial 4.64.11, Ovid *Tristia* 1.5.69–70, Cicero *de Lege Agraria* 2.96, Propertius 4.4.35) and Cicero is here credited with toiling on all seven at once: *laborat* even suggests (as Ferguson notes) the labours of Hercules, also undertaken to rid the world of pests.

240–244　**as much … as**: the speaker sets up a correlative clause (*tantum … quantum*) which contrasts the achievement of Cicero and that of Octavian, with contrasting verbs – the decorous *contulit* for Cicero and the aggressive *abstulit* for Octavian. He also asserts that Cicero's earning of the title 'father of the fatherland' was more meritorious as it was given freely by *Roma* (stressed in epanalepsis) and not under duress as was the case with Octavian.

240　The **toga** stands in synecdoche for his civilian status as contrasted with military uniform (cf. 10.8–9). **within the walls** (*muros intra*) fits this well, as Roman legions were not permitted to be marched inside the *pomerium* (city boundary).

241–4　**name and title** (*nominis ac tituli* – here partitive gentives with *tantum*) as things to be earned are very much at the heart of this poem: the future emperor Augustus is here downgraded with his lowlier birth-name Octavius (changed to C. Julius Caesar Octavianus on his adoption by Julius Caesar and then elevated with the honorific title Augustus when he became emperor in 27 BC) and compared on equal terms with the equestrian consul Cicero. Octavian is also credited with tireless efforts in the vivid juxtaposed imagery *udo/caedibus adsiduo*. **Leucas** was an island close to Actium where Octavian won the massively significant battle of Actium on September 2nd 31 BC; **Thessaly** alludes to the battle of Philippi in 42 BC when the 'Second Triumvirate' of Octavian, Antony and Lepidus routed the men who had assassinated Julius Caesar.

241　The mss. reading *in* cannot be right and I have printed Jahn's emendation *sibi* as the best of many suggestions.

242　Philippi is not in fact in **Thessaly** but in Macedonia: Pharsalia in Thessaly was the scene of the battle between Caesar and Pompey in 48 BC and writers after Virgil (*Georgics* 1.489–92) tend to confuse the geography, seeing the two battles as 'two decisive steps in one progress towards the principate' (Mynors (1990) 95).

243–4   **father of the fatherland**: the title *parens/pater patriae* was awarded to Romans who had served the state well: Romulus was the original 'father of the state' (Livy 1.16) and later Camillus was so called in 390 BC (Livy 5.49: see Ogilvie (1965) 739). Cicero was spontaneously hailed with this title by Q. Catulus in a packed senate (Cicero *in Pisonem* 6) and Augustus received the title in 2 BC (*Res Gestae* 35, Suetonius *Augustus* 58, Dio 53.18: see Yavetz (1984) 13–14) and later emperors were offered it (and feigned reluctance to accept it) almost as a courtesy: see Suetonius *Nero* 8 on Nero, Pliny *Panegyric* 21.1 on Trajan, *CAH* xi.143 on Hadrian. The epanalepsis of *Roma ... Roma* provides rhetorical emphasis worthy of Cicero himself, increased by the explanatory epithet *libera* which is two-edged: on the one hand, Rome gave Cicero this title because she was now 'free' from the threats of Catiline, but on the other hand republican Rome was not yet bound to obey the whims of the emperor. **Rome** is personified, as often in moralistic writing (see 7.138n.)

245–53   The other **man from Arpinum** was Gaius Marius (157–86 BC: see *OCD* s.v. 'Marius C.') who (like Cicero) rose from provincial equestrian obscurity to become a *nouus homo* who won the consulship seven times, reorganised the Roman army and became one of Rome's most significant military figures: J. later (10.276–82) discusses his career as one of ultimate failure but here sees him as a model of meritocratic success.

245   **Arpinum** (cf. 237–8n.) was in the area occupied by the Volsci tribe – a race who were 'long enemies of Rome, unassimilable to its system of (imposed) peace and command' (McGill (2020) 30: cf. Livy 7.27.7) and who produced the warrior (and enemy of Aeneas) Camilla in Virgil's *Aeneid*. **on the ... hills**: *in monte* suggests hard work in a hard landscape, as at 11.89, 11.159–60 (and the tough primitive wife is a *montana uxor* at 6.5) as well as recalling Cicero who *in omni monte laborat* at 239.

246   Marius' degraded status is vividly described: he works for **wages** (*mercedes*) for somebody else (*alieno*) to the point of exhaustion (*lassus*) in ploughing (*aratro*) – unlike the noble man who would hire others to work his land. Plutarch (*Marius* 3) echoes the idea of Marius' tough upbringing.

247   The vivid language continues now that Marius is an army recruit: the staff is **knotty** (*nodosam*) to make it even more painful, and it is used with such force that it shatters (*frangebat*) on his head – producing (presumably) blood-loss and disorientation as well as disgrace: even Thersites was only

beaten on the back and shoulders (Homer *Iliad* 2.265). The **vine staff** (*uitem*) was carried by a centurion in the army and was a common instrument of corporal punishment (cf. e.g. the centurion Lucilius (136n.) who regularly broke his staff on the bodies of his soldiers – but he too only hit them on the back (*tergo*)). The imperfect tense of *frangebat* suggests that this was a regular occurrence and the heavy spondees of this line evoke the seemingly endless pain as well as the slowness which provoked the centurion's wrath. *frangebat* has Marius as subject and so must be passive in sense ('caused to break') as at 6.479 (contrast the active sense at 8.136).

248 **slow ... sluggish**: the key adjectives *lentus pigra* are juxtaposed for emphasis. **pick-axe**: the sentence ends with the low word *dolabra* – an uncommon word found nowhere else in Latin poetry. The activity being described is that of digging up earth to build up a mound around the camp (*castra*): see Watson (1969) 66–68.

249 **Yet**: *tamen* marks the surprise that so lowly a private could achieve so much as to save the city from the **Cimbri**: a Germanic tribe who (along with the Teutones) invaded Italy in 102 BC and were defeated by the combined forces of Marius and Q. Lutatius Catulus in 101 BC (see Demougeot (1978)). **state emergency**: *pericula rerum* is an epic phrase (Silius 15.113) here magnified by *summa*, and *excipit et solus* marks his achievement as one individual (although he in fact acted with his colleague Catulus (see 253n.)) and feeds into the *topos* of 'one man saved the state' as in Ennius' famous judgement (*Annales* 12.363) on Fabius Cunctator ('one man by his delaying tactics restored the state to us', echoed at Virgil *Aeneid* 6.846 and Livy 30.26.9). **takes on**: *excipit* is (as Courtney notes) an effective zeugma: with *Cimbros* it means he 'sustained their attack' (*OLD* s.v. 'excipio' 11a: cf. Virgil *Aeneid* 11.517, Horace *Odes* 4.9.23) while with *pericula* he 'took the dangers on his shoulders' (*OLD* s.v. 11c). Other writers also comment on the panic which accompanied the German invasion (Sallust *Jugurtha* 114, Appian *Illyr.* 4.11) and Plutarch tells us (*Marius* 16) that Marius declared his intention to 'to turn back this cloud and thunderbolt of war and save Italy'.

250–2 The praise of Marius' achievement goes on: *protegit urbem* amounts to calling Marius 'protector of the city': he worked **alone** (*solus*) to protect the 'quivering city' (as Cicero did (238–9)) against an enemy of gigantic physical size (*numquam maiora cadauera*) who arrived as terrifying enemies and ended up being left as food for the crows. The Romans regarded Germans as larger than themselves (see Caesar *BG* 1.39, Tacitus *Germania* 3, 20, *Histories* 5.14, *Agricola* 11, Plutarch *Marius* 11, Seneca *de*

Ira 1.11.1–2) and defeating a bigger enemy (like David versus Goliath) is of course a greater achievement: here J. expands and makes vivid the *topos* by his focalisation of the crows and the corpses with the largeness now increased to being the largest ever seen (*numquam ... maiora*). J. elsewhere (13.164–6) shows fascination with German distinctive racial characteristics.

251 The mss. reading *Cimbros stragemque* was accepted by most editors until Nisbet ((1995) 249–50) cast doubt on it and some editors now prefer Nisbet's suggestions *cumulos stragemque* (Braund) or *stragem tabemque* (Willis). The repetition of *Cimbros* is not in itself exceptional (cf. *Roma* at 8.243–4, *Syrophoenix* at 8.159–60, *audeat* at 16.9–10, *puero ... pueri* at 14.47–8). The word-order reveals the scene by degrees: 'Marius takes on the Cimbri and protects the city; and then (somebody else) was flying towards the dead Cimbri, something which saw them as corpses (the biggest ever) – namely <u>crows</u> (*corui* in emphatic position at the end of the line). *Cimbros stragemque* forms a hendiadys meaning 'slaughtered Cimbri' (cf. 9.47n.).

251–2 The defeated Germans are now depersonalised into a single *stragem* (**slaughter**) and then a mass of **corpses** (*corpora*). *attigerant* here has the sense of 'get a taste of' (*OLD* s.v. 'attingo' 2b: cf. Tacitus *Annals* 4.54, Virgil *Eclogues* 5.26) and the alliteration of *cadauera corui* suggests the pecking of the birds. Birds of prey (and dogs) feasting on the corpses of enemies or executed criminals is a *topos* of ancient literature, from Homer (*Iliad* 1.4–5) onwards: see e.g. 14.77–80, Sophocles *Antigone* 29–30, Lucretius 4.680, Ovid *Ibis* 168–9, Silius 13.597, Petronius 116.9. What makes this passage special is the focalisation whereby we see the enormous corpses through the incredulous eyes of the greedy birds.

253 **aristocratic ... second**: the key words frame the line (*nobilis ... secunda*) as the speaker stresses the point that the noble man came second to the ignoble Marius. The *collega* in question was Q. Lutatius Catulus (see *OCD* s.v. 'Lutatius Catulus (1), Quintus') who never forgave Marius for eclipsing his victory at Vercellae in 101 BC. Plutarch (*Marius* 27) tells us that the Roman people wanted Marius to have all the glory but that he shared his triumph with Catulus (Cicero *Tusculan Disp.* 5.56) if only out of fear that the soldiers would refuse to play along with a solo triumph (Plutarch *Marius* 27). **Laurel** was used to decorate the brow of the general(s) celebrating a triumph (see Pliny *NH* 15.133–5, Beard (2007) 246–47 for possible explanations) just as it was also used to decorate the doorposts at weddings (cf. 6.79) or other joyous occasions (10.65). *secunda* properly applies to *nobilis* but here agrees in hypallage with *lauro*.

254–8 **plebeian**: Cicero was *ignobilis* (237) but still of equestrian stock: Marius started as a day-labourer in the mountains (245–6): now the Decii are 'emphatically plebeians' (Braund (1988) 120) with the term repeated in anaphora, and the next great man is more ignoble again (259). Publius Decius Mus and his son (with the same name) both died willingly to save the Roman army: the father in 340 BC fighting the Latins (Livy 8.9.8) and the son in 295 fighting the Samnites (Livy 10.28.15): both offered their lives in a ceremony called *deuotio* in which a man offered his life to the gods of the underworld in exchange for the safety of the state, and their patriotic self-immolation became the stuff of legend – see 14.239n., Cicero *Rab. Post*.2, *de Natura Deorum* 3.15, *pro Sestio* 48, Virgil *Aeneid* 6.824.

254 **souls**: *anima* properly means the animating spirit (Lucretius 3.117–129) but is used in non-philosophical contexts for 'souls of the dead' (*OLD* s.v. 'anima' 6, as at 2.156, Virgil *Aeneid* 6.817–18, Lucan 1.447, 6.786) which looks forward to their self-sacrifice in 257, as well as being a laudatory term for a person's 'spirit' (*OLD* s.v. 'anima' 8: cf. the scornful *animae uiles* in Virgil Aeneid 11.372, Lucan 5.683).

255 **names**: *nomina* is stressed in enjambement, suggesting that the only 'low-born' part of these men was their name: and *tamen* again (cf. 249n.) shows the surprise that such noble acts could be done by lowly folk.

255–7 The formulation of the *deuotio* is enunciated over (almost) three lines, the wording close to the 'common combination *sociis et Latino nomine*' (Courtney *ad loc.*), with the *auxiliis* referring to the Samnite allies: the phrasing is unfortunate, as Livy tells us (8.3.8) that the occasion of the conflict was a 'rebellion of the allies and those of the Latin name' (*sociorum nominisque Latini*). The vast benefit gained from the sacrifice is enacted by the repetition of *pro totis ... pro / omnibus ... omni* and the formal archaic language of *dis infernis terraeque parenti* gives the sentence a solemn tone which is close to that quoted in Livy (8.9.8: *deis manibus tellurique*). The enjambement of *omnibus* and its separation from *pro* (cf. 5.33, 6.58) adds to the elongation of the phrasing which enacts the vast numbers being helped.

258 This line has been marked as an interpolation by many editors. If genuine it does little more than paraphrase the point of the previous four lines, but the thought is interestingly reversed: the many troops being saved by the Decii were regarded by the Decii themselves as worth more than their own lives. *pluris* is a genitive of value.

259–60 **man born of a slave-girl**: Servius Tullius (578–535 BC) was the sixth and the last 'good king' of Rome – being succeeded by Tarquinius

Superbus who murdered him at the instigation of his daughter Tullia. Perhaps because of his name Seruius (~ *seruus* ('slave')), Roman sources speculated that he was the son of the Latin captive Ocrisia and an unknown father (Livy 4.3.12, Dionysus of Halicarnassus 4.1) and he was said to have enfranchised freedmen as well as a host of other political innovations which smoothed the path to the republic which was established on the expulsion of Tarquinius (see 7.199–201, Livy 1.39, Horace *Satires* 1.6.9 (with Gowers (2012) *ad loc.*), *OCD* s.v. 'Tullius, Servius', Ogilvie (1965) 156–57). The poet enhances the surprise here: the low birth is mentioned in two words (*ancilla natus*) but the achievement is amplified over the following eleven. Livy (1.48.8) tells us that Servius was a hard act to follow and that 'just and legitimate rule died with him': the speaker's choice of words is more economical, as *ultimus ille bonorum* means literally 'last of the good kings' but also suggests 'the pinnacle of good kingship' (*OLD* s.v. 'ultimus' 7: cf. 2.34, 12.55, 15.95). The *trabea* was a ritual purple **robe** associated with Romulus (Ovid *Fasti* 1.37, 2.503–4, *Metamorphoses* 14.828, Virgil *Aeneid* 7.612–3, 11.334) and later worn by the *Flamen Dialis, Salii,* consuls, augurs and equites on state occasions (see 10.65n.); the *diadema* (**crown**) was the symbol of regal power (see 13.105n., Suetonius *Julius Caesar* 79.2, *Caligula* 22, Horace *Odes* 2.2.21, Seneca *Thyestes* 599), while the *fasces* were the ceremonial **rods of office** (see 8.23n.). **Quirinus** was the title given to Romulus after his deification (Ogilvie (1965) 84, *OCD* s.v. 'Quirinus': cf. 3.67, 11.105, Horace *Epodes* 16.13 (with Watson (2003) *ad loc.*), Virgil *Georgics* 3.27, *Aeneid* 1.292): the name is used here not only for metrical convenience (*Rōmŭlī* would not scan in a hexameter) but also for the religious associations of this saintly monarch.

261–8   The last king of Rome was Tarquinius Superbus (Livy 1.49–60, *OCD* s.v. 'Tarquinius Superbus', Ogilvie (1965) 194–97) who was ousted by a conspiracy led by Lucius Junius Brutus following the rape of Lucretia, perpetrated by a son of the king. Brutus' sons then plotted to restore Tarquin to the throne (Livy 2.3–6): the conspiracy was revealed by the aptly-named slave Vindicius (Livy 2.5) and two of the sons were executed on their father's orders, an act which found memorable expression in Virgil *Aeneid* 6. 817–23. Once again the *nobiles* (offspring of the consul) behaved badly while the state was saved by a slave.

261   **betrayed ... tyrants**: the line begins with the key word *prodita* (here transferred in hypallage to the unpolitical bolts of the gates) and ends with the emotive term *tyrannis* (plural referring to his family as well as himself):

the imperfect tense *laxabant* is conative as the conspiracy did not succeed and the heavy spondees convey the striving.

262   **in exile**: after his expulsion from Rome Tarquin went to Caere in Etruria, from where he sought alliances to restore himself to power: *exulibus* is used as an adjective agreeing with *tyrannis* and the enjambement well evokes the break in the king's power. *iuuenes* here means 'sons' (as at 3.158, 10.310, 14.121: the equivalent form of *filius* (*filii*) could not be fitted into a hexameter) and the choice of word is deliberate as young men were expected to have high ideals (263) but also allowed to make mistakes (cf. 8.163–4) and learn from them: the justice (*iustis ... poenis* 267–8) of their father makes no such allowances, although he is never referred to here as 'father' but only as 'consul' (for the clash of personal and political duty cf. 14.255n.: the theme was a *topos* in the rhetorical schools (*ad Herrennium* 4.66, Quintilian 5.11.7, Seneca *Controuersiae* 10.3.8). The sons in question were Titus and Tiberius Junius Brutus (Livy 2.5).

262–3   **who should**: the monosyllables ending 262 add archaic gravity to the sentiment which expresses the typical Roman expectation that young men ought (*deceret*) to act for idealistic political motives (*pro libertate*) even though the nature of the act is highly uncertain (*aliquid*) and the outcome doubtful (*dubia*) – these key terms here juxtaposed. *libertas* remained a key word in Roman politics (see Wirszubski (1968)) and satire (e.g. Persius 5.73) although J. generally makes sardonic use of it (3.299, 6.140, 6.216–8, 7.116, 8.177).

264–5   The speaker invokes the heroic young of the distant republican past with allusion to some famous tales from the days when Lars Porsenna was trying to bring back the monarchy to Rome. Publius Horatius **Cocles** single-handedly warded off the Etruscan enemy while his allies destroyed the bridge behind him – and then swam full-armed through the current to safety. Gaius **Mucius** Scaevola entered the Etruscan camp to kill Porsenna but was taken prisoner and threatened with death. To show his contempt for pain he thrust his right hand into the fire – an act which so impressed Porsenna that he released him and the man gained his cognomen *Scaevola* ('left-handed': cf. Martial 1.21). Cloelia was a woman hostage given to Porsenna: she escaped and **swam** across the Tiber. The three tales are narrated together in Livy (2.10–13) and Manilius (1.779–81) and Cocles and Cloelia are also found together on the shield of Aeneas (Virgil *Aeneid* 8.646–51) where the 'sons of Aeneas rushed onto the sword for the sake of freedom (*pro libertate*)'. The three tales are sufficiently well-known to need little explanation for J.'s audience and form a small tricolon crescendo here: Cocles and Scaevola are named, while Cloelia (unnamed) has her identity revealed by the line devoted to her tale. **border of the empire**: the river Tiber is poignantly referred to as *imperii fines*, reminding the audience of the time when Rome simply meant Rome and possessed no world-wide empire bounded by major rivers such as the Rhine, Danube and Euphrates (see notes on 8.51–2, 8.169–70).

266–8   The poet sets up a strong contrast between the slave (*seruus*) who foiled the plot and deserves mourning and *illos* (the sons of Brutus) who were executed without compunction.

266   **hidden**: *occulta* (stressed like *prodita* at 261) goes with *crimina* which here means 'wrongdoing' (cf. 8.215–6n.) and the slave's spitting out the facts is conveyed in the plosive alliteration of *patres produxit*.

267–8   Female mourning for the young is usually connected with heroic death in battle (e.g. Homer *Iliad* 24.723–76, Virgil *Aeneid* 9.473–502, 11.215–6, Horace *Odes* 3.2.6–9, Livy 2.7.4) or for the untimely dead (Tacitus *Annals* 3.1–4) or as a sign of wifely fidelity or lack of it (Petronius 42.7, 111–2): for the whole topic see Hopkins (1983) 219, Edwards (2007) 172–74. The mournful tone here is helped by the spondaic rhythm of *matronis lugendus*. It may seem odd here as Vindicius was said to have been rewarded with money and freedom (Livy 2.5.9) and his death is not recorded: the point here is the topsy-turvy contrast between the state funeral envisaged for the heroic slave and the grim execution for the *nobilis* criminals, who were given the sort of punishment normally reserved for slaves (they were stripped, beaten with rods (cf. *uerbera*) and struck with an axe (cf. *securis*: cf. 136–7n., Virgil *Aeneid* 6.819) according to Livy (2.5.8). **legal**: *legum* reminds us that laws 'denote constitutional as opposed to arbitrary regal power' (Courtney) which was a bedrock of ancient republican theory (cf. e.g. Plato *Crito* 50a7–54d1, Thucydides 3.37.3, Lucretius 5.1143–50, Tacitus *Annals* 3.26.3, Seneca *Ep.* 90.6) while *prima* reminds us that this was the dawn of the republican era.

269–75   Coda: better to be a good peasant than a bad noble – and we are descended from shepherds (and worse) anyway. The paragraph is framed by the key verbs *malo* and *nolo*.

269–71   **Thersites** (Homer *Iliad* 2.211–77) was the recalcitrant soldier who speaks against Agamemnon and is reviled physically and regarded as 'the most disgusting (αἴσχιστος) man to go to Troy' (*Iliad* 2.216): he is a byword for low repute and ugliness (Ovid *Ex Ponto* 3.9.10, 4.13.15) and in the myth in Plato's *Republic* (620c2) he chooses to be reborn as an ape (but cf. *Gorgias* (525e) where he is regarded with more understanding). **Achilles** was the greatest Greek warrior, son of a goddess (Thetis) and a mortal: his wrath drives the plot of the *Iliad* and the contrast of the two men is one which J. returns to 11.30–1. In Homer the contrast is not one of birth (see Geddes (1984) 22–23) but one of military rank, behaviour and appearance: but the speaker here uses the pair as vehicles for the contrast of origins. The language here is peremptory and personal to Ponticus, with the jabbing repetition of *tibi sit…tu sis*. The scansion *mālŏ* is not unusual in satire: 6.167, 14.153 and also 6.223 (*uolŏ*), 10.72 (*interrogŏ*), 10.250 (*orŏ*), Persius 5.84, 5.87, Horace *Satires* 1.9.17 (*uolŏ*): note how modal verbs like *uolo, malo* can (as here) take a simple subjunctive (*sit*) without *ut* (AG §565, K-S ii.1. §127.11) but J.'s usual practice is the infinitive (as at 3.40, 4.69, 6.464–5, 7.157, 7.209–10, 10.97).

270   grandson of Aeacus … armour of Vulcan: Achilles is magnified by his ancestry and his achievements here: his impressive patronymic (*Aeacidae*) alludes to his grandfather Aeacus who was a son of Zeus, a glorious man and one of the judges in the underworld (Plato *Gorgias* 524a, *Apology* 41a, *OCD* s.v. 'Aeacus'), while his acquisition of the divine armour from Hephaestus (Vulcan in Latin: see Homer *Iliad* 18.429–617) shows his military prowess and ongoing divine favour and sets up a daunting prospect for Ponticus to grasp (*capessas*: cf. *OLD* s.v. 'capesso' 1b, Virgil *Aeneid* 3.234, 11.324: cf. *Aeneid* 8.535 for *Uolcania arma*).

271   The glorious hero of 270 is now simply named as **Achilles** when the emphasis falls on *te Thersitae similem*. The reproduction of similar men is evoked by the repetition of *similis … similem*.

272–3   Livy (1.8) tells us that Romulus, fearing that his new big city would be empty, increased the population with a ruse which other city-founders had used ('who collect a lowborn and unpretentious crowd and then lie about them being born out of the earth' (cf. 46n.)): he opened up an **asylum**, to which 'there fled from the neighbouring folk an entire mob – with no distinction between freeborn and slave – all greedy for a new life' (cf. Livy 2.1.4, Virgil *Aeneid* 8. 342–3, Ovid *Fasti* 3.431–2). This asylum (Ogilvie (1965) 62–3) was on the Capitoline Hill and still referred to as such by Tacitus (*Histories* 3.71). The lengthy phrase leads up to the bathetic word *asylo* and the repetition (*longe repetas longeque reuoluas*) enacts the labour of going so far back in time. *reuoluas* suggests unwinding a scroll: cf. 6.452, 10.126, 15.30 and the enjambed *nomen* provides the crucial find at the end of the search – only to discover that it comes from what is *infamis* (see 173–6n.).

274–5   the first ... name: the solemn spondees of line 274 and the balanced framing of the line (*maiorum ... tuorum*) leads to the bathetic final line where the ancestor is shown to be a shepherd or something too shameful to specify. Tending sheep was obviously not in itself disgraceful and pastoral poetry is predicated on the simple country life of livestock and agriculture (cf. e.g. Propertius 2.1.44, Horace *Epode* 2.61–2, Virgil *Eclogues* 1.21) which did not exclude music and poetry (Hesiod *Theogony* 22–5, Theocritus 1.7–8, Virgil *Eclogues* 6.4–5, Lucretius 5. 1387): it is the coy *praeteritio* with which this poem ends (for *dicere nolo* cf. Lucilius 17.570–1W, Catullus 67.45, *ad Herennium* 4.50.24, Propertius 3.6.22) which inflicts the fatal blow to any noble's self-esteem, hinting at the more explicit accusations of writers such as Minucius Felix (25.2) who saw the asylum as proving that Rome was packed with 'reprobates, criminals, wicked men, assassins and traitors' (cf. Dionysius of Halicarnassus 1.89: a kinder view at Plutarch *Romulus* 9.3). *dicere nolo* makes an apt conclusion for this verbose satire.

SATIRE IX

'Juvenal's finest creation, the contemporary but inexpressibly foul creature Naevolus, the lusciously male self-prostituting hero of poem 9.'

Henderson (1997) 96

'The 9th Satire deals with a disgusting offence, one of the main sources of corruption in the ancient world.'

Ramsay (1950) lxiv

'…in respect of literary artistry it is Juvenal's masterpiece'

Courtney (2013) 373

This is the only one of J.'s satires in dialogue form – a form used by Horace to good effect in most of *Satires* Book 2 (2.1, 2.3, 2.4, 2.5, 2.7, 2.8) and by Persius in 1 and 3 – although most of J.'s Satires make use of direct speech in a less formal way and Satire 3 is almost entirely a speech in the mouth of a named interlocutor. This poem is a perfect example of the poet using the *persona* method to dramatise his points and to characterise his speaker without revealing himself, and it is fascinating to see how the speaker gives Naevolus more than enough rope to hang himself, offering him reassurance and concern to elicit Naevolus' secrets but keeping an ironic distance from the plaintive responses uttered and at times (e.g. 102–112) overtly mocking Naevolus' naiveté.

Many scholars have seen the primary satirical target in this poem as the 'indignant but selfish, amoral and unscrupulous Naevolus' (Braund (2004) 349). Naevolus is a sexual braggart (34, 43–4, 72–8) who seems to think that a patron will provide him with a living. He is in effect a male prostitute for whom the clock is ticking (125–9), who has a high opinion of himself (124) but who lacks the insight to see that his share-price cannot remain high. He drops literary allusions into his speech in a pretentious manner and has unrealistic notions of his financial needs (140–146), blaming bad luck rather than poor judgement for his poverty.

Others have seen Naevolus as more of a fool than a knave and argued that the 'real' target is the patron who is exploiting him, although of course Naevolus is our only source of information on this. The cuckolded patron brags about 'his' children even though they are another man's, he veers from gushing affection to calculated meanness in a matter of a few lines (36–40), his impotence almost costs him his marriage (75–6) and he keeps dodgy company (62).

Both are of course held up to criticism – the one for duping his *cliens* and the other for being so pathetic and workshy – and they deserve each other. The speaker's final words (130–134) are an indictment of a Rome in which a man like Naevolus will never lack for customers and in which the system of patronage has degenerated into one of mutual exploitation (note the pointed use of the word *amicus* in 130). The speaker says all this without voicing distaste (unlike *Satire* 2) leaving any moral judgements to be drawn by the reader since the world of the poem is one of amoral and pragmatic place-seeking.

Discussions of this poem include: Bellandi (2009), Braund (1988) 130–77, Courtney (2013) 373–75, Flores Mitello (2019) 297–313, Geue (2017) 100–13, Highet (1954) 117–21, Plaza (2006) 155–66, Schmitz 122–27, Tennant (2003), Uden (2015) 74–85, Winkler (1983) 107–29.

1–7 The poem opens in the manner of a Platonic dialogue with introduction of the narrator and his interlocutor and dramatic details of Naevolus' appearance. The three figures with whom Naevolus is compared in lines 1–7 all have significant characteristics for the poem: Marsyas made claims which were unfulfilled and ended up in agony, as did Naevolus: Ravola engages in (to the Romans) transgressive sexual behaviour (as does Naevolus), and Crepereius Pollio is looking for others to help him, as Naevolus will be advised to do (130–131).

1 **Naevolus** is a 'significant name' from *naeuus* ('a discoloured mark on the skin, mole, birthmark' *OLD* s.v. 'naeuus') and so equates to 'Mr Warty': for significant names cf. Umbricius in 3, Fuscinus in 14. The name Naevolus occurs in Martial several times: he is a shy speaker (1.97), an extravagant dresser (2.46), a pathic (3.71, 3.95) and only friendly when he is worried (4.83). **brow clouded over**: *fronte obducta* is a meteorological metaphor found also in Horace *Epodes* 13.5: Watson ((2003) *ad loc.*) compares Homer *Iliad* 17.581, 18.22, Horace *Epistles* 1.18.94. *obducere* literally means to 'cause to cloud over' (*OLD* s.v. 'obduco' 6b: cf. Lucretius 5.777): the metaphorical use is found also in Seneca (*de Clementia* 2.5.4, *de Ira* 3.25.4).

2 **Marsyas** was a Satyr who claimed to be a better musician than the god Apollo: in the ensuing contest Marsyas was **defeated** (*uictus*) and punished

by being flayed alive. There was a well-known statue of his death in the Roman Forum (close to the praetor's tribunal) which showed the Satyr with wineskin in left hand, right hand raised and an agonised facial expression: see Horace *Satires* 1.6.120, Martial 2.64.8. The image was also found on Trimalchio's dinner-table (Petronius 36.3) and his name was even linked to corporal punishment of pupils (Martial 10.62.9). The elevated comparison of Naevolus with a mythological image ('the Roman Statue of Liberty' (Gowers (2012) 247)) will lead bathetically onto the disgusting figure of Ravola – and Satyrs were proverbially priapic as befits Naevolus.

3 why: *quid tibi cum* is colloquial Latin: cf. Plautus *Aulularia* 631, *Menaechmi* 323, 369, Martial 1.77, Cicero *pro Caelio* 33.11, Propertius 3.3.15, Ovid *Metamophoses* 1.456.

3–4 why ... beard: the phrasing is clever, moving from Naevolus' facial expression (*uultu*) to the shame of Rauola's *os impurum* as vividly seen in his wet beard: the juxtaposition of *inguina barba* enacts the activity while *uda* adds vivid detail. The name *Rauola* derives from *rauus* ('tawny' or 'grey', used often of wild animals). **Rhodope** is the name of a mountain range in Thrace but is also found as a Greek name 'associated with disreputable women' (Courtney). For the prurient fascination with cunnilingus cf. Martial 1.77.6, 2.84.3, 3.81, 4.43, 7.67.17, 9.92.11, 11.47.8, Henderson (1991) 185–86.

5 We give ... pastries: Guyet, Pinzger and Markland (followed by many modern editors) marked this line as an interpolation (as the sequence of thought is strained) but it was found in the text of J. by the time of Servius (on Virgil *Georgics* 3.360, *Aeneid* 7.115). Housman read it as joined to the previous line and assumed that the narrator (*nos*) beat Ravola ('like a slave caught licking the pastries'), while Willis, Clausen, Ferguson, Braund punctuate it as a separate generalisation in the manner of an afterthought conveying yet more contempt for Ravola, with the word *lambenti* linking the two lines. **slap**: *colaphus* is a Greek loanword (κόλαφος) and the source of modern words such as French *coup* and Italian *colpo*: it is found in comedy and satire (e.g. Plautus *Captiui* 88, Seneca *Apoc.* 15.2.2). For the use of *incutio* with words for 'blows' or weapons (*OLD* s.c. 'incutio' 1d) cf. 3.246, Seneca *H.F.* 88, *Nat. Quaest.* 2.12.5. **pastries**: a *crustulum* (diminutive of *crustum*) was a small cake often given as a bribe to children (cf. Horace *Satires* 1.1.25, Seneca *Epistles* 99.27). The slave could lick the cake and then return it to its place without being caught – something which was often suspected (cf. Lucilius 629W, Horace *Satires* 2.4.79, 2.6.109):

less culpably, slaves also ate the left-overs when clearing away plates from the dinner (Horace *Satires* 1.3.80-82). **licks**: *lambenti* after line 4 adds a layer of innuendo, given the common use of the verb in sexual contexts: cf. 2.49, Martial 2.61.2, 3.81.2, Adams (1982) 136, 140.

6–8 **Crepereius Pollio** is mentioned at 11.43 as a bankrupt *eques* who 'goes begging with his finger bare' (i.e. having lost or pawned his equestrian ring). Here he is prepared to offer three times the normal interest rate but is such a bad risk that even this insane sum will not tempt the lenders to lend him cash.

6–7 The language is elliptic: understand '<the face of> Crepereius'. The swiftly dactylic line, the enjambement which leaves Pollio to the next line, and the plosive alliteration in line 7 are suggestive of the desperation of the man. *erit* must have a 'prospective' sense of 'will turn out to be' (as at 1.126, 2.47, KS II §36.2).

7 The standard **rate of interest** (*usura*) was 12% *per annum* (Pliny *Epistles* 10.54), although lower rates were known (cf. *CAH* xi. 783, *OCD* s.v. 'interest, rates of', Crook (1967) 211–13) and Cicero (*ad Atticum* 1.12.1) thought 12% excessive: Crepereius here was (allegedly) prepared to borrow at an interest rate of 36%. A still more outrageous moneylender was the Fufidius described by Horace (*Satires* 1.2.12–17) who charged 60% interest on loans, targeting especially the young.

8–9 **goes round**: the verb *circumit* is not essential to the meaning of the sentence but adds a note of desperate motion leading to the crushing negative *non inuenit*. **idiots**: *fatuus* is an adjective commonly used as a noun (*OLD* s.v. 'fatuus' 1b) and means a 'clown' or 'house fool' at Seneca *Epistles* 50.2. The speaker then produces a rhetorical question (*unde…?*) and the key terms *repente/ tot* are juxtaposed over the enjambed line-break. *rugae* are wrinkles produced by frowning rather than by old age (cf. 13.215, *OLD* s.v. 'ruga' 2b).

9 **content with a modest lifestyle**: *modico contentus* sounds close to the Epicurean ideal of the *paruum quod satis est* as found in Democritus (fr. 284DK), Lucretius (5.1117–1119) and the language of pastoral idealism (e.g. Virgil *Georgics* 2.461–74, Horace *Odes* 2.18, 3.1.17–48, Tibullus 1, Propertius 3.2.11–16). The point here is explained in the word *equitem*: to qualify for equestrian status a citizen had to have an estate worth at least 400,000 sesterces (cf. Pliny *Epistles* 1.19), which was a large sum but by no means exceptional (see 14.323–4n.). The owner could therefore be described as content with what was (statistically speaking) not excessive, a

point which is raised again at the end of this poem (see 140–146nn.) **playing the role**: *agebas* has a theatrical sense as at 8.186, *OLD* s.v. 'ago' 26, Horace *Satires* 2.6.111, Ovid *Ars Am*.1.611.

10   *uerna* means **home-bred**, as of a slave who was born at home rather than bought from abroad: cf. 1.26. It is often linked with low and even childish humour (cf. Seneca *Epistles* 51.10, Martial 1.41.1–2, Petronius 24.2, Tacitus *Histories* 2.88) and the juxtaposition with *equitem* neatly points out the frank lack of pomposity afforded by the apolitical rich man with no loss of his status as an *eques* – as seen at once in the setting of the dinner-party. The juxtaposition of *mordente facetus* (as also *salibus uehemens* in line 11) neatly conveys the combination of aggression and cleverness which is also often the mark of satirical wit. The contrast between the depressed state of Naevolus now and his former self is cleverly established with the sort of clever language which a wit would himself use.

11   The jokes are as 'home-bred' as the joker himself, a point enhanced by the metaphor of jokes being 'born' **inside the city**. *sal* (literally 'salt') was an old metaphor for 'witticism' (cf. Catullus 13.5, 16.7, Horace *Satires* 1.10.3, Phaedrus 5.5.8, Martial 12.95.3, *OLD* s.v. 'sal' 6b): the metaphor is of course apt for this description of a *conuiua*. The *pomerium* was the sacred city-boundary (see *OCD* s.v. 'pomerium').

12–15   **Everything … hair**: we have to understand parts of the verb *sum* in these lines and this 'telegram' style has the effect of conveying surprise. The list of oddities begins with the overarching generalisation (*omnia nunc contra*) and then itemises the visible aspects of Naevolus' appearance (face, hair, skin, legs) which justify it. Apuleius (*Florida* 1.3.6) describes Marsyas in similar terms ('foreign, with an animal's face, brutish and hairy, his beard unwashed, covered with prickly hair') and the inference of Naevolus' mental state from his physical appearance is also found at Theocritus 14.1–6 where love-sickness is manifested in emaciation and unkempt hair.

12   **opposite**: *contra* here is adverbial (*OLD* s.v. 'contra' 10a) as at Seneca *Epistles* 7.3, Tacitus *Histories* 2.97. The opening of the line with *omnia nunc* may be an allusion to Virgil *Eclogues* 7.55 (*omnia nunc rident*) – poetry which will later (9.102) be more overtly cited. The line concludes with three pejorative adjectives: *grauis* (*OLD* s.v. 'grauis' 7c) has the sense of 'depressed' and stands in contrast to the grinning joker of lines 10–11, while *horrida siccae* describes his hair which is unkempt (cf. 6.10, 8.116, 14.194–5n.) and also lacking in the fashionable oils which would have made his appearance sleek and attractive. Romans used oil on their hair especially

for parties (Horace *Odes* 1.4.9, Tibullus 1.7.51, Propertius 2.4.5, Cicero *in Pisonem* 25) and so Naevolus' hair reveals that he is no longer living the life of a *conuiua*.

13   **forest**: just as *comae* means both 'hair' (*OLD* s.v. 'coma' 1) and 'leaves' (*OLD* s.v. 3), so here *silua* is a natural metaphor for hair grown out of control, and the juxtaposition with *comae* enhances the effect. Oil was used on the bodies of Romans at the baths and the resulting 'gloss' (*nitor*) was seen as a sign of health and cleanliness (cf. Horace *Epistles* 1.4.15, Pliny *NH* 31.84 and for Greek equivalents see LSJ s.v. 'λιπαρός'). The juxtaposition of *nullus tota* emphasises that Naevolus' body is totally lacking this quality: obviously the narrator can only see the parts of Naevolus which are visible but infers that if those visible parts are unoiled then *a fortiori* the invisible parts are also.

14   **The Bruttian strip of hot pitch** was used for depilation: elsewhere J. expresses deep contempt for male depilation but he also expects men to take care of their appearance (see 8.114–5n.). The Bruttii lived in what is now Calabria in the 'toe' of Italy and were known for producing a form of medicinal **pitch** (Columella 12.18.7, Calpurnius *Eclogues* 5.80, Pliny *NH* 24.37). *fascia* is a **strip** of material or band cf. 6.263, 14.294, while *uiscum* is sticky **pitch** (*OLD* s.v. 'uiscum'2b). In two manuscripts (G and U) this line is found twice (after line 11 as well as in this position) and the mss. have a variety of variant readings possibly caused by scribal unfamiliarity with the word *Bruttia*.

15   **legs ... hair**: untrimmed hair is growing as much on Naevolus' legs as on his head. The line is well balanced and expressed, possibly reminiscent of Lucretius 5.956: *frutico* ('to sprout branches') is here metaphorical, picking up *silua* from 13, while the harsh sounds of *squalida crura* evoke the rough bristles. *squalidus* is elsewhere (11.80) used of a ditch-digger.

16–17   **Why ... home?**: the speaker asks another question beginning *quid* (as at 3) but the sense here is more 'why?' than 'what?' (*OLD* s.v. 'quis¹' 16: cf. Petronius 57.1, Catullus 52.4) and again the verb is omitted. Sexual exhaustion will turn out to be the cause of his being thin: the physical effects of sexual love were well documented (e.g. Catullus 6.13, 51, 89) and the lover was expected to be thin and sickly-looking according to Ovid (*Ars Amatoria* 1. 723–38). The style here is cumulative, with the juxtaposition of *macies aegri* and *tempore longo* picking up *ueteris* – and *olim* picking up both. *ueteris* (cf. 7.170) and *olim* (cf. 3.163, 6.90, 6.281, Horace *Epodes* 14.7, *OLD* s.v. 'olim' 2a) have the sense of 'from a long time ago' while *tempore longo* indicates that the disease has been present for a long time: the phrase *tempore longo* (ablative of 'time how long' as at 6.474, 10.239, KS II §79 *Anm.* 12 and = *diu*) and the pleonastic phrasing of line 17 enacts the lengthy and burdensome illness.

17   **three days**: the reference is to what the Romans (who counted inclusively) called 'quartan fever' (*febris quartana*, τεταρταῖος πυρετός) which would strike the patient every third day (see 4.57, Martial 10.77.3, Cicero *ad Fam.* 16.11.1, Celsus 3.16, *OLD* s.v. 'quartanus' 1, Hippocrates *Aph*.2.25, Plato *Timaeus* 86a): 'quartan' fever was preferable to 'tertian' fever which struck every other day. The present tense of *torret* after *tempore longo* has the sense 'has been tormenting': the verb is used of literal heat and thirst (Lucretius 3.917, *OLD* s.v. 'torreo' 2a) as well as the metaphorical fever of love (e.g. Catullus 100.7, Horace *Odes* 1.33.6, 3.9.13, 3.19.28, *OLD* s.v. 'torreo' 2b) and here causes the line to be framed with words of fever. *domestica* (cf. 14.32, 15.64) is a fine metaphor to suggest that fever 'set up house' with the patient, but note also that Fever was 'an established *numen* of Roman religion … with a shrine on the Palatine (Pliny *NH* 2.15f.)' (Eden (1984) 88).

18–20   **You could … to suit**: ancient medicine depended on the physicians' ability to read internal illnesses from external symptoms, and the link between mental and physical decline was known from Homer's Anticleia onwards (*Odyssey* 11.200–203): cf. e.g. Lucilius 678–9W ('we see how the man who is sick in mind sends signals with his body'). Note here the anaphora of *deprendas… deprendas* and the placing of the binary opposites *tormenta* and *gaudia* in similar position on consecutive lines. *depre(he)ndo* denotes the 'detecting' of something which is not obvious (cf. 4.142, 6.285, 6.640, 7.112, 9.3, *OLD* s.v. 'deprehendo' 4) and the enjambement enacts the unending pain suffered, contrasted with the brevity of the allusion to joys.

19–20   **the face … to suit**: the speaker produces a summative generalisation. *habitus* is the perfect word here, meaning both the 'expression' of the face (*OLD* s.v. 'habitus' 2, citing this passage) and also the inner condition of the body (*OLD* s.v. 1, cf. Celsus 2.10.7): elsewhere in J. it usually indicates garb or clothing (e.g. 2.124 (with *sumit* as here), 8.202) and so there is also a light metaphor at work in the face 'putting on each set of clothing' to suit its mood. *inde* means 'from that cause': see 7.103–4n.

20–21   *propositum* is a grand word to use for Naevolus' louche former **lifestyle** (cf. 5.1, 10.325), while the implicit movement in *flexisse* (*OLD* s.v. 'flecto' 8) is picked up and dramatised in the metaphor of *contrarius ire*.

22–24   **you used to…**: Naevolus is reminded of his old habits of frequenting (*celebrare* 25) religious sites which had a reputation as meeting-places for affairs: women were seen as more prone to religious enthusiasm and so would be unaccompanied by men (see 6.511–547). The shrine of **Isis** (cf. 6.529–30) was in the Campus Martius (cf. 6.489 (where Isis is described as a 'procuress' (*lena*)), Ovid *Ars Amatoria* 1.77–8, 3,635–6, Martial 11.47.4) and her worship had an erotic dimension according to Witt ((1971) 85–86), *pace* Plutarch (*On Isis and Osiris* 351f–352a). The temple of **Peace** was built by Vespasian (Suetonius *Vespasian* 9, *CAH* xi.967–8) after the Jewish War (Pliny *NH* 34.84, 36.27): it held works of art such as the statue of **Ganymede** (see 9.46–7n.) mentioned here. The **foreign mother** Cybele was a divinity whose rites were brought in (*aduectae* cf. Livy 29.10.5) from Phrygia in 205 BC (see 8.176n.). Her rites were celebrated by women in ceremonies which men were forbidden to attend, and her priests were castrated men (*galli*): see 6.511–21. **Ceres** was the goddess of harvest and food who had a temple on the Aventine Hill (cf. *OCD* s.v. 'Ceres'). Like Cybele she was worshipped especially by women (see Watson and Watson (2014) on 6.50).
22   **Ganymede**: the line ends with the four-syllable name *Ganymedem* as at 7.6, 8.229: the homoerotic connotations of the name look forward to line 26. *repeto* (sc. *memoria*) means to 'recall' (*OLD* s.v. 'repeto' 6c).
23   **Palace**: *Palatia* here refers to the temple of Cybele on the Palatine Hill (*OLD* s.v. 'palatium' 2b). *secreta* 'gives a suggestion of mystery appropriate to the *Magna Mater*' (Nisbet (1995) 250: who however suggests reading *Matri*). There is also apt incantatory assonance in *Palatia matris*.
24   **Ceres'**: the name of the goddess stands for her temple (cf. 14.260). Ceres was especially known for chastity (Statius *Siluae* 4.3.11, Spaeth (1996) 112–16) and women were told to abstain from sex before her rites. The parenthetical rhetorical question assumes that adultery on her site was thus a *ne plus ultra* of female degradation and the choice of *prostat* underlines this as it connotes prostitution (1.47, 3.65, 6.123, 8.226, *OLD* s.v. 'prosto' 2).
25   **Aufidius** Chius appears as an adulterer also in Martial (5.61.10). **adulterer**: *moechus* is a transliterated Greek word (μοιχός) for an adulterous lover, used by J. for both men (e.g. 2.27, 6.24, 6.100) and women (e.g. 2.68, 6.278). The P manuscript tradition reads *scelerare* here ('to incriminate') but *celebrare* makes more immediate sense, is more in keeping with the 'urbanity' of tone here (as Courtney notes): and also lends something of its sense of 'praise' (*OLD* s.v. 'celebro' 6) to the nearby word *notior*.
26   **bend … over**: *inclino* was used especially for 'positioning of the pathic

(male or female)' (Adams (1982) 192: cf. 10.224, *Anth. Pal.* 5.54.2, Apuleius *Met.*9.7). Naevolus is seen as the dominant partner in these affairs and so his shame would be less than that of the pathics whom he is meeting, but it is possible that some same-sex relationships were sanctioned by the republican *lex Scantinia* (2.44) – a law which Domitian had reintroduced vigorously (Suetonius *Domitian* 8.3, cf. 11.29, Statius *Siluae* 5.2.102, Dio 67.12.1, *CAH* xi.79) and ridiculously (see 2.29–33). It is also important to note that Naevolus can hardly complain about his homosexual duties as a *cliens* as he does (43–4) if he has been performing these same acts freely with others.

27–46   Naevolus' 1st speech: the rewards accruing to a sexual *cliens* are paltry. The effort is not worth it as the 'payments' are unequal to the efforts.
27–8   **Many find ... the effort**: the language here is close to that of 7.96 and 9.124, but the contrast here is made in chiastic form: *utile ... multis: mihi nullum ... pretium. operae pretium* is colloquial in tone (cf. Petronius 27.2) while *uitae genus* is found in prose both medical (e.g. Celsus 1.1.1), philosophical (Cicero *de Officiis* 1.120, Seneca *Epistles* 24.22) and rhetorical (Seneca *Dial.*5.15.3, [Quintilian] *Decl. Maiores* 8.7.22): see *OLD* s.v. 'genus' 10. *inde* means 'from that source': see 7.103–4n. The clash of ictus and accent in *at mihi*, the enjambed phrasing and the plosive alliteration all convey his anger.
28–31   **greasy cloaks ... seam**: Naevolus itemises the rewards received in a grudging manner, with pejorative terms to convey his distaste.
28   The *lacerna* was a **cloak** worn over the toga to protect it (and the wearer) from bad weather (see 14.287n., 16.45): such garments were sometimes given by patrons to *clientes* who had to brave the elements to accompany them: cf. Persius 1.54, Martial 6.82.9–12, 7.92, Horace *Epistles* 1.19.38. The garments here are described as **greasy** (*OLD* s.v. 'pinguis' 2) or else 'coarse' (*OLD* s.v. 'pinguis' 6) and the infrequency of the gifts (*aliquando*) marks another criticism.
29   This line has been suspected and the sense of the sentence would run better without it: it is possible that the scribe wrote *munimenta togae* as a gloss to explain *lacernas* and *duri crassique coloris* to explain *pingues*, only for the next scribe to think that these words were by J. *munimentum* is a military term for 'fortification' used here metaphorically (as at 6.O11): *color* (*OLD* s.v. 'color' 6) would have to mean 'appearance' with a possible nod to the lack of expensive dye in garments made in Gaul rather than in Tyre (a contrast also made in Martial 4.19, 6.11.7–8 where the speaker laments that '*pinguis Gallia* clothes me').

30   Naevolus uses the jargon of the textile industry to convey his knowledge
(cf. Ovid *Metamorphoses* 6.58 *percusso … pectine*) and also to provide some
effective 'p' and 't' alliteration: the cloaks are **beaten** (*OLD* s.v. 'percutio'
1b) with the **comb** (*OLD* s.v. 'pecten' 2a) of the **weaver** (*OLD* s.v. 'textor').
The line is framed with pejorative terms as the process is done **badly** (*et
male*) and the weaver's Gallic origin marks him as inferior, as at Martial
4.19.1: see *CAH* xi. 724–5, 752–3.
31   **Silver** (*argentum*) was used as coinage (hence French 'argent': cf.
12.49, Horace *Satires* 1.1.86, Persius 3.69, *OLD* s.v. 'argentum' 4) but
here Naevolus is referring to silver plate with some pretence to being a
connoisseur. Silver-plate was a valuable commodity (cf. 1.76, 3.220, 6.355,
7.133, 8.123, 9.141, 11.41, 12.43, 14.62n.) and was given as a gift (Persius
2.52–3, Martial 5.19.11, 8.71, 10.14.8, 10.57, 11.105). This silver was thin
(*tenue*) and its source was an **inferior** (*OLD* s.v. 'secundus' 11c) **seam** (*OLD*
s.v. 'uena' 6). See *OCD* s.v. 'metallurgy, Roman'.
32–3   Naevolus blames **the Fates** for his miserable life (cf. 7.190–202),
just as later on (148–50) he accuses 'fortune' of turning a deaf ear to his
prayers. His statement is made all the more ponderous by the anaphora of
fata… fatum and the heavy sibilance of line 33 as well as the coy euphemism
(**those parts**: cf. Adams (1982) 44–45) which will be spelled out in detail in
line 34. *sinus* here refers to **clothing** covering the lap/groin as at Petronius
24.7, Seneca *Contr.* 4. pr.11, while *partes* is quite common in allusion to
sexual organs (*OLD* s.v.'pars' 6a): *partibus* is a possessive dative with *est*.
The **stars** are commonly credited with agency in determining our future: see
7.194–6n. **let you down**: *cessant* (*OLD* s.v. 'cesso' 3c) suggests that good
fortune is a positive choice of the stars which they may fail to provide.
34   *neruus* primarily means a 'sinew' or 'muscle' as at Lucretius 2.905 and
was commonly used to mean **penis** as here (cf. 10.205, Lucretius 4.1043,
1115, Horace *Epodes* 8.17, 12.19, Petronius 129.8, Adams (1982) 38): the
length of the organ is well enacted in the extended phrasing *longi … nerui*,
the heavy spondaic rhythm, and the effective adjective **unprecedented**
(*incognita*). **get you nowhere**: *faciet* has the basic meaning 'achieve' (cf.
8.1, *OLD* s.v. 'facio' 25) but the word is often used in sexual contexts (e.g.
7.240, Adams (1982) 204).
35–6   **Virro has seen you**: the obvious place where a man might be seen
naked was in the baths (see 6. 374–6, 11.156–7, Petronius 92.8–9, Martial
9.33, 11.51) and Virro was not alone in drooling over the large members on
display there: cf. Martial 1.96.11–13, 2.51.4, Seneca *QN* 1.16.2–3. *spumanti*

... *labello* is reminiscent of the foaming mouths of mad people such as Heracles (Euripides *Heracles* 934) and Orestes (Euripides *Iphigenia among the Taurians* 328) who were hallucinating (cf. 13.14n.) and so is hyperbolic for the salivating of a lustful viewer. Virro was named as the stingy patron in Satire 5, but since his name is used there as a type ('Virro and the other Virros' 5.149) his name may be generic rather than specific. The name is here (as Braund (1988) 242 n.32 points out) apt as *uir* is the Latin for 'male' (cf. Martial 1.96.6) and so looks forward to ἄνδρα in 37. Note also the use of spondees as Virro drools in line 35, the diminutives (*labello* and *tabella*) mocking his effeminacy and the strongly enjambed verbs (*uiderit ... sollicitent*) showing the immediate transition from sight to harassment.

36 Wax tablets (*tabellae*) were a good medium for **love-letters** (see 6.233, 14.29, Ovid *Amores* 2.5.5): the messages here are affectionate (*blandae*), constant (*assidue*) and frequent (*densae*: *OLD* s.v. 'densus' 3) in an accumulation of persistent importunacy leading to the enjambed verb *sollicitent* (cf. 16.28).

37 '**for the man ... faggot**': the Greek is an altered quotation from Homer *Odyssey* 16.294 (=19.13): Odysseus is telling his son Telemachus to hide the weapons from the suitors and suggests that he use the excuse that he fears that they may get drunk and disorderly 'and bring shame on the feast and on your wooing – for iron of its own accord draws a man to it'. The gnomic line may allude to the magnetic and thus magical properties of iron (see Cary and Nock (1927) 125–26) and was translated by Valerius Flaccus (*Argonautica* 5.540): here the epic line is used for comic and bathetic effect with substitution of κίναιδος (*cinaedus*: '**faggot**') for σίδηρος ('iron'): Plaza ((2006) 161) adds a further dimension to the passage by pointing out that the Latin equivalent of σίδηρος (*ferrum*) is a term for 'penis' as we see at 6.112 where the poet tells us (in connection with female admiration of gladiators) that 'women love *ferrum*'. Roman satire makes frequent use of Homer's *Odyssey* (cf. 14.19–20, 15.13–26, Horace *Satires* 2.3.14, 2.5.76, 81, *Epistles* 1.2.23, 9.64–5 (Polyphemus), 2.56, Martial 1.62.6) but Naevolus does so more than most (cf. 45–6n., 64–5, 81, 103, 149–50) and it is possible to read this literary resonance as another aspect of his self-inflation, as in his head he is a Ulysses dealing with sexually predatory men such as Virro. Certainly the topsy-turvy world of the second half of the *Odyssey* (where the apparent beggar was in fact the master and the apparent masters (the suitors) were the real beggars) mirrors Naevolus' conception of his situation where the patron is socially superior but sexually pathic, while the *cliens* is socially inferior

but sexually dominant. The Greek also hints at Virgil *Eclogues* 2.65 (*trahit sua quemque uoluptas*: 'each man is drawn by his pleasure'): see 9.102n.

38   But what monster…?: Naevolus fires off a rhetorical question of the 'what is worse than…?' kind (as at 4.86–8, 6.185–7, 8.231–2, 11.2–3: at 6.190 he asks simply *quid ultra?*) *ulterius* (*OLD* s.v. 'ulterior' 5) usually means 'further' or 'more', as at 1.147, 4.20, 7.30n., 15.118, Virgil *Aeneid* 12.938, but it can also denote 'more extreme' in a moral sense as at 2.34 (*ultima*), Catullus 88.7–8 (*ultra*), Livy 30.42.19–20 (*ulterius*). **monster**: a *monstrum* is often a prodigy or sign from the gods (e.g. 2.122-3, 13.64–70n., *OLD* s.v. 'monstrum' 1) but J. uses the term of people (cf. 4.2, 6.286, *OLD* s.v. 'monstrum' 4) or their behaviour (15.121) when they are (to him) beyond the norm: for the whole topic see Plaza (2006) 305–36. **stingy effeminate**: the line ends with two adjectives, either of which may be acting as a noun – we may read it as referring either to an effeminate miser or to a miserly effeminate – but since Naevolus' main complaint is the lack of reward Braund ((1988) 241 n.18) is probably right in seeing *mollis* as the noun. *mollis* here denotes effeminacy in men (cf. 2.47, 6.63, 6.366, 6.O23, Catullus 25.1, *OLD* s.v. 'mollis' 15): for the figure of the *auarus* cf. 7.30n.

39   'I gave you…': Naevolus quotes his patron's words in derision as he counts off the growing list of his gifts (*haec … deinde illa … mox plura*) in a tricolon crescendo of meanness, with the final limb both suggesting 'yet more' (*plura*) and also giving the agency to the receiver (*tulisti*) rather than to the giver. The 'counting' pattern ironically recalls the famous list of kisses at Catullus 5.7–10.

40   does his sums…: *computat et ceuet* is a verbal dramatisation of the key phrase *mollis auarus* from 38. **wiggles**: *ceuere* (often linked with its female equivalent *crisare* as at 6.322: see Adams (1982) 136–37, Mussehl (1919), Butrica (2006) 30–35) is usually rendered in modern parlance as 'to twerk': cf. 2.21, Persius 1.87, Martial 3.95.13: for the action cf. 6.O19, Petronius 23.3.

40–42   reckoning … accounts: the theme of 'counting' is dominant as it is in the mind of the patron and his client. A *calculus* was a stone used in making calculations on a type of abacus or counting-board: the phrase *calculum ponere* is common (*OLD* s.v. 'calculus' 3b: cf. Petronius 115.16, Seneca *Dial.* 11.9.1, *Epistles* 81.6) for 'reckoning up'. Note here how the orders are being given out in peremptory jussive subjunctives followed by an imperative (*numera*) and finally another jussive subjunctive (*numerentur*): the affectionate *tabellae* of 36 have now been replaced with the harsh *tabulae* of accountancy. The *pueri* here are slaves known as *calculatores* (*CIL* 5.3384, Justinian *Digest* 38.1.7).

41–2 Five thousand sesterces is one quarter of the sum which Naevolus later claims he needs to live (9.140) and half the amount of which Calvinus has been defrauded in Satire 13 (see 13.71–2n.) – on the other hand a labourer would be lucky to earn 1000 sesterces in a year and so his claims here to be badly off also fall flat. Note the anaphor of *numera ... numerentur* as Naevolus introduces his own 'balance sheet' of effort invested against profit accrued.

43–4 easy...: *facile et pronum* (cf. 13.75) is pleonastic: *pronum* has the primary sense 'falling forward' and so equates to 'as easy as falling down' (cf. *OLD* s.v. 'pronus' 7b). The obscenity of these lines has caused some scholars to doubt their authenticity, although the poet here as often avoids using primary obscenities (Adams (1982) 221): *penis* is less of an obscenity than its synonym *mentula* (see Adams (1982) 35–36) and the rest of the sentence is made up of words which are perfectly respectable in themselves. The juxtaposition of *uiscera penem* enacts the deed and then the grotesque ending of the sentence (*occurrere cenae*) spells out in graphic detail what is being envisaged. **decent**: *legitimum* (emphasised in enjambement) has the sense of 'genuine' (cf. Petronius 21.4, 117.5, *OLD* s.v. 'legitimus' 5) and helps to characterise Naevolus as proud of his endowment.

45–6 ploughs was not uncommon in the ancient world as a metaphor for sexual intercourse (cf. *fossa* at 2.10 and Adams (1982) 154) and *fodio* has both an agricultural sense (*OLD* s.v. 'fodio' 2) and a clear sexual sense (Adams (1982) 151–52). There may also be a covert allusion here to Achilles' words to Odysseus in Homer (*Odyssey* 11.489–91), where the hero says that he would prefer to be 'the hired serf of a man who owns no land and who has no great livelihood, than to be the ruler of the dead' – see 37n. for other references to the *Odyssey* in this poem.

46–7 But you...: it is unclear who speaks these lines and ancient texts did not generally mark a change of speaker. Naevolus may be here addressing his patron to argue that sex with him is no longer the pleasure it might once have been: or else the speaker is reminding Naevolus of his status as a former beauty. The language is a cumulative string of laudatory words for effeminate male beauty: *tenerum* (used of a eunuch at 1.22: cf. 6.O24, 8.16, 12.39) denotes youthful freshness at 6.548, 7.237, 14.215, while *puerum* often means 'catamite' (cf. e.g. Martial 11.8.12, 11.78.4, Petronius 11.1, 20.8, 28.4, *OLD* s.v. 'puer' 3). *pulchrum* need not mean 'effeminate' (cf.

7.190, 10.196, 10.345) and can even denote 'morally fine' (16.57, Virgil
Georgics 4.218) but the extended phrase *dignum… caeloque* can only apply
to Ganymede who was the beautiful Trojan youth taken by Jupiter to Olympus
as his cup-bearer (*OCD* s.v. 'Ganymedes'). The tale of Ganymede was told
in epic (Homer *Iliad* 20.232–5, *Homeric Hymn to Aphrodite* 202–17) and
other poetry (Theognis 1345-8, Ibycus fr. 289, Pindar *Olympian* 1.43–5,
10.103–5) and alluded to in Virgil (*Aeneid* 1.28) Horace (*Odes* 4.4.4) Ovid
(*Metamorphoses* 10.155, 11.756) as well as in satire and epigram (5.59,
9.22, Petronius 92.3, 17 times in Martial). J. here uses an effective poetic
hendiadys in *cyatho caeloque* (where 'the cup and the heavens' means 'the
heavenly cup': for hendiadys cf. 3.211, 5.77, 6.84, 8.251, 10.284, 11.123,
12.60, 13.167, 14.9. The transliterated Greek term (κύαθος: cf. 5.32, 13.44)
and the reference to the 'heavens' alludes poetically to the Greek legend
without needing to name the catamite. *dignum* adds a touch of pretension:
he considered himself to be no less beautiful than Ganymede.

48–9   Will you men…: Naevolus widens the apostrophe to the whole class
of *molles auari* and reinforces his indignation with the anaphora of *uos*, the
exasperated combination of a future tense with *umquam* and the sharp final
point which shows from the patron's refusal to pay for his pleasures that (*a
fortiori*) he will never show kindness to another human being (cf. 12.130
for a similar jibe). His own status is ironically reduced: *asseculae* were of
low status (cf. Cicero *Verrines* 2.1.65, 2.3.30, *ad Atticum* 6.3.6) but this
one is described as *humilis* (cf. 8.44) which lowers him even further, and
the enjambement throws emphasis onto the parallel noun *cultori* (cf. 7.37:
see *OLD* s.v. 'cultor' 4, 'colo' 7b). **gratify**: *indulgeo* has the basic sense of
'show kindness towards' (*OLD* s.v. 'indulgeo' 2) and is asking for kindness
to be reciprocated, but there may also be a hint of the Greek χαρίζομαι which
is often used in erotic contexts (e.g. Plato *Symposium* 182a, *Phaedrus* 231c,
256a, Aristophanes *Ecclesiazusai* 629, *Knights* 517, Henderson (1991) 160).
49   *morbo* is interesting, suggesting that his sexual behaviour is an
infirmity or natural weakness rather than a conscious choice of lifestyle:
see 2.16, 2.50, Manilius 5.155, Seneca *Epistles* 83.20, *OLD* s.v. 'morbus'
3b. *donare* is placed in contrast to *indulgebitis* in 48 and *iam* suggests that in
the past the patron was not so stingy at least with his own pleasures.

50–1   Look: Naevolus addresses himself in the second person singular.
umbella is found only here and at Martial 11.73.6 and the parasol here marks the
patron's effeminacy, with *uiridem* perhaps ironically suggesting the word *uir*
('male'). The colour **green** is also significant: Hopman ((2003) 569) comments

that 'green is a marker of bad taste and sexual deviancy when worn by men (Williams (1999) 129)' and cites 2.97, Martial 1.96.9, 3.82 as further evidence. *sucina* were **balls** of **amber** which ladies would rub for their sweet smell (cf. 6.573, Ovid *Metamorphoses* 2.366, Martial 3.65.5, 5.37.11, 11.8.6): the generous size of these presents is brought out by the enjambed epithet *grandia* and the verb *mittas* (suggesting the transporting of amber rather than simply handing it over): this could also suggest that Naevolus' patron is shameless in not hiding these effeminate items, were it not for *secreta* in 53.

51   **birthday**: Romans gave each other presents on their birthdays (cf. 12.1n., Balsdon (1969) 121–2) and also at certain festivals such as the *Matronalia* in March (see 53n.): cf. Ovid *Ars Amatoria* 1.405–6 for the pairing. **to send**: *mittas* is a potential subjunctive (*NLS* §119). This line is metrically smooth until the caesura but the rhythm thereafter is bumpy: *quotiens redit aut madidum uer* has five speech accents in 3.5 feet and only one of them (*aut*) coincides with the metrical ictus. The speaker mentions rainy spring to evoke the season of festivals which were especially celebrated in February, March and April (Balsdon (1969) 68).

52   The *cathedra* was a ladies **chair** (1.65, 6.91, Martial 3.63.7, 12.38.1–2) and this male occupant would need to have a long one (*longa*). *strata* is the past participle of *sterno* and here (as at 6.5, 10.335, 16.44) means 'to cover with cushions' (*OLD* s.v. 'sterno' 2).

53   **the ladies' day**: the 'female Kalends' refers to the *Matronalia* on March 1st which was a festival in honour of Juno when women often received gifts from their husbands (Plautus *Miles Gloriosus* 690, Balsdon (1969) 124, Scullard (1981) 86–87 +n.102): the evidence suggests that the rites were exclusive to women, and *secreta* suggests that he is not advertising his effeminacy. There is also a sensuous quality to the central verb *tractat* (cf. 6.102, *Priapea* 80.2, Adams (1982) 186–87)). The line is a form of 'golden line' where a central verb is framed by two nouns and two adjectives in symmetrical arrangement (N-a-v-a-N).

54–5   **little bird**: the *passer* (στρουθός: Thompson (1936) 160–62, Fordyce (1961) 87–89) was sacred to Venus (Sappho fr. 1.9) and considered over-sexed (Pliny *NH* 10.107, Otto (1890) s.v. 'passer' 1, Henderson (1991) 129): it was famously the pet (*deliciae*) of Catullus' *puella* (Catullus 2.1). The word was also used as an endearment between lovers (Plautus *Asinaria* 666,694, *Casina* 138) and here is sarcastic: there is also a contrast between the pet bird and the wild hawks of the next line. **Apulia** in the 'heel' of Italy was good land for livestock and its sheep produced 'Canusine' wool of fine quality (Watson and Watson (2014) on 6.150, Martial 9.22.9, Suetonius *Nero* 30.3). For 'Apulian plains' as a potential (if unrealistic) reward for a *cliens* see Martial 10.74.8. The lines are forceful, with spondaic rhythm, the jingle of the parallel verbs *seruas … lassas* ending consecutive lines and the anaphora of *tot* marking a strong tricolon crescendo as Naevolus sketches an inventory of his patron's holdings. The list suggests that the patron has large estates: mountains would be used for summer grazing of the flocks (see Watson (2003) on Horace *Epodes* 1.27–8 and cf. Horace *Epistles* 2.2.177–9), *praedia* are whole 'farms' (e.g. Horace *Satires* 2.3.168, 2.6.56, 2.7.110) while *pascua* denotes 'grazing land' in general (cf. e.g. 12.13, Lucretius 5.1248, Virgil *Eclogues* 1.48, *Georgics* 3.213, Calpurnius *Eclogues* 2.18). His sheep are (it would seem) more fortunate than his *cliens*.

55   The *miluus* was a bird of prey usually identified with the red **kite** (ἴκτινος (Thompson (1936) 119–21)): its powers of long and rapid flight (Ovid *Metamorphoses* 2.716) made it a proverbial marker of enormous estates as at Petronius 37.8, Persius 4.26, Martial 9.54.10 (Otto (1890) s.v. 'miluus' 4) which is here amplified by the verb *lassas* as the patron's estates would exhaust even the kite's prodigious stamina. The bird is also known for its rapaciousness (Otto (1890) s.v. 'miluus' 1: Martial 9.54.10, Petronius 42) which also suits the patron himself who 'outdoes' the birds in both respects. The noun is scanned as a dactyl (*mīlŭŭs*) in earlier Latin (e.g. Ovid *Metamorphoses* 2.716, Persius 4.26) but here must be scanned as a dissyllabic word (*mīluōs*) as at Ovid *Halieutica* 95.

56–7   All three places mentioned are close to Naples in the *ager Campanus*, 'the most fertile territory in Italy' (Livy 7.38: cf. Cicero *de Lege Agraria* 2.76: see *OCD* s.v. 'Campania'). **Trifolium** (Pliny *NH* 14.69) was known for its wines (Martial 13.114), the coastal town of **Cumae** was a thriving Greek colony famous for its corn (Ogilvie (1965) 269, 291), home of the prophetess the Sibyl (3.3, 8.125–6n., Petronius 48.8) and the destination of Umbricius in Satire 3 (3.2–3, 3.321), while **Gaurus** (cf. 8.85–6n.) is a mountain close to Lake Auernus (Lucan 2.667–8) and a place where vines grow (Statius *Thebaid* 8.544–5, *Siluae* 3.5.99)). The epithet *inanis* possibly indicates a volcanic crater (and suggests that Gaurus is to be identified with Monte Barbaro) but also makes a neat contrast with *implet* in the same position on the previous line – the 'empty' place manages to 'fill' its owner.

58   **seals … jars**: a *dolium* was a storage container large enough to house a Cynic philosopher (14.308–9n.) and used to store unfermented (or partially fermented) wine (*mustum*) before it was transferred to *amphorae* (cf.

Propertius 3.17.17–18). The *dolia* were sealed with pitch (Columella *de Re Rustica* 12.18.5, Palladius 10.11.1, Ulpian *Digest* 19.2.19, Martial 11.18.24: cf. Horace *Odes* 1.20.3 with Mayer (2012) *ad loc.*) to keep the wine drinkable for long periods (on the whole process see Thurmond (2017) 164–72). The rhetorical question (*quis plura?*) dramatises the simple statement into a challenge to the interlocutor, while the juxtaposition of *dolia musto* (as at Propertius 3.17.17) enacts the placing of the wine in the jar. The future participle *uicturo* is ambiguous: it could be from either *uiuo* ('long-living') or *uinco* ('conquering'): the former is the obvious point being made (as sealing jars extended the life of the wine) but there is also a hint of the latter in the case of this supreme viticulturalist.

59–60 **How much ... land**: after the long list of the patron's estates Naevolus restates his own efforts (*exhausti*) and asks for a 'small' reward (*iugeribus paucis*). The phrase *quantum erat* (cf. Martial 2.46.9, Ovid *Metamorphoses* 4.74, *Tristia* 3.3.31) makes use of the indicative where we might expect a subjunctive (AG §437a, KS 1. §44) but also perhaps carries the literal meaning as Naevolus has asked for his rewards in the past (39–40). Here the services rendered are less bluntly alluded to with the powerful juxtaposition *exhausti lumbos*: *exhaurio* has the literal meaning 'drain of fluids' (*OLD* s.v. 'exhaurio' 1) – which is close to the mark in Naevolus' case – while *lumbos* makes the site of his fatigue all too explicit (cf. 6.314, 8.16, Persius 1.20, 4.35, Catullus 16.11, Martial 5.78.28–9, Lucretius 4.1267, *Priapea* 19.4, Adams (1982) 48: cf. 9.136n.). The Roman *iugerum* was a unit of land of about 0.27 hectares (two-thirds of an acre): J. later (14.163) claims that 'two *iugera*' were enough as an allotment for veteran soldiers in former times. The phrasing here recalls Horace *Odes* 2.15.1–2 and Martial 4.64 (Braund (1988) 241 n.20). Property such as Horace's Sabine farm (*Satires* 2.6) and Martial's Spanish estate (12.31) was sometimes given by patrons to clients: see White (1978) 90–91, Saller (1983a) 251.

60–62 **Is it better...?**: the rhetorical question pits the idyllic conventional scene of the rural (heterosexual) family (complete with child and pet) over against the (to him) indecent figure of the castrated priest of Cybele. Naevolus sentimentalises the rural family with heavy use of diminutives (*casulis... catello*) and the mixture of affection (*cum matre*) and playfulness (*collusore*) is reminiscent of similar scenes at 3.171–9 (esp. 176), 11.151–3 and 14.166–72. The urban satirist is often given to pastoral idealism when it suits his argument, and the details here of toy-houses and puppies can only be for emotional purposes.

60	The mss. read *meliusne hic*: 'here' would mean 'in Rome', while 'this rustic child' supposes a specific child. I (with Courtney and Willis) have printed Housman's *melius nunc* (with *nunc* in the sense of 'as things are [since you are going to leave the estate to this *gallus*]': see 5.141, 12.57, *OLD* s.v. 'nunc' 10, Persius 1.36. Also worth considering is Castiglione's *melius, dic*: J. likes the peremptory short imperative (3.295, 6.29, 6.393, 7.106, 8.56, 9.54, 10.338, 11.33, 13.33, 14.211) but does not use it elsewhere as a single-word parenthesis.

61	The heavy use of 'c' alliteration adds emphasis and also aurally prepares for the *cymbala* which crash in the next line. There is no mention of a father in this household: on the evidence of this poem he is unlikely to be Naevolus' patron. **little cottages**: a *casa* is already small, and diminutive *casulae* are even smaller (cf. 11.153, 14.179, *Moretum* 60, 66, Petronius 44.16): toy-houses made from sticks are envisaged here (cf. Tibullus 2.1.24, Horace *Satires* 2.3.247, 2.3.275, Aristophanes *Clouds* 879, Balsdon (1969) 91). The *catulus* was a **puppy**, and the form *catellus* is the diminutive form of this diminutive animal (cf. Martial 1.83.1), suitable as a playmate for the tiny *infans*, like that of Trimalchio's catamite (Petronius 64) or of the heartless wife who loved hers more than her husband (6.554): for Roman lapdogs see Martial 1.109, Toynbee (1948) 34–36, Toynbee (1973) 108–22.

62	**legacy … cymbals**: the cosy scene is exchanged for the disturbing image of the *gallus* (cf. 8.176n.), alluded to here by his characteristic beating of *cymbala* which was a distinctive feature of the worship of Cybele (cf. Catullus 63.21, 63.29, Lucretius 2.618, Propertius 3.17.36, Virgil *Georgics* 4.64). **friend**: *amicus* is a word of great resonance in Latin: from a basic meaning of 'personal friend' it comes to mean a 'political associate' (*OLD* s.v. 'amicus²' 3) but here the meaning is simply that Naevolus' patron has friends like himself and so prefers the eunuch decadent above the 'normal' Naevolus. There is also a stab of criticism in the child becoming simply a *legatum* (**legacy**) to be passed on to a very unlikely father-figure. The line is elegantly phrased, with three nouns sandwiching two verbal forms.

63–4	**you're a pain**: Naevolus quotes his patron (as at 39) with a bald statement of irritation – and then answers him with a clever metaphor (*pensio clamat*), a variation of vocabulary (*posce … appellat*) and a reference (see next n.) to Homer's *Odyssey*. **pain**: *improbus* is a strong word (see 13.53n.), used of Eppia who fled Rome to be with her gladiator lover (6.86), of a child-abuser (10.305) or a neighbour stealing land (16.37). *posco* (*OLD* s.v. 'posco' 1e) has the sense of 'ask for just deserts' as at 1.98, 5.65, 6.125,

8.246 and for the patron to regard this as *improbus* is by definition excessive and unfair. Note here the string of 'demanding' verbs (*poscis … clamat/ posce … appellat*). *pensio* (*OLD* s.v. 'pensio' 3) is '**rent**-money' (cf. Martial 3.30.3, 12.32.3, Suetonius *Nero* 44.2) and the plosive alliteration enacts the 'shouting' (*clamat*) described. *appellat* here has a similar sense of 'demand payment' (cf. 7.158n., *OLD* s.v. 'appello' 5) and while slaves did not receive wages they did require feeding (14.126) and could also expect some money (*peculium*: cf. 3.189, Virgil *Eclogues* 1.32, *OLD* s.v. 'peculium' 1a, Hopkins (1978) 125–26).

64–5 Naevolus uses a reference to the *Odyssey* (see 37n.) to vivify his statement that he only has one slave. **Polyphemus** was the cannibalistic one-eyed giant who imprisoned Ulysses and his men in Homer's *Odyssey* (9.105–566): the hero intoxicated the giant and then blinded his one eye with a sharpened stake, allowing him and his men to escape. The language is poetic: there is the four-syllable name ending line 64 (cf. 7.6–7n., 8.103) which is itself Homeric (cf. *Odyssey* 9.407, 9.446) and *acies* is a poetic word for 'eye' (Lucretius 2.420, Virgil *Aeneid* 4.643, 6.788, *OLD* s.v. 'acies' 4b). **crafty**: *sollers* (which replicates Homer's common epithet of πολύμητις ('of much guile')) alludes especially to the hero's invention of the name 'Nobody' (Homer *Odyssey* 366–7, 408–412: there is a pun on the Greek word μῆτις which means 'cleverness') to ensure his escape. *per* has the sense of 'by means of which' (*OLD* s.v. 'per' 14).

66 I need … another: to possess only one slave is an embarrassment to Naevolus, but the idyllic family group in 14.167–9 also only has one and Hopkins ((1978) 108) acknowledges that more mouths to feed (*pascendi* here) would be a problem for poor families (see further Balsdon (1969) 107). The line is structured around the key words *alter … hic … ambo* as Naevolus does the maths and lands on the enjambed gerundive *pascendi* which is the awkward problem (cf. 14.126n. and 3.141, 9.136 for the use of *pasco*).

67–9 Naevolus thinks forward to having more than one slave (*puerorum*) but being unable to house them properly. His desperation and bid for sympathy are couched in rhetorical questions with anaphora of *quid*, a parenthetic *oro*, feigned sympathy for the cold conditions suffered by the slaves and poetic language and parody.

67 winter blows: *bruma spirante* (an ablative absolute) shifts attention from the food (*pascendi*) to the clothing required for the slaves. The language is poetic: *spiro* is used (*OLD* s.v. 'spiro' 5) of winds blowing (Lucretius

6.428, Virgil *Aeneid* 4.562) and lawyers' lungs also (7.111), while *bruma* is a poetic word for 'wintry weather' (cf. 6.153, 14.273–4, Horace *Odes* 4.7.12, *OLD* s.v. 'bruma' 2). The parenthetic *oro* (*OLD* s.v. 'oro' 1f) has the force of 'please' and facilitates another *quid* straight after in enjambement.

68   say: the rhetoric is striking, with the conceit that the speaker will be speaking directly to the 'shoulder-blades' and 'feet' affected by the wintry weather: for the effects of cold on the shoulder-blades cf. Seneca *Epistles* 63.11. **icy blast**: The *aquilo* was notoriously cold (cf. e.g. Virgil *Georgics* 2.113, Horace *Odes* 3.10.4, *Satires* 2.6.25) and the most violent of the four winds (Watson (2003) 346). The same combination of month, season and wind was made by Martial (1.49.19–20).

69   'stay ... cicadas': the quotation is a parody of Virgil *Aeneid* 1.207 (*durate et uosmet rebus seruate secundis*: 'stay firm and keep yourselves for favourable times') where Aeneas is seeking to encourage his men who have been blown off course and landed in Africa. The cicada was associated with summer: cf. Lucretius 5.803, Ovid *Ars Amatoria* 1.271.

70–89   Naevolus moves on to his second major point: having established (43–4) that he has served his patron as his lover, he now reveals that he has also served his patron's wife (cf. 2.59–60) and so both saved his patron's marriage and also given him children. The theme of the surrogate sexual partner recalls Catullus 67, Martial 12.91: and J. has earlier (6.81) explored the embarrassment of men rearing children who are visibly not their own. Petronius' Trimalchio similarly claims to have served both his master and his mistress when he was a slave (*Satyricon* 75.11) and it was not unknown for Roman ladies to have sex with their slaves (cf. 6.279, Tacitus *Annals* 12.53, Petronius 45.7): but Naevolus is not a slave and his actions are therefore governed by choice rather than compulsion.

70   But even though...: the language is forensic in style as Naevolus moves his attack into more incriminating territory: *dissimulare* means to 'conceal' or 'turn a blind eye to' a state of affairs and is common in oratory (32 exx. in Cicero's speeches), while *mittas* here means 'disregard, ignore' (Cicero *pro Murena* 33, *pro Sulla* 70, *pro Flacco* 79, *OLD* s.v. 'mitto' 5): *cetera* refers to 'all the other <services I have given you>' and prepares for the introduction of the new point. The anaphora of *ut* (here meaning 'although' as at 9.103, 10.240, 13.100, Martial 2.41.4, *OLD* s.v. 'ut' 35) is another forensic device.

71   what price: *metiris pretio* is an effective juxtaposition. *metiris* (*OLD* s.v. 'metior' 5) has the sense of 'appraise, assess' and commonly has an ablative of the means or criterion of assessment (e.g. Horace *Satires* 1.2.103, *Epistles* 1.7.98, Seneca *Epistles* 110.4.6): here Naevolus is only interested in money (*pretio*) and the only question is 'how much?' (*quanto*).

71–2 **the fact that**: *quod* introduces the conditional clause which acts as the object of *metiris* (cf. 3.153, 5.12, 9.83, *OLD* s.v. 'quod' 4). **obedient and loyal**: *deditus ... deuotusque cliens* is a powerful statement of loyalty and affection (cf. Seneca *de Beneficiis* 3.5.2): *deditus* can have the sense of marital devotion (cf. 6.181, 6.206) which is ironic here, while *deuotus* can denote devotion to the point of being bewitched (Tibullus 1.5.41, Horace *Epodes* 16.9, Ovid *Amores* 3.7.27, *OLD* s.v. 'deuoueo' 3b) and certainly beyond the call of duty (Horace *Odes* 4.14.18, Lucan 3.311). The juxtaposition of *cliens uxor* enacts the union which is going to be described in the following lines.

73–4 **you cannot…**: the speaker moves into didactic mode (*scis certe* brooks of no denial) with a lengthy indirect question following the main verb *scis*, using three question words to introduce the three relevant considerations of how (*quibus modis*), how often (*quam saepe*) and with what bribes (*quae pollicitus*). *ista* refers to the sexual act between Naevolus and his patron's wife: the pronoun often has a pejorative ring (cf. 2.75, 2.136, 6.191). *saepe* cannot be right as Naevolus is describing a single occasion and the scribe's eye was perhaps distracted by *saepe* in the same place in 73. Most modern editors print Housman's *nempe* which makes better sense and is common in J.'s argumentative style (cf. 3.95, 8.57, 8.164, 8.80, 10.110, 10.160, 10.185, 13.181).

74–5 **girl**: the term *puella* indicates a young wife (as at 2.59, 6.258, 6.O32, Catullus 17.13, 62.23, Horace *Odes* 3.22.2, Tibullus 1.6.15, Watson (1983) 135–37) but also carries erotic connotations of the 'beloved' as often in elegy (e.g. Catullus 2.1, 3.3, Propertius 3.2.2, Tibullus 1.2.5, 1.8.50, Ovid *Amores* 1.1.20). The juxtaposition of the enjambed *amplexu rapui* after the pathetic *fugientem* gives a touch of violence to the encounter and certainly suggests a lack of consent, thus adding to the self-characterisation of Naevolus as sexually over-energetic (cf. 34).

75 *tabulas* (*OLD* s.v. 'tabula' 8a) refers to the wedding **contract** which was sealed by witnesses at the wedding itself (cf. 2.119, 6.200, 10.336, Treggiari (1991) 140 n.72, 165) and acted as proof that the wedding had taken place. *tabulas rumpere* (literally 'to shatter the contract') means 'to divorce' as at Tacitus *Annals* 11.30.2.

76 **move out**: The mss. *signabat* has been doubted by editors on the grounds that only the witnesses sealed the contract and that she would be unlikely to be entering into a new marriage while still in the patron's house: the second point could be overcome if the imperfect tense had a conative or inceptive sense (8.261, *NLS* §100 (ii)) quality ('she was all for sealing' once she had moved out) but the first point remains a difficulty and Eden's *signabant* (referring to the witnesses and requiring an unstated change of subject (Eden (1985) 349) is difficult to accept. I have printed the emendation *migrabat* of Highet ((1952) 70) which amplifies and instantiates *fugientem* as the wife was now (*iam*) moving (6.171) back to her father's house: this is a common usage in J. (cf. 3.163, 6.171, 6.O8, 7.7, 11.51, 15.151). The corruption can be explained by a scribe confusing 'r' for 'n' and writing *mignabat* which was then 'corrected' to *signabat* with a glance at 2.119.

76–8 The language again depicts Naevolus in unflattering terms as a sexual machine who is proud of his prowess. He made the act last all night (*tota ... nocte*), made the couch rattle and made both the patron and his wife cry (*plorante ... uox*). *uix* might suggest that even he found this difficult – but then the word probably indicates simply that this was a superhuman effort requiring the whole night to accomplish.

76   bought back: the metaphor of *redemi* has a range of meanings: to ransom, recover, pay a debt: here the sexual 'debt' which the patron cannot pay has been paid by Naevolus. The image of sex lasting all night is common: 10.235, Catullus 88.2, Ovid *Heroides* 16.215, Petronius 21.7, 81.6, Martial 9.67.1, 12.65.1–2.

77   weeping: the patron weeps outside the door in an inversion of the 'serenade' (*paraklausithyron*) common in love elegy (e.g. Horace *Odes* 3.10, Propertius 1.16, *Anth.Pal.* 5.23, 6.71)): as Copley ((1956) 140) notes, this passage recalls Horace's scathing version of the genre at *Satires* 1.2.64–7 (where the noble suitor is beaten up outside his beloved's doors while her lower-class lover is inside) and the situation was ripe for ridicule (Catullus 67, Lucretius 4. 1177–84, Persius 5.164–6, Martial 10.13, Aristophanes *Ecclesiazusai* 960–75). The patron here is only excluded from his lover by his own impotence (cf. Catullus 67.20–22).

77–8   witness: inanimate objects are said to be witnesses to sexual misdeeds here and at (e.g.) Catullus 6.10, 67, *Anth. Pal.* 5.181.12, 5.4.5–6, Cicero *pro Cluentio* 15: here there is a pun on *testis* (meaning both 'witness' and 'testicle', with the word emphasised by the 't' alliteration) and the surprise that there was a 'real' witness in the form of the patron himself after the unreal witness of the *lectulus*. The diminutive form of the word is mock-affectionate and increases the humiliation of the patron, as does the framing of the line with the second-person pronoun (*te* ... *tu*) and assonant jingle of *lectulus et tu* with its offbeat rhythm suggesting finger-jabbing.

78   **noise**: the line focusses on the sounds coming from behind the door from the bed and the mistress, with both *sonus* and *uox* understated terms for the sounds in question. The use of *dominae* is sardonic – she was the wife of his patron and so in that sense his 'mistress' but she also acted as a sexual 'mistress' in this case. The offbeat rhythm of *dominae uox* is perhaps intended to imitate the sounds of passion.

79–80   Naevolus produces a generalised *sententia* to justify his actions, claiming that he has actually saved his patron's marriage and pointing to 'many' other cases where the same is true. The marriage is described with a tricolon crescendo of authoritative metaphorical terms, all contributing to the sense and seeking to convince us that Naevolus is an expert in this matter: the union is struggling to stay fixed (*instabile*), it has started to be pulled apart (*dirimi*: used of divorce at Suetonius *Julius* 43.1, *OLD* s.v. 'dirimo' 4) and it is on the point of being dissolved altogether (*OLD* s.v. 'soluo' 17b). His evidence-base for this statement is large (*in multis domibus*) and his goal is the 'saving' of a union. The final word gives the punch-line as this 'saviour' is bathetically indicated as *adulter*.

81–3   **where ... which ... no**: Naevolus produces a tricolon crescendo of rhetorical questions to introduce the bombshell argument that he had given his patron children to boast about and profit from.

81   **turn to**: *circumagas* suggests the 'wheeling around' of stars (5.23), or troops (7.164), or physical going out of one's way (Horace *Satires* 1.9.17), while in Tacitus (*Histories* 3.73.6) it has the sense of being 'swayed' by arguments. The image here is of the evasive patron changing tack as he tries to wriggle out of his obligations. The wording of *prima aut ultima* recalls (as Courtney notes) Homer *Odyssey* 9.14: the phrase suggests that the patron will not know where to start in his defence (cf. Virgil *Aeneid* 4.371, 677, Valerius Flaccus 7.433–5) and the contempt is enhanced with the plosive alliteration and the added resonance of *ultima* (suggesting the lowest of the low as at 8.44, *OLD* s.v. 'ultimus' 9).

82–3   **Do I get...**: Naevolus ironically goes into 'abandoned heroine' mode with the sort of language used elsewhere in Latin by such women as Ariadne (Catullus 64.132–201), Scylla (Ovid *Metamorphoses* 8.108–42), Medea (Ovid *Heroides* 12) and Dido (Virgil *Aeneid* 4.305, Ovid *Heroides* 7) who were deserted by their menfolk: Winkler ((1983) 139 n.78) suggests that this passage is possibly modelled also on Encolpius' lament over Giton at

Petronius 80–1. The point of the parody is to underline that Naevolus – the bisexual super-stud – is in fact relegated to the female role by this effeminate patron: he claims even to give birth to children (*nascitur ex me*) with the diminutive form (*filiolus*) showing almost parental affection (cf. 6.390): the reader is reminded of the same-sex marriage denigrated in similar ironic language at 2.132–42 or the marriage of the emperor Nero to Pythagoras at Tacitus *Annals* 15.37. Rhetorical repetition is used to the full: line 82 is framed with anaphora of *nullum*, followed by anaphora of *quod* on 83 in emphatic positions (at the start of the line and immediately after the caesura) and the itemised listing of *filiolus ... filia*. The ending of 83 hammers the point home with the monosyllables *ex me*. The prosody *ergō* is also found at 3.281 but is elsewhere in J. scanned *ergŏ* (see 8.37–8n.)

84   bring them up: *tollis* is often taken to refer to the father 'picking up' the newborn baby from the floor and thus acknowledging the child as his own (*OLD* s.v. 'tollo' 2a) but Shaw (2001) and Watson ((2014) on 6.38) have cast serious doubt on this ritual and the word here has the ongoing sense of 'bring up'. **newspapers**: *acta* here refers to the *acta diurna* (see 7.104n.): there may be a slight pun in using the term *libris* ('books') to record the birth of children (*liberi*) and *spargere* is chosen ironically as the word literally means to 'scatter seeds'. The line is framed with second-person singular verbs denoting the sense of personal agency which Naevolus attributes sarcastically to his patron who is not in fact the real agent of the procreation.

85   proof: an *argumentum* is something which proves a case (*OLD* s.v. 'argumentum', 'arguo'). Here the news of the children 'proves' the patron's virility (*OLD* s.v. 'uir' 1c). Romans would hang garlands on the doorposts to celebrate a wedding (cf. 6.51–2, 79) or other joyous occasions (10.65, 12.91, Seneca *Epistles* 67.11–12, Tacitus *Annals* 15.71, Dio 63.29.1).

86   you ... gossip: the juxtaposition of the verbs *es dedimus* makes it clear that Naevolus is the real agent of the paternity. *fama* could denote positive 'fame' or 'celebrity' (e.g. 7.39, 7.79, 8.76, 10.114, 10.125, 10.140, *OLD* s.v. 'fama' 7) but *opponere* (cf. 2.39) here shows that *fama* refers to the hostile gossip which claimed (correctly) that the patron was unable or unwilling to have sex with his wife: for the pejorative sense of *fama* cf. 1.72, 14.1, 14.152, *OLD* s.v. 'fama' 6b. The subjunctive *possis* is in a relative final clause ('something for you to be able to use to counter the gossip').

87–90   Men who had legitimate children enjoyed legal and financial **privileges** after the Augustan moral legislation (the *lex Iulia de maritandis ordinibus* and the *lex Papia Poppaea*) which sought to promote marriage and childbearing (see e.g. Horace *Carmen Saeculare* 13–20): the childless could only inherit half of any bequest (Gaius *Inst.* 2.286) and the remaining half would 'fall' (cf. *OLD* s.v. 'caducus' 10) to members of the family or (failing that) to the state (Tacitus *Annals* 3.28). Having one child was enough to guarantee that the patron could inherit fully, but men with three or more children – even gladiators (Suetonius *Claudius* 21.5) – enjoyed even greater benefits (such as priority in holding office or securing a province) and this distinction was conferred on men such as Martial (2.92, 3.95.5–6, 9.97.5–6), Pliny (*Epistles* 10.2) and Suetonius (Pliny *Epistles* 10.95): see *OCD* s.v. 'ius liberorum', Treggiari (1991) 60–80, Wallace-Hadrill (1981), *CAH* xi. 870–74. Naevolus builds up his point from the general and vague (*iura ... heres*) to the capacity to inherit fully (*omne*) to the further potential bonus of *caduca*, to the crowning social and financial glory of having the *ius trium liberorum*, dangling the necessary third child (to add to the *filiolus* and *filia* of 83) as an incentive for him to continue using his services. The argument (cf. *redemi* at 76) is made in strictly financial terms, suitable for the *mollis auarus* (38) who *computat et ceuet* (40).

87   The line is framed with the key terms *iura* and *heres* and the central phrase (*propter me*) hammers home Naevolus' claim in a solemn spondee.

88–90   *nec non* (8.103n.) is an elevated way of saying **'what's more'**. *dulce* – a word often used of children (e.g. 5.139, 6.38, Lucretius 3.895-6, Horace *Epodes* 2.40, Virgil *Georgics* 2.523–4, *Aeneid* 4.33) – is here applied to the financial rewards which they might bring the miser. The repetition of *caducum/caducis* at the end of successive lines, juxtaposed with adjectives of quality (*dulce*) and quantity (*multa*) is effective, as is the emphasis thrown on *commoda* and its alliterative framing of line 89. The *ius trium liberorum* was much sought after and here Naevolus teases his patron with the prospect of making up the number to the requisite three with anaphora of *si* and his final word *impleuero* is itself a *double entendre* as the verb was used of inseminating women (Ovid *Metamorphoses* 6.111, 11.265, *Ars Amatoria* 1.325, Lucan 8.409). There is a pause after this word to accommodate the change of speaker which adds emphasis to this verb.

90–1   **You have**: the speaker interrupts Naevolus with reassurance and a further question to express interest and to elicit more information and begin a new topic. The sentence is not necessary – Naevolus could simply have continued without interruption – but the vocative *Naeuole* serves to remind the reader who is speaking and allows him to add a touch of irony with his mock-sympathetic remark (*iusta ... tui*), complete with clash of ictus and accent (*ille quid affert*), and omission of *est*, to feign excitement. *dolor* is mental rather than physical pain as at 11.52, 13.12, 13.131. *affert* here has the metaphorical meaning of 'bring forward an argument' (*OLD* s.v. 'affero' 13).

92   **He ignores … donkey**: the patron's callous attitude is brought out by the framing of the line with the key terms. The verb *neglego* is elsewhere (5.16) used (as here) of the patron who ignores his *cliens*, and the mockery of Naevolus is brilliantly expressed in the comic caricature of the two-legged donkey who is simply a replacement (*alium*) for himself, with the key noun *asellum* postponed to the end of the line for bathetic effect as at 11.97. The donkey, which occupied 'the bottom rung on the equid hierarchy' (Watson and Watson (2014) 178, citing Griffith (2006) 227–28), was proverbial for the size of its penis (cf. *Priapea* 52.9–10, Apuleius *Metamorphoses* 3.24, Petronius 24, Archilochus 43 – a feature claimed also by Naevolus at 9.34): it was a beast of burden used for thankless drudgery and also an unlikely sexual partner for the desperate women of 6.333–4 and Apuleius *Metamorphoses* 10.19.3. It was also proverbial for stupidity (Otto (1890) s.v. 'asinus, asellus' (i), (ii)) which also fits Naevolus' self-criticism here ('he finds another mug').

93   **alone**: *soli* is dative singular (AG §113). *memento* is the 'future' form of the imperative of *memini* (cf. 5.71, 6.572 – see 8.134n.), giving perhaps 'a tone of mock-solemnity' (Watson and Watson on 6.572) and also (like *fige* in the following line) adopting a didactic tone (cf. Lucretius 2.66 (with Fowler (2002) 150), Horace *Satires* 2.4.12). The interlocking of *haec soli commissa tibi* neatly enacts the enclosure of the knowledge in the person.

94   **complaints**: the key word *querelas* is emphasised at the end of the line: *querela* elsewhere in J. (13.135, 16.19) denotes 'grievances' such as would be addressed in courts. **lock**: the imperative of *figo* in this metaphorical sense (*OLD* s.v. 'figo' 8) has here a didactic and censorious tone as at 5.12, 11.28, Horace *Odes* 3.15.2, Virgil *Aeneid* 3.250, Seneca *Epistles* 16.1, 75.7, 113.32.

95   **lethal**: the grandiose language continues: instead of using a simple adjective, Naevolus uses the periphrastic *res mortifera* (cf. 2.102, 3.165, 4.35, 6.357, 8.198) and *mortifera* leads ominously onto *inimicus* – only to have the line rendered bathetic with the ending *pumice lēuis*. For attitudes towards male depilation (and the use of the pumice stone to achieve it) see 8.16n.

96   **entrusted … burns with hatred**: the line is marked by the juxtaposition

of three verbs showing that the first action leads at once to the others. For the use of the pluperfect tense of *commiserat* (when we might expect a perfect) cf. 5.76, 6.281, 7.152, 10.272, 15.16, KS II.1 §35.2: the use of this tense makes the sudden present tenses (*ardet et odit*) all the more striking. *ardet et odit* (cf. Seneca *Medea* 582) recalls other such combinations of verb + *odi* as 15.71, Lucretius 3.1069, Horace *Epistles* 2.1.22, Ovid *Tristia* 3.1.8.

97   **thinking that**: *tamquam* protests Naevolus' innocence in a feigned counterfactual (cf. 3.47): the poem so far proves that Naevolus has indeed revealed all too much of what he knows.

97–99   **sword ... club ... torch**: a bucolic diaeresis introduces a catalogue of violence which Naevolus fears from his effete patron, with the three forms of harm ranged in a tricolon crescendo of parallel infinitive constructions all dependent on *non dubitat*. The action begins with the seizing of a weapon, then personal injury with a different weapon, and finally damage to property. *sumo <arma>* is a common verb to denote taking up arms (in this case a blade) against somebody (e.g. Horace *Odes* 3.2.19, Ovid *Metamorphoses* 11.382, *OLD* s.v. 'sumo' 1b) and this exact phrase (*sumere ferrum*) occurs at Ovid *Heroides* 16.373, while the changing weaponry (*ferrum/ fuste* juxtaposed over the line-break) both adds to the arsenal and also throws in harsh 'f' alliteration (cf. 7.190–4n.).

98   A *fustis* is a **club** (6.416, *OLD* s.v. 'fustis' 2) while *aperire* here is to 'split open' (cf. 4.110, Seneca *de Ira* 1.2.2, *OLD* s.v. 'aperio' 5). The juxtaposition of *caput candelam* adds more alliteration: a *candela* is a 'candle, taper' usually used for lighting (e.g. 3.287) or to signify a funeral (Persius 3.103) but here this tiny flame can cause arson which could sentence those inside the house to death by targeting the door (see 13.145–6n.).

99–100   **poison**: after the risky overt violence of physical assault and arson, Naevolus adds the cynical aside that the safer option of poisoning is available to a man who is rich, with the key word *ueneni* postponed to the very end of a loquacious sentence. The combination of *contemno* and *despicio* is common in oratory (e.g. Cicero *in Verrem* 1.1.9, 1.1.43, *in Vatinium* 38.1, *de Oratore* 3.80, [Quintilian] *Decl. Minores* 17.11, Apuleius *Metamorphoses* 7.27, Pliny *Panegyricus* 33.4) and adds a sententious air.

cost: *annona* is often used of the city's corn-supply and is here (as at Horace *Epistles* 1.12.24) used simply to mean 'the market-price', but the word is chosen sarcastically both 'as if poison were a commodity in regular supply with a price fixed each year' (Courtney) and also as a sardonic hint at what the stingy patron would put into the mouths of his clients to 'feed' them.

cara also has (alongside its obvious sense of 'expensive') the additional hint of 'dear to one' (cf. 3.53, 10.350) suggesting (with *numquam*) a lack of any affection.

101   Senate of Mars: the *curia Martis* is a Latin form of the Athenian Council of elders known as the Areopagus (ὁ Ἄρειος πάγος: see *OCD* s.v. 'Areopagus') which endured for over one thousand years as a major organ of law and government and was amended in the time of Hadrian (*CAH* xi.622). The Areopagus was proverbially discreet with its secrets: Ἀρειοπαγίτου σιωπηλότερος ('more silent than an Areopagite') or Ἀρειοπαγίτου στεγανώτερος ('more guarded than an Areopagite') were an ancient Greek equivalent of 'as silent as the grave' (Themistius *Orationes* 21.263a, Alciphron 2.3, LSJ s.v. Ἄρειος πάγος, ὁ'). The future tense *teges* is a form of imperative (see 8.37–8n.) and the juxtaposition with *occulta* (cf. 7.200, 8.266) enhances the theme of secrecy.

102–123   The speaker reasons with Naevolus that keeping secrets is impossible in a slave-owning household: cf. Martial 2.82, 7.62, Petronius *fr.* 28.

102   Corydon: the speaker opens with an allusion to Virgil (*Eclogues* 2.69: *a Corydon, Corydon quae te dementia cepit?* ('ah Corydon, Corydon, what madness has taken possession of you?'): see also 9.37n.) in which the youth Corydon speaks to himself, trying to shake off his unrequited passion for the boy Alexis. The romantic infatuation of Virgil's character is ironically evoked in this exposure of Naevolus' cynical use of sex for money: and Virgil's reassuring final line ('you will find another Alexis, if this one scorns you') is echoed in lines 130–131.

102–3   The rich cannot keep their affairs **secret**: their slaves will gossip and furthermore their lives attract more interest than those of the poor. The key verb *esse* is stressed in enjambement – secrets cannot 'exist' at all (as at 6.366, 13.86, 14.123, Propertius 4.7.1) – and the verb *putas* mocks the naiveté of Naevolus.

103–4   slaves … marble: the list of speakers is in descending order of plausibility from the human (*serui*) to the animal (*iumenta … canis*) to the inanimate (*postes et marmora*). Slaves obviously overheard and saw things which would reflect on their masters if recounted (e.g. Seneca *de Beneficiis* 3.27) and they could be required to testify against their masters in court – giving rise to Seneca's wise judgement (*Epistles* 47.4) that slaves who are allowed to speak <u>with</u> their masters will not speak <u>against</u> them. The evidence of slaves could of course be public-spirited and welcome as in the case of Lars Porsenna (8.261–8). **beasts**: *iumentum* is a beast of burden (mules at 3.316, 4.5, 7.180, 8.154, cattle at 14.147) and the fantastic notion of them speaking is perhaps yet another (cf. 9.37n.) nod towards Homer who has horses prophesy the death of Achilles (*Iliad* 19.404–417). The **Dog** is a noisy animal (e.g. 6.415–16, Lucretius 5.1066, Horace *Epodes* 5.58, Virgil *Aeneid* 5.257, Petronius 64.9, Martial 12.1.1) but they are not elsewhere credited with speech. The conceit of talking **door-posts** recalls Catullus 67 and Propertius 1.16: doors are more commonly the addressees of speech than its agents (e.g. Ovid *Amores* 1.6.73–4). **Marble** was used in rich Romans' houses (cf. 11.175n., 14.88–90n.) as flooring (6.430, 11.175), wall-coverings (Seneca *Epistles* 114.9), columns (14.307) and statues (8.55, 8.230): here (as at 1.12) the use of the marble is unspecified and the stone is given the power of speech. Walls are elsewhere personified as potential witnesses of criminality (see e.g. Cicero *ad Fam.* 6.3.3, *pro Cluentio* 15.6, *pro Caelio* 60.7, *Philippics* 2.69) and the notion of the house speaking out goes back to Greek tragedy (e.g. Aeschylus *Agamemnon* 37–8, Euripides *Hippolytus* 418, 1074, *Andromache* 924–5). *ut* is concessive (see 9.70n.)

104–6   **Close…**: the speaker produces six instructions in quick succession, three in direct imperatives and three jussive subjunctives, in a tone which is didactic and authoritative. The first four orders are brief and concern things, while the final two concern people and spread over the whole of line 106. The purpose of the passage is to evoke all possible measures to ensure the privacy of the rich man – safe from prying eyes either outside his house or within it.

104–5   Rich Romans under the early empire began to use a form of glass (*lapis specularis*) in the windows of their houses (Paoli (1990) 155–56) and even of their litter-chairs (3.242, 4.21) but *claude* suggests that *fenestras* here means **shutters** (for this sense see Persius 3.1–2, Horace *Odes* 1.25.1, Ovid *Amores* 1.5.3, *ex Ponto* 3.3.10, *OLD* s.v. 'fenestra 1b). **gaps**: *rimas* in that case refers to gaps in the shutters which would admit light (cf. Persius 3.2 Martial 1.34.6, 11.45: the word is used in Seneca (*Epistles* 86.8) for tiny windows in a bath-house): covering these with *uela* would block out light and thus prevent people seeing into the house. Ornamental *uela* could be hung on walls of a bridal suite (6.228) but these *uela* are for privacy as at Martial 11.45, where also the 'smallest hint of a *rima* is sealed up'. *ostia* represent the double **doors** on the outside of the house (cf. Horace *Satires* 1.1.10) which in rich houses had a janitor known as an *ostiarius* (Petronius 28.8). The final two words of 105 are textually uncertain: one group of manuscripts reads the future imperative form *tollito lumen* but this is a form used very rarely in J. and the other reading found in the manuscripts is a sudden plural imperative (*tollite*) which is also difficult. Nisbet ((1995) 250–51) has proposed emending to *tolle lucernam* which removes the problem of the verb by substituting *lucernam* for *lumen*: *lucerna* is exactly the sort of oil-lamp which was used in Roman times (cf. 6.131, 6.305, 7.225, 8.35) and formed a metaphor for twilight (10.339).

106 the place: *dele medio* (*OLD* s.v. 'medium' 3b) is colloquial for 'from the scene' and is as old as Ennius (*Annales* 8.263W) and common in comedy (e.g. Terence *Phormio* 967) and prose (e.g. Cicero *Verrines* 2.2.177, Petronius 38.14, 59.1, Seneca *Epistles* 93.10). *recumbo* can mean 'to recline at dinner' (3.82, 5.65, 6.434, 6.448, *OLD* s.v. 'recumbo' 3) and so may simply mean 'have no dinner parties', glossing the generalised *e medio ... omnes* with a specifically Roman reason for having people at one's home: it is tempting however to see it as referring here to the practice of slaves sleeping as guards outside the master's door (Braund (1988) 254 n.115 refers to Apuleius *Metamorphoses* 2.15, Martial 11.104.13–14).

107 The cockerel was expected to crow three times before dawn (Otto (1890) s.v. 'gallus' 2, Ammianus 22.14.4, Aristophanes *Ecclesiazusae* 390) and *gallicinium* was a common word for 'dawn' (e.g. Petronius 62.3, Apuleius *Metamorphoses* 8.1). *ad* + accusative here means 'at' (*OLD* s.v. 'ad' 21b) and the sentence is construed thus: the *caupo* will know (*sciet*) what (*quod*) the rich man (*ille*) is doing at the time of the cock crowing for the second time.

108 know ... hear: the didactic tone continues with assertive future indicative verbs juxtaposed for added effect (*sciet audiet*). The timescale is short indeed – *ante diem* means 'before day has fully started' leaving little time for the news to travel after cock-crow – rendered slightly more plausible by the adjective *proximus*. Inn-keepers do not receive a favourable press in Latin literature, often seen as crooked men who water down their wine (Horace *Satires* 1.1.29, 1.5.4) and even murder their guests (Cicero *de Diuinatione* 1.57): there is a memorable vignette of an obnoxious *caupo* at 8.159–62.

109–10 made up: not content with retailing what they have heard and seen, the chorus of kitchen-servants also invents stories against their master. *pariter* and the asyndetic list of job-titles suggests the men egging each other on to invent stories. The *libarius* was a maker of the cake known as a *libum* (cf. 3.187) which was used in sacrifices (Horace *Epistles* 1.10.10) and to celebrate birthdays (Ovid *Amores* 1.8.94, *Ars Am*. 1.429, Martial 10.24.4), while *archimagirus* is a word taken directly from late Greek (ἀρχιμάγειρος) meaning 'chief cook'. The language here suggests the pretensions of this rich man with his imported expensive Greek slaves, the expansive five-syllable noun (as at 7.123, 7.148) ending 109 and the spondaic *carptores* beginning 110 with ironic pomposity – all pointing to the irony that these men hate him. **carvers**: the *carptor* was a slave who carved the roast meat (also known as *scissor* (Petronius 36.40) and *structor* (5.120, 11.136–141)). Here there is an obvious pun on the two senses of *carpo*: to 'carve food' (*OLD* s.v. 'carpo' 6) and also to 'criticise' or 'tear strips from' a person (*OLD* s.v. 'carpo' 9).

110–12   **For what...?**: the tone of harsh criticism is conveyed in the 'c' alliteration and the indignant rhetorical question which uses litotes (*quod ... non dubitant componere*) for the assertion that slaves will invent anything. The lengthy words and fifth-foot spondee of 111 lead neatly to the enjambed *baltea* which enact the slaps with its emphatic position at the end of the question and the start of the line. Slaves were routinely beaten ('philosophers merely advised that it should not be done in anger' (Hopkins (1978) 119 n.41): cf. 13.104n.)) as well as being subject to other punishments: cf. 6. 219–224, 474–507, Seneca *Epistles* 47.4, De Ste Croix (1981) 48-9. The beatings were carried out with a range of implements (6.479–80): here the weapon is a sword-belt (*OLD* s.v. 'balteus' 1) and its plural form (while being metrically necessary) may also connote the multiple beatings inflicted.

112–13   **Some...**: a further litotes (*nec derit qui*: cf. 3.302–3) introduces the unspecified man whose intake of alcohol has made him loose-lipped – a well-attested side-effect of alcohol (cf. e.g. Horace *Odes* 3.21.14–16, *Epistles* 1.18.37–8, *Ars Poetica* 434-5, but critiqued at Seneca *Epistles* 83.8–15). *te* may be the indefinite second person ('one') rather than specifically Naevolus, as often found in verbs (e.g. 5.54, 7.50, 9.18). The **crossroads** (*compita*) are a common haunt of *flâneurs* and gossips: cf. Horace *Satires* 2.3.25–6, 2.6.50, Livy 34.2.12, Ovid *Amores* 3.1.17–8, Martial 7.97.12, Propertius 2.20.22, Gellius 1.22.2. The vocabulary and word-placing are expressive here: the juxtaposition over the line-end of *quaerat/ nolentem* reflects the tug-of-war going on, while the reluctance in *nolentem* is focalised further in *miseram* (agreeing grammatically with the ear: for the word cf. Horace *Satires* 1.9.8, 1.9.14). *uinosus inebriet* is a further juxtaposition stressing the image of drunkenness with (again) the hapless ear the object of the inebriation.

114–115   **what you**: the speaker refers back to what Naevolus asked of him at 101, with parts of *ille* used to frame the sentence in a pleasing chiasmus which would be diluted if we punctuated after *taceant* as suggested by Nisbet ((1995) 251). *roges* is a jussive subjunctive (cf. 1.14, 3.276, 7.9, KS 1.186 §47 (c)), while *taceant* is a subjunctive in an indirect command: *quidquid* is here equivalent to *id quod* (as at Petronius 86.3).

115–117   **swigging**: slaves were notoriously bibulous in Roman comedy (e.g. Plautus *Aulularia* 623, *Amphitruo* 425–32, *Miles Gloriosus* 818–58) and Falernian wine from the region of Mt Massicus in Campania was an expensive vintage and a strong wine (cf. 4.138, 6.303, 6.430, 13.216n., Horace *Odes* 1.27.10, 2.11.19). The enthusiastic drinking is brought out by the choice of verb *potare* which suggests **swigging** rather than more decorous drinking (cf. 5.30, Watson and Watson (2014) on 6.9). There is also a neat jingle whereby the slaves prefer to *prodere* than to *potare* with both infinitives in similar positions on consecutive lines, and the close placing of *arcanum ... subrepti* brings out the element of secrecy in both cases.

117   **Saufeia** was described (6. 320–22) as an enthusiastic participant in the rites of the Good Goddess Cybele – rites which were said to be fuelled by alcohol (2.86–7, Watson and Watson (2014) on 6.315). *faciens* here has the sense of 'conducting a sacrifice' (cf. Virgil *Eclogues* 3.77, *Aeneid* 8.189, *OLD* s.v. 'facio' 24b) and *pro populo* also denotes public rather than private worship which all suits the Saufeia of *Satire* 6. The imperfect tense of *bibebat* suggests that her drinking was habitual and the name Saufeia shows that she belonged to a wealthy aristocratic family (cf. Martial 2.74.1, Shackleton-Bailey (1965) on Cicero *ad Atticum* 1.3.1). Martial (3.72) viciously attacks a woman of this name.

118–20   **You should…**: the thought is ironic: we ought to live good lives so that slaves will find nothing to say against us. This ignores the point made at 109 (that slaves invent stories) and is clearly intended to be a mockery of Naevolus' sensitivity and a challenge to one who will not find it possible to live a good life for even the most selfish of reasons. For the garrulity of slaves see 9.103–4n.: to describe this is as **the worst part of a bad slave** is a grotesque exaggeration, given the brutality and economic damage wreaked (with much justification) by rebellious slaves such as Spartacus. There is a major textual crux here and 119 is most likely to be an interpolation. Courtney plausibly suggests that the trouble started with a scribe writing *tunc* for *tum*, thus adding one syllable too many to the line, leading to later scribes either writing *tunc his* (Φ) or *tunc est* (P) which restored the prosody but wrecked the meaning. Line 119 was added by a helpful scribe as a gloss on the lonely *causis* in 120 (although it does not rescue the sense unless we also delete 120–121; it was also placed after 123 in Φ, and *idcirco* is not a word J. ever uses elsewhere) and most editors since Housman have bracketed 119 and restored *tum*. Problems remain: the plural *causis* is explained with one singular reason and Braund may be right in her suggestion ((1988) 254) that we omit the whole section and print:

> *uiuendum recte est ut linguas mancipiorum*
> *contemnas: nam lingua mali pars pessima serui.*

tum est is a strong elision but elision before *est* is not uncommon in satire: cf. e.g. 1.17, 1.30, 1.86, 1.125, 5.1, 14.276.

120–1 **tongues**: note the effective repetition of *lingua* in successive lines. 120 ends with the pompous five-syllabled word *mancipiorum* (cf. 109–10n.) leading to the enjambed verb *contemnas* and followed by a generalisation whose plosive alliteration and hissing sibilance enhances rather than conceals its vacuity.

122–3   These lines have also been suspected and deleted by some editors, but the thought is worth keeping as it presents the paradox that the slave-owner is less free than the slave. This Stoic notion found expression in (e.g.) Persius 5.73–131, Seneca *Epistles* 47.17, 51.9, Cicero *Paradoxa Stoicorum* 5.33–41, Horace *Satires* 2.7, Martial 2.53. The slave owner has to feed (9.67) and clothe (9.68–9) his slaves, but there is also a pun at work: the slave-owner keeps them safe (*custodit*) with money (*aere*), but *aere* may also hint at the bronze shackles with which he keeps the slave under guard. J. later (14.15–17) returns to the notion of the *animae* of slaves. **food**: *far* was archetypically plain food (5.11 (*farris canini* 'dog's bread'), Persius 3.25, Horace *Satires* 1.5.68–9, 1.6.112). *illis* is read by Courtney as ablative of comparison with *deterior* ('in a worse state than those <slaves>') but is better read as an ablative of separation after *liber* ('not constrained by those <slaves>': *OLD* s.v. 'liber' 4).

124–129   Naevolus replies with an elegiac lament on the transience of youth and pleasure. The brevity of youth and the rapid approach of death, especially as seen in the imagery of flowers and the setting of a party, are themes familiar from ancient lyric and elegiac poetry (e.g. Horace *Odes* 2.3.13–16, 2.11.5–10 (with Nisbet and Hubbard (1978) *ad loc.*), Propertius 2.15.51–4: see e.g. Lyne (1980) 192–200) and the maudlin Trimalchio gives his own take on the theme at Petronius 34.7–10. Naevolus is no doubt anxious about the fading of his sexual prowess which has so far been his

ticket to patronage (cf. 34, 43–4, 72–78) and dresses up this performance-
anxiety in the borrowed garb of the elegiac poet.

124–6   useful: Naevolus replies in terms of utility (cf. 27 *utile*) but it is
financial loss (*damnum*) which is the real essence of his *spes deceptas*. **trite**:
commune here means 'not specific to my case' or 'run of the mill': Naevolus
thinks that he is a special case (an accusation levelled also at Calvinus
(13.140–142n.)). *modo* (see 8.125n.) is contrasted with *nunc*. **the duping
of my hopes**: *spes deceptas* is an example of the so-called *ab urbe condita*
construction where the participle bears the weight of the meaning.

126–8   swift ... hurrying: the theme of haste is pronounced in *festinat
... decurrere uelox* leading us to expect a word such as 'life' (see Nisbet
(1995) 24): instead we read the enjambed *flosculus* whose diminutive size
perhaps supports its transience and also justifies the adjective *breuissima*
in 127. *decurrere* (see *OLD* s.v. 'decurro' 5c) has the sense of 'run its
course'. *flosculus* can refer to a boy in the 'bloom of youth' as in the case of
Iuventius (Catullus 24.1) or Attis (Catullus 63.64) but is here metaphorical
for the brevity of life as well as looking forward to *serta* in 128. The brevity
of happiness is enacted by the placing of *breuissima* in the middle of an
extended misery of *angustae miseraeque ... uitae*. **part**: *portio* is used of a
'share' of life/time also at Seneca *Epistles* 49.4, *Dialogi* 6.21.2.

128–9   drinking ... girls: the thought is close to Horace *Odes* 1.11.7–8
and the apparatus is conventional for the ancient symposium (6.297, 11.122,
15.50, Plautus *Asinaria* 803, Lucretius 4.1132, Cicero *in Catilinam* 2.10.16,
Balsdon (1969) 49–51). The style is suitably elegiac with the anaphora of
dum, the asyndeton of *serta unguenta puellas*, the juxtaposition of *poscimus
obrepit* to mark the simultaneity of the actions and the ending of the sentence
(and the joy) with *senectus*. For the notion of old age/death 'creeping' up
on us cf. Lucretius 1.414–5, Cicero *de Senectute* 4, 38, Plautus *Pseudolus*
686. *non intellecta* is well chosen: taken literally it means 'without being
observed' (*OLD* s.v. 'intellego' 3) but in the context of drinking and sex it
also suggests mental stupor.

130–134a   have no fear: The speaker's final words to Naevolus again seek
to reassure him that he will not lack for sexual partners since contemporary
Rome is a magnet for men who would enjoy his services: cf. 2.168. The
language is ironically rhetorical: the strong negatives of *ne ...numquam*,
the sibilance and pleonasm of *stantibus et saluis his collibus*, hyperbole
(*undique ... omnes*) and the catalogue of transport in *carpentis et nauibus* all
support the crude realities of *pathicus* and the brusque idiom *digito ...caput*.

130 **faggot**: *pathicus* (referring to a man who assumed the passive role in anal intercourse) was a pejorative term (2.99, Catullus 16.2, 57.2, 112.2, see Adams (1982) 133). *ne* + imperative is a common form of prohibition in early Latin and Latin poetry (AG §450a).

131 The **hills** are the seven hills of Rome (cf. 6.296, Horace *Carmen Saeculare* 7) which usually stand for the permanent basis of Roman society and culture but which here are supporting sodomy. For the notion that Rome is a cesspit of vice flowing in from all over the world cf. 3.62–66, 6.295–7, Tacitus *Annals* 15.44: this builds on a standard argument of republican moralists that vices were imported along with luxury goods from overseas and especially from Greece (e.g. Cicero *de Republica* 2.7–8, Sallust *Catiline* 10, Edwards (1993) 92–97; cf. 11.100n.). Sometimes the conceit is reversed whereby noble foreigners are corrupted by their contact with Rome (e.g. 2.160–170).

132 *conueniunt* is surely correct as the firm prophecy of the future tense *derit* relies on the fact that suitable candidates are already assembling. The huge numbers involved are brought out by the hyperbole of *undique* and *omnes* and also by the expansive phrasing *et carpentis et nauibus* (cf. Horace *Epistles* 1.11.28–9, *Odes* 1.6.3) which by its very length suggests the vast convoy: a *carpentum* (cf. 8.147) was a two-wheeled carriage pulled by two mules (cf. Paoli (1990) 230 with illustrations).

133 **scratch their head**: touching the scalp with one finger was reckoned to be a sign of homosexual availability (cf. Plutarch *Pompey* 48) and J. may be thinking of a passage in the Elder Seneca (*Controversiae* 10.1.8) where he describes a man 'who wrote a poem against Pompey – who was victorious over land and sea – scratching his head with one finger'): this poem has been identified as Calvus *Fragment* 8 ('Magnus, whom all fear, scratches his head with one finger. What do you think he wants? A man.'). Otto ((1890) s.v. 'digitus' 12) suggests that the effeminate man only uses one finger to scratch his head in case he disturbs his hair-arrangement: cf. also Seneca *Epistles* 52.12.

133–134A A major textual crux. There may well have been a lacuna between 134 and 134a, as *haec exempla* (135) has no referents in the preceding lines and we would expect *exempla* to refer to a list of people (of either sex) who might have offered Naevolus more than his current patron. *altera maior / spes* suggests that (after the duping of his earlier hopes (125–6)) a new source of income is available to Naevolus from the hordes of pathics coming into Rome and Housman ingeniously proposed reading:

altera maior
spes superest: turbae, properat quae crescere, molli
gratus eris…

('another greater hope still awaits you: you will be pleasing to the
effeminate mob which is growing rapidly')

Willis prints Buecheler's emendation *alter amator … gratus erit* (excising
134 altogether) which would mean 'alternative lovers will find favour (with
the patron?)' and feeds Naevolus' paranoia about being supplanted: an
amator is a virile lover (and not a pathic) and could well supplant the fading
Naevolus. Clausen deletes *gratus eris … dentem* and so leaves Naevolus
relying on the new customers flocking into Rome to replace his current
patron, while Courtney speculates that Naevolus is being told to turn his
attention to lonely <u>women</u> as a source of income (cf. 1.37–41: we know
that Naevolus is bisexual from 22–6 and 72–80): Courtney suggests that a
lacuna after *spes superest* gave examples of men and women engaging in
this business. The change of sexual target would render 130–133 pointless
unless there were indeed a substantial lacuna in which the wider vistas of
female bedmates were opened up.

   rocket-wort: *eruca* is 'an acrid cruciferous herb used as an aphrodisiac'
(*OLD* s.v. 'eruca'): cf. *Priapea* 47.6, 51.20, Horace *Satires* 2.8.51, Ovid *Rem.
Am.* 799, Martial 3.75.3, Celsus 4.16.3, Columella 10.1.1.109, 10.1.1.372,
Pliny *NH* 19.154, [Virgil] *Moretum* 84. The phrase *imprime dentem* is
unusual for the simple act of chewing and it may be that the speaker is again
using a light sexual innuendo to this sexual expert: love-biting was well-
known (Catullus 8.18, Lucretius 4.1080, Plutarch *Pompey* 2.2) and Horace
(*Odes* 1.13.12) has the similar phrase *impressit … dente … notam*.

135–50   Naevolus concludes the poem with a final series of complaints.

135–6   **Clotho** and **Lachesis** are two of the three Fates (*Moirai* in Greek),
the daughters of Zeus and Themis who spin the thread of human destiny
(see *OCD* s.v. 'fate' and cf. Hesiod *Theogony* 904–6, Plato *Republic*
10.617b–21a,). Clotho (Κλωθώ 'the spinner') and Lachesis (Λάχεσις
'dispenser of lots') are named by (e.g.) Hesiod *Theogony* 905 and the *Ilias
Latina* 891: both are regularly mentioned as agents of fate – Lachesis at
3.27, Ovid *Tristia* 5.10.45, Seneca *Apocolyntosis* 4, Pindar *Olympian* 7.64,
while Clotho has a speaking role in Seneca *Apocolocyntosis* 3.3 – but here
they are viewed as symbolic of Naevolus' life-expectancy in an interesting
ironic distortion of mythology and logic. Naevolus cannot change his fate

by any efforts on his part – he is simply fated to stay alive by his sexual efforts – and his image of the Fates being 'happy' (*gaudent*) is most unlike the usual representation of these grim goddesses (e.g. Catullus 64.305–381, Tibullus 1.7.1, Virgil *Aeneid* 10.814–5, Horace *Odes* 2.6.9, *Epodes* 13.15–16) as well as being at odds with his subsequent account of the deafness of *Fortuna* (148-50). The sentence ends with a typically crude explanation of the joy with the bodily parts named and juxtaposed for effect (as at 43 *uiscera penem*) and a caricature of the penis 'feeding' the stomach (an image found also in Martial (9.63.2)).

137–8   Naevolus now affects religiosity and addresses his **household gods** (see 8.110n., 12.87–90) in a further play for sympathy from his interlocutor: the language reminds us that his household is poor (*parui…minuto… tenui*) and his attitude is one of pious affection for these divinities (*nostri*: cf. Plautus *Trinummus* 39 Catullus 31.9, Ovid *Rem.Am.* 302) whom he addresses with an emotional vocative *o* (cf. e.g. Lucretius 2.14, 3.1, Virgil *Georgics* 2.458, *Aeneid* 1.437) especially used in prayers (Horace *Odes* 1.9.8, 1.32.13 with Nisbet and Hubbard (1970) *ad loc.*). The worship of deities with combinations of **incense** (*ture*) **grain** (*farre*: cf. Persius 2.75) and **garland** (*corona*) was common (cf. Horace *Odes* 3.23.3–4, Ovid *Fasti* 4.409–10) but here poor Naevolus can only promise either the incense or the grain, and *far* was notoriously plain fare (9.122–3n., 14.155n.). The worship is poor but the language is rich: note the expressive use of assonance in *ture minuto ... et tenui ... exorare corona* expressive of the register of religious ritual. Horace's money-lender (*faenerator*) Alfius is also one to idealise the worship of the Lares in his idyllic fantasy (*Epodes* 2.65–6): see Braund (1988) 258 for further references.

139–40   Naevolus, having reminded the gods of his piety (137–8) now makes his prayer for deliverance from a poor **old age** (picking up *senectus* from 129): J. later (10.188–288) gives a powerful account of the miseries of old age with especial focus on the loss of sexual potency (10.204–9, 238–9) and Naevolus is right to be anxious if this is how he makes his living. *figam* is a metaphor from hunting (cf. 1.23, Martial 1.49.13, *OLD* s.v. 'figo' 2) but may also have sexual connotations if only because it is regularly used of Cupid piercing lovers (e.g. Ovid *Ars Am.* 1.23, Tibullus 2.1.71, Martial 9.56.3: see Saller (1983b) 74). The language of *quando ego...?* recalls the plaintive rural longing of Horace *Satires* 2.6.60–62

140   The **mat** (cf. 5.8) denotes the status of a beggar and the **stick** suggests the infirmity of old age (Calpurnius Siculus 5.13, Ovid *Metamorphoses*

6.27, 8.693, 14.655, Seneca *Hercules Furens* 696, *de Clementia* 2.6.3.11, Martial 4.53.3).

140–146 Naevolus unpacks *aliquid* from 139 and lists the items which (he claims) will free him from destitution in his old age. **twenty-thousand at interest**: There has been considerable debate about whether the 20,000 sesterces refers to capital or interest, and *pigneribus positis* (**with pledges secure**) could make sense with either translation. Most editors (and White (1978) 89, Bellandi (2009) 482–3 n.21 + *OLD* s.v. 'faenus') assume that it refers to the annual **interest** payable on his capital invested, calculating that an equestrian capital of 400,000 sesterces would produce 20,000 at the lowest rate of interest which was 5%. Elsewhere (14.322–4) J.'s speaker suggests that 400,000 is a sum one could be content with, but that passage is of little help here as the avaricious reader is expected not to agree (14.335) and the speaker goes on to state that if equestrian income is not enough then even the wealth of Croesus will be insufficient (14.328–3: cf. Horace *Satires* 1.1.62 'nothing is enough'). Saller (1983b) has argued strenuously that *faenus* can mean 'capital' rather than interest (citing e.g. 11.40, 11.48). He points out that we are nowhere told that the figure represents <u>annual</u> interest (rather than monthly) and takes *faenus* to mean *in faenore* ('money lent out at interest' as at Horace *Satires* 1.2.13, Valerius Maximus 4.8.3) or simply as 'capital' (as at Tacitus *Histories* 1.20): it is certainly odd to read this one item as 'income' but all the other items as 'possessions'. If Saller is right, and Naevolus loaned out his 20,000 sesterces at the top rate of interest (12%: see 9.7n.) he would have to live on an annual income of 2,400 sesterces which is above the pay of a legionary under Domitian (900 sesterces: see Watson (1969) 151) but considerably less than the 5000 sesterces paid out to him by his patron at 9.41 for an unspecified period of work – and certainly insufficient to buy the possessions which he goes on to list. These possessions are not 'the assets of a very modest but not desperately poor man' (Saller (1983b) 74): how many people of low income would acquire litter-bearers, let alone silversmiths and painters? The silver vessels are also such as to attract the critical notice of a Fabricius (see 142n.) and the diminutive *uascula* is ironic in the extreme. Juvenal has left the matter ambiguous and either assumed that it was clearer to his contemporaries (than it is to us) or else was unconcerned by the uncertainty. It is also arguable that the haziness is part of the characterisation of Naevolus who is spluttering his demands with abundant plosive alliteration (141) and daydreaming about riding into the Circus on the strong arms of his men. His wishlist is for things of superficial value (hefty attendants to show off at the Circus, a silversmith and an artist) rather than the sort of practical things which might deliver him financial security – such as land and slaves to work it. His speech is ironically self-revelatory as the work of a greedy pretentious parvenu (cf. Winkler (1983) 122, Braund (1988) 156, Rosen (2007) 235) but also bears the evidence of a man who is further along the homosexual spectrum than he might care to admit (cf. 9.26): being carried ostentatiously in a litter-chair is stigmatised frequently (1.32, 1.64–5. 3.239–42, 6.353, 10.35) and here the mention of the 'strong' men adds to the attack, while a concern with the arts is itself a sign of a suspect aestheticism (2.85, 2.99–107, 11.90–119).

interest: the key word *faenus* and its noun *faenerator* ('money-lender') had extremely pejorative overtones for the Romans (see Watson (2004) 122–3 on Horace *Epodes* 2.67) and Romans made attempts to restrict the practice with little success: Naevolus (who mocked the calculating ways of his patron (9.38–42)) is morally no better than his master but (it would seem) much less successful at acquiring and keeping wealth, as his list makes clear.

141 **goblets of pure silver**: the phrase *argenti uascula puri* is used again at 10.19 where the argument demands that this is a small amount of wealth to risk carrying in the street: the diminutive *uascula* would suggest small vessels and Naevolus is trying to give the impression that he does not want much – only for this to be blown in the next line.

142 C. **Fabricius** Luscinus was censor in 275BC and regarded as a pillar of society (see 2.154, 11.90–1n.). He expelled P. Cornelius Rufinus from the senate for owning silver plate in excess of 10lbs/4.5kg (Livy *Epit.* 14) and so these *uascula* cannot be small. The description of Fabricius as *censor* and the juxtaposition with *notet* brings out the legal process: *noto* is the standard term for stigmatising forbidden persons or objects by the censors (*OLD* s.v. 'noto' 3a). The bucolic diaeresis introduces the next item on his list and it is significant that his men are to be *fortes*: perhaps Naevolus is himself susceptible to masculine attraction.

143 The **Moesi** were a Thracian tribe who lived in what is now Northern Bulgaria and Serbia: the province of Moesia was created in 29 BC and was later subdivided into two (see *OCD* s.v. 'Moesia') and Roman legions were stationed there in the time of J. It is not clear why Naevolus specifies precisely this tribe to supply his men except for the general tendency of speakers in J. to romanticise the strength and sturdy character of men from

the northern provinces or from the rural parts of Italy (cf. e.g. 11.151–61). Two men would have to be *fortes* to carry Naevolus in his litter-chair into the Circus – the litter was usually carried by six (1.64, Martial 6.77.10) or even eight (Martial 6.84.1, Catullus 10.8) men, and Braund ((1988) 259 n.134) suggests that for this reason these men are bodyguards rather than litter-bearers, although there is a precedent for **two** at Petronius 96.4. The language is interesting: the slaves are to 'direct' (*iubeant* has a sense of Naevolus' passivity in the arms of these men) him to 'take his position' (*OLD* s.v. 'insisto' 3) in the 'shouty Circus' (for the noise cf. 8.58–9 where the Circus is called *rauco*, 11.197–8, Martial 10.53.1) where his safety (*securum*) is clearly in doubt, all suggesting a degree of sub-optimal weakness on his part. **necks in position**: *loco* often has the sense of 'hire out' (as at 8.185, *OLD* s.v. 'loco' 7 and cf. 6.353) but might also mean 'place' (*OLD* s.v. 'loco' 1) and *ceruix* (as the body-part most engaged in contact with the pole) is metonymic for the carrying of the litter-chair (cf. 1.64). If *loco* means 'hire' then the Moesi would be hired for the occasion rather than owned as slaves and thus sit oddly in the middle of a list of possessions and so I have read the phrase as 'their neck(s) in position' (cf. 6.351). Heinrich emended *locata* to *locatum* (going with *me*) to remove this uncertainty. *ceruix* is used elsewhere of male strength (3.88, 10.260), of vulnerability in the face of death (10.120, 12.14) and of both (10.345: Silius has to offer his 'lovely white neck' for execution once he has been propositioned by the emperor's wife).

145   **also**: *praeterea … et alter* is a good piece of characterisation, suggesting that more ideas are coming to him as he speaks – a sequence which he ends abruptly with the peremptory *sufficiunt haec* (after a bucolic diaeresis) at the end of 146. **stooping**: *curuus* supplies emphatic alliteration and indicates an artist of many years' experience rather than a beginner (the word is commonly used to indicate old age (Kißel (1990) 790 on Persius 6.16)) as well as the vivid vignette of the man bending over his work (cf. Seneca *Epistles* 58.25 for the close work involved). A *caelator* would be employed to engrave plain silver (cf. Cicero *Paradoxa Stoicorum* 1.13.4 (with reference to Fabricius), Pliny *NH* 34.85, *CIL* 8.21106) and greedy men like Verres were said to have such men in their service (Cicero *in Verrem* 2.4.54, 2.4.63).

146   **pictures**: *facies* is understood by Courtney to mean 'wall-paintings', but is more likely to mean (as Braund, Green and Ramsay translate) 'portraits'. Naevolus will presumably rent out these slaves to others and thus earn steady income from their work (as suggested by Friedländer (1895) and

Courtney ad loc.), allowing him an alternative income from the sex work of which he is now tired. **in a trice**: Green suggests that Naevolus is here referring to 'instant painting' which Encolpius blames for the decline of art (Petronius 2.9: cf. Schmeling (2011) *ad loc.*, *OLD* s.v. 'compendiaria' 2). **many ... in a trice**: *multas ... cito* shows that Naevolus is more interested in quantity than in quality. The present indicative *pingit* shows that this is the man's regular activity (cf. 7.185, 11.130–1).

146–7 **this will be enough**: *sufficiunt haec* marks the end of the wishlist, as if Naevolus has suddenly snapped out of a daydream. *quando ego pauper ero?* is taken by most editors to be a plaintive plea for an improvement in his lot, whereby *pauper* denotes 'having a modest sufficiency' (Watson and Watson (2014) on 6.295, citing Seneca *Epistles* 87.40) akin to Epicurean contentment with the 'little that is enough' (see 9.9n.) and seeing *paupertas* as a state preferable to total *egestas* ('destitution': cf. Cicero *Paradoxa Stoicorum* 45, Seneca *Epistles* 17.6, 58.1 for the distinction) which is deemed 'disgraceful' (*turpis*) by e.g. Virgil *Aeneid* 6.276, [Seneca] *Octavia* 833. This is in the context hard to reconcile with the demands made: 'he wants the interest from an equestrian census, but he stipulates that his investment is to be well secured: his plate is to be more than 4.5kg' (Courtney) and nobody would reckon that owning two artists was necessary to be deemed *pauper*. Braund ((1988) 259 n. 136 suggests an alternative punctuation which would allow Naevolus to say 'these are sufficient since I shall [always] be poor' but (even allowing for the added 'always') this too falls foul of the fact that his demands go well beyond the realm of *paupertas* and scholars have to read the words as ironically showing Naevolus' self-delusion. Roman readers may well however have understood the lines as following and glossing the last sentence: 'These will do: when will I be poor [if I have these items]?'

147–8 **pathetic prayer**: for the phrase *uotum miserabile* (i.e. a prayer which is not going to be granted) cf. 3.276, but contrast Statius *Thebaid* 2.642 where the 'pathetic prayer' is realised (in death): the adjective *miserabile* recalls *miserabilior* at 9.6. The language of these two lines stutters almost to incoherence, with absence of verb in *uotum miserabile*, monosyllabic words ending 147 with clash of ictus and accent and *his* standing elliptically alongside *spes* with the presumed sense 'hope for these [things to be realised]'. *Nec ... saltem* here has the sense of *ne quidem* (*OLD* s.v. 'saltem' 2, *OLD* s.v. 'ne' 6, KS 2.§159 *Anm.*5(c): *ne quidem* is not found in J.) and the phrase has a powerful sibilance (*spes his saltem*).

148 The goddess **Fortune** had one temple in the Forum Boarium and a huge

one at Praeneste (cf. 14.90n.) and is a regular presence in J. as the goddess who can create the topsy-turvy world he describes and whom philosophers dismiss: cf. 3.40, 6.605, 7.197, 10.52, 10.285, 10.365–6 (=14.316), 15.95. Here there is a double sense, in that *fortuna* can also mean '(great) wealth' (as at 6.287, 11.176, 13.10, 14.113, 14.328, 16.34, *OLD* s.v. 'fortuna' 12) or 'high class' (8.74): *uocatur* can either mean 'is invoked' as a goddess (*OLD* s.v. 'uoco' 1b) or else 'is demanded' (*OLD* s.v. 'uoco' 6). What poor Naevolus really wants is *fortuna* ('money') and expects *Fortuna* to deliver it with him offering her a share of the winnings in a *uotum* (as Courtney suggests): and he does not take the effort even to do this praying, leaving it to unspecified others to pray on his behalf, the long spondees of 148 indicating the effort involved.

149–50   The subject of the verb is *Fortuna* and the lines refer to an incident in Homer's *Odyssey* (12. 39–52, 158–200: see further *OCD* s.v. 'Sirens') when Odysseus/Ulysses put wax into the ears of his men so they could row his ship past the irresistible song of the Sirens without being drawn to their doom. The hero had himself strapped to the mast so that he alone could hear the song and live. The image was common in Latin: cf. 14.19, Cicero *de Finibus* 5.49.3, Horace *Satires* 2.3.14, *Epistles* 1.2.23, Ovid *Ars Am.* 3.311, *Rem. Am.* 789, Seneca *Epistles* 31.2, 56.15, Petronius 127.5, Martial 3.64.1: the phrasing here recalls closely that of Propertius 3.12.34 (*Sirenum surdo remige adisse lacus*). The point here is that the wax had to be totally noise-cancelling and so *Fortuna* is as deaf to his prayers as the sailors were to the song (*cantus*). The Sirens were often located on Sicily (cf. Seneca *Hercules Oetaeus* 189–90) or S. Italy (cf. Statius *Siluae* 3.1.64, Petronius 5.11). The poem ends with two fine epic lines recounting an epic saga: note the sudden perfect tense of *affixit* following the present tense *uocatur* (showing that when *Fortuna* is being called she has already made her ears deaf), the collective singular *remige* (cf. 3.142, 3.306, 6.150, 10.155, Virgil *Aeneid* 5.116, Ovid *Met.* 8.103), the expressive verb *effugit* (cf. *euasit* at 9.65) and the heavy spondees to describe the act of pushing the wax into the ears in line 149 followed by the ship picking up speed to escape with the dactylic *quae Sĭcŭlos*. The poem ends with the significant idea of deafness (*surdo*) as does *Satire* 13: *Satire* 3 ends with the image of being an *auditor* and *Satire* 8 ends with the idea of silence. The philosopher Democritus is said (10.53) to hold up the middle finger to Fortune (cf. 13.20), and the reader is urged (10.363–6) to adopt courage and good sense rather than wait for Fortune: it is apt that this poem ends with Naevolus whining that the goddess (like his patron) will not listen to his pointless prayers, and that the *cliens* is as deaf to good sense as his patron is to his needs.

SELECT INDEX